D1385628

LESLIE STEPHEN

LESLIE STEPHEN

His Thought and Character
in Relation to his Time

by

NOEL GILROY ANNAN

Fellow of King's College, Cambridge

LONDON
MACGIBBON & KEE
1951

First published 1951

DRAWING BY SIR LESLIE STEPHEN, CHARACTERISTIC OF
THE ILLUSTRATIONS HE SCATTERED ON THE MARGINS OF
HIS BOOKS

Made and printed in Great Britain
by THE PITMAN PRESS LTD., BATH
for MACGIBBON & KEE, LTD.
2 Guilford Place, London, W.C.1

PREFACE

When F. W. Maitland, perhaps the greatest of all English professional historians, wrote Leslie Stephen's commemorative biography, he said: 'He is too big for me for one sort of writing and too dear for another,' and he added: 'Someone will some day do for him what he to our admiration did for many others: illustrate in a small compass his life by his books, his books by his life and both by their environment.'

This I have tried to do. Maitland did his work so well that a new biography would be superfluous; and though I have seen some letters which were not accessible to him, such new biographical material has added little to the facts which he collated. I have, however, felt at liberty to quote passages from letters and from the manuscript of the autobiography which Stephen wrote for his children, to which Maitland had access but which obviously he did not feel able to use in a commemorative biography. That I have been able to do so is entirely due to Mrs. Clive Bell, who lent me this manuscript, put at my disposal all the papers in her possession, lent me the family photographs reproduced in this book, one of which was taken by her great-aunt, the well-known artist, Mrs. Cameron, and was always kind, helpful, and dispassionate. I owe her much and thank her.

This book, then, is a critical study of Leslie Stephen rather than a biography. It was originally submitted in a shorter form for the Le Bas Prize Essay and there 'in a small compass' I attempted to follow Maitland's instruction; but I found that the background of Stephen's times cast such a shadow over the man that he was in danger of partial eclipse; and I therefore added the two biographical chapters and expanded those on his moral experience. Nevertheless, the background—the tradition of thought to which Stephen belonged—is essential if his thought is to be intelligible; and conversely Stephen is the touchstone to his environment. To understand Stephen is to understand Evangelical morality and Victorian rationalism, the two strongest influences of the age. In him we can hear the dominant of the Victorian tonality. He is a minor figure in the British empirical school that descends from Locke through Hume and John Stuart Mill to Russell; but he looms much larger when he is seen as a member of the new intellectual aristocracy, of the great Stephen connection which links the Clapham Sect with the original Bloomsbury circle, and of that ethical and intellectual tradition which was expressed most finely in the writings of Mill and George Eliot. In this tradition Stephen made the classic exposition of agnosticism; and he attempted in a wider sphere than philosophy to illuminate and humanise the morality which he had learnt in his Evangelical and utilitarian up-bringing. In Stephen's writings and in the events of his life this way of regarding and judging the world springs to life.

I wish to thank the editors of *The Times*, *The Times Literary Supplement*, and *The Listener* for permission to reproduce certain passages. I am also indebted to many friends and colleagues for help, comment, and suggestions, which I have acknowledged, where possible, in the notes at the end of the book. But I must thank the following here by name: Miss Dorothea Stephen, for giving me the little drawing by Leslie Stephen, reproduced on p. iv, characteristic of the illustrations which he scattered on the margins of his books; Mr. E. M. Forster, for the loan of Henry Thornton's private diary; Mr. J. Roach, for the loan of two letters of Sir James Fitzjames Stephen; Professor N. Sykes, for elucidating several theological points; Mr. Isaiah Berlin and Mr. S. E. Toulmin, for help on certain philosophical problems; Mr. John Saltmarsh, for the benefit of his learning on nineteenth-century Cambridge; Mr. D. Loukes, Assistant Librarian of King's College, for kindly reading the proofs; Mrs. Joan Bennett, Mr. Matthew Hodgart, and Mr. P. N. Furbank, for reading and advising me on various passages; my wife, for her encouragement; and, lastly, Mr. George Rylands, for reading this book twice in draft and in proof, and giving it that severe and affectionate criticism which is, perhaps, the only kind of criticism that can help anyone to write less badly.

N. G. ANNAN.

London, January, 1951.

CONTENTS

ILLUSTRATIONS

To
Nigel Clive

CHAPTER I

THE EARLY YEARS

AMONG all the changes in the structure of Victorian society few are so interesting as the emergence of an intellectual aristocracy which has profoundly influenced English politics, education and literature during the past hundred years. Certain families establish an intellectual ascendancy and begin to share the spoils of the professional and academic worlds between their children. These children intermarry and form a class of able men and women who draw into that circle people of intellectual distinction. The same blood can be found appearing among the headmasters of the public schools and the Fellows of Oxford and Cambridge Colleges; the same tone of voice can be heard criticising, teaching and leading middle class opinion in the periodicals; and the same families fill the vacancies among the senior permanent officials in a Civil Service open to talent. Most of these families rise by time-honoured methods. The younger son of a line of yeoman farmers or country parsons goes into trade or industry and flourishes. His children fall under the spell of evangelical religion, which inspires them with moral purpose and teaches them, when they in their turn mature, to remember the peremptory duty laid upon parents to teach their children diligence and responsibility. As a result the next generation is enabled by its parents' efforts to compete successfully for the prizes of school and university life, and the learned professions are open to them. They have to work for their honours: competitive examinations discipline their minds and force them to show their mettle. But their intellect is trained principally at home where from their childhood they are accustomed to hear their fathers and uncles discussing abstract questions with friends. When their turn comes to marry they often choose the daughter of one of their father's circle whose tastes and fortune are similar to their own. Or one of the sons may introduce a fresh strain by marrying a thoughtful

girl from an upper class family such as the Balfours; one
of the daughters may attract the younger son of a nobleman,
a Cecil, a Russell or a Lyttelton. Their minds are disciplined
at Oxford and Cambridge, they talk a common language
and share similar experiences which enable them to develop
intimate friendships with each other. In these ways an
aristocracy of intellect forms.

Leslie Stephen was born into this class, and to understand
him we must study his provenance. Class on the impersonal
level is the key to conduct because it defines the way in
which a man is treated by his fellow men and how reciprocally he treats them. It is justifiable to stress its importance because, in England especially, a man's social status
has always been a touchstone to his standard of values.
English novelists from Henry Fielding to E. M. Forster
can fairly be described as obsessed with class distinctions;
and this is natural because in England movement from a
lower to a higher class has been marked by just that degree
of possibility and yet of difficulty which makes people
acutely aware of class differences and produces a tension
that is felt all through society. Leslie Stephen's class can
justly be called intellectual because the standards by which
it measures its relations with other classes are based on
mental and moral attributes and not primarily on the
attributes of wealth or birth. It can also be described as
aristocratic because its members feel ultimately secure;
secure in that they are satisfied that their standard of values
transcends all others; secure in that they are well to do.
They see no reason to imitate the manners of any other
class and therefore they inherit the natural ease of manner
(in their case the natural tone of voice in which they address
the public) that characterises an aristocracy. Of course,
like any other class, they have their vices. Pre-occupied
with the intellect, they often respond uncertainly to beauty;
when they cannot relate new forms of art to their own
comparatively narrow experience, they dismiss them, and
they are apt to censure other people's behaviour when it
is foreign to their own traditional morality. But because
they judge people by an exterior standard of intellectual
merit, they can welcome a newcomer to their class and thus

escape the aristocratic vice of picking people up like trinkets
only to drop them when they cease to be entertaining or
useful.

In this aristocracy of intellect two connections are particularly fascinating. The first and more famous, resembling in
complexity and power the old Whig Cousinhood of the
eighteenth century, provides a staggering galaxy of talent
and centres upon the four families of Trevelyan, Macaulay,
Huxley and Arnold. Sir George Trevelyan is a nephew
of Thomas Babington, Lord Macaulay, and his son,
G. M. Trevelyan, marries the daughter of Mrs. Humphry
Ward, a niece of Matthew Arnold. Mrs. Humphry Ward's
sister, Julia Arnold, marries Leonard Huxley, son of T. H.
and father of Julian and Aldous Huxley. A separate branch
of the Macaulays marries the daughter of a well-known
clerical family, the Conybeares; the wife of Dr. Arnold of
Rugby is a Penrose and one of her nephews, who are mostly
schoolmasters, is a Fellow of the Royal Society and his
daughter becomes Principal of Holloway College, and later
of Somerville College. In modern times a Trevelyan and
a Huxley marry into another vast clan, the Darwin-
Wedgwood-Allen connection, which has in recent years
gathered to it a Keynes and a Cornford. The second of
these genealogical tangles, which more directly concerns us,
is the Stephen alliance. Sir Leslie Stephen is the brother
of Sir Fitzjames Stephen, the eminent jurist and Anglo-
Indian administrator, and the uncle of the young parodist
J. K. Stephen and of Katharine Stephen, Principal of
Newnham College. The Venns and Diceys, both celebrated
academic families, are his first cousins, and his Stephen
collaterals excel in the law. Sir Leslie marries firstly a
daughter of Thackeray and secondly a Jackson. Julia
Jackson, who has Vaughans and Prinseps as uncles, is a
niece of Lady Somers and Mrs. Cameron, the photographer,
and is the aunt of H. A. L. Fisher, Cabinet Minister and
Warden of New College, and of Mrs. F. W. Maitland, wife
of the historian, who later marries Sir Francis Darwin.
The daughters of Sir Leslie's second marriage are Vanessa,
the wife of Clive Bell, and Virginia, the wife of Leonard
Woolf; the sons are Thoby and Adrian. Adrian marries

Karin Costelloe, the niece of Logan Pearsall Smith and of
Alys, first wife of Bertrand Russell; she is also the sister of
Ray Strachey and the step-daughter of Bernard Berenson.

Now, these two connections share a common spiritual
heritage. Both Macaulays and Stephens are descendants
of the Clapham Sect. The Clapham Sect was the derisive
name which Sydney Smith conferred on a circle of wealthy
Evangelicals who practised what Wesley had preached, and
spread the gospel of what was to become the widest religious
movement in Victorian England. They struggled to abolish
slavery; as a part of that struggle they dispatched to the
tropics missionaries who altered the course of British colonial
history; they organised Evangelical philanthropy; and
their enthusiasm for humanitarian causes sent ripples across
the surface of English life and inspired such people as
Shaftesbury and Florence Nightingale, herself a descendant
of a member of the Sect. Leslie Stephen was such another
offspring. Like the Gladstones the Stephens were originally
Scots farmers, and James Stephen was the son of a small
merchant who had come south to seek his fortune. But the
merchant had failed and the son was thrown upon the world.
Somehow he scraped a legal education, and after a long
courtship during which he was first forbidden his sweet-
heart's home and then could not decide between her and
another whose physical charms were more obviously
appealing, he eventually married his first love and joined
his brother, as he thought for good, in the West Indies.*
His legal practice, however, prospered, and in 1794 he was
able to return to England where he settled in London and
rose to be a Master in Chancery. But he had brought back
with him more than legal experience. For during the time
of his sojourn in the Barbadoes, the spirit of the English
Common Law had worked in his bones and had aroused
a hatred of slavery. He had not waited until his return to
make this known. On one of his visits to England he had
met Wilberforce and during the remainder of his stay in
the Barbadoes he had clandestinely supplied Wilberforce
with facts for his campaign against the Slave Trade. Now
that he had settled in England he was able to join him

* For the story behind this romance, see Notes *infra*.

openly and add his practical knowledge of the system of slavery to that of Zachary Macaulay. Stephen fought for the slaves in the House of Commons, to which he was elected twelve years after his return, and soon began to find himself drawn further and further into the circle of earnest men in Clapham. It was Wilberforce who comforted him on the death of his wife and four years later supplied the widower with a widow to marry—his own sister. This second marriage decided the provenance of the family. Stephen moved to Clapham, fervently embraced the Evangelical faith, and became a central figure of the Sect. Like them he was a staunch Tory and defended the government of the day against the attacks of the Whigs and Radicals; Spencer Perceval, Prime Minister, was his intimate friend and when shot down in the lobby of the House, died in Stephen's arms; and Stephen visited his assassin in gaol to pray with the criminal. Though virtually a self-educated man, still rough in his ways and heated in his language whenever he was opposed, so fanatical in his advocacy of the cause of the slaves that he would reproach Wilberforce for any act of courtesy shown to the opposition, Stephen was accepted without question by the Sect; he had risen in the world to an assured position.

If Stephen was still a rough diamond, the circle in which he now moved was cultivated and serene. The Clapham Sect, wrote Leslie Stephen's father, were the sons of men who had been thought enthusiastic fools and, though no less earnest themselves in their religion, were never afflicted by the narrow piety of those Evangelicals who despised the fruits of the intellect as a sign of the purer light. They were business men with sound incomes and wide interests. Wilberforce was a man of charm and breeding who disliked a gloomy Sunday. Zachary Macaulay corresponded with Mme. de Staël, Broglie and Chateaubriand. Granville Sharp learnt in his youth as a draper's apprentice 'to love the Quaker, to be kind to the Presbyterian, to pity the Atheist, and to endure even the Roman Catholic'; and perhaps this descending scale of compassion had something to do with winning for himself the position of patriarch of the anti-slave movement. But the real leader of the Sect was Henry Thornton, and his house in Clapham became the citadel of Evangelicalism within whose walls the anti-slave campaign was planned, forces mobilised and deployed, and the network of Evangelical organisation spread over England. Thornton was a vastly able man, a banker who also understood the theory of finance and wrote a treatise on the subject of such excellence that Bentham abandoned his enquiries into the matter. Thornton was not the kind of Protestant who divorced his religion from his business ethic. He spoke in Parliament against the unequal pressure of taxation on rich and poor and 'raised his own contribution to the level of his speech' by giving six-sevenths of his income to charity until he married, after which he gave one-third.* Thus, although James Stephen himself lacked polish, his friends were distinguished, and his children, contemporaries of the Wilberforce boys and of the young prodigy, Tom Macaulay, were schooled by their Wilberforce step-mother and listened to the conversation of men who were public figures with a great taste for discoursing on moral and religious topics.

It was Master Stephen's third son, James, who clave most strongly to the traditions of Clapham by marrying into the Sect and by becoming their chronicler. Being eleven years old when his father re-married, he was spared the more rigorous side of his step-mother's educational theories; for she was a woman who held that a child ought to have read Bishop Butler's *Analogy*—the greatest English theological work of the eighteenth century—before the age of seven. His father sent him to Trinity Hall and bequeathed him to the care of the fervent Evangelical Joseph Jowett, great-uncle of the future Master of Balliol, an elegant Latinist and Professor of Civil Law, noted, as it was said, for the perennial

---

* Other prominent members of the Sect were: the Venn family; Charles Simeon, the famous Cambridge preacher; E. J. Eliot, brother-in-law of Pitt; Lord Teignmouth, devout but temporising Governor-General of India; Sir R. Inglis, Chairman of the East India Company; Sir William Smith, art-connoisseur and opponent of religious disabilities; Lord Glenelg, Secretary of the Colonial Department (1835–1839); Robert Grant, Glenelg's brother, who championed the cause of Jewish emancipation; and Charles Bradley, who held an incumbency in Clapham from 1829–52 and was father by two marriages of a score of children, including G. G., F. H., and A. C. Bradley, and Margaret Woods, author of the excellent short novel, *A Village Tragedy*.

freshness of his interest in young men.* But the younger
Stephen was not impressed with his education. The 'three
or four years during which I lived on the banks of the Cam
were passed in a pleasant, though not a very cheap, hotel.
But had they been passed at the Clarendon, in Bond Street,
I do not think that the exchange would have deprived me
of any aids for intellectual discipline or for acquiring
literary and scientific knowledge.' Young Stephen was
called to the Bar and since his father was able to transfer
some of his clients to him, the briefs began to pile up in his
chambers. In 1814 he married the daughter of the Rev.
John Venn, Rector of Clapham. The Venns were the stuff
out of which intellectual families are made; they had been
clergymen since the reign of Elizabeth and they stood at
the centre of the Evangelical movement within the Church
of England.† The sanguine temperament of the Venns
matched the *parvenu* energy of the Stephens, and while the
second James Stephen had inherited the thin skin and quick
temper of the Stephens, Jane Venn possessed the common-
sense and cheerfulness of her own family. It was from
their marriage that Leslie Stephen was born on the 28th of
November, 1832, barely a month after the death of his
grandfather, the Master in Chancery.

By the time James Stephen reached maturity the great
days of Clapham appeared to be over. Evangelicalism was
gaining ground everywhere and the party had already one
bishop in the House of Lords. The Slave Trade had (in
theory) been abolished and the struggle over the administration of the Act had been won. But there still remained
work to do. Could not the slaves in the British Colonies be
freed? Stephen dedicated himself to the task. In 1825 he
accepted the post of Counsel to the Colonial Office and Board
of Trade, gave up his private practice, and for twenty-two

* It was Jowett who composed, or rather arranged from Handel, the
Cambridge chime, now known throughout the world as the chime of Big Ben.
    † John Venn's father, Henry, can almost be said to have invented the
Clapham Sect. The contemporary of Whitefield and Wesley he was, like them,
much moved by Law's *Serious Call*, and during his curacy at Clapham spread
the light to Henry Thornton's father. His book the *Complete Duty of Man* was
accepted by all Claphamites as the classic exposition of Evangelical theology.
Charles Simeon was his disciple and inherited his eloquence. His son, John,
returned to the scene of his father's first triumphs and was rector of Clapham
from 1792–1813.

years he laboured in Colonial affairs, to become one of the great colonial administrators of the age. Permanent civil servants soon learn to despise those whom the fortunes of politics set over their heads. Politicians appear to fall neatly into the two categories of knaves or fools whose desires are to be thwarted or humoured as occasion serves. Stephen was hardly a popular figure in that he displayed all the weary contempt of the able civil servant for his chiefs, and in addition his very virtues excited envy and fear. An encyclopaedic memory gave him command over the details of the politics, administration and constitution of all the colonies, and the various Secretaries of State who flitted briefly in and out of office were compelled to rely on his fabulous comprehension. Politicians began to complain that here was a man who had not won his power in the political arena and yet was able to influence governments. For Stephen was an official with a policy: whereas the Government policy was to 'meliorate' the position of the slaves, Stephen intended to free them. When therefore about the time of the Reform Bill, the agitation to free the slaves led by Zachary Macaulay was obviously bound to lead to legislation, strong feelings were expressed that Stephen should have no hand in the matter. The Secretary of the Colonies, Lord Stanley, determined that he would keep the permanent official in his place. He rejected Stephen's counsel, intimated that he himself was a man of ability and let it be known that he had decided to draw the bill himself. But Stephen was to have his revenge. The task proved quite beyond the powers of the nobleman, and on a Saturday morning Stephen was summoned to do the job at top speed. He returned home; began to dictate that afternoon; worked for the first and last time in his life over Sunday; and laid the draft bill in sixty-six clauses before his chief on the Monday morning. So far from diminishing, his influence grew and became sadly apparent during the four year tenure of office by the Claphamite, Lord Glenelg. Just before Glenelg was appointed, the Under-Secretary to the office, whose work had been done by Stephen for years, complained to Lord Melbourne that his subordinate was trying to supplant him. 'It looks devilishly like it,' replied the Prime Minister—and left it at that. Two years later, during Glenelg's period of office, the unfortunate man resigned and Stephen took his place as Under-Secretary. The nickname of Mr. Over-Secretary Stephen is intelligible.

Omniscience and high rectitude do not endear a man to his lesser contemporaries. Crabb Robinson had noted that Stephen, as a youth, spoke of his worldly prospects 'with more indifference than was perhaps right in a layman,' and described him as a 'pious sentimentalist and moralist.' He did not conceal the fact that he thought his own policies right and those of his opponents iniquitous; and this was more than usually irritating because his mind, trained to appreciate legal and moral distinctions, seeded objections like weeds to choke his opponents' proposals and bred innumerable arguments to garnish his own proposals. His ministers found themselves too often arguing from a brief which was so subtle that it confused rather than convinced their colleagues. 'The truth is,' he said to his subordinate, Henry Taylor,* who was urging him to take the simple course of action in some matter, 'the truth is I am *not* a simple man.' He was not. He was sensitive to the odium which he incurred, and as this was coupled with a natural shyness which he strove to conceal, the complexity of his mind was displayed to the worst advantage. He had a nervous trick of talking with his eyes half shut that made him seem maddeningly condescending. His shyness took the form, as it sometimes does, of inordinate loquacity. To overwhelm with words was a way of shaking off bores and choking critics; Taylor tells how Stephen once brushed off a caller by talking to him without pause for breath for half an hour and bowed him out of the room before the man had uttered a word. An official's unpopularity, however, is rarely explicable simply in terms of his personality, and the abuse which Stephen endured was partly created by the changing relations between the permanent officials and Ministers of the Crown. Whereas it had been possible for

* Sir Henry Taylor (1800–86) played for years an important role in the Colonial Office. He wrote an Elizabethan pastiche drama, *Philip van Artvelde*, which at one time had a certain *réclame*, and an admirable treatise on the art of rising in politics, entitled *The Statesman*.

the former to be regarded as superior clerks in the eighteenth
century, an age of legislative reforms transformed their
status. We accept the preparation of bills by the bureaucracy
as inevitable to-day and think that a Minister is entitled
to tell his permanent officials of the general idea of a new
measure and to expect them to implement it *in toto*. The
fiction that the Minister formulates policy and that his
Civil Servants execute it, is preserved only by the Civil
Service itself. In fact the senior officials not only direct
day-to-day policy, but by their familiarity with the problems
of their department lay down long-term policy. In their
view it is for the Minister to indicate that he wants the
policy to be changed, and only by hard work and political
insight can the Minister see what changes should be made
and how they are to be effected. In Stephen's time this
had not begun to be recognised. Ministers did not take
kindly to that sort of hard work, and even Gladstone complained that he had been sent to school again to study figures
when he was appointed to the Board of Trade. Nevertheless,
the old days of staffing Whitehall with gentlemen by patronage and supporting them by clerks and messengers were
passing. Statistics were almost becoming popular in times
when Anti-Corn Law League pamphlets lay on the drawing-
room tables of the middle classes. The man who prepares
and can handle statistics has the measure of the amateur
statesman who has never learnt the technique of criticising
them and, in general, the official who prepares the details
of a legislative measure necessarily is the master in argument.
Government was gradually becoming more professional,
more dependent on the expert, and the new experts such
as Stephen and Chadwick were to feel the blast of unpopularity delivered by the representatives of vested interests
who were unable to attack their proposals on technical
grounds and had to resort to arguments of general principle.
Even so, the Colonial Governors who had to execute
Stephen's policies were not always obscurantists. Reformers often expect that the measures, into which they
have thrown so much energy and spirit, must achieve not
only the legal and administrative changes which they
propose but also that change of heart vital to the success

of a measure. Stephen saw his great bill for the liberation
of the slaves as the end of the campaign when it was really
the beginning. He remained impervious to the despatches
from the West Indies which complained that the problem
of slavery began only after its abolition—that the transition
from slavery to freedom was not just a change in legal
status effected by a stroke of the pen, but a social process.
'As the question at present stands,' wrote a Governor of
Trinidad some years later, 'a race has been freed, but a
society has not been formed.' Grievously biased as many
of the opposition were, Stephen's critics were making valid
points which could not be met by clever drafting or by
sapient memoranda, and were hard therefore for a man like
Stephen to endure.

Thus, Stephen suffered at the hands of men far less liberal
and humane than himself and he resented their attacks to
which, as a Civil Servant, he could make no reply. He
affected to despise his profession and told Taylor to abandon
Government service and stick to literature. The harder one
slaved the odder politicians thought it that one did not
slave harder. In the world of letters work was judged on its
merits: in politics expediency and the innocuous proposal
were the governing criteria. It is, perhaps, not surprising
that at the end of his career Stephen opposed the project
for throwing open the Civil Service to competitive examination; not because he approved of patronage but because
his experience convinced him that the low state of public
morality would defeat such a desirable change. Nevertheless
there remained a place where he could find release from
the world of affairs and rest his jangling nerves. At home
he could relax with his wife and dandle his children on his
knee. He refused to enter society, he declined the *entrée* to
Holland House. In later years he might be found at one of
Macaulay's breakfasts with Monckton Milnes, Charles
Buller, the Wilberforces, Hallam, Milman and Thirlwall,
enjoying the brilliance of the talk though finding it undeniably frivolous. But, in general, if clever men wished to
see him, they could come to his house. And they did come.
James Spedding, one of the early Apostles, Nassau Senior,
the economist (a next door neighbour), John Stuart Mill,

and Greville, the diarist, were glad to listen to his flow of conversation. John Austin, the Utilitarian jurist, his literary wife and their remarkable daughter, Lucy, who kept a skull and a rifle in her bedroom, were also frequent callers. Stephen, however, liked best the simpler Clapham company of his brothers-in-law, Henry and John Venn, the Diceys and Garratts and his own brothers. The home was his natural habitat; and it was a home where children were educated.

Leslie Stephen was the fourth of a family of five children. Herbert, the eldest son, was a good deal his senior and died at Dresden in his twenty-fifth year; the second child a daughter died in infancy before Leslie was born. He grew up under the shadow of his equally famous brother, James Fitzjames, and with a younger sister Caroline Emelia. The family lived in what is now Hyde Park Gate in a Kensington bordered on the west by market gardens and country lanes. Their playground was Kensington Gardens. Leslie was his mother's favourite, perhaps because he had inherited all his father's sensitivity. He burst into tears if reproached, he would not hear stories with unhappy endings, he hid his face rather than look upon a picture of the Crucifixion. He adored listening to poetry and would repeat it to himself long after he had been put to bed, humming the lines or, as he called it, 'playing the band.' So potent was the effect that his whole frame would shake while it was being read, and these transports of emotion exhausted his slender reserves of energy. His mother who taught him his early lessons, noticed that he was bright at arithmetic; but she also marked how languor and pallor stole over his face after a bare half-hour. Eventually a doctor was consulted who diagnosed that great Victorian malady, incipient brain-fever, and prescribed a regimen of Brighton—and no more poetry. Sir James Stephen was never a man to shirk the call of duty: he moved the whole family to Brighton and travelled down from London for the week-ends. It was less inconvenient than it might have been, for Fitzjames was already there at a private school run by an Evangelical clergyman. Leslie joined him there and was rewarded by readings of the *Arabian Nights* in place of *Marmion*.

The pious air of an educated upper-middle class Evangelical family in the last century is breathed no more to-day. The descriptions of an Evangelical childhood left by Stephen or G. W. E. Russell belie the more publicised memories of gloomy severity or cruelty recorded by Ruskin, Samuel Butler or Augustus Hare. The Stephen children led happy, gentle lives. Christianity flowed about them and they bathed in it. There were no fervid prayer-meetings, no witch-hunting for sins, no probing the heart and titillating the conscience, no tense expectation of the moment when each child should announce that he was saved and demand that his elders should celebrate his conversion. The children were never troubled by the thought of their mother waiting for them to receive an 'illumination.' They learnt to pray at her knee, to join every morning and evening in family prayers, to read the Bible as the best of all story books. The children believed that Jesus lived because their parents talked to Him each day; and their conviction that Jesus was journeying through the world, but always at hand, was extraordinarily vivid—as if another member of the family were living under the same roof. They followed the events of His life through the Church year; the long slow weeks of Lent, leading to Passion week when the story of how He passed each day was retold, to the great culmination of Good Friday when Jesus redeemed mankind and made His offer of salvation to them, appeared as but yesterday. But they learnt more than a religion of emotion. The Catechism, simple theology and family prayers, stamped their imagination with the graver and more terrible images of the Christian faith. Hell existed and God punished sinners. Not that such a fate awaited them. They were children and Jesus loved them. How then, asked their mother, could they offend their dearest Friend by fits of temper and obstinacy? No doubt religion often went to their heads. All children are at some time or other prigs and the form that the priggishness takes depends on their upbringing. Leslie was no exception. He once refused to ride on a donkey to church because it was wrong to make the beast work on Sunday and he obviously enjoyed the feeling of sanctity as his father argued vainly to persuade him that such views were extreme. But it was exactly such priggishness that Sir James Stephen was determined to eradicate. He would not have his children grow up patent Christians, formalists and cheats. They were to be taught that morality is not to be found by obeying a set of rules and that life is a continual effort to do one's duty to other people. The children were brought up to notice that their father was a man of principle. 'Did you ever know your father to do a thing because it was pleasant?' his mother asked Fitzjames, who replied, 'Yes, once—when he married you.' But it was true. Sir James Stephen was inexorably suspicious of pleasure. He drank little; ate the lightest of meals; and asking himself once why it was that he continued to take snuff and receiving no satisfactory reply, ceremoniously emptied the box out of the window. 'He once smoked a cigar,' wrote Leslie, 'and found it so delicious that he never smoked again.' Home-life was austere. They went neither to theatres nor dances but, here again, their father was at pains to point out that such pursuits were not sinful, although for people like themselves they were not 'convenient.' On no account were they to lay up treasure to themselves that they were better than others. The Stephen household was far more liberal than most Evangelical households at that date; and the customary apparatus of instruction, the penny-bank, the missionary stories, the charitable work among poor children and the Sunday School, were quietly ignored. Their sense of duty was so ingrained that they believed themselves to be living the freest of lives. The Stephen boys noticed something else about their father: they saw that he never exposed his heart.

This fear of an excessive display of the Christian virtues may have determined Sir James Stephen's choice of a public school for his sons. Arnold was at that time at the height of his fame at Rugby and Sir James might have been expected to send his sons there; indeed he took Fitzjames with him to see Arnold, but decided in favour of Eton. Whether he felt that Rugby encouraged boys to become prigs or whether he feared the reproaches of his more solid Evangelical relatives to whom Arnold's intellectual Christianity was suspect, is not clear. More probably he doubted the doctor's sanguine verdict on Leslie's health after the boy had been a year at Brighton. The doctor had advised a boarding school 'to have the sugar taken out of him,' but Sir James had other ideas. He saw that Leslie was still delicate and he had heard of the abuses of the public schools.* To ensure that his boys would not be contaminated and since Leslie was still only nine and a half, he therefore decided to take a house at Windsor, from which he could commute to London, and his sons attend Eton as day-boys. He accordingly called on Dr. Hawtrey, the headmaster, outlined his scheme and asked whether there was any prejudice against day-boys. Dr. Hawtrey sagely shook his head, and on the 25th of April, 1842, both boys entered the school.

Experts in one field are all too ready to take on trust the judgments of experts in another field. The headmaster's *ipse dixit* was enough for Sir James Stephen, whereas the most casual enquiry would have told him that day-boys, as they always have been in boarding schools, were despised. The public schools for the past twenty years had been redefining the term 'free education.' At Shrewsbury small tradesmen who demanded that their sons should be educated free or at a low cost in the local grammar school, had been defeated by first Butler and then Kennedy, headmasters who interpreted a free education to mean a liberal training in classical scholarship and not instruction in book-keeping. This was less true of Eton which had in the eighteenth century established its claim to educate the sons of the ruling class, but it still counted for something. A day-boy was suspect because he might be the son of a Windsor grocer or footman at the Royal Household who was attempting to break into the upper classes by insisting that his sons should be educated in their home town. Young boys exaggerate the prejudices of their parents, and at Eton in the 'forties the length of the journey which a boy made to the school

---

* Sir James feared for the spiritual health of his sons as they passed out of the influence of the home. Giving thanks to God for Herbert's safe return from his first spell of duty in the Navy, he told his wife 'He has brought back with him less (at least so it seems) of the contagion of that fearful calling than my fears had foreboded. He has returned with his affections active and simple. . . .'

each half-year was thought to be directly correlated with
the breadth of the paternal acres. Moreover, the Eton
authorities mistrusted Sir James Stephen. He was a
reformer, an occult power behind Royal Commissions, and
an Evangelical. Eton despised reform, loathed interference and belonged to the High and Dry party in the
Church. If Sir James's first consideration was the well-
being of his sons, he could not have taken a more disastrous decision than to send them to an Oppidan house as
day-boys.

Both Fitzjames and Leslie were bullied systematically
from the day they arrived. College was the place for poor
boys or the sons of Windsor parents, not the Oppidan
houses, which were reserved for gentlemen; and this fact
was driven into their heads and bottoms.* They were
unprepared in every way for such treatment. They had
not been brought up in some high-spirited upper-class
family, they were middle-class boys who had been taught to
converse seriously, to read omnivorously and to admire Scott
and Wordsworth; their companions were the sons of
squires who preferred field sports to such pursuits. As a
day-boy Leslie rose at six, read the Bible at his mother's
side, and returned home each evening to prepare the next
day's lessons, so that to the end of his time at Eton he never
made a single friend. He was too small and fragile to be
able to defend himself. Living at home, however, shortened
the hours in which he was exposed to bullying, and the
tough Fitzjames did something to protect him though, as
Leslie said afterwards, he fought other boys so often that
his terminal bill for top-hats must have been phenomenal.
At all events it was no use looking to Dr. Hawtrey for help.

* They were fortunately preserved from the torture endured by small
boys at the hands of the Sixth Form in Long Chamber in College into which
they were locked with their fag-masters from 8 p.m. to 8 a.m. secure from
any interruption by a master. So appalling were the conditions of bad food,
dirt and squalor under which they lived that the year before the Stephens
went to Eton, only two candidates presented themselves for election to College
although thirty-five places were vacant. During their time in the school, new
lodgings were built for Collegers and under Provost Hodgson the horrors of
Long Chamber gradually mitigated. Fitzjames Stephen was years later to
plead in the Ecclesiastical Courts for a Colleger, Rowland Williams, accused
of writing a heretical essay in *Essays and Reviews*, who was literally scalped in
Long Chamber and remained disfigured for life through being tossed in a
blanket.

Hawtrey was a humane man who deplored violence and once told a sixth-former that it was bullying that turned Shelley into 'a perfect devil.' But he was a snob; bullying was a tradition, and tradition was sanctified; and his appeals to the boys' better nature delivered in an eccentric pronunciation were ridiculed. In Hawtrey's defence it should be said that even Arnold despaired of boyish brutality, for though Arnold hoped to turn out Christian gentlemen, he thought it beyond his powers to make Rugbeians Christian boys while still at school.

By the standards of the day an Eton education was sound, and a high proportion of prizemen and classics who took first-class honours at the University were Etonians. Etonians enjoyed a reputation for a quick brilliance and elegance in their classical work, and above all a peerless ability to turn out elegiacs. A good copy of verses was the summit of achievement. Beginning in the lowest forms by stringing nonsense words together to imprint scansion upon the mind, an Eton boy would show up a copy of longs and shorts once or twice a week for the five or seven years of his school-days, so that classical prosody was drummed into him until it became second nature. But other schools had begun to outstrip Eton. The Etonian scholar could master grammatical forms, but the pupils of Vaughan at Harrow or Kennedy at Shrewsbury were learning syntax and philology. Shrewsbury boys, in particular, were famed at the university for their minute scholarship and mechanically perfect Greek iambics, and for a precision of mind which left its mark on everything they touched: so much so that they were noted for a special aptitude at whist which they played with astonishing accuracy and expressionless countenances. Hawtrey had begun to reform the classical curriculum, but as one might expect, in the most discreet manner, and the changes he effected were designed rather to lower the number of boys in a class than to raise the standard of scholarship. He did his best, however, to instil respect for a good composition or set of verses, he encouraged the teaching of ancient history, and since he spoke excellent French and fair German and introduced allusions from these languages into his lessons, he may have conveyed to a

few of his pupils that the Muses inhabited other countries
than England, Greece and Rome.*

But Hawtrey's teaching touched only the Sixth Form, so
that neither Leslie nor Fitzjames ever benefited as they both
left the school too young. Leslie was clever at his work
and went up the school rapidly, but the Eton curriculum
did not suit his talents. Scarcely any mathematics were
taught and he picked up French at home. The teaching of
modern history or literature or even English grammar was
unknown. The *Edinburgh Review* commented in 1845, 'A
Parliamentary return of all that is taught at Eton during
ten years of pupilage in the nineteenth century—what
books are read, even at the head of the school, Ovid, Vergil,
Horace and Homer—ought (if anything can) to surprise
the public into some uneasiness on the subject'; and the
writer added that matters were not much better elsewhere
in that Arnold had introduced remarkably few changes
into the public school courses of study. It was at a later
date that the admirable practice was introduced of sending
boys to their tutor for private reading which might include
English literature. Leslie had no such luck. He lodged with
Dr. Balston, and Dr. Balston was a single-minded man.
'If you do not take more pains,' he said to Fitzjames, 'how
can you ever expect to write good longs and shorts? If you
do not write good longs and shorts, how can you ever be a
man of taste? If you are not a man of taste, how can you
ever hope to be of use in the world?'

This epitome of usherdom brought Leslie's Eton days to
an end. At the end of 1846 when he was just fourteen he
was prizeman of his division and had been moved up to
Upper Division, Fifth Form. But this did not satisfy Dr.
Balston. He wrote to Sir James complaining that, while
Leslie was diligent and well-behaved, his elegiacs were a
disgrace and his compositions lacked polish. Without taste,
Dr. Balston repeated, the boy could not appreciate beauty.
Sir James with memories of Leslie's voracious appetite
for poetry thought that he responded to beauty better

* His attempts, wrote A. D. Coleridge, 'were received with broad smiles
and vague, incredulity. "The modern Germans" said he, "have borrowed
from Homer's ἴφθιμος γυνή—*eine wackere Frau.*" Inextinguishable laughter.
Hawtrey: "What on airth is there to laugh about?" '

than most boys of his age, and had the courage to do
what few fathers dare. He had already taken Fitzjames
away when he discovered that he was unhappy, and now he
removed Leslie on the grounds that if Eton could not in
five years ground his son in elegiacs, to persevere was stupid.
Dr. Balston went his way unmoved and twenty years later
had the satisfaction of resigning as headmaster rather than
sanction a reform of the curriculum.

Both boys had hated their schooldays but they reacted
differently. On the day that he left, Fitzjames tore off his
white tie, stamped it into the mud and slouched into the
ante-chapel to scowl at the boys as they entered. But in
later life, like so many Englishmen, he revised his opinion
and thought that bullying had made a man of him. 'I was
on the whole very unhappy at Eton,' he admitted, 'and I
deserved it; for I was shy, timid, and I must own cowardly';
he liked to recall the time when he realised that the only
salvation for a boy lay in his fists, 'the process taught me for
life the lesson that to be weak is to be wretched, that the
state of nature is a state of war, and that *Vae Victis* the great
law of Nature.' When the day came he sent his son, the
immortal of the Wall Game, J. K. Stephen, to College.
Leslie was far more critical. He refused to worship at the
shrine of the public schools and used to say that when
schools boasted of having produced such and such a man,
what they really meant was that they had failed to extinguish
him. Their teaching was contemptible. 'The average lad
of eighteen who comes up to the Universities from one of our
great places of education shows a negation of all useful
knowledge which is, in its way, a really impressive phenomenon.' And he took the opportunity of a celebrated public
scandal at Winchester in the 'seventies—the case of 'Tunded
Macpherson' where a boy had been mercilessly flogged by
prefects—to speak about the tortures suffered by small boys
and the honest Dobbins of *Vanity Fair*; bullying would not
be stopped until men stopped 'dwelling more fondly upon
their schooldays in proportion to the remoteness of their
memory.' He rarely spoke of Eton and sent his sons to
Clifton and Westminster. On the other hand, he thought
that, bad as it was, a public school was the best English

education available, and he would not have gone so far as many intellectuals in the first third of this century who declared that the only reason for enduring a public school was that it made the rest of one's days comparatively happy since no disaster later in life could ever parallel the horrors of adolescence. Leslie Stephen believed in discipline and self-reliance. Latin grammar was as necessary as physical exercise; force, vitality, energy, manliness had a better chance of surviving at a public school than elsewhere. In other words he realised that it was not entirely Eton's fault that companionship in games and walks—sunny summer afternoons and eating enormous teas in winter—had been denied to him. And on another curious point Leslie and Fitzjames were agreed. However tough Eton might have been, it was satisfyingly free from moral uplift. The Chapel Services taken by the Provost and Fellows were so dry that no boy ever connected the religion he professed in Chapel with the life he led in the school. Indeed it was difficult at times to perceive the slightest connection between the two in the sermons which were preached to them. 'The subject of my discourse this morning, my brethren, will be the duties of the married state,' droned one old fossil, and his discourse, it need hardly be said, bore no resemblance to those frank talks delivered by housemasters of the present age. This lack of religious zeal was to arouse comment at a later date, but Dr. Balston, as usual, saw no need for change; he did not want to run the risk of a sermon in which one phrase might swerve from the canons of good taste. Asked when he was headmaster whether he did not think that preaching was an excellent means of influencing the boys, 'No,' he replied, 'I was always of opinion that nothing was so important for boys as the preservation of Christian simplicity.' Now, Leslie Stephen saw that, though one might raise an eyebrow at his tutor's assumption that the young thugs who boarded with him had remained in a state of primitive innocence, there was much to be said for the kind of honesty which did not pretend that religion was connected with the ordinary boy's life of cribbing, lying, cheating, elegant stealing and brutality. He personally deplored the famous Rugby earnestness and disliked boys

'who conceive themselves to have imbibed a moral as well
as a social superiority, and who go through the world ever
afterwards as volunteer missionaries, brandishing their
exalted moral sense in the face of all spectators.' Eton was
free from cant. The *alma mater* was a bloated old harridan,
boisterously merry, unashamedly dirty, who did not try to
conceal her failings by sneaking off to the conventicle to
thank God that she was better than others. This is an odd
tribute to pay to one's school, but more interesting than
most.

Until he went up to Cambridge Leslie studied with
private tutors and spent a few terms at King's College,
London, where he attended F. D. Maurice's lectures to
improve his mathematics. More and more able young men
spent a year or two there before entering the old universities,
but the majority of the students were hard-working middle
class boys of London parents. The painful lack of refine-
ment that marred Leslie's elegiacs was less of a handicap
and he also learnt modern languages and history. But his
attendance was fitful. His health was still erratic; the
doctors pursed their lips knowingly, expressed fears of
brain fever and murmured—fresh air—seaside—exercise.
So he passed the months fishing in Scotland or idling at
Torquay with his parents. There was a humiliating interlude
in a gymnasium swinging Indian clubs; and his sister's
dancing-mistress lent him a chest-expander. Leslie at this
time was a tall, lanky boy who had outgrown his strength,
awkward and unwilling to open his heart to a soul. Despite
his parent's care, despite his Windsor Park pony and his
Chinese mice, his boyhood had been lonely. He adored his
mother but he found his father unapproachable. Sir James's
health had broken down, and now knighted, a Privy
Councillor and retired, he was permanently at home and
looked to his younger son to accompany him on his walks.
The walks raised up barriers between them: Sir James's
conversation was a monologue and, when it ceased, a lugu-
brious silence enveloped them. Fitzjames remained his
father's favourite, for Fitzjames held independent views,
spoke his mind, damned the consequences, but garnered
parental wisdom. Always in Leslie's youth the figure of

Fitzjames loomed above him; broad and strong, successful and competent, knowing his own mind and already the friend of the best men of his generation at Cambridge. In contrast Leslie felt that fellows thought him a muff. The dull days, however, were drawing to an end. He was to leave his family and go to Cambridge. He would return to his first love, mathematics, and serve at a court where common sense and logic were king and queen and where that odious flunkey, Good Taste, was told to kick his heels in an ante-chamber. He would have a room of his own and a chance to make some friends. Even so there were risks. He was to read for Honours in an exacting subject; and devout relations prayed, with good reason and no lively hope, that he might survive the Cambridge climate. His health persuaded Sir James that the intellectual competition of his brother's college, Trinity, with its blue ribbands of freshman and scholarship examinations and prizes would overstrain him, so he was entered for his father's old college, Trinity Hall. In the Christmas term of 1850, when he was still seventeen, Leslie took up residence in college; the chest-expander was left in a cupboard at home.

2

It may sound odd that Leslie's parents feared that reading for an Honours Degree would overtax his strength but their anxiety was well-founded. Undergraduates at Cambridge fell academically into two sets: men who read for Honours in mathematics or classics,* and the majority or *polloi* who read for a pass degree and 'went out in the poll.' It was no surprise to see able men take the poll examination.† Sir

---

* The Moral Sciences and Natural Sciences Triposes, created in 1851, attracted very few men at this time.

† Before 1849 any man who wished to sit for the Classical Tripos had first to be classed, i.e. qualify as a Junior Optime, in the Mathematical Tripos. There was always a number of unfortunate classics who failed to be classed in mathematics and were consequently debarred from attempting the Classical Tripos; their only course was to go out in the poll. After 1849, a man needed only to qualify for an ordinary degree in mathematics or to obtain a first class in the poll examination to be allowed to take the Classical Tripos. Even so, a man whose studies had been interrupted by illness or other troubles would very likely abandon his hopes of an Honours Degree and take the poll examination.

James Stephen had taken the alternative course of going
out in law and Fitzjames, having twice failed to win a
Trinity scholarship—an examination taken during undergraduate residence—decided to go out in the poll since his
failure had ruined his chance of a Fellowship at his College.
Most reading men spent at least seven or eight hours a day
at their books, so that work for an Honours Degree required
a healthy constitution.

Indeed the Mathematical Tripos was designed partly to
test exactly how long a man had worked each day. All
questions in every paper were compulsory and more were
set than a man could reasonably be expected to answer
within the time. They consisted of propositions, or *bookwork*, and problems, and the trick was to know the bookwork
by heart and dash it down on paper as quickly as possible
to leave the maximum time for the problems. For instance,
there were seventy-five propositions in Conic Sections alone
which might be set, and yet not more than seven would be
likely to appear in the examination. A hard-working man
would learn the lot by heart in order to be safe. In Stephen's
time, the papers were spread over eight days amounting
to forty-four and a half hours' work in all. During the first
three days candidates were examined in elementary subjects
and forbidden to use analytical geometry or the calculus;
there was a short interval while the weaklings were weeded
out; and all who passed were then permitted to sit for the
second part of the examination. A good Wrangler, or first-
class man, could be expected to *floor* the bookwork in the
early papers and tackle nearly all the problems. The trial
of knowledge and ability came in the second part. But it
was still primarily a test of wide knowledge rather than of
skill and ingenuity, for the examiners reckoned that only
twelve hours of the forty-four and a half should be spent on
problems. Much of the preparatory work consisted of
practising manipulations which would increase the rate of
solving and writing out the solutions of propositions. Part
of the test lay in the speed at which a candidate could work,
and this in turn depended on how fast he could make his
pen skim over the sheets of paper. Hence it paid to learn
endless propositions by heart so that not a moment would

3

be wasted in the examination room in thinking them out. The reckless were soon entangled in horrid snares. A good man, tempted to attempt too many questions, would lose marks for accuracy; another, tackling problems which were worth more marks, would get bogged, and fail to score enough marks on the bookwork. The Tripos was a trial of memory and nerves.*

True to their sporting instincts the English had contrived to turn even the university examinations into an athletic contest. Everything depended on marks, and the year Leslie Stephen took the Tripos, the candidates were each given a slip of paper on which marks were assigned for bookwork and riders in order to indicate the relative difficulty of the different questions. Candidates were arranged in strict order of merit from the Senior Wrangler down to the last Junior Optime or holder of the Wooden Spoon; and below him lay the hapless men who were *gulfed*, or allowed degrees, and those who were plucked outright. It soon became known who were in the running for the top places in the first class. You studied 'Calendar,' as it was called, just as bookies study form, and bets were laid on the favourites. Weeks before the examination the pundits would know how the best men had been shaping, what their coaches predicted and how their health had been standing up to the long grind. A rumour would fly about that a small-College man had made wonderful progress during the vacation and that the Johnian and Trinity bloodstock had better sharpen their pace. As they came into the straight, men would work fifteen hours a day or

* The scope of the papers was about as wide as the present Mathematical Tripos Part II except that there was more optics and astronomy, far less analysis and, of course, no thermodynamics. But the type of work required was greatly different. The Tripos in Stephen's time was designed for the hard and fast worker. Far more bookwork was demanded and the problems were not nearly so remote from bookwork as they are to-day; in fact no man who had gone thoroughly over the ground would find himself faced with a problem which could not be related to a similar problem in his books, whereas to-day a Junior Optime has no hope of answering some of the problems which demand ingenuity and a certain degree of originality of mind. It is more difficult to compare the Cambridge mathematical student of the 'fifties with his contemporaries at the Polytechnique; but the most sanguine estimate in favour of the English suggests that while the first ten Wranglers might be the equal of the Frenchmen, the average undergraduate was below the continental standard.

more and their coaches would spot likely questions and urge them on to a final spurt; one or two would strike it up as high as twenty hours a day in the last week and totter into the examination room with flasks of ether or brandy in their pockets. Examination day dawned in the first week in January and prospective Wranglers prayed for a mild spell of weather. For if there was a sharp frost the Senate House would be so cold that a good man might get *frozen up*, his hands so blue that he could not write at speed, and valuable marks would trickle away before he could recover. The Peterhouse outsider would be seen to be writing for dear life, and the sight would throw his Trinity rival off his stroke. When the great mathematician, Arthur Cayley, took the Tripos in 1842 his rival from St. John's was seen ostentatiously to leave the Senate House a full hour before the end of the allotted time for the paper. A friend rushed up to his rooms that evening, 'Cayley! Cayley! they tell me Simpson floored the paper this afternoon in two hours. Is it so?' His backers had no cause for alarm; the future Senior Wrangler, who was soaking his feet in a tub, replied imperturbably without altering his position, 'Likely enough he did. I floored it myself in two hours and a half.' College loyalty ran high and tutors and gyps would pick up gossip about the fortunes of their men; the coaches would prognosticate; and the punters hedged. A long fortnight intervened and then the results were posted. There was money in it for the victors. The first ten Wranglers stood an excellent chance of a Fellowship even at Trinity and St. John's; a man from a small College could hope for a Fellowship if he were placed among the Wranglers. A high Wrangler could set up as a coach with propriety and a first or second Wrangler had a testimonial of ability that would open doors for him in London. Leslie Stephen estimated the value in hard cash of a high place at about five thousand pounds in all.

Such was the career on which Leslie embarked, and so far from his health breaking under the strain it steadily improved and troubled him no more. At the end of his first year he won a scholarship at Trinity Hall and had obviously settled to his work. His next task was to choose a good coach. College teaching was inadequate and tutors spent their hours of instruction ramming the elementals into the heads of the average undergraduates. A flier went to an outside coach whose reputation rested on his record of successes. A good coach could work up a clever man whose training had been neglected, or cram a man of good memory but no great brilliance, or drive a nimble-witted fellow by cracking his whip. Much depended on him, and many men preferred a coach with a rough tongue who would slang his pupils to victory. The great coaches flung part of their personality into their best men and worked through them. Probably because he was a small-college man, Stephen was not accepted by the leading coach of the day, William Hopkins, who in twenty-two years of teaching produced one hundred and seventy-five Wranglers of whom seventeen were top of the examination.* He chose instead to go to the Johnian, Isaac Todhunter, and in the vacation was tutored by his cousin, James Wilberforce Stephen, a Fourth Wrangler. Todhunter was a character: quaint, crotchety, sour, uncouth, surrounded by cats and canaries, he worked with true mathematical precision: Chapel at 7.30, pupils from 8.15 until 3 o'clock, a walk which never varied until dinner at 4, and from 5.30 to 10 another stream of pupils. 'He lived,' wrote Leslie Stephen 'in a perfect atmosphere of mathematics; his books all ranged in the neatest order, and covered with uniform brown paper, were mathematical; his talk, to us at any rate, was one round of mathematics; even his chairs and tables strictly limited to the requirements of pupils, and the pattern on his carpet, seemed to breathe mathematics. By what mysterious process it was that he accumulated stores of miscellaneous information and knew all about the events of the time (for such I afterwards discovered to be the fact) I have never been able to guess. Probably he imbibed them through the pores of his skin. Still less can I imagine how it came to pass that he published a whole series of excellent educational works. He probably wrote

---

* Hopkins's successes were so habitual, writes Winstanley, that when on one occasion his highest man was only eighth Wrangler, his servant, according to report, remarked 'Master ain't placed this year.'

them in momentary interstices of time between one pupil's entering his sanctum and another leaving it.' Todhunter lived for his work, and though he told his wife on their wedding-day that his devotion to mathematics melted beside the love he bore her, he nevertheless introduced her to Hamilton's Quaternions on their honeymoon. Stephen went to him twice or three times a week for catechetical lectures and was stirred to compete against his fellow-pupils by Todhunter's weekly papers. 'Push on. Push on,' his coach would say, and Leslie pushed on to such effect that he turned himself into a reasonable mathematician. After a labour of ten terms he took the Tripos and was placed twentieth in the list of Wranglers or half-way up the first class out of a field of a hundred and forty-three men.

It was a sound performance, since he had the bad luck to strike a particularly brilliant year. The Senior Wrangler was E. J. Routh who later far outshone both Hopkins and Todhunter as a coach and produced an astonishing list of successes among his pupils.* The Second Wrangler was the genius Clerk Maxwell who first reduced the properties of the electro-magnetic field to exact measurement and discovered that the velocity of the transmission of the forces in this field was the same as that of light—a discovery which Einstein declared was the most important in physics since Newton's time. The place immediately above Stephen was occupied by Aldis Wright, the editor of Shakespeare. But Stephen defeated his cousin Edward Dicey, who later became editor of *The Observer*, and the future Lord Harting-ton, and sundry budding archdeacons. His triumph duly brought its reward though it was a reward which later proved to be double-edged. Stephen naturally hoped for a Fellowship, but another Trinity Hall man who stood above him in the list of Wranglers had prior claims and was at once elected to a lay Fellowship. The college, however, was determined not to lose sight of Stephen who, they thought rightly, had the makings of a good college tutor. It so happened that another Fellowship at this moment fell

* For twenty-four consecutive years a pupil of Routh's was Senior Wrangler. He produced twenty-eight Senior Wranglers in all and hundreds of his pupils were placed in the first class.

vacant; Stephen's name was put forward and he was
elected at Christmas 1854. The award was of the type
which required the holder to take Holy Orders.* And this
he duly did in the following year.

He still found it difficult to meet people easily. As an
undergraduate he kept a bull-finch in his room to sing to
him and was known by his contemporaries as 'a tall, gaunt,
and shy man who read mathematics, and hovered on the
edge of a conversation without boldly taking his part.' But he
was fast coming out of his shell. In the Union debates he
spoke frequently and but for Todhunter's remonstrances
would have held office in his third year. Politics had begun
to interest him and as a radical he displayed the contempt
for the conservatism of his elders which a young man ought
to show. He belonged to a small circle of men mostly in his
own college, but the Diceys were another link with the
university world. He began to develop his own style of
talk; he would express his opinion with the utmost vigour,
and then relapse into silence, ready to pulverise some
sententious judgment in a sentence. Not all who met him
approved; he was ambitious to be invited to join the Apostles
but no invitation came, though Leslie might have been
expected to join this select gathering. His brother had been
an active member, two of Leslie's friends belonged to the
society, yet the Apostles passed him over. Intimate friendship came hard to one who was as shy as he was, but his
shyness was a symptom of something far more crucial.
Something in his personality grated on his intellectual
equals and made them feel that he was not of their own
flesh and blood.

They were right. Stephen did not care to be an intellectual. Above him loomed the ghost of Fitzjames's reputation and Leslie had to lay it before he could be himself;

* Not all Fellows were compelled to take orders; all but two in Trinity and
all but four in St. John's were so obliged, but in Trinity Hall only two out of
twelve were clergymen. The remainder were usually absentee lawyers who
resided twelve days a year at Christmas for audit. The University Commission of 1852 pointed out that this was sanctioned by practice rather than
by the College statutes which seemed to lay down that certainly four and
probably eight of the twelve Fellows should be in orders; but as the statutes
were so obscure they ought to be revised. This was accomplished in 1860
with Stephen's help.

and as so often happens, the ritual of exorcism transformed
the exorcist.* He was not disturbed by his brother's mental
prowess with which he knew that he could compete on
equal terms. His father certainly thought him the cleverer
of the two. But he was ashamed of his nervous sensibility
and boyish ill-health. Throughout his life he despised
weakness in any form. Weakness must be overcome: he
admired his cousin, Albert Dicey, for 'the triumph of an
active intellect over a ridiculously incapable body.' Stephen
wanted to appear to his contemporaries as an athlete who
incidentally owned a competent thinking-box. So he went
in for the river. True, he rowed exceedingly badly and
though he still continued to row when a young don he
could never rise higher than the second boat. His real
triumphs were achieved as a coach when Trinity Hall went
head of the river in 1859 and again in 1862. None could
rival his wind and fire and his long legs could keep up with
the boat mile after mile along the tow-path as they paddled
down the river towards Ely. Clad in a filthy shirt and grey
flannel trousers with a large purple patch in the seat, and
damning the eyes of any cox on the river who did not give
way, the Rev. Leslie Stephen was a sight to make Victorian
eyes blink. The fact that he had taken Holy Orders did not
disturb him a whit. His great-grandfather Henry Venn
a few days before he was ordained in 1747 had played for
Surrey against All England and at the end of the match
gave his bat away to the first comer saying, 'I will never have
it said of me, Well struck Parson.' Leslie belonged to a
different generation, and it is he and not Charles Kingsley
who should be regarded as the founder of muscular Christianity. He was also a formidable athlete, a great walker
for whom a stroll to London and back to attend a dinner
was nothing extraordinary. He once challenged a friend to
run three miles while he walked two and won by two hundred
and thirty yards. Stephen invented the Sports and won

---

* Leslie Stephen nursed no feeling of resentment against his brother whom
he honoured and whose biography he wrote. The book, however, betrays his
lack of sympathy with Fitzjames's mind which was in some ways subtler than
his own. It gives the impression of a man sparring at a distance from his
opponent; parrying and feinting skilfully enough but never squaring up to
him.

the mile in 5·4 and the two miles in 10·54. He challenged another friend to run to Baitsbite along the towpath while he leapt over ditches and plunged through hedges cross-country on the other side of the river, and was only narrowly defeated. One day the Vicar of Eaton Socon complained that 'his parish had been invaded by four lunatics who, he was told, were clergymen from Cambridge.' It was Stephen with some friends testing his muscles on yet another feat of endurance. Sir James Stephen's careful plan to send Leslie to a small college so that he should not overtax his strength had somehow miscarried; the delicate boy had been turned into a fanatical athlete.

Rowing remains such a popular pastime at the universities because it gives the otherwise inept what they want but cannot get from games. The happiest hours of rowing are when it is over; the sensation of having overcome the weariness and desperation which afflict an oarsman in rowing a course produces after the event an extraordinary quality of pleasure. The will has triumphed over the body. This pleasure is also strongly tinged with the knowledge that one has endured hardship with one's friends. In rowing, far more than in cricket or football, where a star player may win a match, nothing can be achieved without team-spirit. The art of rowing in an eight is to make the boat run smoothly and this depends to a remarkable extent on the psychology of the crew. Weeks of coaching may improve individual oarsmen yet the boat may deteriorate, since its progress depends on the crew's state of mind. An atmosphere of comradeship must therefore be created in the boat-club. The crew eat together in Hall; as an essential to success, they are encouraged to consider themselves superior to their fellows; and a good oar may be dropped from the club if he does not fit in. This intense feeling of comradeship and reliance upon each other makes the boat run smoothly—so that if one man relaxes the pressure of his feet on the stretcher or brings his oar through too high, the other members of the crew almost unconsciously deviate from their normal stroke so as to prevent the boat from rolling or running in jerks.

The real leader of the boat is the coach; for though

stroke dictates the rate of striking, he is quite unable to increase the boat's speed unless the crew are so co-ordinated that they immediately respond. The coach's job is to get the men into the proper attitude of aggressive self-confidence so that they overcome in a race their natural feeling of exhaustion and despair. The crew must believe in victory not only during the race but throughout training. In rugger a first XV will nearly always beat a second XV simply because the individual skill and knowledge of the players is superior. But a second boat will almost always beat a first boat in a trial because the second boat, knowing that to be beaten is no disgrace, rows without nerves, while the first boat fears defeat, knowing that victory will not heighten their prestige. Everything therefore depends on the coach. He must be tyrant enough to be obeyed without question, persuasive enough to prevent sulkiness or loss of self-respect, sensible enough not to demand too much hard work in the early stages when the boat is running poorly and before the crew can see the results of hard work, and careful enough not to bring the crew on too fast which will lead to staleness and instil groundless doubts and fears into the crew's mind taking weeks to eradicate. The coach is virtually a member of the crew and plays upon it like a minstrel on his harp.

Stephen has a place among the great rowing coaches. He may have rowed badly but he knew how it should be done. He could invent ingenious analogies and similes to catch his crew's imagination; he knew when to slang a man and when to praise; and his fertile mind was always thinking out new ways of improving rowing technique so that he never grew stale. Rowing gave Stephen the pleasure of intense comradeship; coaching gave him in addition the delights of leadership. It gave him self-confidence and the pleasurable knowledge that others had confidence in him as well. This was what he was to require during the rest of his life. He had subdued his sensitiveness and could count himself one of those 'manly affectionate fellows' whom he had learnt to admire at Trinity Hall. During his years at Cambridge no fitter epitaph could have been designed for him than that of the first rowing man in literature, Elpenor

in the Odyssey; 'Fix upon the mound of my grave the oar
that in life I pulled among my comrades.'

Stephen felt that he had triumphed over his nature; but
as so often happens the price of the triumph was not realised
until many years later. An instalment, however, had to
be paid almost at once. The transmogrification into a
tough lost Stephen friends in a place where people are too
often judged by the company they keep. Trinity Hall was
not distinguished academically or socially. It was filled
with amiable young men of whom the brightest intended
to be lawyers and the remainder came to Cambridge to
enjoy themselves. Night after night Stephen's rooms were
filled with the din and jargon of rowing men comparing the
form of the boats. 'You took me for a sanctimonious prig,
and I took you for a rowing rough, and I don't know which
was nearest the mark,' a contemporary told him in later
years. He was not aggressively anti-intellectual but indi-
cated strongly that affairs of the mind should be kept like a
kettle on the hearth humming a private song to itself, to be
displayed only when some public occurrence had stoked
the fire so fiercely that the kettle had to blow off steam.
His utterances on such occasions were explosive and
delivered with a solid portion of contempt for the opinions
of all concerned—himself included. This apparent contempt
for other men's opinions in a discussion, even for the value
of discussion itself, had probably led the Apostles to reject
him. Yet though he disappointed the Apostles, the hearts
of Trinity Hall rejoiced. The undergraduates saw that their
tutor's heart was in the College and, what was more, in
their personal pursuits. It was Stephen who presided at
Bump Suppers and wrote the College Boating Song, and
they noticed that his enthusiasm was as frenzied as their
own when the boat went head of the river. 'I shall never
forget the joy with which he caught hold of my hand and
shook it,' said the stroke of the boat on that occasion. 'He
very nearly upset us all into the river, and, if I had not used
some strong language, I believe he would have done so.'
Undergraduates could forget that he was a parson, for
Stephen was ready to take the lead in every new enthusiasm.
The first sports meeting between Oxford and Cambridge in

1864 was permitted largely through Stephen's influence. At the time when Tennyson was calling Riflemen to form, Stephen enrolled as a Volunteer and his rooms resounded to the crash of arms drill. Happily the idlest undergraduate in the College, whose rooms were below the Tutor's, did not miss his opportunity and sent his gyp to present his compliments to Sgt. Stephen and beg him to conduct 'Order Arms' with a little less noise as his studies were being disturbed. Moreover, the undergraduates saw him as their champion; though he was in authority he deflated it by referring to the Master as 'old stick-in-the-mud,' and by despising openly the fusty, dusty dons who opposed rowing and athletics because young men enjoyed them. The freedom with which he expressed his views somewhat scandalised Ben Latham, the Senior Tutor and founder of Trinity Hall's distinction. Latham winced to see a College official galloping round Parker's Piece in some race and losing so many garments in the process that parsonical decency was imperilled. But it was Stephen and not Latham who was the major influence in the College during the 'fifties. Not that he adopted any of the subtler means by which a tutor can achieve popularity. His letters to pupils were models of forthright bluntness and if they could not see the affection that lay behind them, *tant pis pour eux*. Nor did he rely on formal entertainment but bawled at them across the court to bring their own commons and have tea with him. He was a character. At one time he developed a mania for dried figs and carried a box of them about with him to friends' rooms where he would perch on a table swinging his legs and munching.

Stephen set a new fashion in dons and must take his place beside schoolmasters, such as Warre of Eton and Bowen of Harrow, who fastened athleticism upon Victorian youth in order to keep them out of mischief. This was the method behind the apparent madness of thirty-mile Sunday walks and College athletics. It was not entirely unreasonable, for the majority of undergraduates were not and never would be interested in the dreary curriculum of the poll degree. Stephen described himself in his undergraduate days as a wearied and disgusted wayfarer along the lanes of mathematics, and the poll men retched at learning gobbets of Paley's *Evidences of Christianity* and the first three books of Euclid by heart. Treated by the University as schoolboys, spending the minimum of time at lectures, resorting to the grossest type of cramming, hemmed in by restrictions, with few diversions to break the routine of Chapel and Hall, they became devoured by *ennui* and refused to behave as adults. What else was there to do except drink at inns, gamble at Newmarket and pick up tarts in Barnwell; or, by way of a change, to bowl over old ladies when out for a spin in a gig and break windows and each other's heads in a hooligan rag? Stephen's cult of athleticism was a palliative for a recurrent disease: a poor remedy, and Stephen knew it. The ruck of undergraduates in each generation require someone who will fight their battles against the purists and disciplinarian scholars, and Stephen, who knew the poll-man better than most dons, did what he could to improve their lot. The changes he proposed in the curriculum were opposed by men who interpreted education in a different sense and pointed out that boys who arrived at Cambridge, ignorant of the elementary principles of arithmetic and geometry, must be taught them. Dr. Paget clamoured for the inclusion of hydrostatics among the subjects for poll-men, contending that 'if hydrostatics were not required, then Bachelors of Arts might go down without knowing the differences between a thermometer and a barometer, and without knowing how to describe the common pump.' Dr. Mayor of St. John's bewailed the fact that the proposed changes in the poll degree would deprive men of the spirit of Greek *mousike* or moral and aesthetic appreciation; and casting a baleful glance at Stephen declared that the changes were inspired by 'pestilent muscular Christianity.' Henry Fawcett, Stephen's greatest friend in the university, believed in mental discipline: he admired the old examinations precisely because they were narrow and thought that young men should train their brains, as acrobats train their muscles, and learn the whole technique of back-somersaults and handstands before trying to swing and soar on the trapeze of the intellect. Stephen's proposals were, on the whole, sensible. We pretend to educate the poll man. Well then, let it be an education and not a soulless farce which undergraduates regard as a stinking bog to be crossed by hiring a crammer. Away with Dr. Mayor and his pretensions that a few classical texts swotted with curses will sweeten the imagination of poll men with *mousike*. Let us rather give them a general course of history and geology and the spirit of the classics. Above all, do not stigmatise the poll man as a lower form of vertebrate life. Open the Tripos to him by providing a pass class. 'An examination (the poll) from which all the best men are by their nature excluded, infallibly produces a low standard among the examinees. The poll system does not simply assume that one man is stupider than another. It deliberately stamps half our students as intellectual pariahs. It writes down every man an ass who can't pass an honours examination. . . . The truth is that all poll examinations will be defective as long as they are entirely divorced from the honour triposes.'

Why did Stephen fail in his attempted reform? Partly because his suggestion to incorporate the poll degree in the Tripos was not particularly happy; to open the Tripos to pass men would inevitably lower the standard of the Honours schools without humanising the standard of the pass degree. Partly because no institution is more difficult to reform than a university whose resident senior members combine a deadly power of dialectic with astonishing stamina and obduracy in debate. The ingenuity in argument, the subtlety in drawing distinctions, the dexterous prevarications, the imperative reasons for procrastination, perpetually bewilder and confound the novice in university administration. The leaders of opinion in Cambridge were all convinced that reform must come; but since each was convinced that he alone could propound the exact solution, the proposals of syndicate after syndicate went down into the dust. Perhaps it was natural that all the reformers, Stephen included, set their sights too low, for the relations between the universities and Church and State were changing too rapidly for them to catch a glimpse of the target. And, finally, the deplorably low level of the average schoolboy's education made reform singularly difficult.

Very little could be done until the University and the Colleges followed Trinity's lead in establishing an entrance examination, thus forcing the public schools to raise their standards; and this they could not do because they restricted entry as far as possible to the sons of gentlemen and rejected in disgust the continental ideal of the career open to talent.

This, indeed, was the crux of the matter. The universities of every country unconsciously assume a purpose in the education they provide. German universities in the nineteenth century, assuming that nothing was more important than the increase of knowledge, tried to bind the best brains of each generation, like slaves, to the grindstone of research. In France the universities and Grandes Écoles during the 'forties forged an examination system designed to provide a standard of qualification for the professions including that of teacher in the State schools. Oxford and Cambridge were peculiar in that they assumed that their first duty was to educate the governing class. Not that there was anything as crudely purposive as special courses of study in politics or commerce—only recognised branches of scholarship were allowed; but before their eyes was the ideal of the educated gentleman who left the university to take his place in the world of affairs. The ideal was no better or worse but born of a different social tradition from that of other countries and other times. It was expressed, not in the courses of study provided, but in the selection of entrants and in the attitude to learning.

Stephen found fault with the English ideal. He had no sympathy for Fawcett's delight in a narrow curriculum. He wished to broaden the field of studies and by this he meant, not the modern craze for integrated courses and all-round education, but a recognition that admirable scholarly disciplines existed, each with its own technique and books, other than classics and mathematics and the newly-founded and despised triposes of the Natural and Moral Sciences. Whatever garden of knowledge you choose to study is surrounded by a wall. The wall is the technique of the subject and to climb it means inevitable drudgery. Why not climb walls which protect gardens of roses rather than force young men to climb those which land them in a plot of cactus? In a series of four articles, contributed to *Fraser's Magazine* after he had left Cambridge, he raised more fundamental questions. Stephen was appalled at the lack of a learned class at Oxford and Cambridge. No one cared if a good man left or stayed, and if he stayed, he had to submit to vows of celibacy, or take Holy Orders or engage in hack coaching. 'Most of the working men of the place are so steeped in the wearisome details of teaching, enforcing discipline, and administering the college funds, that they have absolutely no time for pursuing an independent course of study': the words have a sinister modern ring. More professorial chairs could be endowed if the financially wasteful system of independent college teaching were abandoned; and this was unlikely to happen so long as professors remained remote from the undergraduate curricula, their lectures 'sprinkled by a few eccentric individuals who have the singular desire to improve their minds.' To compare Oxford and Cambridge with the intense intellectual activity of German universities would be humiliating. And why was this? Because Cambridge's educational values were morally wrong. Fawcett liked to boast that Cambridge treated Fellowships as prizes for those who won the tripos races without any nonsensical regulations about research attached to them. But, according to Stephen, this very system of competitive triposes and prize fellowships, often held *in absentia*, was ruinous. It turned triposes into tests of mental agility; examiners were so frightened of cramming that any subject which could be got up was excluded; and nearly all subjects of interest can, of course, be got up—after a fashion. Stephen felt that the mania for testing ability, a quality required for the ordinary kind of worldly success, had so maimed the Cambridge ideal of education, that any suggested improvements in the system were judged by the degree to which they increased the spirit of competition for Honours and prizes. No wonder English lawyers and theologians were so notoriously narrow-minded.

In this respect Stephen was ahead of his colleagues. 'In the 'sixties,' wrote Maitland, 'he was already advocating the reforms that were effected by the second commission in the 'eighties.' Stephen did not demur, however, at the restriction of entry to the sons of gentlemen. To criticise a past generation for not accepting what we ourselves have only just accepted as normal is supercilious folly; and to argue that Stephen should have advocated open entrance examinations and have crusaded for the abolition, not only of the religious tests, but also of the unspoken class tests, would be to ask him to step out of his own generation into our own. G. M. Young has said that the Oxford and Cambridge ideal of the educated gentleman was almost the sole barrier against an all-encroaching materialism and professionalism; and certainly it did much to make earnest people of all classes think of education as something valuable in itself and not as a short-cut to political power or crude self-advancement. Stephen was not at fault in his acceptance of the ideal but in his interpretation of its possibilities. He wanted dons to be more learned and undergraduates to be given the chance to benefit from this learning, but he did not hope that this would change the character of the under-graduate. On the contrary, he was satisfied with the young men as they were. For Stephen himself was subtly tainted with the English contempt for culture and the world of ideas. Learning and literature were well enough, but what Stephen feared was the atmosphere of mind that they generate in the young. Were there not weeds and deadly nightshade, mandragora and fennel, hidden among the flowers of learning which only an adult mind could distinguish and reject? He had visited Heidelberg after taking his degree and the experience confirmed him in his notions of insular superiority: the only other man he had seen sculling on the Neckar was an Englishman. He thought the English undergraduate, playing cricket and rowing, infinitely superior to duelling philosophising German louts or spindly French intellectuals arguing about politics and art. And so he informed Matthew Arnold that the English had every right to call themselves 'the best breed in the universe' because there weren't many better. What nobler type of boy was there, for instance, than Tom Hughes's young brother, Harry, whose funeral sermon Stephen preached at Trinity Hall when he broke a blood

vessel at athletics and died young? True, it had taken all
Stephen's powers to push him through his examinations, yet
'without any special intellectual capacity, he somehow
represented a beautiful moral type . . . absolutely unselfish
. . . so conspicuously pure . . . so unsuspicious of evil in
others . . . sweet and loyal in his nature . . . [which
inspired among other undergraduates] profound respect, at
least, for the beauty of soul that underlay the humble
exterior.'

It is right to tell the clever and the successful not to
despise simple and unaffected young men, but a different
matter to set up such young men as the ideal. The longer
one examines Stephen's judgments on youth the more they
appear to be vitiated by sentimentalism and dread of
intellectual verve and fancy. Like so many of his contemporaries Stephen worshipped 'character' as a Kantian
Thing-in-itself, and failed to realise that character, uninstructed by the intelligence or informed by the emotions,
is liable to be exerted on the side of injustice and intolerance.
Guts and open-heartedness without some knowledge of the
world are not enough, and to believe that 'manly and affectionate fellows' could 'fight a good battle in the world' was
to glorify will-power as an end, not a means, and to forget
that education means opening, as well as training, the mind.
'I don't care a straw for Greek particles, or the digamma. . . .'
mused Tom Hughes's Squire Brown when he sent Tom to
Rugby. 'If he'll only turn out a brave, helpful, truthful
Englishman, and a gentleman, and a Christian, that's all
I want.' But you cannot produce Stephen's or Squire
Brown's ideal unless you acknowledge the value of *mousike*,
even though you may not define it in terms of Mr. Mayor,
and the digamma. Stephen's ideal among intellectual
undergraduates was the hard-headed man who stood for
no nonsense—a type too often blind to the subtler kinds of
sense. He was determined to admire nothing, and though
men were none the worse for taking time off to read literature
or talk politics, he advised them to 'stick to your triposes,
grind at your mill, and don't set the universe in order until
you have taken your bachelor's degree.' This is the voice
of the pedagogue who cannot understand that affectation,

4

mockery, frivolity and extravagance are ways in which young men can criticise life seriously.*

In fact Stephen's conception of the ideal is what he wanted to be himself and what he hoped he was. Stephen was best known at Cambridge as a radical and an ardent party man. The genial toughs whom he taught were insufficient for his needs; he sought intellectual companionship and found it in the circle which centred round Henry Fawcett. Two years Stephen's junior at Cambridge, Fawcett moved to Trinity Hall shortly after coming into residence and was elected a Fellow in 1856. He later became Professor of Political Economy, entered Parliament and served in the administration of 1880 as Gladstone's Postmaster-General where he introduced the parcel post. The two men became close friends, and after Fawcett was accidentally blinded by his father in a shooting accident, Stephen cared for him with feminine tenderness. In those days, wrote Stephen, there were two main circles among the younger men, the literary set who read Tennyson, *Jane Eyre* and sometimes Browning; and the more serious thinkers who discussed *Sartor Resartus* or followed F. D. Maurice as liberal theologians. Fawcett would have nothing to do with either. He denounced Carlyle as reactionary and Maurice as muddle-headed, and set himself up as a descendant of the Philosophic Radicals. His mind was uncommonly clear and he admired Cambridge teaching for its distrust of obscurity and ambiguity. 'This shallow stuff does not go down here, does it?' he used to say. Leslie Stephen fell under his spell and together they declared war on what they called 'dyslogistic' words such as sentimentalism and declamation. Anyone who denounced them as Philistines was told roundly that this 'was a name which is best definable as that which a prig bestows on the rest of the

---

* In politics alone the young were to be given their head: he himself in his old age did not regret his youthful republicanism. 'A man should be ashamed rather of not having felt in his youth the generous impulses which make him sympathise with whatever appears to be the cause of progress.' He would have understood the motives which led his grandson, Julian Bell, to abandon pacificism and, though no Communist, to drive an ambulance in the Spanish Civil War, in which he lost his life: his grandson exemplified 'what a young man ought to become—an enthusiast for the newest lights, a partisan of the ideas struggling to remould the ancient order and raise the aspirations of mankind.'

species.' The universities were traditional in politics, and
though Cambridge had long-standing connections with
the Whigs, radicals were few and far between. Blindness
had not dimmed Fawcett's high spirits; six foot three and
broad in proportion, he rode to harriers and skated fifty
miles in a day across the Fens. Together the two firebrands,
as young dons should, enjoyed themselves at the expense
of the Old Guard. They fastened in particular upon Dr.
Geldart, the Master of Trinity Hall, an ancient mega-
therium, who liked his bottle in the evening and asked only
to be left in peace. But now he resembled a barnacled
dreadnought, straddled by salvoes from port and starboard,
his young radical colleagues on the one hand and on the
other his wife, a formidable Mrs. Proudie of the Evangelical
persuasion. One day she sent her husband into a College
meeting with strict instructions not to grant the Chaplaincy
of St. Edward's, in the gift of the College, to F. D. Maurice
on the grounds that he held lax views on the subject of
Eternal Punishment. Stephen and Fawcett guessed what
had happened and innocently enquired the exact nature of
the allegedly heretical passages. The Master, unable to
make a signal to base, foundered with all hands, and to
their delight Maurice was appointed. Far from disliking
him the rebels regarded Dr. Geldart with unassailable
affection; and when he lay on his death-bed Fawcett
visited him and so invigorated the old gentleman that he
called for a bottle of port and his fishing tackle to the infinite
scandal of Mrs. Geldart who forbade a repetition of the visit.*

Fawcett's good-natured hard-headedness, however, provided a mingy diet. Uninterested in science, theology or the
arts, he was the kind of utilitarian who gloried in using the

---

* Mrs Geldart found it most difficult to get her husband into a seemly
frame of mind. 'I don't know why it is,' she complained, 'but I can't get poor
dear Charles to take any interest in the arrangements for his funeral.' As a
good Evangelical she waited anxiously for her husband's last words which
would indicate that his thoughts were fixed on higher things, but Dr. Geldart
remained lamentably mixed with the dross of this world. Feeling the death
pangs hard upon him, the flame lit up for the last time. 'You will let the
undergraduates have some of the old sherry,' he gasped, and thereupon expired.
Mrs. Geldart, writes Thomas Henry Thornely, was so appalled that she called
for an autopsy and joyfully exclaimed, when the surgeons proclaimed that
there was evidence that the Master's mind had become unhinged at the end,
'Clearly not responsible! Clearly not responsible!'

felicific calculus like a sickle and preached free trade, co-
operatives, social equality of the sexes, and the removal of
religious tests. Spiritually, however, he was nearer to James
than John Stuart Mill and his chop-logic destruction of cant
and sham. Intellectually, Stephen lost by his attachment to
Fawcett nearly as much as he gained. Fawcett confirmed
him in many of the prejudices of his class, for instance, in his
insularity; he learnt to devour French literature only later
in life. In the formative years Fawcett drove Stephen so
far towards the centre of the circle that he never quite had
the strength in maturity to struggle towards the periphery.
A great critic should stand to one side of his age so that he
can see it in perspective. When we think of Dr. Johnson or
Matthew Arnold, Tocqueville or Chateaubriand, we can
appreciate the advantage a critic enjoys who is not committed to any one of the prevailing ideologies which the
majority of men unconsciously choose. The distinction is
between an attitude and an answer to life. The former is a
process of thought. It may rest on a highly dogmatic
structure such as Christianity, but the critic will be aware of
his duty to revalue, re-open his mind, and keep the antennae
of his sensibilities as responsive to new experience as possible.
He will always be rearranging old material in new shapes,
never satisfied that he has settled Hoti's business or properly
based Oun; he will avoid slipping into a mechanism of
thought which does the job for him like an adding-machine;
and he will judge every new problem on its own merits and
not equate it with some similar experience in the past.
The latter—the answer to life—is not to be despised. It is
essential to politicians who would be unable to conduct
their business without it. It assumes that the major questions
are settled once and for all and that all change is in effect
a modification of the prototype on the floor of the factory.
It provides firm ground for the controversialist and by no
means implies inferior capability. Still, it is less helpful
than the former outlook to a critic, however suited it may
be to others. Stephen was handicapped by his early
allegiance to the utilitarian system and it was some time
before he disentangled himself from Fawcett's influence.
Despite their similarity of outlook, there was, however, a

noticeable difference between them. Fawcett believed that
the best way of learning a subject was to lecture on it.
One evening, he announced after Hall, 'Now, I am interested
in Socrates, and want to know more about him, so I am
thinking of giving a lecture upon him.' 'But, Fawcett,'
said Stephen, 'have you read his works?' 'No, but I mean
to.' Stephen, on the other hand, was steadily reading
philosophy. By 1860 he had read Mill and Comte, Kant
and his English adapter Sir William Hamilton, Hobbes
and Locke, Berkeley and Hume and most of the main
intellectual works of the day; but since his secret activity
was unknown to most of his contemporaries they were
somewhat surprised when he was appointed in 1861 to
examine in the comparatively newly created Moral Science
Tripos.* This interest in philosophy was in the end to cut
short his career in Cambridge.

Stephen's Christianity had never been fervent. He had
never adhered to the Evangelical party whose foremost
members, by the middle of the century, were noted for their
piety and philanthropy rather than for their intelligence,
and whose committeemen were often despicable bigots with
a taste for persecution. Even his father had fallen out with
them. After his retirement from the Colonial Office, Sir
James Stephen had published a volume of essays in one of
which, like Tennyson, he faintly trusted the larger hope that
sinners *might* in some remote aeon be relieved of their
suffering in hell. This hapless blunder was seized upon by
people outside as well as inside the Evangelical camp. Shortly
after Sir James's retirement the Prime Minister on
Macaulay's advice appointed him to the Regius Professor-
ship of Modern History at Cambridge and the conservative
party sniffed at the appointment. Would not Sir James now
be in a position to pervert the youth of the country? Dr.
Corrie, the Master of Jesus College, wagged his head at
Archdeacon Hardwick. 'Who would have thought we
should have seen a live Gnostic walking about the streets
of Cambridge? You know, my friend, in healthier times

* This tripos included philosophy, political economy, jurisprudence and
some history. The office of examiner could hardly be described as exacting
since in 1860 there were no candidates at all, and in the first nine years of its
institution only sixty-six men took honours.

he would have been burnt.'* In Leslie's second year as an undergraduate a Grace was offered at a congregation to enquire into Sir James's beliefs and probe for *falsa doctrina*, though the Grace was not put to the Senate. Two years later, in 1853, F. D. Maurice, whose lectures Leslie had attended in London, was bitterly attacked in the Evangelical press for holding similar views and was expelled from King's College, after a series of shabby interviews with the Principal, Dr. Jelf. This treatment of two men whom he knew to be deeply religious naturally turned Leslie towards the moderates.

The remarkable fact about the episode of Sir James Stephen's religious beliefs was not that a protest was made, but that the Grace was never put to the Senate. In Cambridge religion was never the issue that it was in the Oxford of Newman and Bishop Wilberforce. 'The average Cambridge don of my day,' wrote Stephen, 'was (as I thought and think) a sensible and honest man who wished to be both rational and Christian. He was rational enough to see that the old orthodox position was untenable. He did not believe in Hell, or in "verbal inspiration" or the "real presence." He thought that the controversies on such matters were silly and antiquated, and spoke of them with indifference, if not with contempt. But he also thought that religious belief of some kind was necessary or valuable, and considered himself to be a genuine believer. He assumed that somehow the old dogmas could be explained away or "rationalised" or "spiritualised." He could accept them in some sense or other but did not ask too closely in what sense. Still less did he go into the ultimate questions of philosophy. He shut his eyes to the great difficulties and

---

* Dr. Corrie was famous for such remarks. When a Dr. Donaldson, whose *Book of Jashar* Corrie had condemned, complained that the Master appeared willing to re-light the fires of Smithfield, Corrie remarked, 'in these economical days he would not be considered worth the faggots.' Born in 1793 he wielded considerable power in the Church. For thirty-two years he was an excellent tutor of St. Catharine's but on failing to be elected Master (though he voted for himself), he was given the Mastership of Jesus College. He also held a lonely Fen living. Dr. Corrie was of a reverent though practical frame of mind. Bishop G. F. Browne, visitor of the living, was somewhat disturbed, on going early one morning to the church, to identify a pungent smell which hung inside it. The verger explained: 'Rector doesn't mind smell of gunpowder. He won't have pigeons flappin' about in t' church, not he.' Corrie died, aged 92, in 1885.

took the answer for granted.' Church-going was to perform an edifying ceremony not to state one's beliefs; and in this spirit Stephen was ordained. 'I took this step,' he reproached himself later, 'rather—perhaps I should say very—thoughtlessly. I was in a vague way a believer in Maurice or in what were called Broad Church doctrines. My real motive was that I was very anxious to relieve my father of the burthen of supporting me.' It was true that Sir James's retirement had reduced his income, but there were other motives as important. Leslie wanted to be independent of his family and to take the prize he had won by trial of tripos. He did not want to follow the strong Trinity Hall tradition of being called to the Bar, so his only alternative was to take Holy Orders; and this imposed no strain on the conscience of an undergraduate ignorant of European thought. Stephen became a clergyman in order to become a tutor and inculcate young men with the principles of 'fearing God and walking a thousand miles in a thousand hours.' It was a higher ideal than the routine acceptance of a Fellowship as a prelude to a College living leading possibly to a Deanery, but it was much lower than the standards set and practised in Oxford under the influence of the Tractarians. There was in Cambridge none of the fierce partisan discussion of theology such as had shown the young J. A. Froude or A. H. Clough in the 'forties where they stood. The 'Sims' or Evangelicals who attempted to carry on the tradition of Charles Simeon were much despised, partly for snobbish reasons as they were generally recruited from sizars and poor undergraduates. The Cambridge Camden Society, whose strategem for restoring the Round Church had been unmasked as a Ritualist plot hatched by the ecclesiologist J. M. Neale,* was no longer a force, and the Oxford Movement had not taken root in Cambridge. Stephen recorded that one undergraduate at Trinity Hall turned his gyp-room into an oratory with candles and flowers, but claims that he was exceptional.

---

* J. M. Neale (1818–66) was a leading Ritualist at one time inhibited from officiating in his diocese by his bishop. The promoter of Anglican sisterhoods, he is best known as a hymnologist: in the first edition of Hymns Ancient and Modern one eighth of the total were his translations or original hymns.

Even infidelity in the 'sixties caused little comment. 'One of our fellows' Stephen noted in a letter 'wrote a book the other day to prove under a very thin veil, that Christianity was a degenerate kind of Gnosticism. Nobody has taken any notice of it, and if he does not insult people's feelings, nobody will.' In a largely clerical society party loyalties and enmities were inevitable, but they were on the level of gossip and university politics rather than of serious disputes about fundamentals. Stephen was thought to be a rather modern clergyman concerned more with ethics than theology, and the sudden collapse of his faith came, therefore, as a shock even to his intimate friends.

He had been ordained in 1855 and a curiously inexplicable interval elapsed before he took priest's orders in 1859 shortly before his father died; the fact that he became a fully fledged parson shows that he had no serious doubts until after that date. By the summer of 1862 he found himself unable any longer to conduct the chapel services. He informed the Master, who went into conclave with the Fellows of the college. Apparently almost all were unanimous in desiring to retain Stephen as tutor until his doubts resolved themselves one way or another, but a senior Fellow feared for the undergraduates' morals, and Stephen resigned immediately; so far from bearing any malice he rightly thought that under the university statutes, it was the only proper course. Fawcett managed to convince his colleagues, quite wrongly, that Stephen's Fellowship need not lapse with the Tutorship and he therefore continued to hold the offices of bursar and steward and coached the boat. But these pursuits soon appeared futile. His prospects of university office were ruined. Declining further and further into agnosticism he left Cambridge for ever at the end of 1864.

We shall see later what led to this change of mind. For it was a change of mind rather than a change of heart. 'From the age of fifteen,' wrote John Henry Newman in his *Apologia*, 'dogma has been the fundamental principle of my religion; I know no other religion; I cannot enter into the idea of any other sort of religion; religion, as a mere sentiment, is to me a dream and a mockery.' Stephen could have

made no such claim, but when he began seriously to consider
the content of his beliefs, he found himself in agreement with
Newman. Facts he had learnt from Fawcett were facts, and
if the dogmas of Christianity did not correspond to them,
then those dogmas were false and should be rejected. The
scales fell from his eyes. As a child Noah's Ark had been
his favourite toy; now, like Bishop Colenso, he found that
'it was wrong for me to regard the story [of the Flood] as a
sacred truth.' He suffered no agonies of doubt, or nights
spent in prayer on his knees; it was like discarding a thread-
bare garment. He suffered pain as every man does who is
faced by a real, and not a hypothetical, moral issue. But it
was more of an irritation with himself, a self-reproach that
he should ever have taken Holy Orders and thus find himself in this predicament, and he knew that people he loved
and respected would be offended. He lingered on for a
little as the broadest of Broad Churchmen and in 1863
was still preaching; but by 1865 he had abandoned all
vestige of belief in dogmatic Christianity.

It was a courageous and honest step to take. There is no
need to exaggerate its importance. Stephen possessed
after his father's death a private income and he was able to
live at his mother's house in London. He had not alienated
all his friends in Cambridge nor was he likely to suffer social
ostracism in London where a freethinker was by no means
unique. Moreover, his resignation did not excite an
immediate reaction in favour of toleration in the university.
In 1867 Fawcett admitted that the resident members who
wished to abolish the religious tests, whereby only Anglicans
could hold Fellowships, were still in a minority. The dons
remained obdurate until Parliamentary agitation forced
them to change their tune. As they saw bills defeated by
ever-decreasing majorities or voted to be read again but
shelved owing to the dissolution of Parliament, they realised
that the change must come, so that by 1869, when Henry
Sidgwick resigned spectacularly from Trinity, the battle
was won, even though two more years were to pass before
the university tests were finally repealed. Stephen's action
had no direct political effect. But it had a moral significance,
and this subtly affected the political atmosphere. In 1870,

testifying before the House of Lords, that wise clergyman and scholar, Lightfoot, saw that the tests were creating a prejudice in the minds of undergraduates against the religion they were meant to protect. 'They see a man prepared to sacrifice his material interests for the sake of conscientious scruples, and it begets a sort of sympathy for non-belief.' Lightfoot saw further. 'It is impossible to shut one's eyes to the fact that a flood of new ideas has been poured in upon the world, and that at present they have not found their proper level; minds are unsettled in consequence, and young men often do not like to pledge themselves to a very distinct form of religious belief.' Lightfoot had for long opposed the repeal of the tests, but the dignified and high-minded resignations of men like Stephen convinced him of the *justice* of the reform. Whatever Lightfoot's attitude had been, the tests would eventually have been repealed, but the manner of their repeal owes something to Stephen and his followers. Unless the opposition is convinced that their opponents are governed by the same considerations of seriousness and principle, government by consent becomes impracticable. Taken at its lowest, Stephen's self-sacrifice compelled his opponents to retreat gracefully and not in a rage lest they outlaw themselves in the eyes of public opinion. Though it is necessary on some occasions to assault one's opponents brutally, good behaviour in politics tends in stable times to breed good behaviour. Stephen's action was an example to others, a pronouncement that it is immoral in all circumstances to bow down in the House of Rimmon when a free choice lies before you. Like many other nonconformists who have sacrificed their position for their principles, he deserves praise.

CHAPTER II

THE MAN OF LETTERS

LESLIE STEPHEN had the good fortune to be born with a temperament which persuaded him that any change in his situation was a change for the better. As soon as he had left Cambridge he made the discovery that university life was a skin poison which raised tetters of irritation or covered one in a blue mould of premature old age. London was a tonic which restored one to health. It was a new experience to be insignificant. At Cambridge 'I walked about in a gorgeous cap and gown, and everyone I met took off their hats to me. Now in London I find that people don't instinctively recognise me. I can walk down the Strand without causing any visible sensation.' Stephen's sarcastic references to the university he had left were not sour grapes; most young dons who tear themselves away from the numbing embrace of that insatiable being, who is at once their mother and their bride, never regret the step they take. The University, Stephen thought, is all too pleasant a place for a bachelor. He lives in a delightful set of rooms with no regular working hours, long holidays and leisure; friends live within a stone's throw, gossip, the ritual of Hall and wine, the walks and sports, the curious avenues of enquiry down which he ambles, are all amiable ways of wasting time. He floats down the years as serenely as the new-mown grass from the lawns which College gardeners cast into the river. Visitors to Oxford and Cambridge imagine that the quiet quadrangles and courts provide the perfect atmosphere for scholarly research. They picture the don seated at his desk, piled high with folios, rising occasionally and pacing across the cobble-stones to check a reference in the library, breaking his labours only to swallow a few mouthfuls of cold meat at the hour when deference must be paid to the demands of the flesh; is it fancy, as we saunter past sets of panelled rooms on a drowsy afternoon, half drugged by the scent of flowers and the hum of summer insects—is it fancy or do we not

hear the scratch of a learned quill on foolscap? And is not
this sound to be heard in room after room, in college after
college?—so that in the mind's eye there rises the vision of
tomes of cultured learning deposited with the regularity of
products on an assembly-line from college rooms into the
press and thence on to library shelves. But in the world of
fact it is quite otherwise. So far from flowing as freely as
the port, the ink freezes on the desk. Some dons are too
indolent; others curl up like snails at the thought of their
colleagues' comments; genuine researchers lose interest in
a problem they have mastered and cannot be bothered to
publish their solution. Those with sociable instincts or a
capacity for administration tire the sun with talking or
submerge themselves in the turbulent waters of university
business; and a few who possess a decent sense of their own
limitations are repelled by the sight of books written by
those who have yet to acquire it. Time and again men
learn that books are best written away from the university.
Only a minority write because they must express themselves; the remainder write only if pricked on by shame or a
sense of duty—which is easily suppressed by arguing that
other duties are more urgent. Leslie Stephen required to
be pushed into writing, and had he stayed at Cambridge,
he would never have become a literary critic or a controversialist. But, in London, living with his mother and
sister in Porchester Terrace, he was induced to write by
two common incentives, want of money and boredom.
Believing (wrongly) that his parson's orders prevented
practice at the Bar—a profession he in any case found
unattractive—he resolved to supplement his income by
journalism.

Here again Leslie was in luck. His brother Fitzjames was
not only a flourishing barrister but one of the leading
journalists in the London periodicals. Fitzjames had
married in 1855 the daughter of the evangelical vicar of
Harrow, J. W. Cunningham, who edited with diminishing
success, the *Christian Observer*. Fitzjames became editor and
wrote articles for this sober journal to improve his style,
though he admitted that 'kind old Mr. Cunningham' had
to insert some phrases to flavour them with the spice of

unction expected by the faithful.* To support his family he
turned to London journalism and worked his way to become
in the 'sixties possibly the most distinguished of all the talented
contributors to the *Saturday Review*. He was a master of the
slashing, exuberant, contemptuous style which made the
paper the outstanding intellectual periodical of the day. It
was he who introduced Leslie to the editor, John Douglas
Cook, and very soon Leslie was writing two articles a week,
the one a review and the other a middle on any subject from
Poor Law Amendment, to Parisian Criminals or the
Redundancy of Women. Cook took all he could get, and
in 1867 gave Leslie a fifty guinea a year retaining fee as a
wedding present. Nor was Leslie confined to the *Saturday
Review*. Within a month of his settling in London a new
afternoon paper costing twopence, the *Pall Mall Gazette*,
was founded, and Fitzjames saw to it that an article by his
brother appeared in the second number. Here Leslie was
again writing in the company of the élite for Trollope,
Kingsley and Matthew Arnold contributed to the literary
side and Froude, G. H. Lewes and himself wrote on politics,
all attempting to realise Thackeray's ideal that there should
be a journal written by gentlemen for gentlemen. The
young newspaper flourished and, incidentally, engaged
Engels as its war correspondent during the Franco-Prussian
war. In 1866 Leslie also began to write for the *Cornhill*
which had been edited by Thackeray, and in addition sent
a fortnightly letter on English politics to the New York
Nation containing descriptions of debates in the House of
Commons and some excellent character studies of its
members.

His normal routine from 1865 to 1871 of three or four
articles a week gives some idea of his capability. He
possessed the gift of Victorian concentration. Snorting,
groaning and scribbling marginalia, he would seem to idle
through a book. Then, taking up a pen and lying almost
recumbent in a low rocking chair which he tipped to and

* More than one view was expressed about the character of Fitzjames's
father-in-law. Fanny Trollope savagely caricatured him in *The Vicar of Wrexhill;*
on the other hand the Duchess of Beaufort wrote: 'It is so delightful to think
of having for our companions throughout the endless ages of eternity such
men as Mr. Cunningham.'

fro as he wrote in a small, neat hand, he would complete
an article of eight thousand words at a sitting. He enjoyed
journalism and was adept at catching the tone of the
paper to which he was contributing. But he had to be
careful, since his religious views and his politics were not
those of a gentleman writing for gentlemen. 'Stephen and
I,' wrote John Morley, himself making his name on the
Saturday Review, 'were shut out from political writing, for
we were both of us in politics inexorable root and branch
men,' and they were warned off controversial subjects
especially as the owner of the paper was a High Churchman. If Stephen wished to air his agnosticism he had to
take to the pages of *Fraser's Magazine*, edited by J. A.
Froude. In 1867 he published the first of his articles on
religious subjects, an analysis of Voltaire's thought, but
though a good number of similar articles appeared in
Fraser's during the next few years, it was not until Morley
took over the *Fortnightly Review* that he found a periodical
sufficiently radical to suit his taste. Meanwhile, he pressed
on with his own private reading. He contemplated an
essay on the United States, but abandoned the idea and
settled down to long evenings of philosophical study and
annotation, Spinoza, Hegel,* Comte, Strauss and Renan.

Amid this mass of work the fortnightly letters to the New
York *Nation* entertained him most, which was not strange
because Stephen had visited the United States at the height
of the Civil War, when in 1863, tired of the gibes of the
Confederate supporters at Cambridge, he had determined
to go to the North and see for himself at first hand American
democracy at work. Leslie Stephen was one of the very
few intelligent Englishmen who found the United States
sympathetic. Still riled by the independence of the colonies,
despising Americans as low-bred boors, a generation of
English travellers from Harriet Martineau to Dickens
confirmed their countrymen in their attitude of superiority.
Stephen realised only too well that this upper class dislike
of the North sprang from dread of democracy. 'The whole

---

* Described as 'in many things little better than an ass.' One is reminded
of James Mill's comment, 'I see clearly enough what poor Kant would be
about.'

affair is looked upon in this country as a breakdown of democracy; that is one of the main causes of the absence of sympathy [for the North],' one of the leader writers on the *Times* noted. Would it not be proved if the North was defeated, that the best form of government was a stable aristocracy of landowning peers and squires, leavened by a number of bankers and merchants and a few men of exceptional intelligence? If this was proved, then movements for extending the franchise were manifestly inexpedient and possibly seditious. Led by the *Times*, upper class opinion was solid for the aristocratic Free Trade South, menaced by a corrupt, protectionist democracy; were not the attempts of the North to raise the issue of slavery hypocritical when their President would not take the stump in favour of emancipation? The North could find support only in the industrial areas of England. When the Federal army ran Russell, the pro-Unionist *Times* correspondent, out of the country, enraged by his accurate reporting of the rout of Bull Run, the last English journalist of importance who might have done something to educate public opinion disappeared; and Delane was at liberty to substitute an editorial policy of animosity against the North in place of a cogent examination of the facts. The *Times* represented official English opinion for Americans and Stephen, therefore, underwent something of an ordeal on his visit. As an hereditary Claphamite he naturally favoured the abolition of slavery, but could not convince Americans, especially after Lincoln's proclamation in favour of emancipating the slaves, that Englishmen did not regard the issue of slavery as crucial. He could point to the fact that John Bright and Morley supported the North and that a fellow radical, Goldwin Smith, had addressed large sympathetic meetings at which the *Times* was hissed, but he blandly told his hosts that Englishmen were incapable of understanding the constitutional issues at stake. Delane saw to it that the North should get no quarter. The evicted Russell declared, 'As I from the first maintained the North must win, I was tabooed from dealing with American questions in the *Times* even after my return to England.'

To visit a country in time of war, more especially of civil

war, is a delicate matter. The easy course is to flatter one's
hosts by telling them what they want to hear, but it is even
easier to scatter unintentional insults by laying one's finger
on their obvious weakness which they by a Freudian
process have conveniently forgotten. The way in which
Stephen was accepted shows what strength of character he
possessed and how his integrity impressed his hosts. He
prided himself on his tough 'realist' attitude to politics
which enabled him to see, that 'the North are destroying
slavery, not because they are abolitionists, but because the
South depends on slavery. That seems to me as plain as
two and two makes four.' His shrewd observations during
his trips to New York, Washington and the battle-front
enabled him to understand American democracy better
than other Englishmen. He was English enough to think
that American statesmen were an inferior breed—by which
he meant that Jefferson and Hamilton were not the equal
of Burke and Canning—and to admit surprise that Lincoln
was 'more like a gentleman to look at than I should have
given him credit for from his pictures . . .'; and when some
years later he contributed to a volume of essays in 1867
advocating a second Reform Bill, he was careful to point
out that the abuses of democracy which the English always
triumphantly pointed to in America, were purely indigenous.* Corruption in American public life disgusted
him, but it took more than average cleverness to see that
machine politics was a concomitant of the continual flow of
illiterate immigrants who looked to the local bosses for
protection; and he added that subtler means of financial
and social inducement to procure favours were not unknown in England. Stephen was a sensible traveller in that
he knew that a few months spent in a country is just long
enough for a man to misunderstand everything of importance, and he resisted Fawcett's appeals to pour out a
flood of radical pamphlets on his return. He realised that

* Stephen made a number of simple points. He began by saying that
democracy need not necessarily swamp intelligence and that to object that
Congress did not bulge with cultivated statesmen was to fail to realise that it
was impossible that it should, when the general level of culture in the country
was so low; and he himself was prepared to rely on the snobbery of the English
electorate, even with full enfranchisement, to return a sound quota of the sons
of the aristocracy to the House of Commons for some time to come.

LESLIE STEPHEN AGED 28 (1860)

JULIA JACKSON, LATER MRS. LESLIE STEPHEN, AGED 14

Englishmen were likely to remain ignorant of America, but he could not forgive the men whose duty it was to lighten that ignorance; and two years after his return he attacked the *Times* in a long and brilliant pamphlet under the worldly-wise anonymity of initials. It was irrelevant, Stephen declared, whether the *Times* were right or wrong about the causes and progress of the war. 'But I contend that I have proved . . . that it was guilty of "foolish vituperation," and as I am weak enough to think anything a serious evil which tends to alienate the freest nation of the old world from the great nation in the new. . . . I contend that I have proved the *Times* to be guilty of a public crime.' And he spoke as he did 'to withdraw our countenance from the blustering imposter who has been speaking all this time in our name without any due authority.' Stephen was quite right. Where there is a serious conflict of interest between two nations, fervent appeals to the principles of friendship and fair-play tend to bring morality in politics into disrespect, because people apprehend that the issues cannot be solved by a simple appeal to the rights and wrongs of the case; but where, as in the case of Britain and the United States, there was no fundamental political rivalry, the *Times* had done wrong to embitter relations needlessly between the two countries. Its factious policy brought retribution in the shape of a lasting distrust by Americans of British foreign policy.

Stephen's American tour gave him something more than the satisfaction of a good nonconformist in championing the right. So far we have seen him as a man with many younger cronies but few intimate friends; deeply attached only to Fawcett or to some odd Cambridge fish such as Joseph Wolstenholme, a mathematician and walker who had the gift of being able to spout thousands of lines of poetry by heart, as the evening fell and the pair of them pounded the last ten miles of the grind back to Cambridge. But now he was beginning to develop a talent for friendship. As he grew older he shunned acquaintances, and the friends he made became devoted to him, so that in their correspondence a great warmth of affection breathes through the written word. In America he made three friends in

particular. Charles Eliot Norton of Harvard and the young
Oliver Wendell Holmes, later the great Justice of the
Supreme Court, were two of them. The third came from
the same milieu, and their letters to each other reveal what
Stephen sought and found in friendship.

This third friend was James Russell Lowell, to whom
Stephen presented a letter of introduction from their
common friend Tom Hughes. Of the bluest-blood in New
England, a scion of Boston, Lowell was already the acknowledged high priest of culture in Cambridge, Massachusetts.
His career had all the auguries of brilliance; the cleverest
young man of his class, rusticated from Harvard for excessive
vitality and bumptiousness, he had redeemed himself by a
dazzling success at the age of twenty-nine with the Yankee
folklore of the *Biglow Papers*. His inherited conservatism
melted on his marriage to a New England beauty, Maria
White, who was the centre of a circle of young radical
Abolitionists. Rejoicing in his ancestry and Americanism,
Lowell was overflowing with bitterness against the insults of
British opinion. 'England *can't* like America do what she
or we will,' he wrote to Stephen after his visit. 'But I think
the usages of society should hold between nations, and see
no particular use in her taking every opportunity to *tell*
us how disagreeable and vulgar we are'; and he spoke
with pride and sorrow of his cousins and nephews who had
fallen in the war and asked Stephen whether they were the
sort of men the *Times* had in mind when it referred to Federal
officers as blackguards. In Stephen, however, Lowell
found more than a sympathetic Englishman. Here was a
fellow bookman who could cap his quotations. Lowell was
already the doyen of American letters with all the Bostonian
faculty for snubbing a hick. 'Who in the world ever heard
of the Claudian Emissary?' exclaimed Howells, exasperated
by Lowell's omniscience. 'You are in Cambridge, Mr.
Howells,' came the chilling reply. Stephen was spared this
side of Lowell's tongue, and he noticed that Lowell was
peculiarly sensitive to his listener's state of mind and
possessed an 'awkward power of penetrating one's obscurer
feelings . . . so acute that he was naturally secure from ever
becoming tiresome. Of all the qualities that make an

agreeable companion, certainly one of the chief is an
intuitive perception of the impression you are making.'
Cambridge, Mass., learnt to commune with Cambridge,
Eng. In Lowell's study at his large Georgian house, Elmwood, the two men would sit, attired in velvet jackets and
puffing at pipes, hour after hour, submerged in an intimate
silence to be broken by a comment on some point which
would lead to a barrowload of volumes, scored with pencil
marks, being scattered over the floor in search of a reference.
Calderon, Boccacio, Dante—Lowell had read them all and
could nod to authors in most dead and living languages.
This was the kind of scholar Stephen could admire, tossing
hay in the meadow by morning, knowing every bird and
flower by name, revelling in Yankee speech and drinking
whiskey-toddy by night. Grunts of pleasure greeted
Lowell's jocular verse and erudite puns, and when the visit
ended they parted with a long, strong handshake at the
corner of the road under the lamp which both men looked
back to with emotion till the end of their days. It was to
Lowell's house that Stephen hurried on his second visit
to America in 1868 when his wife had fallen ill, and it was
to Stephen that Lowell went to recuperate from his official
duties during his appointment as Minister to the Court of
St. James in the 'eighties. Lowell stood godfather—or, as
Stephen preferred to say, in quasi-sponsorial relation—to his
daughter Virginia, and Stephen obeyed a summons to
Elmwood to visit him for the last time in 1890, the year
before he died; he had invited Stephen because he thought
him 'the most lovable of men.'

What were the causes of this affinity? Their common
Puritan stock had much to do with it. They both shied
from indecency in literature; they both thought that a
biographer had betrayed his trust if he unveiled any weakness which should have been left in modest obscurity. Great
was Lowell's rage when Froude claimed that Carlyle was
sexually impotent and that the great prophet's marital life
was a model of incompatibility. Stephen was equally
shocked; to publish such stuff now was 'a needless outrage.'
Lowell deplored the fact that 'biography, and especially
that of men of letters, tends more and more towards these

indecent exposures . . . There are certain memoirs, after
reading which one blushes as if he had not only been
peeping through a key-hole but had been caught in the
act.' Stephen echoed him in his review of the published
Browning love letters. Sometimes it is almost impossible
to distinguish between the two voices in the Elmwood
study, especially when they mourn to each other the loss of
their wives; each of them has sacred places to which they
would fain make pilgrimage—the heavily sardonic phraseology is identical. Their attitude to sinful pleasure was also
similar; commenting on Stephen's essay about the New
England Calvinist theologian, Jonathan Edwards, Lowell
wrote 'If he had only conceived of damnation as a spiritual
state, the very horror of which consists (to our deeper
apprehension) in its being delightful to who is in it, I could
go along with him altogether.' Stephen was, also, just
the man to be taken in by the false honesty, the over-ripe
confession spoken in a deprecating, mock-modest tone that
is the sincerest form of self-flattery, which Lowell so often
employed; as when Lowell admitted that he had as a young
man put a pistol to his head but did not have the courage
to pull the trigger, 'of which I was heartily ashamed, and
am still whenever I think of it.' This kind of revelation
would convince Stephen that his host was a manly fellow,
too brave to commit suicide, but too honest not to admit that
fear to some extent deterred him. Politically shallow, they
both purported to be radicals, but they were radicals by
convention. Lowell's youthful attacks on law, order, and the
Constitution were forgotten even faster than Stephen's republicanism. Neither had any likings for Kings or lords, but they
defined democracy as government by the cultivated, educated
minority. Lowell believed in a Bostonian conception of
democracy which was fast passing, if, indeed, it had ever
existed. He told Tom Hughes that he would never give up a
thing if it had roots, and Stephen noted that in the civil war
the barb which festered in Lowell's mind longest was the
English assumption that all Americans were low-bred immigrants. On his return from his diplomatic mission abroad,
Lowell bewailed the state of American democracy ruined by
corruption and the Irish; it was a 'kakistocracy rather, for the

benefit of knaves at the cost of fools.' Insensibly he moved
closer to the ideals of the country he had so bitterly criticised.
As Minister in London he found himself at home, admired
for his after-dinner speeches and courtly felicities, a natural
hidalgo. He could still see through the English and pray
Americans to retain some of their dynamic vulgarity, and
he was astonished by the innuendoes of certain low-bred
politicians that he had been bought by English culture.
'These fellows,' he complained, 'have no notion what love
of country means. It is in my very blood and bones. If I
am not an American, who ever was?'

Lowell was an American of a special caste and what
Stephen took to his heart was less America than New
England. The last of a line of Cambridge Brahmins when
the strain was running thin, his youthful rebellions had
always been a little forced, as ill-fitting as his poetical
effects were contrived, and after his wife's death, Harvard
reclaimed him as a professor and tamed her wayward son.
His poems echoed every poet in turn. Economics, trade
unions, science ('I hate it as a savage hates writing, because
I fear it will hurt me somehow'), were all anathema.
Stephen's agnosticism disturbed him. 'I find no fault,' he
wrote, 'with a judicious shutting of the eyes' and he complained that Stephen seemed to think that there was something dishonest as well as undignified in drifting about
on the hencoop after Science had scuttled the old ship of
Faith. He liked to lie in an intellectual easy-chair and guzzle
books, adhering 'to the old notion of literature as a holiday.'
At his best he helps us to enjoy the books he loved: his
essays, now neglected, on Chaucer, Dryden, Wordsworth
and Izaak Walton are worth reading. But when Lowell
cannot lean on the word genius, he is undone. Deprecating originality in anything which he could not place,
he was imprisoned by the good form standards of his
class.

Mercifully, however, few people select their friends for
their intellectual merits alone. Reading between the lines
of Stephen's letters to Lowell, we detect a certain reserve:
Stephen praises Lowell's writing primarily for evoking
memories of Elmwood. Stephen understood better than

Lowell his relation to the world, and their political development, though similar, was notably different. At the height
of his radicalism Stephen fought an election for Fawcett
at Brighton, edited an election newspaper and cursed and
swore when Fawcett went down in defeat. The Reform Bill
of 1868, however, and the legislation of Gladstone's first
administration sated his appetite. The crudity of reformers
repelled him; by 1874 he found Fawcett's optimism unbearable and thought that but for the accident of their
sojourn at Cambridge they would never have become
friends. He lost interest in politics because he saw that the
principles which he had applied with such zeal in the
'sixties had degenerated into formulae and that he lacked
the ability to give them meaning. Liberal principles were
merely 'pretexts for acting in a convenient way'; when
British trade needed peace, Liberals were Quaker pacifists,
when foreign competition turned Britain imperialist, Quaker
precepts were condemned as cowardly. He agreed with
Morley that politics were not an art or a science but a
dodge, and he commended Bagehot's 'good, sweeping,
outrageous cynicism' and his dictum that illusion is a
necessity in politics. Lamenting the Gladstonian faith in his
old age, Stephen wrote:

> We are sometimes invited to regret the insensibility of
> Englishmen to 'ideas.' The regret may be softened by the
> reflection that in politics an idea means a device for saving
> thought. It enables you to act upon a little formula without
> taking the trouble to ask whether it be or be not relevant
> to the particular case.

Stephen disliked a life in which illusions and compromise
were the realities, and principles, appearances. Unlike
Lowell who was bewildered by the developments in American
politics, Stephen knew that he was temperamentally unsuited
to the game and was wise enough not to waste his energies
on a frustrating pursuit.

2

The Leslie Stephen who settled in London in 1865 was
still recognisable as the boy who had gone up to Cambridge
fifteen years before, though in the United States he had

grown a beard, the bright red straggling growth with which he was afterwards to be inseparably connected in people's minds. He still inwardly distrusted himself. Freed from celibate university life, and now in his middle thirties, he wanted to marry. But who—surely no one—could wish to marry him? 'I was shy, diffident, and fully impressed with the conviction acquired at Cambridge that I was an old don.' Bachelors, especially Cambridge bachelors, are apt after the age of forty to go one of two ways. Either they become old-maids, fussy, prudishly and primly garbed, valetudinarians whose cupboards bulge with tonics, pills and lotions, or they gyrate in orbits of ever wilder eccentricity, their trousers supported by string, their socks attached to combinations by paper-clips, their rooms an asylum, the walls padded by decades of unread newspapers and letters from scholars long since dead. Receipted bills are filed by flinging them up on the top of wardrobes, forgotten mutton-chops moulder beneath a mountain of discarded research, and some ancient beldam forbidden to disturb the dust of ages eventually becomes the sole companion of their dying years. Such visions of the future appalled Stephen and inspired him to look about before he should be 'dried up into a hopeless mummy, "walking about to save funeral expenses," and with a soul that ought to rattle like a dried pea in a pod.' He hoped he was not too far gone to be revived, but feared that he would remain a bachelor.

At this time two young ladies were much on the mind of literary hostesses in London. William Makepeace Thackeray had died in 1863 leaving two daughters, Anne Isabella and Harriet Marian, living by themselves in Onslow Gardens. In March, 1865, they lunched with Lady Stephen, and in June Leslie and his sister with Fitzjames and wife took them by train to Henley where they hired a boat and rowed down the river to Maidenhead. Leslie also met the sisters at the house of his father's successor at the Colonial Office, Herman Merrivale, and at George Smith, the publisher of Thackeray. Mrs. Gaskell saw Leslie and the Thackeray girls together at the latter house and prophesied that he would marry. The two sisters were by no means alike. Annie's face was round, plain and bonny, her figure short and dumpy, and conversation poured from her in floods: vivacious and entertaining, she was already hatching a clutch of novels. Of Minny, on the other hand, her father wrote that at twenty-one she was 'absurdly young for her age for she still likes playing with children and kittens and hates reading and is very shy tho' she does not show it and very clever tho' she does not do anything in particular and always helps me out of scrapes which I am always getting into.' She was an English rose, a Victorian girl unspoilt by education, 'pure-minded' said Leslie Stephen, 'as happily many are pure-minded' and free from any taint of coarseness or conceit of self-consciousness, 'which destroy the true ring of the natural affections.' It soon became obvious that Leslie was taken with her, but how was he to be made to conquer his diffidence and be brought up to the mark? A vile lioniser of Buckle and Herbert Spencer, a certain Mrs. Huth, nearly spoilt the match by her 'cork-screwing' questions, and when Stephen refused to answer, decided on other tactics. Knowing that he was going to Switzerland to climb in the summer, she arranged that all four of them should meet at Zermatt. Rather vexed— though he was later to think kindly of Mrs. H.—Stephen agreed. 'One of my sacred places ever afterwards was a point where the road winds round a little bluff near Täsch. Thence I descried the party approaching on mules . . . and walked back with them to Zermatt . . . I began to know that my fate was fixed.' Nevertheless, there was a certain hesitation in meeting it; he hastened away to keep a date with Bryce, the historian, in Vienna, where also, inci-dentally, he began his long friendship with George Meredith. Back in London in the autumn he waited but could not bring himself to decide. Then, hearing a rumour that the Thackeray girls were annoyed with him for not call-ing, he pulled himself together. The day came when 'I lunched by myself at the Oxford and Cambridge club, thought over the whole affair in a philosophic spirit and went to 16, Onslow Gardens.' He proposed and was accepted. Mrs. Huth congratulated herself; everyone rejoiced; and on the 19th of June, 1867, they were married in a seemly but rather unusual manner, described by

Leslie's mother as 'a most original wedding—at 8 o'clock
in the morning . . . nobody invited, but a large number of
friends and acquaintances assembled.'

Love for Stephen was a simple emotion. Passion, obsession,
delusion, could never steal upon him unseen, breed about his
heart and possess him; the fascinating and alluring and
those attractions that are mysteriously generated by the
temperament and physique, were alien to his nature and
repelled him. Love meant devotion: to adore and to be
adored. But on the level of humdrum existence he found it
difficult to translate this devotion into sympathy and
understanding. Stephen regarded his wife as a soothing
creature who would dissipate worry, attend his needs and
bend to his will, but discovered to his surprise that marriage
cannot be circumscribed by a series of rules and concepts.
Minny had a determined chin and, since they had returned
to live at Onslow Gardens with Annie, Stephen found that
he had also married a sister-in-law. He might have managed
Minny alone, but Annie was beyond his control. She had
the habit 'which I cannot unreservedly applaud' of looking
on the bright side of things. Gay, utterly haphazard, for
ever in a muddle, she was unable to distinguish facts from
her own interminable fancies. She wrote novels—but were
they, Leslie asked himself, as good as they should have
been? 'Once when a story of hers was published in Australia,
the last chapter got into the middle and nobody found out—
in Australia, at any rate.' The Stephens decided that her
Irish blood had somehow overpowered her father's strain:
they would tame and reform her. They told her she was a
sentimentalist and erratic; Fitzjames advised her on a
systematic course of reading, 'Macaulay, Gibbon, etc. It
was well meant advice, but,' said Leslie, 'I could afterwards
have told him, utterly useless.' Fitzjames reviewed one of
her stories by comparing her to Jane Austen 'with ponderous
insistence upon the negative merits' of Annie's tiny offering.
It was then that Minny spoke up. 'Fitzy,' she exclaimed,
'does not see that Annie is a genius!' Annie and Minny
were by no means pliable, and since Minny sided with her
sister, Leslie found himself to his chagrin only half her
master. 'Annie and Minny used to call me the cold bath

from my habit of drenching Annie's little schemes and fancies with chilling criticism.' Stephen could never realise that the weighty analysis applied to destroying a chapter of Buckle had no relevance in his sister-in-law's world. But there was worse to come. Annie not only muddled her facts, she muddled her figures. She was, he complained, far too generous and 'imprudent in money-matters.' She even went so far as to spend the money that she earned from the publication of her stories. She could not pay her share of the household expenses and often led Minny into making rash purchases. He made scenes with her over unpaid bills, she promised to amend, but somehow the promises, slipped her mind. Worst of all, she *would* talk in the evenings when he wished to be silent and of these occasions he said in self-defence, 'she was always the aggressor.' Stephen could be memorably silent, and the arrival of guests was no deterrent. 'I am, I think, the most easily bored of mankind,' he offered as an excuse, and the cheerless obmutescence which would descend about him was an omen of a sudden exit to his study leaving his wife to cope as best she could with the guests. Edmund Gosse has described one of these evenings. Indeed, he could hardly forget. Bidden with Robert Louis Stevenson to dine, the two young aspirants hurried round expecting to meet the literary world of London. Instead they were greeted by the Stephens and Annie Thackeray. Their host remained bowed and speechless throughout the whole of dinner and, at first bewildered, they found themselves mesmerised into a similar state of oral paralysis. It was left to Annie to stir the torpor of the evening in a shrill mono-logue. Eventually her fabulous departure from factual truth stirred Stephen to reproof, and as his sister-in-law was exclaiming, 'Indeed, I tell my maid everything,' he groaned, 'Oh, yes Annie, and we do wish you wouldn't,' relapsing again into the twilight of his thoughts while Annie's peals of laughter rang round the icy dining-room.

Yet, although the presence of a sister-in-law is not the natural recipe for a happy marriage, the marriage was a success. Leslie was proud of his wife and wrote her delightful letters. His Cambridge friends had quizzed him on his

choice, 'Miss Thackeray is the youngest, isn't she, Stephen?
Yes. Does she write as well as her sister? No. Doesn't she
write occasionally? No. Doesn't she help her sister to
write? Wouldn't she write well if she did write etc. etc.
etc. which I succeeded in stopping by inextinguishable
laughter.' Another letter survives scribbled with the point
of a fork on the menu of a dinner of the Political Economy
Club, 'My dearest Minny, I am suffering the torments of
the damned from that God-forgotten Thornton, who is
boring on about supply and demand, when I would give
anything to be with you. He's not a bad fellow, but just
now I hate him like poison. O-o-o-o-o-o-oh!' He cooed
over her affectionately, entranced with his new and rather
frightening acquisition. She had a peculiar charm of her
own, wayward and changeful and quaintly picturesque.
Her mind was untrained but her intuition was sharp and
the good sense of her judgments perpetually astonished
her husband—after he had decided to act contrary to her
advice. In December, 1870, she gave birth to a daughter,
Laura, and Stephen rejoiced in the happiness of family
life. Writing to Holmes, he said, 'Did you ever remark
what a beautiful object a small baby is? I never did before,
but I see it now. As for a mother and child in the attitude
of a Madonna, I can only say that the sight goes some way
to reconcile me to papists. . . .'

Family life forced him to work even harder at his
journalism, and though enjoyable, he began to find it
unsatisfying for at the back of his mind an idea for a large
scholarly work was germinating. He ground away on the
Saturday Review, sneering at virtue and enthusiasm, as he
put it, but the routine became meaningless. Ought he to
live on bread and water and produce a *magnum opus* establishing certain everlasting laws of human nature until
somebody else proved the contrary, or ought he to have an
occasional glass of champagne and write only leading
articles which did not prove anything in particular? His
family urged him once again to study for the Bar and he ate
dinners in a desultory fashion hoping that nothing would
come of it. In 1871, however, it was suggested that he might
take on the editorship of *Fraser's* in Froude's place; he

consulted George Smith who promptly offered him
Thackeray's old magazine the *Cornhill*. Naturally Minny
and Annie were pleased that the family connection should
be kept and he accepted. The editorial salary of £500
a year enabled him to give up some of his journalism
and settle to the task of writing the book which was to
become the *History of English Thought in the Eighteenth
Century*.

The *Cornhill* was a family magazine, published monthly,
and designed for the drawing-room tables of the upper-
middle class. The contents usually included two serialised
novels, sundry articles of current interest, and one of
Stephen's essays in literary criticism which he later published in *Hours in a Library*. 'What can one make,' he
grumbled, 'of a magazine which excludes the only subjects
in which reasonable men can take any interest: politics
and religion?' Stephen was not the man, however, to
quarrel with his fate and the mixture was handed out as
before. The mixers, at any rate, were not to be despised:
nearly all the major mid-Victorian poets, novelists and
critics contributed, but on the whole, however, the *Cornhill*
public preferred the romances of his friend, James Payn,
to enjoy whose novels, as Stephen admitted, one had to
be unsophisticated. He told Thomas Hardy that the
heroine in *The Trumpet Major* married the wrong man.
'I replied,' said Hardy, 'that they mostly did. "Not in
magazines," he answered.' And Sully was forbidden to
mention Schopenhauer because the ordinary reader might
vaguely scent infidelity in a German name. As an editor
Stephen asked for nothing but a quiet life and bowed his
head to Dr. Bowdler's demands. He considered himself a
slave to popular stupidity and soon deluged Hardy with
apologetic requests when three lady subscribers wrote to
complain of an improper passage in a serial of one of his
novels. *May* 1875: Delete 'amorous' substitute 'sentimental.' *August:* 'I may be over-particular, but I don't
quite like the suggestion of a close embrace in the London
churchyard.' *October:* 'Remember the country parson's
daughters. *I* always have to remember them. I think you
have much improved the rose-leaf incident.' Hardy

expostulated to his editor, pointing out that after the publication of the book the *Times* had commended one of the very passages Stephen had suppressed, and Stephen was reduced to irritated silence till he closed the interview by saying that he spoke as an editor and not as a man, and that Hardy had no more consciousness of these things than a child. But, in fact, Stephen spoke as a man more than he cared to admit. As a good journalist Stephen realised that it was part of his trade to pander to the taste of the *Cornhill* public, and that it was not incumbent upon him to alter the character of the magazine, granted that he regarded his post primarily as a safe job which gave him leisure to write. But, curiously enough, his own taste often coincided with that of his public. Or, rather, his appreciation of literature operated on two levels. His mature judgments are to be found in his critical essays, but in his letters and articles odd phrases occur which suggest that he himself found no difficulty in sympathising with the *Cornhill* subscribers. Writing of an obscure author, Margaret Veley, he said, 'the end of her novel was painful, whereas most readers—and I do not say that they are wrong—like things to be made pleasant.' He enjoyed a thoroughly sentimental novel in the same way that many intelligent men to-day pore over detective stories. And on matters of sexual propriety in novels Stephen took, as we shall see, a severe view. The connection between Hardy and the *Cornhill* was broken in 1877 because he feared that the opening situation in *The Return of the Native* might develop into something 'dangerous' for a family magazine; and from his detestation of the attitude of French novelists towards sex, it is clear that many rejections and excisions which he excused on editorial grounds, were agreeable to him for personal reasons. Was not part of his pride in Minny due to the fact that her pure-mindedness was rooted in ignorance which made him in this particular the master of her soul?

The *Cornhill* remained a side-line and during the 'seventies Stephen's mind was principally concerned with religious controversy. In 1875 he performed a symbolic act. One spring day he summoned Thomas Hardy to call on him in his study no matter what hour, and late that night, after the long climb up the stairs to the top of the house, Hardy found Stephen pacing up and down the room. The only light was a solitary lamp on the reading table. The dressing-gown which Stephen was wearing over his clothes accentuated his height so that he looked like a seer in robes as he passed in and out of the shadow, the lamp illuminating his prophetic face each time he passed the table. On it there lay a document. It was a deed by which Stephen renounced his Holy Orders and Hardy had been called to witness his signature. Like most men who are fighting for a matter of principle Stephen was depressed by the lassitude, indifference and ignorance of intelligent men to what he conceived to be the vital issues, and as usual with reformers he was disappointed most with the followers in his own camp. Though he had met Huxley some years previously and liked him, he could write to Charles Eliot Norton that he found him and Morley alone fully sympathetic. He felt isolated in his agnosticism. A reprint of his articles in *Fraser's* which he called *Essays in Free thinking and Plain speaking* had recently been published, but apart from a whiff of grapeshot from the Broad Churchmanship of the *Spectator*, most journals refused to notice it. He was perpetually astonished at the hardiness of the most exotic of Anglican plants; in the 'sixties he commented on a lawsuit brought against the Ritualists to decide 'what clothes they may wear, and the only way of deciding it is [to find out] what clothes people wore in the days of Charles I'; and ten years later he found the same disputes flourishing as he watched his brother defend Ritualist priests in the courts, and solemnly argue whether the sacramental bread should be cut thick and square or round and thin. 'And David Hume has been dead for a century! I blush for my race!' Such matters seemed to him grotesque and he let them pass to concentrate his attack on the main theological defences of the Church. Later in life he was to fret that his plain-speaking might have wounded someone's feelings, just as in his literary criticism he argued that disagreeable topics should be excised from novels for the same reason; but at the time he was vexed that he seemed to make no

impression on the public's hide. Whether or not he gave
offence, he was received socially without visible embarrass-
ment on the part of his hosts. The circles in which he
moved, were unalarmed, and he complained that some of
them regarded his controversial activities as an aberration
and himself as a 'respectable radical, partly misled by female
influences and given to chaff the parsons.' The only positive
effect of his preaching to which he could point was humili-
atingly comic. An old family acquaintance, Archdeacon
Allen, wrote to him in pain and fury to protest against his
book and then sent Stephen's civil reply to Newman
demanding chastisement. Newman declined to enter into
another controversy and returned the letter; crying
vengeance the Archdeacon touted both Stephen's and
Newman's letters around and eventually tried to involve
William Thompson, the Master of Trinity. The Master
lived up to his reputation for sardonic humour by ignoring
the Archdeacon's demand and by offering instead to buy
Newman's letter for the beauty of its style which he valued
at seventy shillings. The baffled Archdeacon accepted in
despair, and the only tangible result which Stephen could
see that his book had achieved, was that the Zanzibar
Mission was that amount the richer by the Archdeacon
bestowing his blood money upon it.

It was at this time that Stephen received a shock from
which he never fully recovered. In 1875 his wife fell ill
during pregnancy and he took her that summer to Switzerland to recuperate. She seemed to improve and he wrote
cheerfully to Norton that they were no longer anxious, but
that same autumn without warning she fell dead on
Stephen's forty-third birthday. He never celebrated his
birthday again. 'I would have died for her with pleasure,'
he told Lowell. 'I scarcely ever saw a cloud upon her
bright face. . . . Well, so long as I can work and help two or
three people near me, I can feel life tolerable; but the old
charm has gone.' More than the old charm had vanished.
He was plunged into appalling gloom; he no longer dined
out; he took no pleasure in any activity and was set fast to
become a recluse. Old Cambridge friends complained that
they had to dig him out if they wanted to see him and the

flow of letters to Lowell and Holmes diminished to a trickle.
He resigned from the Cosmopolitan and the Century
Club, where he used to meet fellow Radicals and anti-
clericals such as Frederic Harrison; and though he kept
up with Morley, he saw him only occasionally. In his
distress he leant upon two women, one a young widow Julia
Duckworth, a next-door neighbour, and the other Annie
Thackeray, who for eighteen months stayed with him to
keep house. Annie remained devoted to her brother-in-law
and was almost impervious to the difficulties of his temperament, but how she endured him at this time is hard to
fathom. Just as he had misjudged Minny's power of
commonsense, he could not recognise that though Annie's
conversation sounded reckless and her mental processes
might differ from his own, she often made sound judgments
on matters which lay within her province. She knew
how to bring up a tiny girl yet directly she took charge,
he began to interfere; he told a foolish German nurse, who
slyly made trouble between them, to disobey Annie's instructions which led to a row, and Julia Duckworth had to
intervene and tell him to behave sensibly.

Moreover, where money and sex entered his life, Leslie
Stephen's reason departed through the window, and
Annie offended against both taboos. Stephen preened
himself on his generosity. He was proud of the fact that he
gave Annie a house costing five hundred pounds and
prouder still when, some years later, he declined her offer
of eight hundred in repayment and accepted only four
hundred. Annie, however, flouted all his conceptions of
sound finance, and he defended himself against criticism
as follows:

At this time, a time I need hardly say of deep melancholy
to me, some of Annie's friends thought, not unnaturally
perhaps, that I was wanting in consideration for Annie.
Her old and affectionate, though not very judicious,
friend, Mrs. Brookfield, reproved me for worrying Annie
about money matters. I was able to make a very simple
statement of facts which showed that I was not substantially
to blame on that head. I cannot say with equal confidence
that I was not occasionally irritable upon details and I

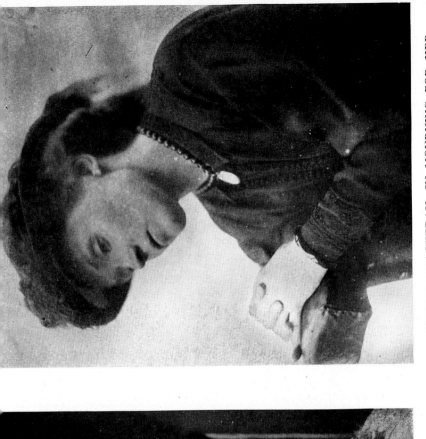

MINNIE THACKERAY, IN MOURNING FOR HER FATHER, 1862. *Photo by Mrs. Cameron*

ANNIE THACKERAY, LATER LADY RITCHIE

LESLIE STEPHEN AND MELCHIOR ANDEREGG, HIS ALPINE GUIDE, *c.* 187

find that I made a scene soon afterwards when Annie brought me some unexpected bills. Julia spoke to me more to the purpose about my want of temper, as we met each other one day; and I took a turn with her in Kensington Gardens where I had the sense to confess my shortcomings and make promises of amendment.

The attitude of men to money is often so bizarre and diametrically opposed to their other characteristics, that to generalise from it is mad. Open-handed characters display the meanest streaks, and it is interesting that English novelists on the whole shy from this awkward theme while the French attack it with gusto. Stephen was not obsessed by wealth and was uninterested in accumulating a fortune. He would lend to young scholars in need and was not thought by his friends to be stingy; and unexpected bills deposited gaily by a spend-thrift are alarming to a family man. Yet he seems permanently to have convinced himself that his family was on the point of bankruptcy. In his last years he plagued his daughter Vanessa's life by accusing her of over-spending on the kitchen books so that she was forced to enter into collusion with the cook to falsify the accounts. Any odd expense in the family was always greeted by a declaration that it would end by them all 'shooting Niagara to ruin.' He staggered his family once by announcing that he had only a bare thousand pounds in the bank. The story got about in the London clubs that poor old Stephen was ruined and Edmund Gosse made discreet enquiries preparatory to obtaining a grant from the Civil List. He discovered that the story was true only if one omitted to include securities and by the bank Stephen meant his current account. This preoccupation with money in the family circle arose partly from his determination to make it clear that those dependent on him were really dependent and partly from his desire for gratitude and appreciation. The sub-conscious process runs: if I can impress upon them that but for me they would be in the workhouse they will love me and appreciate my talents all the more. Stephen's thrift was inherited from his Evangelical forebears and money, of course, was the key to status in the middle class which by the 'eighties was unlocking all doors into the upper class as readers of Henry James's *The Awkward Age*, or Trollope's *The Way We Live Now*, or Ouida's *The Massarenes* will recall. Whatever the cause might be, it put an additional strain on his family.

But worse was to follow; Annie collided with the canons of sexual conduct and was so imprudent in her behaviour before her engagement that Stephen breathed a prayer of relief that her innate pure-mindedness saved her from a fatal judgment. She began to see much of a charming boy, Richmond Ritchie, who had just gone up to the university and set her cap at him to such effect that he was swept off his feet by her gaiety and high spirits. Rumours of an affair began to circulate, and then, 'at last the catastrophe occurred. To speak plainly I came into the drawing-room and found Richmond kissing Annie. I told her at once that she ought to make up her mind one way or the other: for it was plain that as things were going there could be only one result. She did, I think, make up her mind and informed me of her engagement that afternoon. As Annie was, I think, seventeen years older than Richmond it was clear that a long engagement would be very undesirable. She could not afford to waste time. . . .' His inhibitions were understandably aroused, since Annie was not only Richmond Ritchie's cousin but his godmother. Stephen forced Ritchie to leave the university without taking his degree and sit at once for the India Office examination. The engagement evoked a major Family Row in which he was much blamed by the Ritchies. 'The fact was that if they hated the marriage, I positively loathed it. I could not speak of it to Julia without exploding in denunciation.' Julia Duckworth, however, told him that his behaviour merely showed that he was jealous of Ritchie's happiness and did not want his household broken up by Annie's disappearance. There was, however, another reason: Stephen's inhibitions were outraged by the marriage of a middle-aged woman to a young boy, and as is common in such cases he made a moral judgment to express an aesthetic revulsion. Thus, he did not in private life abate one tittle of the horror which he expressed in public for sexual irregularity. It never crossed his mind that meanness could be considered a worse vice than sexual passion, in that meanness is a negative, selfish desire to grasp and keep, while sexual passion is often aroused by a positive desire to give and love.

From this we can see photographs of two Stephens gradually emerging as the developer is applied to the negative. There is the photograph of the staunch friend 'most lovable of men' and, superimposed, the vexing paterfamilias. In the year after Minny's death it looked for a time as if the former would fade from the negative and the world would be left with the picture of a self-tortured misanthrope in love with his own condition of sorrow. He almost enjoyed telling Norton that his pleasure in friendship had withered and he deliberately nursed his unhappiness. Annie had now left to be married and by his own choice he ate his Christmas dinner alone in 1877. His doting sister, Milly, rushed to his assistance, but she loved not wisely but too well. She had, indeed, following her brother's example, left the Church of England, but was soon to join the Society of Friends and her state of mind as expressed in one of her published works, *Light Arising: thoughts on a Central Radiance*, was unlikely to console her brother.* Her visit sunk him in a yet deeper gloom, and perceiving that she could not help him, she wept in concert: 'tears always came too easily to her . . . though affectionate she was a most depressing companion.' The experiment lasted three weeks and then her health broke down. She was replaced by a German house-keeper recommended by the Huxleys, who was also to look after Laura. In the midst of this domestic chaos suddenly all was to change.

During his two years as a widower Stephen had on more than one occasion, as we have seen, relied on Mrs. Duck-worth for comfort and advice. Once again it was the Hughes family who had in the first instance introduced them, when Tom Hughes's sister had told Leslie before he married Minny that he ought to consider Julia Jackson carefully. She was then a young girl of ethereal beauty and whom Burne-Jones had chosen as the model for his painting of the Annunciation. Her mother had been one of the seven Pattle sisters famous for their good looks and descended from

* See Notes to this chapter *infra* p. 296 for an account of Caroline Stephen.

a dashing French nobleman who had settled in India after the Revolution. Stephen used to meet Julia in London at her uncle's, Thoby Prinsep, who patronised the arts and took both Burne-Jones and G. F. Watts at different times into his household. 'The house,' wrote Stephen, 'had a character of its own. People used to go there on Sunday afternoons; they had strawberries and cream and played croquet and strolled about the garden, or were allowed to go to Watts' studio and admire his pictures. . . . And there used to be Leighton and Val Prinsep and his friends who looked terribly smart to me.' In a word, Stephen found it not his sort of world and both the Prinseps and he were a little shy of each other.* Everyone danced attention upon Julia; she had proposals from Holman Hunt and the sculptor, Woolner, and Stephen dared hardly think that she would cast her eyes in his direction. When she became engaged to Herbert Duckworth, he felt 'a sharp pang of jealousy,' possibly because Duckworth was only a year younger than himself; and hearing Duckworth described as 'the perfect type of public school man' confirmed Stephen in his self-distrust and convinced him that such beautiful creatures as Julia Jackson were not for crotchety intellectuals like him. But Duckworth died in 1870, leaving his widow with three small children. 'I was only twenty-four,' she told Stephen, 'when life all seemed a shipwreck,' and when Stephen found himself in the same predicament they were drawn to each other. She was still strangely and exquisitely beautiful with wide, wise eyes, which had seen suffering, eyebrows that lifted naturally away to the temples, and an expression sad and poetical. He remembered how even when he married Minny he had been keen to make a good impression on Julia. Soon he began to realise how dear she was to him, discovered he was in love, and on

---

* Not because the Prinseps were aesthetes. Val Prinsep, on the contrary, could bend a poker in his hands and despised 'artistic effeminacy.' To a lady gushing that a sky in one of his paintings was too beautiful, he replied, 'Yes, madam, I thought I had got in a rummy effect.' D. G. Rossetti, who loathed him, wrote:

> There is a big artist named Val,
> The roughs' and the prizefighters pal.
> The mind of a groom, and the head of a broom,
> Were nature's endowments to Val.

the 5th of February, 1877, proposed.* Julia, taken by
surprise, refused him but after an exchange of letters agreed
to remain friends on the understanding that marriage was
out of the question.† But Stephen returned to the attack
and, after further complicated correspondence over a year
and with many doubts, she finally agreed. They were
married on the 26th of March, 1878.

3

Happiness once again fell upon Stephen like a May
shower; but, burnt by the desert sun of solitude and
anguish, he had learnt to change his ways. His love for
Minny had been protective, jocular, cossetting. In Julia
he recognised a deeper and more sensitive character than
his own and one who had borne sorrow, as he would have
wished to bear it, but could not. He worshipped her with
unalterable devotion—'Good God, how that man adores
her,' said Henry James, and Meredith told Stephen's
daughter, 'He was the one man to my knowledge worthy
to have married your mother.' Indeed, worship was what
he sought in marriage: a living image before whom he
could pour out the flood of devotion that could find no
outlet in religion. He idealised her and longed to sacrifice
himself for her—which in the day to day routine of
home life he was quite incapable of doing. In one of the
letters which he wrote to Julia imploring her to marry him,
he said:

You must let me tell you that I do and always shall feel
for you something which I can only call reverence as well
as love. *Think* me silly if you please. Don't say anything
against yourself for I won't stand it. You see, I have not
got any saints and you must not be angry if I put you in
the place where my saints ought to be.

* Stephen's highly developed topographical sense made him note where
and when this occurred. The lunch at the club in a philosophical spirit
had encouraged him to propose to Minny, and it was on this day as he was
walking into town that he stopped outside Knightsbridge Barracks and 'suddenly said to myself "I love Julia." ' The mood came upon him in singular
places.

† For a detailed account of Stephen's courtship see Notes to Chapter II
infra, p. 297.

In this period, so full for Stephen of domestic happiness and
sorrow, he wrote the works on which his fame as a scholar
and thinker rests. During his first marriage he had been
writing a long essay on the religious thought of the preceding
century and this grew in scope until he published in 1875
the *History of English Thought in the Eighteenth Century* in two
volumes totalling 925 pages. The subject had been suggested
to him by an essay by Mark Pattison on some aspects of
the religious thought of that century, but before he had
finished Stephen had analysed the thought of the Deists and
the orthodox apologists, the political, moral and economic
theories of the age as well as, briefly, its imaginative literature. It still stands as a major contribution to scholarship
and in a sense will never be superseded in its scope. He
followed this work up with another tome. He had begun in
the 'seventies to write under Morley's editorship for the
English Men of Letters series to which he contributed during
the next twenty-five years studies on Johnson, Pope, Swift,
George Eliot and Hobbes each of which was thrown off
in a twelve-month while he pondered over weightier matters.
From 1876 to 1882 he worked on the *Science of Ethics* and
directly that was published, he began to plan his *English
Utilitarians*. The year 1882 marked a new phase in his
literary life. George Smith broke the news to him in the
autumn that the *Cornhill* was running at a loss and that
the circulation had dropped from 25,000 to 12,000 during
Stephen's editorship. A good editor should have a flair
for sensing changes in public taste and Stephen, preoccupied
with his own writing, was too content to run in the old
grooves. The *Cornhill* public were tired of the serialised
novel, and wanted less solid reading, a more ephemeral
magazine for half-hour snatches between the games,
amusements and new pastimes which the late Victorian
age was discovering. Stephen at once resigned but though
chagrined naturally at Smith's losses and his own failure,
he had no need to worry. *The History of English Thought in the
Eighteenth Century* had put him on a pinnacle in the literary
world; and Smith knew himself to be justified in inviting
Stephen to edit a vast new project, the *Dictionary of
National Biography*.

Smith had originally planned a compendium of universal biography but 'from that wild attempt' he admitted, 'I was saved by the knowledge and sound judgment of Mr. Leslie Stephen.' Stephen knew that the difficulties attending the birth and delivery of a national biography were grave enough. The past was already littered with the corpses of infant dictionaries which had perished at the tender age of the third or fourth letters of the alphabet, and so Stephen as editor laid down a series of rules. Contributors must complete their articles within six months, they must curb irrelevance and, most famous rule of all, must keep eulogy within bounds: 'No flowers by request,' as Alfred Ainger put it. He solved the problem of inclusion by deciding that names which were only names should not qualify. For instance, one must draw a distinction between bibliography and biography; the mere fact that a man had published a book did not in itself qualify him for inclusion. By printing twice a year in the *Athenaeum* the names which were considered worthy of inclusion and by asking readers to suggest additions, Stephen escaped the charge of editorial partiality, and soon the venture was under way.

Then the nightmare began and letters arrived in dozens. He was haunted by families with requests to include obscure relatives. The inevitable clergyman wrote enclosing a list of 1400 hymn-writers each of whom was entitled to a place. Antiquarians and bookworms moved in to the assault. One of the minor triumphs of the Dictionary was Stephen's success in taming the pedants. True, in the first volume, he was not alive to all the possibilities and when one looks up King Alfred one is greeted with the entry 'Alf— see Aelf—' and the harmonious names of Elgiva and Elfrida have been transmogrified into Aelgifre and Aelfryth. This mania for Anglo-Saxon spelling had been imposed on Stephen by the arch-pedant, Professor Freeman, and there was a danger that the ordinary reader would fail to find many Anglo-Saxon names when their customary spelling had been so changed. But Freeman was not to enjoy his triumph long. The vision of a line of kings, such as Athelstone and Ethelbert, stretching out to the crack of doom and masquerading in diphthongs, so seared Stephen's eyeballs that he was prepared to risk a breach with the professor rather than let unnatural orthography prevail and common sense perish. He accordingly proposed a compromise: that names would be found under their ordinary spelling and their scholarly aliases inserted in brackets. Freeman would have none of it: was it not an insult to his championship of our Saxon heritage? He would resign rather than contribute an article on Athelstan spelt with an A. Stephen accepted the resignation with alacrity and the professor departed in a huff.

Such a task of organisation could not be borne by one man, and Stephen had the good fortune to pick an excellent assistant in Sidney Lee. Even so, the undertaking appears extraordinary to-day, when such a venture would be financed from university funds or public trusts and undertaken by a team of scholars and assistants, that Stephen and Lee between them were able to keep rolling from the press a volume a quarter and that George Smith was prepared to finance the enterprise at a loss of £70,000 on an outlay of £150,000. Moreover, the state of English historiography at that time must not be forgotten. The *English Historical Review* did not exist and the history schools in the older universities were in their infancy. The editors could not fall back on a regiment of academic historians and cadres of Ph.Ds. trained in the methods of research. In this respect England was far behind Germany and France. As a result there was a good deal of unevenness in the contributions; inaccuracies and misprints crept in, and Stephen had neither the patience nor the stamina for office work and proof-reading. Another blemish was the disparate treatment of sources by the contributors which more careful editing might have eliminated.

Nevertheless, the Dictionary was a triumph: this work of 29,120 articles in 63 volumes by 654 contributors, *monumentum aere perennius*, is Stephen's most enduring bequest to posterity. Creighton and Gardiner, Tout and Firth and, above all, Pollard, gave of their best and the level of the contributions is astoundingly high: German and French scholars generously admitted the Dictionary's superiority to their own national compendiums. It was an enterprise free of literary log-rolling and of the worst features of seminar research. For Stephen's greatest rule was that each life was to be readable, a biography in itself, not a compendium of sources or a disquisition by a scholar on disputed points. Contributors were ridden on the lightest of reins and encouraged to enliven their style. On one occasion this vivacity brought its reward. In writing George Eliot's life Stephen described Tito, the hero of *Romola*, as one of her 'finest feminine characters' which drew from a phlegmatic reviewer the comment that presumably Romola herself was meant. Maitland grimly observed: 'A Dictionary should not be strewn with such mantraps.' Long before the completion of the task, however, Stephen had been forced to resign.* The work indeed crushed him. Most of his days were now spent in cursing the handwriting and prolixity of the contributors. He himself contributed 378 articles 'almost any one of which might have earned an American Ph.D. degree,' Allan Willard Brown mournfully remarks. In 1885 he took no holiday, his own handwriting grew spidery and difficult to read, and the headaches which racked him after Minny's death returned. Throughout his letters the execrations roll like thunder. 'An accursed Doctor of Divinity has been cheating me' . . . 'that damned Diction-ary is about my bed and spies out all my ways, as the psalmist says' . . . 'I am knee-deep in dictionary and drudgery' . . . 'A hideous package from the Dictionary has come which I have not yet had the courage to open' . . . 'the damned thing goes on like a diabolical piece of machinery, always gaping for more copy, and I fancy at times that I shall be dragged into it, and crushed out into slips.' His friends, accustomed to his groans and delighting in his outbursts of invective against some obtuse contributor, laughed at the act Stephen put on for their benefit. But his

* Stephen edited the first twenty-six volumes of the Dictionary, Lee the remaining thirty-seven; and Lee continued his task and brought out the supplements of 1901 and 1912. The planning and organisation of the enter-prise, and its character, was largely Stephen's work; but much of the credit is due to Lee who was superior as an editor and under whose direction the Dictionary expanded ever more majestically each year. Lee was also able to benefit from the mistakes of the earlier volumes and to draw on a widening circle of contributors. Stephen, however, continued to contribute articles to the Dictionary after his retirement.

wife did not laugh. She loathed the Dictionary and saw
that it was killing Leslie. Switzerland did him no good and
in the summer of 1889 he collapsed in the Athenaeum; when
another winter holiday in the Alps in 1891 ended in influenza,
she persuaded him to give up the editorship entirely, as 'it
is impossible with his nature for him to do half work.' For
years now he had been outwriting his strength and the old
therapy of mountaineering and walking holidays was ceasing
to work. His wife soon took another step. In 1894 he visited
the Alps for the last time.

Stephen's name was known to many Englishmen who
had never read a word of his controversial or critical works.
He was one of the heroes of the new sport of the upper-
middle class in mid-Victorian England, the conquest of
the Alps when the exploits of great climbers were followed
with almost the same avidity as those of cricketers in the
succeeding generation. Although Rousseau was the first
(in Stephen's words) 'to set up mountains as objects of
human worship' and pioneers, such as Albert Smith, were
climbing in the 'forties, the golden age of mountaineering
did not begin till the 'fifties when the French railways
reached Basel and Geneva, and Switzerland came to be
hardly more than a day's journey from London and the
fare less than ten pounds. The London lawyer or business
man, the don or clergyman, could reach their playground
quickly and cheaply and the sport itself was inexpensive:
in 1855 a single climbing expedition with five porters and
three guides cost a couple of friends only four pounds each.
In true English fashion the enthusiasts formed a club;
and though Stephen was not one of the original members of
the Alpine Club, founded in the autumn of 1857, he was
elected in 1859, became President in 1865, edited the Alpine
Journal from 1868–72 and spent some twenty-five holidays
in the Alps. Stephen was one of the protagonists in the days
when the great peaks fell one by one before the skill of these
pioneers in a new kind of exploration. The technique of the
sport was still in its infancy and there was no question of
selecting well-known climbs or ice-walls as tests of skill;
conquest was all and climbers had to pick their own routes
to the summits. Stephen was the first man to climb the

Schreckhorn and could claim a number of other peaks as
his own. Everyone spoke of him as one of the great climbers
of his day; better perhaps on ice and snow than on rocks,
but a master of both; a climber who delighted in long, steep
snow slopes, as well as in cutting steps, and able to manage
the loose scree of the Bietschorn. His long legs, like a pair of
compasses, moving at the slow, steady, guide's pace, his great
reach, his power of resistance to cold and fatigue, and his
sanguine temperament, gave him great advantages. Unlike
some of the brotherhood he was opposed to guideless climbing
and he chastened the English Alpinists by telling them that a
third-rate guide was always superior to a first-rate amateur.
This was untrue and, in any case, Stephen never climbed
with any but the three best guides in Switzerland.* But the
remark is characteristic of Stephen's dislike of boasting and
his habit of denigrating his accomplishments. As an
Alpinist he was the soul of orthodoxy: that is to say he
loudly condemned climbers racing each other up mountains,
and frequently did it himself.

Stephen went to the Alps to climb and for no other reason.
Ruskin might stay in the valleys to worship and sketch and
curse the vulgarity of the mountaineers rushing home 'red
with cutaneous eruption of conceit, and voluble with con-
vulsive hiccough of self-satisfaction'; but, though Ruskin
in London was 'one of the people who frightens me to
death, and makes me want to sink into my shoes and forces
me to be sulkily silent,' in the Alps he was a figure of fun, an
absurdity who criticised Stephen for the sacrilege of smoking
a pipe on the top of a peak. Nor had Stephen much use
for the other body of opinion—the scientists—who had
done much to advance Alpine adventure. He rallied them
for toiling up the slopes laden with clinometers, barometers
and prismatic compasses, 'fanatics who by a reasoning
process to me utterly inscrutable have somehow irrevocably
associated Alpine travelling with science'; Tyndall was so
offended by such remarks that he resigned from the Club.

* One of them, Melchior Anderegg, became a privileged person and was
twice invited to England. He pained Stephen by declaring that the vista from
the railway carriage of the endless chimney-pots of South London was a finer
sight than any Alpine horizon; but his preference for the waxworks at Madame
Tussaud's to the splendours of Westminster Abbey entranced his host.

Stephen was single-minded in his devotion to the point of rudeness. He cut Olive Schreiner, the South African novelist, when she was staying at the same hotel, simply because she was a celebrity. One day H. A. Morgan, explaining why he could not accompany Stephen on a climb, was interrupted by a young lady who most inappropriately began asking details of the excursion Morgan had promised to arrange for her. 'I see what you prefer, to coming with me over the mountains!' Stephen snapped, and with a look of contempt strode down the path to Zermatt. He was always a jealous lover.

The charms of mountaineering resemble those of a great courtesan; in addition to her physical attractions, and the raptures she inspires, she possesses that indefinable quality of mystery which, once felt, binds her devotees to her helplessly for life. It is a power which is exerted with peculiar poignancy over intellectuals. Like love, mountaineering makes it possible for the intellectual to experience things which would otherwise be impossible: danger, intense comradeship, manliness, physical pain in pursuit of a tangible objective, and the sensation of being at one with Nature. Psychologically the intellectual is always conscious of his isolation. He is not at one with the human race: the world is forever out of joint and he is conscious that he cannot escape. Remove him from civilised society and plant him in the silence of the snows and his neuroses fall from his back like Christian's burden—but in *this* Pilgrim's Progress Evangelist carries not the Bible but the Book of Nature in his hand. Stephen was a Wordsworthian. He communed with Nature and Nature 'helped' him. That was why he insisted on climbing in silence, not in order to cogitate on the march, but so as to bathe his mind in the healing springs of Alpine scenery. His indignation with Fitzjames was boundless when, on the only occasion the brothers climbed together, Fitzjames talked *Saturday Review* all the way to the top and down again. Sometimes his silence was due to natural causes; when one of his party chaffed him as they were starting on a long ascent at 2 a.m. in a cold mist, he announced, 'I hope no one's such a fool as to suppose I'm in a good temper at this hour in the

morning.' More often his silence was of a depth that
struck his companions more forcibly than words. His
most valiant Alpine friend and the only foreigner apart
from his guides whom Stephen ever got to know, the French
painter Gabriel Loppé, described how on the Titlis, 'Tout
vibrait à nos yeux tant notre émotion était profonde. . . .
Stephen silencieux, remuait à peine les lèvres pour dire à son
neveu le nom de quelques unes de ces grandes cimes qui font
l'orgueil de la Suisse. Trois-quarts d'heure furent bien vite
écoulés, il fallut partir; chacun reprit son piolet, et nous
descendîmes en silence. . . .'

    Stephen was a Wordsworthian—which is a very different
thing from being Wordsworth. He communed with Nature
but also came to achieve, to walk farther and faster than
other men, to conquer mountains. He liked to note the
varieties of flowers and plants, or to identify the other peaks
visible from the summit. Whereas Wordsworth's eye was a
kind of hole in the head through which the impressions he
received from Nature passed directly to his heart, Stephen's
was a categorising eye; it was as if he needed a direct
contact with things in order to make him human again
after living too long with people. Achievement, of course,
is the essence of mountaineering. Climbing gives, to those
who need it, the reassurance that they are men—men still
capable of defeating the tyranny of life. Stephen's youthful
determination to be an athlete was a rationalisation of a
more deep-seated fear: a doubt whether he was capable of
achieving anything. Mountaineering gave Stephen the
chance to announce to the world that, like Carlyle, he had
proclaimed the Everlasting Yea and that he gloried in the
struggle for existence. It was no accident that he chose
mountaineering as the background of his profession of faith.
In *A Bad Five Minutes in the Alps*, he pictures himself hanging
over a precipice and asking himself the value of life. As he
hangs on the ledge, knowing that he will, as his joints crack,
be hurled into eternity, what is there left to believe in?
Christianity, proclaiming the utter sinfulness of man and
threatening damnation, is at once dismissed. Pantheism,
either of the new scientific or ancient Eastern variety, is also
unsatisfactory; the assertion that the self on death merges

with Nature and is, as Omar Khayyam declares, no more than a bubble among a million similar bubbles poured by the eternal Saki from his bowl, affronts our sense of individuality. And if this is too pessimistic, the Religion of Humanity is too optimistic in its brash comfort that each man plays his part in helping the human race to progress. 'Humanity will blunder on pretty much as it did before . . . [it] was too big and distant, and too indistinctly related to me, to lift me for one minute above the sense of that awful personal crash which was approaching so speedily.' No: at such a time all creeds fail us.

The one suggestion which was of some sort of use came from a different and very undignified source. Years ago I had rowed and lost a race or two on the Thames, and there was a certain similarity in the situations, for there comes a time in a losing race when all hope has departed, and one is labouring simply from some obscure sense of honour. The sinews of the arms are splitting, the back aches, and the lungs feel as though every blood-vessel in them were strained almost to bursting-point. Whatever vital force is left is absorbed in propelling the animal machine; no reason can be distinctly given for continuing a process painful in a high degree, dangerous to the constitution, and capable of producing no sort of good result; and yet one continues to toil as though life and happiness depended upon refraining from a moment's intermission, and, as it were, nails one's mind—such as is left—down to the task. Even so the effort to maintain my grasp on the rock became to me the one absorbing thought; this fag end of the game should be fairly played out, come what might, and whatever reasons might be given for it.

Fight the good fight and you will live; and if you must die, then look back with pleasure and pride at the strife. Mountaineering dramatises the struggle for life. 'The game is won,' writes Stephen, 'when a mountain-top is reached in spite of difficulties; it is lost when one is forced to retreat.' But mountaineering is not just a trial of endurance. Greater even than on the river is the emotion of comradeship.* For here, more than glory is at stake, it is life or

* There is an affinity between the physical and psychological adjustments which a crew must make in rowing to get the boat to run smoothly, and those which mountaineers make when roped together on a climb.

death, and the rope round your waist speaks of the friends
above you and below on the rocks who will save your life
in the certainty that you will as willingly lay down your
life for them. Those friendships last longest in which two
men have endured and suffered danger together; no
matter how often they quarrel in later life, neither can
forget the intense emotion they have experienced together.
The monotonous regularity of regimental reunions, so
inexplicable to wives, at which a man foregathers with old
acquaintances, with whom he has in civilian life nothing in
common, is one indication of the strength of the bonds
which unite men who have once faced danger together—or
who imagine that they did. For the Victorians, mountaineering was one of the few ways in which pacifist liberals
could experience emotions similar to those they envied in
soldiers and mariners. 'An Alpine journey' wrote the
pioneer, J. D. Forbes, in the *Quarterly Review* of 1857, 'is
perhaps the nearest approach to a campaign with which
the ordinary civilian has a chance of meeting.' Danger,
indeed, is one of the physical pleasures of life; and if men
cannot obtain it in one way they will invent new ways of
finding it. In addition the Alpine comradeship was at once
a freemasonry and an opportunity for Stephen to relax,
joining in rags and stump-cricket or playing *fly-loo* in some
little inn with his companions and the guides, 'which means
that everyone puts down a piece of sugar and a ten centime
piece before him, and the one on whose sugar the first fly
settles, gets the money.' The Victorian public school
mystique of games permeated the Alpine brotherhood and
influenced their attitude to the sport. Play is sanctified if it
can be shown to be work—work which teaches a moral
lesson. 'Properly speaking,' said Carlyle, 'all true Work is
Religion.' Writing of an ascent of Mont Blanc, made in the
company of Huxley and two other friends, John Tyndall confessed: 'We were about to try our strength under unknown
conditions, and as the various possibilities of the enterprise
crowded on the imagination, a sense of responsibility for a
moment oppressed me. But as I looked aloft and saw the
glory of the heavens, my heart lightened, and I remarked
cheerily to Hirst that Nature seemed to smile upon our work.

"Yes," he replied, in a calm and earnest voice, "and, God willing, we shall accomplish it." ' Stephen was an apostle of the religion of work and subscribed to the doctrine of vicarious labour through play.

Stephen, as G. W. Young declares, did much to make mountaineering respectable in England by showing that it was not a series of foolhardy pranks but a laborious, hardy and ennobling pursuit. He also canonised it as the great pursuit for the introspective: the pursuit which helps to solve the problem which sometimes besets them—how to show that they are good-hearted fellows when they lack the skill and grace to play games or the accuracy, up-bringing and inclination for field-sports. Climbing bolsters the ego, for no mountaineer can be a muff. It would be ridiculous to suggest that every climber takes to the mountains to nurse his neuroses, and the early Alpinists were drawn to Switzerland for a variety of reasons: the Italian princesses, for instance, who made some well-advertised climbs originally went there to hunt ibex and chamois. But in Stephen's case there was more to it than a love of Nature or adventure, and behind his Alpine essays lurks a strange uneasiness. He worshipped the emotions he had experienced in certain places, not Nature. Yes, the emotions themselves; Stephen was an Alpine sentimentalist first and last, and he luxuriated on his memories. Like the road junction under the lamp where he clasped Lowell's hand, which was sacred, so was the trysting place with Minny at Täsch sacred; Wengen Alp was sacred—the list of holy shrines in fact is interminable. He was in love with his own feelings and would indulge for hours in nostalgic recollection. If you carefully seal an emotional experience into a bottle of preserves, you will find when you open it in winter time that it tastes different from fresh fruit; there is a sugary almost sickly taste and something will have to be done to disguise it. Stephen disguised his sentimentality by a simple recipe. He made jokes.

The *Playground of Europe*—a holy book to mountaineers— in which he published the best of his Alpine essays is full of jocular humour—sometimes admirably satirical at the expense of Ruskin's devotional exercises or of mountaineers'

bombast, but often false, *voulu* and facetious. Facetiousness
springs from the desire to conceal, from being ashamed to
expose one's emotions. It is also an attempt to have things
both ways. Stephen liked to show that he was moved by
the Alps, that they alone could stir him to blaze forth in a
purple passage. No sooner, however, has he launched himself on a flight of fancy than, 'I am verging on the poetical';
down comes the balloon and he brings himself ostentatiously
to earth. We all applaud—here is a man who can do the
tall talk and yet is on our level. How excellent to shrug off
the scientists by saying in wretched weather on the top of a
mountain, 'As for ozone, if any existed in the atmosphere,
it was a greater fool than I take it for.' There are, however,
some fine passages in which Stephen can match the great
Victorian word-painters. He did not compete with them;
indeed he deplored Ruskin's endless similes and rococco
imagery. He preferred to paint the Alpine scenery in
separate strokes of purple, almost meticulously, and to
awake in his reader that emotion, so familiar to the mountaineer, of man's insignificance among these lonely peaks
which seem to echo Obermann's cry, 'Eternity, be thou
my refuge!' The following is an extract from *Sunset on
Mont Blanc* which Stephen though to be his best piece of
prose:

And suddenly began a more startling phenomenon. A
vast cone, with its apex pointing away from us, seemed to
be suddenly cut out from the world beneath; night was
within its borders and the twilight still all round; the blue
mists were quenched where it fell, and for the instant we
could scarcely tell what was the origin of this strange
appearance. Some unexpected change seemed to have
taken place in the programme; as though a great fold
in the curtain had suddenly given way, and dropped on
to part of the scenery. Of course a moment's reflection
explained the meaning of this uncanny intruder; it was
the giant shadow of Mont Blanc, testifying to his supremacy
over all meaner eminences. It is difficult to say how sharply
marked was the outline, and how startling was the contrast
between this pyramid of darkness and the faintly-lighted
spaces beyond its influence; a huge inky blot seemed to
have suddenly fallen upon the landscape. As we gazed

we could see it move. It swallowed up ridge by ridge,
and its sharp point crept steadily from one landmark to
another down the broad Valley of Aosta. We were
standing, in fact, on the point of the gnomon of a gigantic
sundial, the face of which was formed by thousands of
square miles of mountain and valley. So clear was the
outline that, if figures had been scrawled upon glaciers
and ridges, we could have told the time to a second;
indeed, we were half inclined to look for our own shadows
at a distance so great that whole villages would be represented by a scarcely distinguishable speck of colouring. . . .
By some singular effect of perspective, rays of darkness
seemed to be converging from a point above our heads
to a point immediately above the apex of the shadowy
cone. For a time it seemed that there was a kind of anti-sun
in the east, pouring out not light, but deep shadow as it
rose. The apex soon reached the horizon, and then to our
surprise began climbing the distant sky. Would it never
stop and was Mount Blanc capable of overshadowing
not only the earth but the sky? . . . But rapidly the lights
went out upon the great army of mountains; the snow all
round took the livid hue which immediately succeeds
an Alpine sunset, and almost at a blow the shadow of
Mont Blanc was swallowed up in the general shade of
night. . . . We were between the day and the night. The
western heavens were of the most brilliant blue with spaces
of transparent green, whilst a few scattered cloudlets
glowed as if with internal fire. To the east the night rushed
up furiously, and it was difficult to imagine that the dark
purple sky was really cloudless and not blackened by the
rising of some portentous storm. . . . In that strange gloom
the moon looked wan and miserable enough . . . and but
for her half-comic look of helplessness, we might have
sympathised with the astronomers who tell us that she is
nothing but a vast perambulating tombstone, proclaiming
to all mankind in the words of the familiar epitaph, 'As
I am now, you soon shall be!'

On other occasions the purple passages seem to be a little
too carefully constructed and accurately phrased, manifestly
inferior to Kingsley. Only an artist, perhaps, can communicate the mysticism of mountaineering, and Stephen
could rarely manage such writing because he was afraid

to appear ridiculous; he usually gives a memorandum of possibilities.*

The Sunday Tramps was the other athletic fraternity to which Stephen belonged and which he founded after his second marriage. He, and the lawyer, Frederick Pollock, and Croom Robertson, the first editor of the philosophical journal *Mind*, were in the habit of taking long Sunday walks and began to invite others. Eventually the Tramps numbered sixty strong though usually not more than ten came out on any one Sunday. The fellowship lasted for fifteen years and chalked up a score of 252 walks.† Among the members were the philosopher, James Sully, and the Positivist, James Cotter Morison; Scrutton and Romer represented the law, F. Y. Edgeworth economics, W. P. Ker criticism, Maitland history and Robert Bridges poetry. Twenty miles was an average stroll and the rule of the order was high-thinking and plain-living.‡ Sometimes, however, they would be fêted at dinner on their way home by Frederic Harrison, Darwin, Tyndall or George Meredith —who had ruined his digestion by walking too often up Box Hill to see the sunrise; but Stephen discouraged such

* Famous as he was, there were occasions when his fame was shrewdly gored. Mrs. W. K. Clifford recalled an occasion in Switzerland when a parson and fellow-guest in their hotel did them some service which she wished to acknowledge. 'I thought I was in some fashion paying back the parson's kindness when I invited him to meet Leslie. But that parson, bless you, had never heard of Leslie and to my horror I heard him say, "Oh, yes, Mr. Stephen, I like some Radicals, I assure you. Now there was Mr. Fawcett—did you ever come across him?" Leslie gave a grumpy "Yes." I settled myself at the tea-table and said firmly, "Oh, but you forget that Mr. Stephen is Mr. Fawcett's biographer." "Indeed?" said the parson in a benevolent voice, "Do you do much writing, Mr. Stephen?" Leslie gave a grunt, and I put in, "Mr. Stephen is editing a little Dictionary," and as that produced no response I added, "The Dictionary of National Biography," for I felt bound to boast a little when I saw my poor friend being sat upon. "Indeed," beamed the parson, "It must be very interesting." The thread of the conversation wandered to the scenery, "There are beautiful walks about here," said the parson, and then he asked the shepherd of the Sunday Tramps in a kind of patronising manner, "Do you care for walking, Mr. Stephen?" Leslie was too much squashed even to answer, and again I struggled to the rescue with "Mr. Stephen is a great walker and a little stroll of twenty miles before breakfast is nothing to him." "Indeed!" said the parson incredulously, "ever do any climbing?" '
† The Tramps were revived in the first years of this century with the blessing of Pollock and others of the old fraternity. G. M. Trevelyan was a prominent member.
‡ Stephen came by his walking honestly. His grandfather, the Master in Chancery on his seventieth birthday, walked twenty-five miles to breakfast, thence to his office and back home on the same day.

sybaritic festivities. He was the general of all expeditions, summoning his troop by cryptic post-cards, planning the strategy of the walks, studying the ordnance survey for short cuts to catch a London train that would land them home for a late dinner, and generally maintaining order and discipline. It satisfied his foible for leadership and his delight in ordering the practical affairs of other men, whom he liked to assure himself were unpractical bunglers. Mrs. Clifford has described the scene of a dinner at the Tyndalls where the Tramps stopped before setting out on the last lap for home. 'Leslie sat at the head of the table and did his autocracy with an occasional grunt or groan if someone said something absurd, but we all knew him to be in his glory. Afterwards we had coffee in Tyndall's study upstairs and then Leslie looked round and said to himself so that all who were near him could hear, 'I must sweep these creatures off,' and five minutes later the Tramps were striding down the road two by two, Leslie's tall figure erect and unfaltering, a pace or two in front.'

His wife brought his friends back into his life again. It was characteristic of Stephen that, when he was broken by Minny's death and spent his days in solitude, he roused himself to make one new friend who needed friendship and was enduring a harder fate than himself, the brilliant mathematician, William Kingdon Clifford, at that date almost at his last gasp from consumption. It was Stephen who got up a subscription to send him to Madeira in the vain hope that he might recover.* His marriage to Julia did not change his circle of friends; the only changes were due to the natural ebb and flow in friendship whereby some friends drift into an alien sea beyond our horizon and are replaced by others who share our interests and situation. Stephen's circle was that of the rationalists, but his closest friendships were with those among them who valued poetic imagination. Of all the host who pass in and out of the pages of Maitland's biography, perhaps Meredith and Morley

* He continued after Clifford's death in 1879 to look after his widow and family, who often stayed at their house in Cornwall. Mrs. Clifford was the author of *Mrs. Keith's Crime*, a novel which created a certain stir and of a number of children's books: one of her stories, 'The New Mother' in *Anyhow Stories* is a classic of the Victorian nursery.

were the dearest: Meredith, accepting that man is Earth-born and at one with Nature, with his creed of cultivating joy and laughter, with his belief that action and feeling unlock all gates and that action and feeling proceed from the Brain; Morley—the young radical Morley of the *Saturday* and *Fortnightly Reviews*, who was one of the few men Stephen could bear to see after Minny's death—with his passionate belief in reason and freedom of the mind, and with a capacity for kindness that impressed two such dis-similar men as Herbert Spencer and Gladstone.* Both these close friends had other similarities: both were too hearty and rhetorical in their protestations, both covered up their humble origins and were Radical snobs, and both were more than usually vain. Friendship for Stephen was an act of private communion; he deliberately shunned society. He could not compete in Julia's At Homes and he rushed from the room at the sound of music. He was blind to the visual arts, hated sight-seeing, and was unhappy in Bohemia. 'I have always been shy of artistic people who inhabit a world very unfamiliar to me,' he confessed to his children. Nature, not art, was Stephen's goddess. For this insular Englishman France was a disagreeable corridor to Switzerland. He despised the polite and deadly conversation about books in London literary society and he detested catechisers who tried to pry quotable opinions out of him. Insensitive to the delicacies and nuances of converse, a stranger to graceful manners, and puritan enough to regard frivolity as a sign of insincerity he was formidable; and when his tall spare figure entered a drawing room, hostesses feared that a blight would wither the conversation. As Augustine Birrell remarked, Stephen's favourite wind was due east. He was an eminent Victorian and after Matthew Arnold's death he was regarded as the first man in the world of English letters. Honours began to shower upon him. Trinity Hall made him an Honorary Fellow; Harvard, Cambridge, Oxford and Edinburgh in turn presented him

---

* Morley used to tell the story, as an example of Stephen's detachment from mundane events, how they spent one Sunday together alone in the country and how just as Stephen was leaving he remarked: 'I suppose you have heard that the French army has surrendered at Sedan and the Emperor is a prisoner.'

with honorary degrees, and he was elected President of the
London Library. Finally in the year of Edward VII's
coronation he was made a Knight of the Bath. He received
these awards, declared Sir Walter Raleigh in the first Leslie
Stephen Lecture delivered in Cambridge, with amused
gratification. The world considered that despite the
labour and sorrow that are the common lot of man, he had
passed a fortunate life.

But the judgments of the world, as we know, are not
worth much. For someone as sensitive and dependent on
the affections of others as himself, the last years of his life
were full of domestic sorrow. Shortly after he had married
Julia a peculiarly agonising affliction weighed upon him.
Laura, his daughter by the first marriage, was beginning to
grow up and seemed at first a backward child; gradually it
dawned on Stephen that she was mentally deficient and
that the insanity of her grandmother Isabella Thackeray
had descended through Minny to her. Then in the 'eighties
disaster overtook his favourite nephew, J. K. Stephen.
Handsome, companionable, charming, J. K. S. combined
the common sense of the Stephens with uproarious wit,
was (and still is) the toast of College at Eton for his prowess
at the Wall Game, Fellow of King's and the author of
Lapsus Calami, a collection of dazzling parodies. Leslie
admired him as his own son and witnessed the distressing
spectacle of seeing him too gradually lose his reason. He
began to suffer from fits of wild excitement and depression;
at times apparently normal, he was expelled from his club
before his illness was diagnosed, and made violent advances
to Stephen's step-daughter, Stella Duckworth. He died in
an asylum in 1892, the promise of his youth blasted in early
years. Meanwhile Fitzjames was clearly weakening. Senility
overwhelmed him and he had to quit the bench; when
Leslie said good-bye to him one day, he noticed for the first
time that his hand was no longer crushed by Fitzjames's
strong grip. Two years after his son's death, Fitzjames
followed him to the grave. So long as Julia was with Leslie
to minister to all his wants and soothe him in his depression
he remained unshaken. One day in April 1895, she
complained that she felt ill and within a few weeks was

dead. Now he felt quite alone. He was to survive her by eight years, but her death made him an old man, looking more and more like a prophet with scanty hair, craggy eyebrows, and eyes staring into space. Deafness imprisoned him, cutting him off from conversation, and visitors to the house now found an old gaunt man with straggling beard and an ear-trumpet, vainly trying to catch his children's chatter, insisting that they shout their jokes in his ear. His faith in the joy of domestic affection was to be tested still further by the President of the Immortals. Stella Duckworth, the eldest of Julia's children, looked after the family after her mother's death and when Vanessa was old enough to take over the management of the house, made a happy marriage. Shortly afterwards she died of peritonitis. His friends, too, had been dying fast about him; first Fawcett, then Lowell, Croom Robertson, and Henry Sidgwick.

Beneath these afflictions Stephen continued to work. In 1890 he published a collection of his maturer controversial essays under the title of *An Agnostic's Apology*. The biographies of Fawcett, Fitzjames and J. R. Green followed, as well as two volumes of addresses to Ethical Societies, while all the time he was working on his last enterprise, the three volume *English Utilitarians*. His Ford lectures, which he was too ill to deliver, were published just before he died. He would write in bed at nursing homes; his book on Hobbes was born between the sheets. He also wrote some entertaining recollections for the *National Review*, republished long after his death as *Some Early Impressions*. But by 1903 the end was in sight; he was stricken with cancer of the bowel and knew that he must die. He picked up his journal for the last time. 'I shall write no more in this book. For some time I have been growing weaker and I fancy I shall do no more work. I have only to say to you, my children, that you have all been as good and tender to me as anyone could be during these last months and indeed years. It comforts me to think that you are all so fond of each other that when I am gone you will be the better able to do without me.' The sight of death mellowed him and his vexatious habits departed. Throughout the year he watched it approaching with open and curious eyes. Huxley had told Morley that he found his dislike of the thought of extinction increasing as he got older and nearer the goal; another rationalist, Herbert Spencer, was much troubled at the end by the Immanence of Space and was in such a state of nerves, Stephen wrote to Norton, 'that he can only talk to anyone for three and a half minutes by his watch and on no exciting topics'; Stephen himself remained calm and awaited annihilation. Just before he died he wrote to bid farewell to George Meredith. Meredith also at the end of his days replied:

My dearest Leslie—Your letter gave me one of the few remaining pleasures that I can have. I rejoice in your courage and energy. Of the latter I have nothing left. Since last September I have not held a pen, except perforce to sign my name. . . . We who have loved the motion of legs and the sweep of the winds, we come to this. But for myself, I will own that it is the Natural order. There is no irony in Nature. . . .

Leslie Stephen died early on the morning of the 22nd of February, 1904. Six months later his children moved from the Victorian house in Hyde Park Gate to the unfashionable squares of Bloomsbury.

4

The present trend in biography bears hard on Leslie Stephen. Biographers concentrate on those aspects of a man's life which their age considers important. A generation, suspicious of worldly success and believing that reality was to be found in the delicate play of personal relations, has dictated to biographers the standard of values by which a man should be judged; hatred for those who tyrannise over other people's lives, mistrust of a powerful will, admiration for humour, integrity and, above all, sensitivity towards other people's feelings, became the cardinal virtues. Judged by this standard Leslie Stephen will be found wanting. So far from practising what he preached about domestic affection, Stephen was insensitive, egotistical and, in a subtle way, tyrannical. In the family, which he worshipped as the sacred entity on which the whole edifice of society and ethics is built, he revealed ironically enough what was hidden from his friends: the inner core of his nature.

To expose the unconscious springs of action is the aim of the modern biographer. Nor is this strange. Clinical psycho-analysis suggested that the contradictions in a man's character can be explained by revealing those subconscious desires which condition the personality. Even more striking has been the influence of the novel on biography. Time and again novelists such as Dostoievsky and Henry James direct our attention to a man's *inner* morality. The novelist is concerned not merely with a man's conscious outward endeavours but with the nature of his will. The will subtly colours all his actions. It is a country beyond the realm of conscious motivation, a country where the writ of religious or social conventions does not run because there reason has no control. A man may honestly desire to be kind, but every act of kindness is vitiated by the subconscious motives behind the act. The novelist is always confronting us with characters who imagine that they are acting from one set of motives but whose wills are really driving them along a different road: their creator exposes them for what they are, hypocrites masquerading as moralists, philanthropists who are narrow-minded tyrants, crooks and scamps who are good-hearted and generous. Following the novelist, the modern biographer claims to reveal what a man really is and not just what the man himself thinks he is or wants to be.*

This preoccupation with the subconscious, this determination to discover what a man is, has led biographers to neglect conscious motives or to regard them simply as evidence for interpreting the subconscious. This is an error. It is an error because it suggests that a man's character is set in a certain mould and that all attempts to change it are wasteful and, in the last analysis, unimportant. It is an error because it sometimes misplaces the emphasis in a man's life. The men

---

* The techniques of the psycho-analyst and novelist are frequently inapplicable to biography and are consequently crudely exploited. The biographer does not have the material, the living mind, on which the psychoanalyst works. Nor does he have the novelist's advantage of creating a character in order to see through him; and therefore it is always doubtful how far the biographer can judge the subconscious springs of action, the colour of a man's will.

and women who suffer most severely from this approach are
those who, like Stephen, were moralists: that is to say,
those who framed laws of conduct for their fellow men,
distinguished virtue from vice, and often into the bargain
tried to make themselves better. Directly some people
hear the word moralist they believe they are on the trail of
a prig, and if in addition the moralist seeks to lead a better
life himself, how pleasing it is to trip him by the heels and
send him spinning! One of the delights of *Tom Jones* is to
see how that prudential philosopher, Mr. Square, having
spent the afternoon laying down the laws of virtue, is
caught in the evening in an outrageous position with a
chambermaid. Is it not futile to attempt to change oneself?
'It is impossible,' wrote Hazlitt, 'for those who are naturally
disagreeable to be otherwise. . . . A vain man who is
endeavouring to please is only endeavouring to shine. . . .
An irritable man who puts a check on himself only grows
dull and loses spirit to be anything.' It is true that many men
are turned by their efforts to reform themselves into cen-
sorious and conceited purists, thereby injuring themselves far
more than they would have done by plodding on unre-
generately as before. But sometimes the only thing that
makes a man of interest are his efforts to reform. His
character may well be of minor importance; the significance
of his life lies in what he tried to become. Charles Smythe
has remarked that Lord Shaftesbury was a man of un-
governable passions, by temperament, proud, imperious,
dictatorial, resentful and ambitious; but his life is the story
of how he mastered these passions by 'the constant, stubborn,
unrelenting dedication of his life to God.' Leslie Stephen,
like Shaftesbury, had his fair share of faults; he was a queer
mixture of conflicting elements which, by strength of will,
he tried to turn alchemically to gold. Of course, both men
fail in their ultimate object—they cannot become the
person they set out to be. Hazlitt is right: men have
certain temperamental strains which they cannot eliminate.
But who in their senses expects anyone to succeed in such a
quest? It is not the measure of men's success or failure
but the *manner* in which they try to change themselves that
is important.

The key to Stephen's character is his effort to change himself. He believed his hypersensitivity to be a weakness and determined to conquer it. The very thought of suffering pained him. He refused ever to visit a hospital; he could not bear to hear the word dentist mentioned; during the Boer War he lay awake at night fancying he could hear the guns on the African battlefields and he would go out of his way to avoid seeing newspaper posters carrying news of the slaughter. As a child he could not bear a word of reproof and if reproached burst into tears. As a man he saw the air thick with imaginary rebuffs and determined never to expose himself. Hypersensitivity, he thought, saps a man's will to go out into the world and do his duty. It must be crushed and destroyed. But as he grew older Stephen doubted whether its ghost had been laid and this bred in him a subtler form of self-mistrust; he knew in his heart that his athletic feats, designed to prove to himself that he could succeed, proved nothing, and that though he had trained his body to endure hardship, his mind was as sensitive as in childhood days. The effort to conquer himself in fact had maimed him: the victory he had won over his own nature was Pyrrhic.

The time has come to count the cost of this victory. It can partly be assessed in his writing. Though as a critic he came to conclusions, his dissatisfaction seeps through the pages; in every essay there is a deutero-Stephen who whispers in the ear of Stephen the critic that all is in vain. No sooner has he laid down a critical canon than he is regarding it quizzically, despairingly. It is not that, in Van Wyck Brooks' phrase, he adopts an Indian-giver style of criticism that takes back with one hand what he has granted with the other; but one can hear a sigh of disbelief that anything that he has written is really worth the reader's effort. But the greater part of the cost fell to the account of his private life since the victory blunted his sensibilities yet left his nature as raw and sensitive as ever. Friends dimly apprehended part of the truth, his family saw all. They became the spectators of his calamity. And this is why we find two different conceptions of Stephen when we come to examine his character, the judgment of his friends who agreed with Lowell that he was 'the most lovable of men,' and the impression left upon his family: the portrait of Vernon Whitford in George Meredith's *The Egoist* and the very dissimilar portrait which appears in the pages of his daughter's novel, *To the Lighthouse.*

Virginia Woolf's Mr. Ramsay is utterly insensitive to the feelings of those immediately about him. He resents his limitations as a scholar and vents his chagrin upon his children. His damning utilitarian insistence on factual accuracy, that whether they like it or not the weather will change and the expedition to the Lighthouse will be ruined, takes the joy out of every childhood fancy and expectation. He is forever jawing with equally unimaginative friends about so-and-so who is a 'first-rate man' and so-and-so who is fundamentally unsound: these alpha-minded, dreary academic categories are meaningless in the only world that matters—the world of human beings who breathe and suffer and love. 'The crass blindness and tyranny in him,' which makes him fling a plate through the window at breakfast because he finds an earwig in the milk, which forbids him ever to praise his youngest son and makes his son hate him, is described with desolating intensity as Mr. Ramsay rows Cam and James to the Lighthouse. 'To pursue truth with such astonishing lack of consideration for other people's feelings, to rend the thin veils of civilisation so wantonly, so brutally, was to her so horrible an outrage of human decency. . . .' Can a man find truth, truth of any value, when he has maimed his feelings, the antennae with which he can sense other people's emotions? It is not that Mr. Ramsay ignores his family for the company of shuffling, sniffling old savants like Mr. Carmichael; he makes un- reasonable emotional demands upon them. He considers himself to be pitied, a man whose life has been wrecked by personal misfortune and who is owed affection and sympathy to sustain him in his great loss. He demands to be told that he is genuinely suffering. 'Sitting in the boat he bowed, he crouched himself, acting instantly his part—the part of a desolate man, widowed, bereft; and so called up before him in hosts people sympathising with him; staged for himself as he sat in the boat, a little drama.' The high-minded moralist turns out to be a ruthless egoist determined to exploit his own suffering and force his family, who are unable to escape, to suffer with him.

The accuracy of this portrait is substantiated in the journal which Stephen wrote for his children and which was called by them, The *Mausoleum Book*, in which he gives an account of his private life. In it he writes of his attempts to subdue Annie Ritchie, his money mania and the countless petty tyrannies with which he exasperated Julia and his children. In his relations with Minny and Julia he adopted two of the classical attitudes of people who demand to be loved: 'People do not really like me, so I will retreat from society and secure myself from any rejection which would mortally wound me'; and, 'You ought to love me because I suffer and am helpless.' Admitting his faults, he puts them down with pathetic honesty—and then tries to justify them. Moods of self-recrimination are followed by explanations of his conduct designed to persuade himself that he was misunderstood. Guilt wells from his pen. He has only to write of Julia and he is pursued by 'hideous morbid fancies' which haunt him that he was at times unkind to her, 'fancies which I know to be utterly baseless and which I am yet unable to disperse by an effort of will. I must live them down.' But he cannot, and the memories return to lie with him at night. 'All this comes back to me—trifles and things that are not quite trifles—and prevents me from saying, as I would so gladly have said, that I never gave her anxiety or caused her needless annoyance.' He worshipped Julia, desired to transform her into an apotheosis of motherhood, but treated her in the home as someone who should be at his beck and call, support him in every emotional crisis, order the minutiae of his life and then submit to his criticism in those household matters of which she was mistress. If a child was late for dinner, it must have been maimed or killed in an accident; and that would be her fault. He would sulk if things did not go his way; if it was suggested that he take a hot bath on coming in soaked with rain from a walk, he would consider his manliness impugned and then like a child pout with injured pride and refuse a piece of his favourite cake at tea. Stephen had cause for guilt. His wife was more remarkable than he. Julia Stephen's memorial was carved by her daughter in the characters of Mrs. Ambrose, Mrs. Hilberry and Mrs. Ramsay; and this is fitting for Virginia Woolf inherited from her mother much of her sensibility and even an echo of her style. Julia's single publication is lost in oblivion yet it reveals her character as surely as Virginia Woolf's portraits. It is about nursing and called *Notes for Sick Rooms*. Imaginative in that it brings to mind all the details unobserved by the sage, it combines an exquisite sensibility towards other people's sufferings with exceedingly practical advice on how to alleviate them. 'The origin of most things,' she begins, 'has been decided on, but the origin of crumbs in bed has never excited sufficient attention among the scientific world'—and from there she analyses the almost impossible task of getting rid of them.* From the snuffing of candles, the arrangement of candles, and the position of

---

* 'Among the number of small evils which haunt illness, the greatest, in the misery which it can cause, though the smallest in size, is crumbs. The origin of most things has been decided on, but the origin of crumbs in bed has never excited sufficient attention among the scientific world, though it is a problem which has tormented many a weary sufferer. I will forbear to give my own explanation, which would be neither scientific nor orthodox, and will merely beg that their evil existence may be recognised and, as far as human nature allows, guarded against. The torment of crumbs should be stamped out of the sick bed as if it were the Colorado beetle in a potato field. Anyone who has been ill will at once take her precautions, feeble though they will prove. She will have a napkin under her chin, stretch her neck out of bed, eat in the most uncomfortable way, and watch that no crumbs get into the folds of her night-dress or jacket. When she lies back in bed, in the vain hope that she may have baffled the enemy, he is before her: a sharp crumb is buried in her back, and grains of sand seem sticking to her toes. If the patient is able to get up and have her bed made, when she returns to it she will find the crumbs are waiting for her. The housemaid will protest that the sheets were shaken, and the nurse that she swept out the crumbs, but there they are, and there they will remain unless the nurse determines to conquer them. To do this she must first believe in them, and there are few assertions that are met with such incredulity as the one—I have crumbs in my bed. After every meal the nurse should put her hand into the bed and feel for the crumbs. When the bed is made, the nurse and housemaid must not content themselves with shaking or sweeping. The tiny crumbs stick in the sheets, and the nurse must patiently take each crumb out; if there are many very small ones, she must even wet her fingers, and get the crumbs to stick to them. The patient's night-clothes must be searched; crumbs lurk in each tiny fold or frill. They go up the sleeve of the night-gown, and if the patient is in bed when the search is going on, her arms should hang out of bed, so that the crumbs which are certain to be there may be induced to fall down. When crumbs are banished—that is to say, temporarily, for with each meal they return, and for this the nurse must make up her mind—she must see that there are no rucks in the bed-sheets.'
Is not the tone of voice similar to that in her daughter's essays?

looking-glasses to the technique of bed-baths and of administering enemas, everything is discussed from the point of view of the sufferer with irony, detachment and common sense. She responded to other people's feelings instinctively; she could heal a child's wound before it was given and read thoughts before they were uttered, and her sympathy was like the touch of a butterfly, delicate and remote—for she knew what it was to live an inner life and respected other people's privacy. Leslie thought himself a practical man but beside her he was a ninny. Leslie thought himself a friend in need, but she knew how to translate sympathy into action. Leslie ploughed furrows of ratiocination to reach conclusions, she had intuitively reached them and acted upon them before he arrived. Thus he was for ever trampling upon her feelings, wounding the person who comforted him, half-conscious of his hebetude, unable to constrain it. Men are to be pitied; and so are we ourselves.

Stephen was an old man when his children were in their 'teens and thus understandably enough, they found him difficult. He lacked the ability, that his wife had to such an extraordinary degree, of apprehending their feelings. He was angelic with children when they were tots, drawing animals, telling stories and writing them letters, but he lacked the patience and imagination to understand them as boys and girls. One day he decided to take over all teaching in the schoolroom and made his children's life so unbearable that he had to be advised to stop. Nothing mattered but that his spirit should live on in them; he was impatient of theirs. Writing to Norton about the son whom his wife most adored, he said, 'Adrian is an attractive, simple little fellow but oddly dreamy and apt to take a great interest in things which are impractical.' The boy, then, must be made to be practical. Adrian in revenge taught himself to imitate his father's voice and, safe in the knowledge of his father's deafness, would strike up before all the family at dinner in the hope of making his brother and sisters giggle; the device worked to perfection until the day when he performed in a growler and discovered that among the peculiar properties of that vehicle was a quality which turned it into a gigantic ear-trumpet, so that his father heard every word. Moans issued from the deeply distressed Stephen, 'Oh, my boy, my boy!' With the merciless insight of children they seized on their father's failings; in particular his habit of dramatising the insignificant into the cosmic. Once as he passed their room stumbling upstairs to his study they heard him talking to himself: 'I wish I were dead . . . I wish I were dead . . . I wish my whiskers would grow.' Mr. Ramsay, tyrannical and self-torturing, demanding that the family revolve round him is the fiction of fact.

Stephen tortured himself by sentimentalising the past and wishing it to be the present. The *Mausoleum Book* is in part an act of commemoration in which he recalls incidents from his married years, places a wreath upon them and embalms them in an electuary of sentimentality. He luxuriated in grief, noting in the book with mournful misgivings the death of each friend, the narrowing circle, the anniversaries of desolation, the happiness that could be no more. Stephen's sentimentality is all the more striking because he diagnosed the emotion in others unerringly and defined it as a mood in which we make 'a luxury of grief and regard sympathetic emotion as an end rather than a means—a need rightly despised by men of masculine nature.' Can it be that he failed to make himself entirely the manly affectionate fellow that he wished to be? Sentimentalism, the enjoyment of emotion for its own sake, is no more a vice than many other similar moods such as nostalgia. But it is often a cloak, a perfumed shroud, donned to conceal the stink of vice, of secret and unknown sins, such as cruelty and coarseness. Stephen was neither cruel nor coarse but his sentimentality concealed his fear of the future, his desire to remain in the past, to remember what had been happiness because he could never know happiness again; and this was inflicted upon his wife and children.

No one can be aware of all his faults, still less change the soil of the temperament in which they grow. Stephen, however, impelled by his Evangelical heritage, searched his soul for faults and tried to change himself. He realised that his habits maddened his family. He knew that they had to tell him things more than twice because, sunk in a brown

TALLAND HOUSE, ST. IVES (THE RAMSEYS' HOME IN
VIRGINIA WOOLF'S 'TO THE LIGHTHOUSE')

VIRGINIA AND ADRIAN STEPHEN, 1886

LESLIE AND JULIA STEPHEN, 1892

study, he did not bother to listen. He acknowledged that
he was fidgety and troublesome, 'and even when alone
in my family, I am sometimes as restless as a hyaena.'
When taxed he made promises to mend his ways and always
failed. But sincerity depends on the relation between our
words and our thoughts, not between our beliefs and our
actions, and none of Stephen's protestations was in the least
hypocritical or pretending to a feeling of sorrow which he
never felt and never wanted to feel. He often consciously
tried to reform, and in order to thicken his thin skin,
dam up the ooze of his sentimentality and face the future,
he adopted two remedies. The first was Carlyle's soporific
of work. All the Stephens ruined their health through
overwork, a symptom of a deep-seated family neurosis.
Although Leslie declared that he had never in his life
worked hard except when taking his degree, added, 'The
only reason why I ever get anything done is that I do not
waste time in the vain effort to make myself agreeable . . .'
he too worked to deaden his feelings. The volume of his
publications is considerable: five volumes of histories of
thought, five books in the English Men of Letters series,
three full length Life and Letters biographies, two short
books of reminiscences, well over a hundred and fifty long
articles and introductions, most of them reprinted, his
contributions to the D.N.B., together with a mass of more
ephemeral journalism, show staggering powers of application.
And, like many of his contemporaries, he was an indefatigable
correspondent.

Wounded sensibilities can be soothed by work which brings
forgetfulness in fatigue. They can also be soothed by
humour. Humour is one of man's most valuable weapons
against the weariness of the world. Some people use it as a
defence against mental exertion and laugh problems away
which they would rather not face; others expose the
weaknesses of their fellow-men to restore their belief in
themselves; a few employ it to enlighten themselves about
their own character and to see themselves in relation to
society. Stephen belonged to the last class. No one saw
himself more clearly in a ridiculous light. As a young man,
he tried to escape acquiring the more ill-favoured of the

academic characteristics, but when he came to London, he
considered himself branded with the mark of the tribe of
dons whom he compared to toads since 'with an unpromising
exterior they both sometimes bear a precious jewel in their
heads.' He was even able to smile at himself on occasions
when most men prefer to romanticise their appearance: he
realised that he was an awkward lover. The comical
and touching way in which he described his courtships is
the mark of one who knew that man, or at any rate himself,
often cuts a ludicrous figure in what should be his most
intense experiences. He employed humour, too, in the way
he questioned emotional clichés: he bequeathed the
deprecating glance to his children in Bloomsbury. Above all,
his humour protected him against self-righteousness. Stephen
realised that a moralist, who keeps before his eyes a goal of
personal perfection, is always in danger of being a prig; the
number of times he mentions that word in his essays betrays
his own anxiety to avoid the charge. Humour, in this connection, is the art of seeing oneself and one's ideals in
relation to other human beings.

Yet though this excellent virtue ministers to the sensibility,
it enfeebles self-confidence in those who doubt their own
abilities. So Stephen lost on the roundabouts what he made
on the swings. His determination never to lie to himself
about himself convinced him that he was a failure and that
nothing he had done would be long remembered. Writing
in the *Mausoleum Book* Stephen said, 'Had I—as I often
reflect—no pretext for calling myself a failure, had I succeeded in my most ambitious dreams and surpassed all my
contemporaries in my own line, what should I have done?
I should have written a book or two which would have been
admired by my own and perhaps by the next generation.
They would have survived so long as active forces, and a
little longer in the memory of the more learned, because
they would have expressed a little better than other books
thoughts which were fomenting in the minds of thousands,
some abler and many little less able than myself. But
putting aside the very few great names with whom I could
not in my wildest fancy compare myself, even the best
thinkers become obsolete in a brief time, and turn out to

have been superfluous. Putting my imaginary achievements at the best, they would have made no perceptible difference to the world.'* If this kind of analysis betrays Stephen's sad lack of self-confidence, its honesty must give us pause. Glancing at the career of the greatest of all Victorian dons, Stephen noted that Jowett was always able to believe in his own achievements. Jowett, as he cryptically put it, had 'not known the greatest happiness': he had not married and begot children. But he had acquired a derivative immortality from his College, and knew that his work would be carried on by his chosen successors. This enviable frame of mind enabled him to retain the illusion which the old usually lose that 'anything you did at your best had any real value, or that anything you can do hereafter will even reach the moderate standard of the old work.' Stephen would not accept this illusion, and his honesty is touched with the annihilating ruthlessness of Turgenev's hero Bazarov, 'If you've made up your mind to mow down everything, don't spare your own legs.'

Nevertheless, it is honest, and their father's honesty and kindliness impressed themselves upon his children. Stephen's defects in the home were certainly grave, not trivial quirks or endearing eccentricities; nor was his the forgivable habit of blazing up in rows which any family worth its salt soon learns how to extinguish. It says much for his daughters and also for him that they did not deny the sweep of his character and his admirable virtues. The portrait of Mr. Ramsay was never intended to be the whole story. On the centenary of her father's birth Virginia Woolf wrote an article for the *Times* in which she gave a very different account. She spoke of his gift of amusing his children by drawing animals and telling stories; and though he was old-fashioned in his views about the vice of luxury and the sin of idleness, and even if he forbade his daughters to smoke cigarettes, he gave them intellectual freedom.

* Cf. *To the Lighthouse* Pt. I 'And his fame lasts how long? Is it permissible even for a dying hero to think before he dies how men will speak of him hereafter? His fame lasts perhaps two thousand years. And what are two thousand years? (asked Mr. Ramsay, ironically, staring at the hedge). . . . His own little light would shine, not very brightly for a year or two, and then would be merged in some bigger light, and that in a bigger still.'

They could read at will in his unexpurgated library. Virginia could study Plato under Walter Pater's sister. Vanessa could choose a career which meant attending an art school. 'Freedom of that sort was worth thousands of cigarettes.' Moreover, he taught his children never to accept the judgments of good form. 'At the end of a volume my father always gravely asked our opinion as to its merits, and we were required to say which of the characters we liked best and why. I can remember his indignation when one of us preferred the hero to the far more life-like villain.' They learnt from him to recognise selfish and trivial opinions. 'A lady, for instance, complained of the wet summer that was spoiling her tour in Cornwall. But to my father, though he never called himself a democrat, the rain meant that the corn was being laid; some poor man was being ruined; and the energy with which he expressed his sympathy—not with the lady—left her discomfited.' It was not his reserve which impressed his children so much as the vigour with which he felt, his love of clear-thinking and his hatred of the stock response. 'He had a way of upsetting established reputations and disregarding conventional values that could be disconcerting, and sometimes perhaps wounding, though not one was more respectful of any feeling that seemed to him genuine.'

These were the qualities which made Meredith and his many other friends love him. And how numerous they were! They were not restricted to his contemporaries or to Clifford or Henley or a dozen others whom he helped. He was granted a privilege often denied to the old: young men such as Desmond MacCarthy enjoyed his company and were kind to him, and H. A. L. Fisher and Maitland who married into the family were men he could respect as well as like. Meredith spoke of his equability; his friends knew that he valued them for their qualities, not for their abilities, and that once accepted they would not be dissected and discarded. His integrity was beyond question. Revenge or malice were beneath him, he despised personal gain and all devious ways of influence or persuasion; and if this magnanimity took him a pace or two out of the world, it invested his actions with a noble simplicity.

Equability and integrity may keep, but never by them-selves make, lasting friends. Nor do his entertaining oddities explain the devotion of his friends. Stephen's famous gruffness could irritate as well as delight. Hardy once wrote in his diary:

Called on Leslie Stephen. He is just the same or worse; as if dying to express sympathy, but suffering under some terrible curse which prevents his saying any but caustic things, and showing antipathy instead.

What was it then that made Stephen the 'most lovable of men'? Partly the knowledge that beneath the hard shell there was a soft heart. Stephen's sentimentalism expressed itself in endearing devotions. Thomas Hardy liked a man to care about the past. The first time he met Stephen, he asked him why he had chosen to live in a new street in Kensington with the pavements hardly laid and the road not yet rolled. Stephen replied that 'he had played as a child with his nurse in the fields hard by, and he fancied living on the spot, which was dear to him . . . I felt then that I liked him, which I had first doubted. The feeling never changed.' That was why Stephen loved to walk round Kensington Gardens and Hyde Park where, wrote his daughter, 'as a little boy his brother Fitzjames and he had made beautiful bows to young Queen Victoria and she had swept them a curtsey.' In the Gardens he had as a child recited *Marmion*; now with his daughters he would shout Newbolt's *Admirals All* at the top of his voice to the astonishment of nannies and park-keepers. But men loved him for reasons deeper than these. Stephen's inner nature was so palpably the contradiction of what he taught that their sympathy went out to him. We admire our friends for their qualities, we often love them for their failings; their failings put them on the same level as ourselves. Looking at Watts' portrait of Stephen one feels that the lower lip of that passionate, tender mouth is beginning to tremble and that Stephen is on the verge of tears. He is shamelessly appealing for love and protection. It was this helplessness in face of bills, servants, parties and the paraphernalia of everyday existence which made women love him. Candida sticks by

Morell because she pities the strong man whose defences have collapsed.

'I only met him once when he was an old man visiting his sister in Cambridge,' said E. M. Forster. 'He said little. Then he noticed that I was looking at him and he turned away.' He feared that someone who might not sympathise would solve the riddle of his personality. To the man himself there is always a riddle. Why do I behave like this? Why am I disliked? Why do I fail? Stephen dreaded exposure and deplored the publication of private papers which reveal to posterity something of a man's inner life. Yet he need not have feared. Partly because he was palpably defenceless against such an enquiry, partly because he valued self-knowledge and set out to cure himself and partly because his character (as distinct from his personality) was massive and impressive, he earns respect. Those who desire a visual image to catch the perplexity of his personality, the grandeur and hardness of his character, the oddness and difficulty of the man, should imagine him in silhouette against the background of his times alone with Nature. His life resembled his favourite pursuit. It was a long climb up the slopes and rocks of thought, plodding slowly on to scale the Alps that towered above him. For Thomas Hardy Stephen's spirit became immanent with the peaks he surmounted, so that the Schreckhorn appears:

> Aloof, as if a thing of mood and whim,
> Now that its spare and desolate figure gleams
> Upon my nearing vision, less it seems
> A looming Alp-height than a guise of him
> Who scaled its horn with ventured life and limb,
> Drawn on by vague imaginings, maybe,
> Of semblance to his personality
> In its quaint glooms, keen lights, and rugged trim.
>
> —At his last change, when Life's dull coils unwind,
> Will he, in old love, hitherward escape,
> And the eternal essence of his mind
> Enter this silent adamantine shape,
> And his low voicing haunt its slipping snows
> When dawn that calls the climber dyes them rose?

This, then, is how we shall view him—as a peak set in the mountain range of a certain tradition of thought. All that any biographer can do is to select an angle of vision or present his subject from different angles. No one is gifted with a vision of 360 degrees, and the reader may object that the portrait is false only if the biographer pretends that the angle of his vision is more obtuse than it in fact is, or if his judgment of human beings in society is shallow. To examine Stephen's personality through his home life is fair provided that we remember that everyone's domestic life is an odd hotch-potch. Nevertheless, there is such a thing as appropriateness in biography. The preoccupation in recent years with the intricacies of personality has led biographers to over-emphasise the sphere of personal relations and to regard that alone as important. Leslie Stephen's life is not in itself strikingly interesting; it is primarily of importance for the light it throws on his intellectual development and on his writing, and to admit this is not to be guilty of pedantry. Nor does it detract from his achievement to say that his writing is most valuable when judged in relation to the tradition of thought to which he belonged and to his environment. To study a tradition of thought through an individual inevitably produces a fresh distortion in that individuals resemble corpuscles in the blood-stream of the social organism, pushed about and coagulating, according to the exertions and diseases of the body they inhabit; yet they are its life. It is worth while seeing how Stephen was gathered into the main intellectual movements of his time and what contribution he made to the Victorian ethos. For in the labyrinth of his conceptions of right and wrong we shall find the man for whom we are searching.

CHAPTER III

EVANGELICALISM

EVANGELICAL morality was the single most widespread influence in Victorian England. It powerfully influenced the Church of England, was the faith of the Methodists, and revived the older Nonconformist sects; it spread through every class and taught a clear set of values. The peremptory demand for sincerity, the delight in plain-speaking, the unvarying accent on conduct, and the conviction that he who has attained a Higher Truth must himself evangelise, leap from the pages of Stephen's books and proclaim him a child of the Evangelical tradition. The intellectual heritage of Evangelicalism has been too readily forgotten. The stream of missionaries, the philanthropy of Wilberforce and Shaftesbury, the soldierly piety of Outram, Havelock and Gordon, are not forgotten; but it is too often assumed to be a religion with a theology simplified to the point of banality which calls men to action rather than strengthens their minds —the enemy of intelligence and learning. It is true that no outstanding intellect emerges among the Anglican and Nonconformist clergy of the Evangelical persuasion, but the histories of the movement, perhaps naturally, do not follow the sheep who stray from the fold. Half the men and much of the enthusiasm of Tractarianism were of Evangelical origin; the most fervent recruits to rationalism came from Evangelical homes. And how many of the middle class intellectual aristocracy are reared in Evangelical families! To understand Leslie Stephen's mind we must see what Evangelicalism bequeathed to him.

The demands of the faith are simple. Man must experience God. He must evangelise among his fellow-men. He must listen to God's word; and since God speaks through the conscience, this means following the inner light wherever it shines.

What kind of God did the Clapham Sect worship and how could one experience Him? The Claphamites took

their lead in theology from their fellow member, Charles
Simeon, the disciple of old Henry Venn, who inclined rather
to Whitefield's Calvinism than Wesley's Arminianism. But
it was a moderate and joyful Calvinism which assumed that
no man could say how many or whom God would elect
and that it was the duty of His evangelists to go into the
fields and feed His sheep. Man is utterly sunk in Original
Sin; so depraved that he hates his God and shuts his ears
to God's call, so that his eternal soul stands in peril of death.
But all is not lost; Christ died for him on the Cross and this
can be his salvation. 'The offer' made by Christ to sinful
man is ever open and he can 'close with it' at any time.
If he allows God's grace to open his heart to his Saviour,
the pains of Hell shall not prevail; but if, stiff-necked and
obdurate, he plunges downward all unheeding, then
Eternal Punishment shall be his reward. The Evangelicals
were acutely aware of the distinct Persons of the Trinity.
Their vision of God was expressed in the final scene of the
first part of Faust where Mephistopheles cries in triumph
over Gretchen, 'Sie ist gerichtet.' 'Gerettet' proclaims the
voice from above. God is both a Judge and a Saviour. In
Majesty and Wrath, He comes to judge the world but at
His side sits Christ who can intercede. In the most famous
of all Evangelical hymns the Calvinist Toplady wrote:

> Whilst I draw this fleeting breath,
> When my eyestrings break in death,
> When I soar through tracts unknown,
> See Thee on Thy Judgment-Throne;
> Rock of Ages, cleft for me
> Let me hide myself in Thee.

So far from being a Paleyan Deity who proves His existence
to men by the ingenious mechanism of Nature, the Evangelical God is a God of miracles. The conversion of every
soul by His evangelists is a miraculous sign of His mercy.
But Christ's compassion must not turn man's gaze away
from the awful vista of His Father's Judgment Seat. Man is
to be judged by other-worldly standards. The God of the
Clapham Sect was an ambivalent God who, however open
to intercession by His Son, had to weigh each soul in the

balance. By God's Holiness the Evangelical meant God's need to judge and, in His mercy, forgive sin; sometimes He might show His judgment in this world as when He worked mightily through wars and plagues caused by inevitable human wickedness. Thus, though the atoning power of Christ's sacrifice was the central doctrine of Christianity, God's judgment—indeed His duty to judge —remained the final reality. If this duty to judge lay so heavily upon their Maker how much more did it weigh upon His children? In the light of this belief Evangelical parents guided their sons and daughters from infancy to distinguish between right and wrong, the good and the wicked, the precious and the worthless. Throughout his life Leslie Stephen never doubted that a man was saved in a moral sense so long as he recognised that it was his duty to exercise his judgment.

Such was the God to whom they prayed. But it was not enough to appreciate that this was the Grand Design. The Evangelicals demanded more—they declared that a man could be saved only if he had experienced God's grace. A man could be certain that God's message of salvation was intended for him personally only by experiencing the moment when grace descended. That moment was his conversion. When a man acknowledged his helplessness, when overwhelmed with the horror of his mortal corruption he cast his sins at the feet of his Redeemer, when he begged Christ to bear the burden as He had promised to His Father on the Cross, then, in a flash, that man might stand upright; not assured indubitably of a place in Heaven— for God's grace might depart and he could yet slide back into the mire of worldliness—but confident in the knowledge that Christ had changed his heart and that he was now, and almost certainly would be, numbered with His saints. God must have touched the heart so that a man *experienced* his own sinfulness and the power of his Saviour. Knowledge of God was an emotional, not an intellectual, understanding. Theology, the arrangement of syllogisms, the creation of principles and philosophies, were fundamentally valueless: no structure of thought could make the design of creation intelligible. The raw stuff of emotional experience was the proof of God's existence. And so, a young Evangelical who developed a turn for philosophy was likely to be drawn towards the Utilitarians who professed to base their conclusions on an empirical examination of human experience. Both Evangelicals and Utilitarians, Leslie Stephen noted, regarded their own version of verifiable experience as final and both were opposed to the study of metaphysics.

To the experience of conversion the Evangelicals added the daily experience of God—the day to day meditation in the silent bedroom, Bible in hand, led a man to know Christ as a friend. It was there that they learnt to train their conscience. High among the tenets of the faith was the injunction that no human intermediary, no priest or State servant, should dare by intervening between man and his Maker implicitly—as the Evangelicals held—to judge God in his dealings with another human being. A sincere man's conscience must be, at the last, the measure of his actions. It must be free to enable him to follow the prompting of the Holy Spirit. How else can he claim to be a moral being, how can he claim God's mercy unless his actions are his own, and not those dictated to him by the external spiritual authority of a visible Church? The Evangelical appeals to the inner light within him for guidance. The Protestant stakes all on the relationship between the soul of the agent and the Judge, and Protestantism is a creed for supermen—for men so secure in God's grace that they cannot stumble.* The particular glory of the faith is that at best its disciples are taught to follow the truth in their hearts. But the dangers are obvious. In a letter to Moncure Conway about his state of mind in 1823, Francis Newman explained, 'I was an Evangelical, but like plenty of Evangelicals beside, both now and then, was resolved to follow the Truth *whithersoever it led me*; and was always indignant when told "you must believe this or that," or you will find it "will lead you further." "*If* that time comes, I shall go further" was my uniform reply.' It was this spirit which led so many of the best brains among the Evangelicals to go further and to secede from the party.

* The great French sociologist, Durkheim, claimed that the rate of suicides is higher among Protestants than among Catholics, because Protestantism places the full weight of responsibility on the individual's shoulders.

But a living religion cannot be expounded point by point. To explain his views, Sir James Stephen told Carlyle, he would have to write an autobiography '. . . to tell of opinions inherited—of the diversities between the paternal and maternal inheritance—of the friends of my youth who, one after another, went down into the grave in the full maturity of the Christian life, and of the Christian faith—of the friends of my later years, in whom the ripening of faith was a tardy and imperfect process—of many books read, which all in turn left me still to search—of the vicissitudes of life, which taught me much not to be found (or not be to found by me) in any books—of Biblical studies and meditations—of habitual exercises of devotion, public, domestic and private—of the reaction on my own mind of the lessons I had to convey to my children—and of influences silently, imperceptibly, yet progressively exerting themselves over my interior self which . . . have wrought that self into a persuasion (that is a heart conviction) from which in this life, I can never now be divorced—a persuasion that the Bible, or rather the greater part of it, is, in some real though indefinable sense, the Word of God—the persuasion that, between the life and death of Jesus Christ and our own reconciliation to God, there is an indispensable, though (I confess) a perfectly inexplicable relation. . .—the persuasion of a real, though wholly incomprehensible, intimacy (amounting almost to unity) of life, and being, and nature between parents and their children, and their more remote posterity—the persuasion thence resulting of an ancestral corruption of our whole race—and the persuasion that, by the adoption of our nature, Jesus Christ has broken the otherwise indissoluble bonds which link us all to sin, and to sorrow, the child of sin.

'To draw out this creed of mine into any series of dogmatical propositions . . . is quite beyond my power. My convictions are, I know, less strong than my persuasions. I am living, or trying to live, more under the guidance of an invisible hand, and under the impulse of indefinable motives, than in submission to any logic, or body of evidences, or weight of authority. If I were of the Society of John Wesley, I should say I am living by my experiences. . . . My creed has for its foundation, superstructure and summit, the sense of unworthiness—of my own personal and individual unworthiness. But yet I think myself bound . . . to tell you as distinctly as I can, that however remote I may be from the character of a Christian, I am bound by links stronger than death to Him from whom that holy name is derived. . . .'

Finally, Evangelicalism is a religion for men of this world. It demands that men shall labour to save their brothers' souls. But how can one evangelise without becoming contaminated by worldly wickedness? How has a man the audacity to show other men their sins knowing all the time that he himself is sinful?

Study the private papers of the Evangelicals and the answer is clear. Henry Thornton of Clapham left a diary which contains the daily entries of his solitary communing. It is a diary of a man in this world, not of it. He does not seek to merge the soul with the One, to lift himself out of the complexity of human existence into the stillness of the infinite where the soul can join itself to God. His religion is a practical religion dealing with practical affairs, and Christ his wise counsellor. A man may work in the world and return with clean hands provided that he is constantly introspective. Each day Thornton examines his life according to the Commandments laid upon him by God's Book. Has he lived according to the Law? How can he amend his acts to follow it more closely? Scrutiny of his actions leads him to resolve to control his will. For the human will yearning after the pomps and vanities of the world must die and become Christ's will. The past is renounced, the old selfish private will dies, and the regenerated will takes control. This state of mind leads, all too often, to a man denying that the old will ever inhabited his body.* But the strength and self-confidence such a belief gives a man

* One can see an interesting throw-back to this Evangelical state of mind in Leslie Stephen's ruminations over the religious crisis that led to his agnosticism. 'I was not discovering that my creed was false, but that I had never really believed it' and 'I . . . became convinced among other things, that Noah's flood was a fiction (or rather convinced that I had never believed it) . . .' Maitland commented on these passages that if you have to 'discover' or to 'become convinced' of the falsity of the story of Noah's Flood, then you have really believed it however baseless the belief may have been. It is an interesting example of how a highly scrupulous mind can deny after 'conversion' that it held certain beliefs which have become morally odious.

is fabulous. Moreover, it redeems him from Guilt. Regarded purely as a therapy, Evangelicalism can be a most
potent healer. Justified by his faith in Christ, a man is
freed from all *ultimate* doubt. He may wrestle with his
conscience and search his heart for shortcomings in his
everyday life. But, unlike a man who believes in justification
partly by works and never therefore quite knows what the
score is—who never knows how many of his bad actions
have atoned for his good actions—the Evangelical's mind
is at rest on the ultimate question. He knows that he is
saved. The knowledge that God does not forget his saints
gives him the strength to labour in the vineyards of the
world.

2

   Thus the Clapham Sect had the confidence to change
the world. They acted in the spirit of the Collects for the
last Sunday in Trinity and the first in Advent; with their
wills stirred up by God, they put on the armour of light,
and learned to live in the world and yet to despise its values.
Secure in the experience of their conversion they were
untroubled by the distractions and vices of London society.
They had seen the obstinate defenders of the Slave Trade,
Nelson among them, retire shattered. High and Dry and
latitudinarian Anglicans hindered and sneered at them,
yet they saw their cause everywhere gaining ground.
Unpopularity and derision often sours zealots and turns
them into cynics or fanatics, but an unpopularity which
gradually evaporates into success and something like
approbation, is a tonic. The Clapham Sect saw that sincerity paid, and they acquired the habit of going against the
grain of their times. Their sincerity sprang from their
determination not to let outward circumstances dictate
their actions. When the time came for Leslie Stephen to
evangelise on behalf of the North in the American Civil
War or to propagate agnosticism, he appeared to have
inherited a double portion of the Clapham spirit.
   He also acquired another quality peculiar to the Clapham
Sect, namely the sense of belonging to a chosen body.
Sydney Smith was wrong in calling them a sect, for a more

orthodox body of men never stepped. They were not a sect but a coterie. Leslie's father admitted that they were a close-knit society up in arms if one of their number was attacked and unsparing in their judgments of individuals outside the clique. They dipped their tongues in vinegar and delighted to smell out a sham. Zachary Macaulay was renowned for his eager frankness and zeal in admonishing his friends and he expected no less from them.* 'Mr. Thornton's letter, in which were only eight lines was long enough to give me the satisfaction of knowing that he had nothing particularly to blame; a negative, but from Henry Thornton no mean, praise.' Thornton's great-grandson, E. M. Forster, has recorded how a young bride, who married into the family, said thoughtfully: 'If there were a spot upon the glorious Sun himself, the Thorntons would notice it.' Moreover, the censoriousness of Thornton and Macaulay was exacerbated by their belief that every moment of time, every word, every friendship, were accountable to God. This self-awareness, this contempt for the opinions of all outside the charmed circle, are the marks of a coterie. There are, however, advantages in clannishness. To belong to a set in which integrity and intelligence are blended, whose members criticise each other vigorously, and which can claim to be educating the country, innoculates a man against the evils of snobbery and the itch to simulate fashionable opinion. The Stephens were content to remain where they found themselves in society: what need was there to climb higher when they were at the top? They lived a public life, but they forswore the lures which public life dangles in front of men, inveigling them to shuffle off their principles. And there was, of course, within the Sect a circle even more

---

* An officer who met Zachary Macaulay was rash enough to say that swearing was a practice which harmed no one. Macaulay was on him like a knife, and subsequently 'feared he might have been offensively strong on the subject'; but he rejoiced to hear that the officer a little later swore no more and 'has become exceedingly restless and uneasy about that and other matters.' Again, visiting a sick friend who said he could not fix on any particular sins, Macaulay 'was at no loss to remind him of numberless particular sins, of the commission of which I myself had been a witness. I set them before him with all their aggravations.' Or, again, a young lady 'showed some very striking marks of a vain mind': whereupon Macaulay spoke his. 'The young lady did not altogether relish my plain but, I am sure, friendly expostulation.' Later he noticed she had put off 'her monstrous, misshapen dress . . . and her lowly looks were, I hope, no fallacious indication of a humbled mind.'

important in their eyes to spiritual development, the family itself. Leslie Stephen learnt to base his whole ethical system on the family. 'The degree in which any ethical theory recognises and reveals the essential importance of the family relation is, I think, the best test of its approximation to truth,' he wrote in an essay in which he answers the question which Johnson posed: which has done the most for humanity, Dr. Johnson or his poor dependent, the doctor Levett?* It is obscure creatures like Levett, answers Stephen, who really inherit the Kingdom of Heaven; a writer should pray to be obscure since public applause demoralises. Humanity owes the greatest debt to the most obscure of all beings in the eyes of the world, wives and mothers, who by their self-sacrifice shape the lives of their husbands and children. So deeply had the Evangelical tradition of the family as the natural centre of worship affected Stephen that he founds the moral health of society upon the institution of the family in his *Science of Ethics*.

Leslie Stephen's thought, therefore, was hewn in Evangelical rock. He relied on experience rather than on a metaphysical vision of the world. He was not shy of preaching as it was the most natural of all duties. He was certain that he ought to make judgments when he criticised. And he looked to his conscience to guide him when doing all three. So much he had gained; but he also rejected part of the tradition. How did Evangelicalism fail him?

Stephen was fortunate in his Clapham upbringing, for the Claphamites exhibited the best side of Evangelicalism. Its dimmer lights, like Thomas Gisborne, might at their brightest exhibit only 'a grave and cheerful complacency,' but its leaders were men of strength and character, and Stephen would not confuse them with the rank and file of the Evangelical party at the time when he was a young man. To Thackeray the Evangelical party within the Church was a by-word for bigotry and a narrow, sneaking

---

* This was the question which provoked the lines in Johnson's poem on Levett which Stephen declared he could hardly read without tears starting to his eyes:

His virtues walked their narrow round,
Nor made a pause, nor left a void;
And, sure, the Eternal Master found
The single talent well-employed.

ADRIAN AND JULIA STEPHEN
HENRY JAMES (1892)

VIRGINIA AND SIR LESLIE STEPHEN (1903)

HORATIO BROWN, MRS. STEPHEN, GERALD AND GEORGE DUCKWORTH
VANESSA, THOBY, VIRGINIA, AND ADRIAN STEPHEN, 1892

morality. Even their great chief, Shaftesbury, confessed, 'I have received from the hands of the [Evangelical] party treatment I have not received from any other. High Churchmen, Roman Catholics, even infidels, have been friendly to me; my only enemies have been the Evangelicals.' The doctrine of the regenerated will in the mouths of men, less humble and honest than Thornton, encouraged hypocrisy and double-dealing; for it is not every man who can lead a changed life while partaking of the normal pleasures of the world. Pusey noted that belief in the regenerated will lead some Evangelicals to speak of their past sins as if they had been committed by another. 'Every man,' said Keble, 'was his own absolver,' and pharisaically those 'born again' looked down on anyone who did not use Evangelical jargon. The initiate had only to mention 'judgments' on sinners, which he had witnessed, or speak with a rapt look about his 'seals,' or converts, which proved that he was 'owned,' or of a child who had merited a 'gracious' whipping, and he was accepted as saved in low Evangelical circles. The doctrine that good works were *evidential*—or in other words an excellent indication that one was of the Elect enjoying perpetual sanctification through the Holy Spirit—exaggerated the importance of worldly success in the eyes of the petty-minded. The close connection between cash and religion, Pharisaism and cant, was the legacy of an emotional religion when it was professed by the ruck of those classes in society who were learning the value—and it was a real value—of Respectability. Far more serious was the Evangelical distrust of the intellect and the imagination. The Stephen family would have laughed at the popular Protestant writer Charlotte Elizabeth Tonna declaring that when she read the *Merchant of Venice* she 'drank a cup of intoxication under which my brain reeled for many a year'; but Leslie's great-grandfather, Henry Venn, had opposed the study of the Hebrew text of the Old Testament and had said, no doubt with the intention of discouraging degrading religious controversy, 'Never, on any account, dispute. Debate is the work of the flesh.' 'The cultivation of the intellectual powers,' said Dean Close, 'can of itself have no tendency towards moral or spiritual good.' Canon Storr went as far as to say that the Evangelicals

9

cared little for the pursuit of truth for its own sake, and the wisest of all the Victorian Nonconformists, R. W. Dale, the Congregationalist minister in Birmingham, admitted that Evangelicals cared only for those truths directly related to salvation. Truth was an instrument for placing men permanently in the right relation to God.

The faults in the rock ran even deeper. Evangelicalism does not satisfy the intellect that asks for knowledge of God apart from personal experience. Directly the sinner is convinced that he is at one with God, no further intellectual effort is required, which led the Oxford Noetics to condemn it as a belief which fostered spiritual pride, Sir James Stephen to deplore its formalism and Dr. Arnold to declare that Evengelicals were good Christians of low understanding, bad education and ignorance of the world. It did not matter that Evangelicalism gave no metaphysical explanation of the riddle of the universe. But it did matter that the one problem it professed to answer—namely the existence of evil in the world—was so often handled in such a gross manner. The Redemption of Man was treated, Gladstone declared, as a joint stock transaction between God and man with Christ as the broker. One acquired 'a saving interest in the Blood of Jesus.' It was a religion whose phraseology was of this world; this made it easier for the uneducated to understand but more difficult for the cultivated to remain inspired. Evangelicalism appeals to the heart but it makes a *rational* appeal. Once a man has closed the deal with God, he is free to rejoice and does not have to justify his state of mind by searching through dogmas. God is recognised by the depth of an emotional experience rather than through the comprehensiveness of belief. The very clarity of Evangelicalism was its undoing. It rested on two stones, the truth of the Bible and the experience of conversion; the Bible was already under attack; and the social milieu in which the children of Clapham lived differed from that in which their middle-aged fathers had received the miracle of conversion. And, as time went on, the Evangelical party in the Church, lashed into a lather by the excesses of the Ritualists, became more and more bigotted so that Archbishop Magee could refer to one of their societies as 'Persecution Company Ltd.', and no intelligent man could view their activities with equanimity. This was why Evangelicalism failed to make a fresh appeal to the descendants of the Clapham Sect.

In the Clapham Sect we can observe an interesting example of an hereditary intellectual strain. Each generation renounce their father's beliefs, but the spirit of the coterie is so strong that there remains an outlook, an attitude, not unlike that of the Sect itself. The second generation of Claphamites witnesses the first defections. It was the Evangelicals in the Oxford Movement such as Newman and Faber, who went over to Rome; the sons of High Churchmen, Pusey and Keble, remained firm. Among the Claphamites the Wilberforces seceded in droves. Three of the four sons of William Wilberforce and both his sons-in-law became Roman Catholics. Samuel alone remained in the Anglican Communion and lived to see his daughter and her husband go over to Rome; and even he returned to the Evangelical fold, says Tom Mozley, as a brand plucked from the burning, but with the smell of burning strong upon him. Shaftesbury had Zachary's son, Lord Macaulay, publicly chastised for negativism in a lecture delivered on Macaulay's death by the celebrated Methodist preacher, Dr. Punshon; and among Macaulay's papers was found a quotation from Conyers Middleton: 'But if to live strictly and think freely; to practise what is moral and to believe what is rational, be consistent with the sincere profession of Christianity, then I shall acquit myself like one of its truest professors' and Macaulay added '*Haec est absoluta et perfecta philosophi vita.*' Sir James Stephen was a liberal Evangelical, and though he told his children that they should treat atheists as men who had insulted their dearest friend, he himself remained on cordial terms with John Stuart Mill and Austin. This was a falling-off from the days when William Wilberforce prosecuted a wretched printer whose name appeared on a blasphemous publication. 'The freedom with which the vessel swings at anchor, ascertains the soundness of her anchorage,' he proclaimed, but he was careful not to put any undue strain upon the chains. 'I am profoundly convinced of the consistency of all the declarations of

scripture,' he explained to Fitzjames, 'but I am as profoundly
convinced of my own incapacity to perceive that they
are consistent . . . I am not here to speculate but to repent,
to believe and to obey; and I find no difficulty in believing,
each in turn, doctrines which seem to me incompatible with
each other. It is in this sense and to this extent that I adopt
the whole creed called evangelical. I adopt it as a regulator
of the affections, as a rule of life and as a quietus, not as a
stimulant, to inquiry.' Fitzjames commented that this kind
of humility came so close to irony that he found it hard to
separate them. Leslie summed up his father's position by
saying that he wore the uniform of the old army though
he had ceased to bear unquestioning allegiance.

If the second generation of Clapham were laxer, the third
would have shocked their grandparents inexpressibly.
Florence Nightingale, grand-daughter of Sir William Smith,
was bitterly attacked for Puseyism by that odious Scots
bigot, Alexander Haldane, who edited the Evangelical
rag, the *Record*. John Venn, the Cambridge logician, took
Holy Orders but in 1883 renounced them.* A. V. Dicey
remained a Christian but cared less than nothing for
dogma. He even doubted the value of the Broad Church
movement and thought that Dean Stanley had lost much by
remaining a clergyman. Sir G. O. Trevelyan followed his
uncle Macaulay and left Christian theology alone; he
admired Henry Sidgwick's theism but he kept aloof from
the struggle between rationalism and religion because he
feared that much good might perish in it. Fitzjames Stephen
fought in the law-courts the cases of Puseyites and Broad
Churchmen impartially. He ceased to believe in the
historical truth of Christianity and attacked miracles and
the logic of Christian belief; yet in a sense he was nearest
to Dean Stanley in believing that the Church should open
its doors to all and liberalise its doctrines. Though he did
not follow Macaulay in holding that the State has nothing
to do with a man's religious beliefs, he believed that the
laymen serving in Parliament and on the Privy Council

---

* His religious convictions remained, however, fundamentally unshaken
and later in life he said that he realised that he could have stayed in the
Church.

should interpret the Church's dogmas: priests existed to supply the enthusiasm.* With these men as with Leslie Stephen, a militant agnostic, we appear to have travelled far from the beliefs of Clapham. And yet there is still the belief in right conduct, in the same ethical standards, in the supreme importance of the individual's relation to the Good.

The change in the fourth generation is more startling. By the beginning of this century the intellectual revolt against Christianity had been superseded by an ethical revolution far more profound in its consequences. The name of the Bloomsbury circle will always be associated with this revolution, and on the surface there seems to be little to connect Leslie Stephen's daughters, Vanessa Bell and Virginia Woolf, or Henry Thornton's great-grandson, E. M. Forster, with the Clapham Sect. On the surface only. Bloomsbury, like Clapham, was a coterie. It was exclusive and clannish. It regarded outsiders as unconverted and was contemptuous of good form opinions. Remarks which did not show that grace had descended upon their utterer were met with killing silence. Like the Claphamites they criticised each other unsparingly but with affection. Like Clapham, Bloomsbury had discovered a new creed: the same exhilaration filled the air, the same conviction that a new truth had been disclosed, a new Kingdom conquered.†
Bloomsbury assumed that worldly values were grotesquely

* For further discussion of Fitzjames Stephen's beliefs see *infra* Chapter VII and Notes to Chapter III.

† The term Bloomsbury has been used as a term of abuse so long that it must be defined. In a paper, entitled *Old Bloomsbury*, Vanessa Bell pointed out that the original circle, which gathered in Brunswick and Gordon Squares between 1904–15, had ceased to exist many years before the term became fashionable and other people inherited its name and reputation. The original members were Vanessa Bell, Virginia Woolf, Thoby and Adrian Stephen (the four children of Sir Leslie); Clive Bell and Leonard Woolf; J. M. Keynes, Duncan Grant and Roger Fry; Desmond and Molly MacCarthy; Lytton, Oliver, Marjorie and James Strachey; Sydney Saxon Turner, musician and civil servant, H. T. J. Norton, mathematician and don; and on occasions E. M. Forster and Gerald Shove, who was a Fabian and a Cambridge economist, and married F. W. Maitland's daughter, whose great-aunt was Julia Stephen.
Thoby Stephen, Bell, Woolf, Turner and Lytton Strachey had all met at Trinity where in 1899 they founded the Midnight Society which met on Saturdays to read plays and poetry at that hour. Keynes was brought into the circle through Strachey and Woolf, and Grant was cousin to the Stracheys. Lady Strachey knew the Stephens well through her friendship with Annie Ritchie. There were, of course, other visitors to the circle but this was the original nucleus.

stupid and wicked. Its members despised wealth, power, popularity and success and were sharp to notice whether someone was on the make. For this reason both Clapham and Bloomsbury infuriated polite society and drew upon themselves a good deal of envious spite. The two sets, of course, held very different views about laughter. The Claphamites were cheerful but only Wilberforce can be said to have known the meaning of the word humour. Bloomsbury's sense of humour was exceedingly highly developed—it was fantastical, gay, satirical, ironic; they were at one with A. V. Dicey when he said, 'It is better to be flippant than dull.' But they combined extreme frivolity with extreme seriousness. Because they did not fall into the academic error of confusing seriousness with solemnity, it did not follow that they were not in earnest. They took the aesthetic movement out of the hands of Oxford dilettantes and gave it backbone; with the help of G. E. Moore's philosophy they created an ethical justification for art for art's sake. In much the same spirit Clapham organised Evangelicalism and gave it direction after the death of Whitefield and Wesley. Finally, both Clapham and Bloomsbury were circles which influenced the whole outlook of their generation. They were each in their time responsible for spreading the new ideas of 'modern' morality.

Moreover, Bloomsbury had its religion. In his memoir, *My Early Beliefs*, J. M. Keynes—himself of Nonconformist stock—described it. 'Our religion closely followed the English puritan tradition of being chiefly concerned with the salvation of our own souls. . . . We claimed the right to judge every individual case on its merits, and the wisdom, experience and self-control to do so successfully. This was a very important part of our faith . . .' From G. E. Moore's ethics they learnt that nothing mattered but 'states of mind.' A state of mind such as being in love, or apprehending beauty, was to be judged by itself and without regard to its consequences, and salvation was to be obtained by 'communion with objects of love, beauty and truth.' Whether the state of mind created by such communion was good or bad was a subject for long discussion in which Moore's celebrated technique of rational analysis was used to decide whether the disputants were asking the right questions or discussing the same things. Now, whereas it had been customary in utilitarian ethics to assume that goodness could be explained in terms of pleasure, Moore discarded this part of the tradition and denied that the amount of pleasure promoted by a state of mind was any criterion for its goodness. In the early days his disciples went even further and tended to argue that a good state of mind so far from being pleasurable was nearly always painful: intensity, passion, creation, produced pain yet were they not the most admirable of qualities? It was therefore thought to indicate a very low and vulgar state of mind if one argued that the amount of pleasure produced by an action had any connection with its goodness or badness.* Thus far the argument followed orthodox puritan lines, but at this point it took a turn towards heterodoxy, for just as in earlier manifestations of puritanism, the emphasis on personal salvation led them into the heresy of Antinomianism. If you are convinced that it is your duty to follow the inner light and to purify your state of mind without reference to any worldly standard, you begin to despise the world so strongly that you ignore your own relation to it; the world may call your actions sinful, but to you they are not, because they proceed from a mind at one with God. Moreover, if you are of the Elect, the unconverted are hardly in a position to criticise you. And so, Moore's morality was jettisoned from his religion and the undergraduates who were to form the Bloomsbury circle went on to deny that there was any close connection between *being* good and *doing* good, or that there existed any moral obligation to consider the effect of one's actions on other people. Moore's precept that the rightness of actions depended on the eventual good which they produced, seemed to them to be a relic of utilitarian orthodoxy, and they held strongly that every state of mind must be judged on its own merits without regard to past or future events.

The new religion was just as strongly concerned with experience especially, writes Desmond MacCarthy, 'those

---

* This was an intellectual judgment which had little direct effect on their habits. Sir James Stephen's resolve never to smoke another cigar because he found his first so pleasant, would have been frostily received.

parts of experience which could be regarded as ends in themselves.' Morality,' he continues, 'was either a means to attaining those goods of the soul or it was nothing—just as the railway system existed to bring people together and to feed them, or the social order that as many 'ends' as possible should be achieved. These ends naturally tied themselves down to personal relations, aesthetic emotions and the pursuit of truth. We were perpetually in search of distinctions; our most ardent discussions were attempts to fix some sort of a scale of values for experience. The tendency was for the stress to fall on feeling rightly than upon action. . . . Nor were we particularly interested in the instincts or the will compared with the play of the intelligence. What was the will but a means, a servant? Or what were the instincts but the raw stuff out of which the imagination moulded a life worth contemplating?' The fourth generation of the Clapham Sect naturally repudiated the moral code of their forefathers. The doctrine of original sin was replaced by the eighteenth century belief in man's fundamental reasonableness, sanity and decency. They violently rejected Evangelical notions of sex, tossed overboard any form of supernatural belief as so much hocuspocus, and set their sails in the purer breezes of neo-Platonic contemplation. And yet one can still see the old Evangelical ferment at work, a strong suspicion of the worldly-wise, an unalterable emphasis on personal salvation and a penchant for meditation and communion among intimate friends.

3

The Evangelical tradition ran strong in Leslie Stephen's veins. What did he himself think of his heritage? Not much. His heart lay with the eighteenth century clergy who thought that religion was part of reason. How could one compare the teaching of Whitefield or Newton with the civilised discourses of the Deists, when Whitefield's one ambition was to induce an ignorant miner to give up drink by preaching the consoling truth that, if he did not, he would burn everlastingly; or when Newton's way of comforting the agonised poet Cowper was to stop him translating Homer

and set him to compose hymns which stimulated his religious
mania? And yet, here was a fascination, a mystery. How
was it possible for a man of intellect to believe the appalling
doctrines of the Calvinists—that God tossed infants with
glee into the bottomless pit and swept heathens and Christians in their millions to the eternal fires reserving for
Himself only a handful of the Elect? Rummaging in the
curiosity-shop of the past, Stephen paused to examine
Jonathan Edwards, the eighteenth century New England
divine and one of the most powerful of all Calvinist theologians. This curio had described himself as a man who
had 'a constitution in many respects peculiarly unhappy,
attended by flaccid solids; vapid, sizy, and scarce fluids; and
a low tide of spirits. . . .' So remorseless were his edicts
against pleasure, his diatribes against children as 'young
loathesome vipers,' and his descriptions of the 'exquisite,
horrible misery' of the damned among whom most of his
congregation would be numbered, that finally even the
children of the Pilgrim Fathers could bear no more and ran
him out of town. Yet Edwards was gifted with an ex-
ceptionally acute mind and his book on the freedom of the
will argues the case for predestination with almost excessive
ingenuity and faces every major theological problem. How
could the boy who had found so many objections to the
doctrine of God's sovereignty and the Elect have come to
accept this ghastly doctrine as 'infinitely pleasant, bright
and sweet'? The answer is that Edwards was not just a
fanatic. Beneath the crust of his religious belief is hidden a
profound moral sense. Metaphysically Edwards works
towards a distinction between those human affections
which harmonise with the Divine Will and those which are
discordant. Religiously he declares that no outward sign—
no vision, no transport of delight, no miracle, no words—
can prove that a man is virtuous, for the essence of virtue
is the love of God for His own sake. The only way in which
a man can guess that a fellow human being has been born
again is by seeing in him signs of increased humility and a
love of Christ, without reference to heaven and hell. Stephen
calls two aspects of Virtue crucial to a sound morality.
Firstly to judge whether John Jones's actions help other

people to lead good lives and how those actions measure
up to the highest standard of conduct. Secondly to ask
what are Jones's motives for his actions. Only if he can be
judged to act for the love of doing good for its own sake and
not for some favour or reward, can we say that he is virtuous.
Stephen thought that Edwards deserved to be remembered
for this revelation alone.

   Stephen's long analysis of this Calvinist should have led
him to realise that Protestantism no less than Catholicism
can be a highly logical and morally satisfying structure,
provided, of course, that the existence of God and its
major dogmas are not questioned. But this is not the case.
Elsewhere Stephen applauded Protestantism for an entirely
contradictory virtue. By insisting that a man must follow
his own conscience, Protestantism made it possible for a
really intelligent man to be done with the whole business.
'Protestantism in one aspect,' Stephen wrote, 'is simply
rationalism still running about with the shell on its head.'
So far from it being a religion with a logical structure,
Stephen now describes it as common-sense morality with a
carapace of superstition. Protestantism compels a man to
examine first principles, Catholicism demands a blind
acceptance of dogma. Stephen assumed without argument
that Protestantism was a revolt by liberals against the
authoritarianism of the Catholic church. The movement
away from rites to sermons, from sacraments to extempore
prayer, must be a revolt towards reason and away from
incantation. Now, this judgment is crude Macaulay.
The connection between Protestantism and freedom of
thought or the development of science is a highly complicated subject; the kind of generalisation that Stephen is
making produces a grotesque distortion of history. In any
case, whether a Catholic or a Protestant determines like
Francis Newman to 'go further,' depends on his temperament and upbringing, not on the nature of his religious
belief. Every generation is faced with certain questions
which seem to be of paramount importance. Will the
religion in which they are brought up be able to suggest
answers to those questions—having regard to all the other
social changes which are taking place in their lifetime? All

one can say is that one religion will help to answer a particular question better than another, but may give a less satisfactory answer to a different question. The particular form of Evangelicalism, in which Leslie Stephen was raised, had grave weaknesses, but this does not explain why the descendants of the Clapham Sect each in turn abandoned the beliefs of their fathers. To equate Protestantism with mid-Victorian Evangelicalism was rhetoric. Nor can we excuse Stephen by pleading that he was only following the historiography of his age. His fellow rationalist, Thomas Huxley, refused to be taken in by Stephen's thesis. To replace Transubstantiation by Consubstantiation was not, Huxley thought, a sign of liberal thought: 'One does not free a prisoner by merely scraping away the rust from his shackles.'

The apparent contradiction in Stephen's thought can be explained by his view of human nature. The Protestant, whose religion tells him to develop and rely ultimately upon his private judgment, *ought* to become a rationalist. How are we to account for the fact that Jonathan Edwards' acute mind did not lead him to this conclusion? Had those flaccid solids and vapid sizy fluids disturbed his balance of mind? Possibly. But more probably because he had the misfortune to be a backwoodsman living out of the current of European thought: by nature a German professor accidentally dropped into the American forests. An emancipated European would face no such difficulty. Let us, therefore, examine the system of thought which Stephen believed had emancipated mankind. Let us look at the second great influence on his life, the impact of Victorian rationalism on his mind at Cambridge.

CHAPTER IV
CAMBRIDGE RATIONALISM

RATIONALISTS are men of a particular cast of mind and much depends on where the casting was moulded. Leslie Stephen, as we have seen, caught the habit of ratiocination at Cambridge, and he always acknowledged his gratitude for the values and the method of thought which Cambridge imparted to her sons. What values and what method? To describe them Stephen resorted to a simple stratagem. Just as Matthew Arnold described what he meant by the grand style in Homer by quoting Francis Newman's translation to show what it was not, so Stephen placed Oxford by the side of Cambridge to illustrate the Cambridge mind.

Even to-day in our more mobile society where easier social relationships and a less rigid class structure have ironed out so many distinctions, one can still perceive faint signs of those temperamental differences which struck Stephen. No Cambridge man can ever compete at Oxford. Directly he sets foot in that city he is aware that he is wearing hobnail boots. Of a coarser and rougher texture, a country cousin from a tranquil backwater served by infrequent trains, he is whipped on his arrival into a dialectical whirligig. He starts one of those frank, intimate, disinterested Cambridge discussions which are intended to clear the mind—and the words are whisked out of his mouth and tossed in the air by jugglers like so many coloured balls until, bemused by the wit and elegance of the display, he falls into a helpless and unnoticed silence. Oxford is a worldly society where a gate from All Souls' opens straight on to London. He cannot discuss politics because in some strange fashion London politics are discussed in terms of Oxford politics and, indeed, appear in the minds of his hosts to be identical. He is a provincial. The very gossip is more pungent and obscure, the savours more delectable, the quadrangles and gardens more orchidaceously romantic. He finds himself among

High Churchmen, whose piety is spiced with irony, and who do not hesitate to perform the pleasurable duty of biting the benighted, in a manner which makes his Latitudinarian ears tingle. Nor can he well discuss literature since, accustomed as he is to emending classical texts after the fashion of Bentley, he is lost in a maze of metaphysical and literary allusions. Aesthetic theories are spun like webs about him and poets' names whizz through the conversation like shuttlecocks; true, all the poets are Cambridge men but that does not mean that he is any better able to discuss them in the Oxford manner.* He likes to take the text, construe the meaning and analyse the poem itself, but as he listens to the talk he reflects lugubriously that his hosts' theories are not susceptible of analysis. For them the poem is an excuse for propounding a philosophy of life, for explaining the inner meaning of poetry, art and life itself. Spinning in circles of ever widening generalisations, he dimly apprehends that Oxford men are asking him to unify religion, aesthetics and morality into a comprehensive metaphysic—can he not hear the call, asks the most persuasive and cultured of all Oxford voices, 'to the true goal of all of us, to the ideal, to perfection?' Will he not admit that beauty is but truth seen from the other side and that all the science of Tübingen (and of Cambridge), is inferior? Why is he not prepared to swear allegiance in this home of lost causes to at least one—which almost certainly, if supported by worldly-wise Oxonians, is not lost? Is there no teacher or prophet to preach a philosophy of life at Cambridge?

The answer to the last question, said Stephen, is simple. There is none. Cambridge appears to be inhabited by nonentities whereas the history of nineteenth century Oxford is the history of its preachers: Whately, Thomas Arnold, Keble, Newman, Jowett, Ruskin, Pater and T. H. Green.

---

* Witness the lamentable figure which three Apostles, Hallam, Monckton Milnes and Sunderland cut, when they debated in the Oxford Union that Shelley was a better poet than Byron. 'The Oxford young gentlemen,' writes James Pope-Hennessy, 'seemed as elegant and unconcerned as their room, and lounged about the fireplace with provoking sang-froid. Worst of all, they alleged that they had never heard of Shelley, and one of them even pretended to think that the Cambridge contingent had come over to support the claims of Shenstone, and that the only line of that poet he could call to mind was one running: "My banks are well furnished with bees." '

To these names there are no Cambridge analogues. Stephen allowed that against Gladstone 'with his great abilities somewhat marred by over-acuteness and polish,' Cambridge could set the clear and energetic, but limited, intellect of Macaulay. By the mystery, charm and hypnotism of their personalities the Oxford prophets cast a spell over the young, fascinating, enthralling, tearing the heart out of their disciples. Rugbeians venerated Dr. Arnold, Newman inspired passionate party loyalty, Balliol men were devoted to Jowett, because these teachers were regarded as great souls at work in the world. This spectacle, commented Stephen, provokes a faint nausea in Cambridge men. They prefer to keep the soul in its place for fear it may breed fads and enthusiasms. Back again, safe and snug in his provincial den, the Cambridge man consoles himself by saying that prophets are half humbug and produce disciples who will be wholly humbug. Let us stop talking for effect and return to studies which are precise and yield tangible results. Above all, let us not attach ideas to a man. To criticise a man's ideas dispassionately is next to impossible if he inspires a Movement. The Cambridge don who, like Stephen, was prepared to give up his time to young men would be their friend, within certain limits their guide, but never their philosopher. In Cambridge ideas were hammered into principles to be judged empirically. The Oxford craving for prophets in Stephen's view weakened the already tenuous hold which Oxford retained on impartial philosophic enquiry. And the man who weakened it most was Benjamin Jowett.

Benjamin Jowett, elected to a Fellowship at Balliol while still an undergraduate, tutor for twenty-eight years and Master for twenty-three, was the greatest of all nineteenth-century dons. His intellectual achievements were considerable; he introduced Hegel to Oxford and stimulated the study of early Greek philosophy, and by his translations made Plato's spirit walk again in England. In mid-Victorian times he was harried by Tractarian bigots for his Broad Church principles which were, as much as anything, inspired by his hatred of persecution. But Jowett was, beyond all else, an incomparable teacher of young men. Statesmen, diplomats, civil servants, proconsuls, professors, philosophers, historians, men of letters, passed through his hands, and to each Jowett imparted the secret of hard work and determination to succeed. His pupils were sometimes paralysed by his shyness and made aware of the dignity he attached to his position. Every sentence they spoke was expected to carry weight and unmeaning remarks were quenched by a chilling reply. His methods of teaching were Socratic—he would pause, poker in hand, and search his man with a question, and so on round the class to show to what logical absurdities sloppy thinking leads. Despising lectures, he put his pupils through the old catechetical mill and sharpened their wits on the grindstone of construe. Yet, though he deplored young men wallowing in poetry and distrusted the influence of T. H. Green's metaphysics, he widened his pupils' literary horizon. They were left with the impression that Jowett thought both poetry and metaphysics important, though they were never quite sure what he himself believed. 'The charm was enhanced,' wrote Pater, 'by a certain mystery about his own philosophic and other opinions'; and in the introductions to his translations of Plato, Jowett did not do much to unravel the mysteries of Platonic thought. The secret of his power lay rather in a kind of slow magnetism. His cherubic features, his bell-like voice, his power to declaim verse beautifully, drew undergraduates and friends to him in legion. He did not let them slip; they were pursued with sympathetic letters demanding to hear that they were doing themselves justice. He not only wanted his pupils to succeed, he did his best to put their feet on the rung of the ladder to success by filling the Master's Lodge in term time with celebrities who might well help his pupils in later life. As he grew older, he sympathised with undergraduate pleasures. As early as 1879 Balliol held a college ball. ('A ball — attachments — matchmaking — matchmaking in College—most inappropriate' muttered a doddering old Fellow.)* He supported the Oxford University Dramatic Society to the fury of his enemy, Freeman, who spluttered with indignation against this 'portentous rage for play-acting.' Nothing was put before the College.

* Henry Sidgwick opposed a similar proposal at Trinity College, Cambridge.

It was his life, his child; and as the list of first classes grew
longer and longer Balliol was acknowledged beyond dispute
to be academically the most distinguished college in
Oxford. Somewhat naturally this bred envy and malice,
and Jowett was often attacked. He was not above enticing
a clever man from another college or indulging in sharp
practice in university politics. 'Parnell is not in it with
him in obstruction,' commented a member of the Heb-
domadal Council. By the time he became Master of
Balliol in 1870 he was exposed to assaults from both flanks.
The old conservatives still regarded him as the arch-liberal
in theology; and now that academic reform had taken the
place of ecclesiastical questions as the centre of controversy,
Jowett, who opposed professorial lectures and research, was
regarded by the younger Liberals as a man who had had his
day. He was an indifferent scholar and, indeed, despised
the whole business: 'How I hate learning!' he once admitted.
Nor had the young conservatives much use for him. The
youthful historian and Tory, Charles Oman, thought he
was 'a noted and much detested figure,' representing
'modernism, advertisement, an autocratic pose, and a
tendency to push the importance of his College beyond the
limit of its undoubted merit.'

But more searching criticisms were to be made. In 1869
a nephew of Anthony Froude, W. H. Mallock, came up to
Balliol. Mallock was a bright young man, later to become
a Roman Catholic and a high Tory; perhaps rather too
bright for Jowett's liking who set him down as a dilettante
and was vexed when Mallock won the Newdigate prize for
poetry. As might be expected, Mallock was not much
elevated by Jowett's sermons, which were unkindly called
by some, Glimpses into the Obvious, and he reached the
end of his tether when Jowett preached a sermon on the
death of an undergraduate who had committed suicide.
Jowett chose as his text the story of the woman taken in
adultery and the greater part of his discourse consisted of a
dissertation on the authenticity of this passage. After
weighing the evidence Jowett came down ever so demurely
against its authenticity and then proceeded to draw the
astonishing moral that we can know little of God's command-

ments, since so many of Christ's words as reported in the New Testament are doubtful; we should, therefore, not hasten to pass judgments on those who commit suicide. The charitable conclusion—typical of Jowett's gentleness—was lost on Mallock. Outraged by the logic of the argument, he published *The New Republic* soon after leaving Oxford which contained a caricature of Jowett.

The New Republic is a country house symposium in which Mallock sets off the leaders of Victorian opinion against each other. Matthew Arnold, Ruskin and Pater; the rationalists Huxley, Tyndall and Clifford; Violet Fane and Jowett, are made to show their paces. In this highly entertaining and malicious satire the deplorable inconsistencies of Dr. Jenkinson's (Jowett's) teaching are mercilessly exposed. Dr. Jenkinson prides himself on winnowing the chaff of superstition from the grain of Christian ethics and he winces when someone has the bad taste to address him as a 'consecrated priest of the mystical Church of Christ.' Yet he starts with surprise when Mr. Luke (Arnold) expects him to agree that personal immortality forms no part of 'the sweet secret of authentic Christianity.' 'You forget,' says one of the house-party in explanation, 'that Dr. Jenkinson's Christianity is really a new firm trading under an old name, and trying to purchase the good will of the former establishment.' Now he is posing as a Christian, now as an ethical positivist abounding in enthusiasm for humanity, and now as an affronted Hellenist when Mrs. Sinclair (Violet Fane) ingenuously suggests that Greek love poems may be hard to construe because they are corrupt. The climax comes on the Sunday when Dr. Jenkinson decides to conduct a service which will be acceptable to everyone present including the atheists. There is, alas, no private chapel, but Dr. Jenkinson is quite ready to pursue his devotions in a small theatre built for amateur productions. The service turns out to be much like the theatricals. In the front row of the stalls, silhouetted against a gay drop-curtain of Faust on the Brocken dancing with a young and naked witch, Dr. Jenkinson offers up prayers, taken impartially from the Koran and the English liturgy, though omitting the Creed. He is about to deliver his sermon when his host

whispers that he has been for the most part inaudible and
suggests that he should preach from the stage. Courteously
thanking him and intimating that it was fortunate that only
the prayers had been missed, Dr. Jenkinson glides behind
the footlights; the curtain is raised and he is discovered
standing in the middle of a gorge in the Indian Caucasus—
the relics of a production of Prometheus Bound—where,
unabashed, he begins to preach taking his text from the
Psalms. 'The fear of the Lord is the beginning of wisdom'
—but only, Dr. Jenkinson goes on to argue, the beginning.
He then proceeds . . . but this profane description must
come to an end. The sermon is a ruthless burlesque of
Jowett's moralised Christianity such as would delight High
Churchmen and amuse agnostics. He was too great a
character to be demolished by Mallock's malice, but the
frontal assault had begun.

Perhaps it is now becoming clearer why Stephen chose
Jowett as the antithesis of the Cambridge mind. He
acknowledged that Jowett did far more for his men than all
the Heads of Houses in Cambridge put together, nor did he
minimise the affection in which Jowett was held and he
added—from Stephen high praise—'The core of the man's
nature was sweet, sound, and masculine.' Moreover, Jowett
avoided the intellectual tyranny which Newman exercised
over his pupils and he encouraged his undergraduates to
grout among the pearls that he cast before them and select
whichever they regarded valuable. 'You might not learn
anything very definite, but you were subject to a vigorous
course of prodding and rousing, which is perhaps the best of
training for early years.' But when Stephen considered his
man seriously, he passed a measured but hostile judgment.
The agnostic first laid his finger on the Broad Churchman's
equivocations. In Jowett's hands Christianity appeared to
demand no more than a recognition of the moral beauty of
Christ's life and a murmured hope that He was divine.
How could a man transform dogmas, which he admitted
were repulsive, into metaphors, allegories, analogies and
rhetoric, when theologians had interpreted them as literal
truths for eighteen hundred years? Aged forty when the
Origin of Species and *Essays and Reviews* were published,

Jowett, so Stephen held, was not too old to change his views. On these grounds Stephen's attack might appear partisan; Broad Churchmen could claim that John Stuart Mill had urged them to continue to sign the Thirty-Nine Articles, even though they did not believe in them, in order to prevent the Church falling into the hands of fanatics; and Arnold's revision of Christianity appeared to Stephen feeble but sincere. Why did Stephen decline to accept Jowett's plea of sincerity?

Stephen thought Jowett an intellectual coward. Jowett used history to escape from his duty to decide how far any philosophy was true.* Had Jowett been a thoroughgoing relativist, had he had the courage to say that Christianity, Hegel, and ethics, were all to be judged *sui temporis* and that no absolute truth existed, Stephen to some extent would have agreed. But Jowett was a Judas to his profession. He opposed Mark Pattison's scheme for endowing research, not so much because Oxford education would suffer, but because he condemned scholarship and learning. He genuflected before the altar of philosophy in the sight of the world but in private he sneered at it. 'Logic,' his pupils quoted, 'is neither a science nor an art, but a dodge'—small wonder that there was so little logical connection between his own thoughts. He was an intellectual harlot masquerading beneath the bombazine of a high-minded ethic. True, he had dabbled in Hegel, who led to 'some interesting points of view not really so much better than others,' and Stephen despised him precisely because he was a dabbler. He never made it clear whether he thought Hegel was true or false;

---

* At the time of Jowett's maturity the game of using history as a stick of dynamite to blow up a system of thought was in full swing. German theologians employed history in one way to demolish orthodox Christianity by the Higher Criticism of the Bible. In another way conservative theorists employed history to oppose liberalism. Savigny and Maine in jurisprudence, and the Austrian school in economics, were attempting to destroy the deductive theories of Bentham and Adam Smith by appealing to tradition and showing that deductive systems have no objective validity and are merely the product of their age. Games, however, can be played only if one never questions the rules, and this particular pastime is endurable so long as one does not ask what *kind* of history is being used. Directly that the selection of historical facts and hypotheses is seen to be arbitrary, and 'tradition' thus becomes what the author wants it to mean, one loses interest. Jowett was playing the game of darkening wisdom with history by declaring that, since most philosophies had some good in them, there was nothing to choose between the lot of them.

he did not care for truth at all. Stephen paused to make a point. ' "He stood" said one of his pupils . . . , "at the parting of the ways," and he wrote, one must add, "No thoroughfare" upon them all.'

Had Jowett not deliberately stopped thinking from fear, he must have left the Church and taken the hard decision to leave his college as J. R. Green at Oxford and Henry Sidgwick and Stephen himself had done at Cambridge. But Stephen suspected that there were other than purely spiritual reasons which kept Jowett in the Church. In a moment of worldly ingenuousness Augustine Birrell criticised Stephen's judgment on Jowett and asked 'Why should [men] sell out of a still going and dividend-paying concern when they have not the faintest idea where to look for another investment for their money? Where was Jowett to go if he gave up Balliol? . . . So he stayed where he was and Balliol got new buildings and a new cricket ground, and turned out a number of excellent young fellows warranted to come and go anywhere except to the gallows and the stake.' Stephen, however, admired men who would go to the stake for their beliefs, with the hoots of society ringing in their ears. He had once met in America the abolitionist, Garrison, 'who was dragged through the streets of Boston for preaching abolition [of slavery] and was only saved by the police with great difficulty.' Stephen thought Garrison a muddle-headed pacifist, but, 'it is impossible not to feel some respect for a man who has been dragged through the streets by a rope.' Jowett was not of such mettle, nor were his pupils. Stephen should have read his Stendhal: 'Good birth . . . destroys those qualities of the spirit which make people be sentenced to death'; and the importance which Jowett attached to good birth explains his conduct. What was it, asked Stephen, that induced him to remain a clergyman and become Master of Balliol? Snobbery. Stephen's irony was not aroused by Jowett's preference for well-bred and titled young men; nor even for Jowett's pleasure at hearing that Tennyson had mentioned his name to the Queen or for thinking the Crown Princess of Prussia 'quite a genius' when she visited him *incognita* to talk philosophy. It was Jowett's calm assumption that the criterion of merit was worldly success. It was his attitude that anyone who had been at Balliol but had failed to make a mark in the world had somehow insulted him and was worthless. Stephen despised Jowett for being all things to all men and for commending 'a good sort of roguery' which consists in never saying a word against anybody however much they may deserve it. Was not his friendship slightly tarnished? Did he not really care less for the man than for his achievements?

Such was Stephen's indictment; but though scrupulously presented, it is the case for the prosecution. For instance, though Jowett's biographer admitted that Jowett placed an excessive value on success, he showed how this obsession sprang from the dread of wasted lives; and the counsel for defence, Geoffrey Faber, pointed out in a recent essay that Jowett's religion was an attempt to find a way between extremes, and was inspired by belief in a personal God and in the validity of Christ's teaching about that God. Moreover, it was cheap of Stephen to sneer at dons like Jowett or W. G. Clark at Cambridge for cultivating poets and novelists and to insinuate that they lionised the literary world in order to show that a don was not by nature incapable of acquiring a pretty taste in verse and fiction. Stephen seemed unable to resist an opportunity to declare that only a healthy hard-headed Philistine could claim immunity from cant and sentimentalism. In Stephen's essay, however, can be seen his own conception of a teacher's duty, which is not only to stimulate his pupils but to inspire them with a passion for enquiry and a determination to discern the true from the false, the profound from the shallow, and to love friends for their own sake and for no other reason. The essay on Jowett is an epitaph, if not on Jowett, then on Stephen's own career at Cambridge in which he implicitly says that it is the duty of a tutor not to batten on his pupils, or court their praise, or pose as a wise adviser and then reject them when they will not follow that advice, or to live his life through them; but to help them when they are in need, to show clearly what he believes and values himself; and then to leave them to judge for themselves. It is a fine creed and worthy of praise.

Stephen's impeachment of Jowett also shows his own method of criticism. Dispassionate enquiry is our only safe guide in this imperfect life. 'The intellect is very well in its way, but the heart is God's especial province,' said Lord Shaftesbury, and Stephen reacting against Evangelicalism at Cambridge was to reply, 'The "heart" is not another kind of reason . . . but a name for emotions which are not reason at all.' Cambridge does not despise generous feelings; as Alfred Marshall declared (in a phrase to which Jowett took strong exception), her dons tried 'to increase the number of those whom Cambridge, the great mother of strong men, sends out into the world with cool heads but warm hearts'; warm hearts by themselves are not enough, and Stephen thought that 'one's conscience may be a dangerous guide unless it condescends to be enlightened by patient and impartial enquiry.'* Cambridge instilled this quality by its emphasis on mathematics. 'As a mere intellectual toy mathematics is far ahead of any known invention,' said Stephen. 'To have been in love with some women is, we are told, to have received a liberal education . . . ; a three years' flirtation with mathematics is supposed to produce the same effect. . . . Our minds have been strengthened and prepared for dealing with other subjects.' The queen of the sciences, the paragon of reason fired by the imagination, mathematics trains the mind to argue with rigour and economy. Mathematics always gives an answer; even though it satisfies a limited enquiry to a previously hypothesised question, still it is an answer. Stephen, Sidgwick,† Clifford, Marshall and Venn all came to philosophy through mathematics and gravitated to empiricism away from metaphysics which flourished in Oxford, the home of Aristotle. It is no accident that whereas Oxford welcomed

---

* It was all very well, wrote Stephen, for Ruskin to thunder away against classical economics but where was the lightning? Nassau Senior and Fawcett believed that scientific enquiry had established certain laws: laws cannot be charmed away by rhodomontade. Stephen claimed (though he can hardly have believed such a naïve excuse) that Thackeray stopped publication in the *Cornhill* of *Unto This Last* simply because Ruskin scouted that spirit of scientific enquiry which alone convinces experts that the purpose is serious.

† Sidgwick was, of course, primarily a classic, but he had been indoctrinated with mathematics for in the year that he was placed top of the Classical Tripos, he was also thirty-third wrangler.

Hegel, Cambridge nurtured Bertrand Russell's new logical method which entailed employing Boolean algebra. Stephen himself swam with the Cambridge tide. His Bible was John Stuart Mill's *System of Logic*.

2

'The young men who graduated in 1850 and the following ten years,' said Stephen, 'found their philosophical teaching in Mill's *Logic*, and only a few daring heretics were beginning to pick holes in his system.' The same was even true of Oxford at that date exhausted by theological controversy. 'It is Mill,' wrote a contemporary historian of philosophy, 'that our young thinkers at the Universities, our young shepherds on the mountains consult, and quote and swear by.' The *Logic* was one of those books which capture the mind of a whole generation. By explaining the relation between the logic of the natural and of social sciences it gave young liberals the same kind of assurance that Marxist dialectic has given in recent years to young socialists. The holes picked in such books by experts are unimportant: the readers have already departed with an armful of arguments as missiles. Stephen in *English Utilitarians* pointed out flaw after flaw in Mill's reasoning but the *Logic* remained the framework for his own opinions.

The important point to note about the *System of Logic* is the title. Before Newton and Locke great emphasis had been laid on formal logic as a means of showing whether propositions were true or false, and philosophers were partly concerned to construct absolutely true statements and then to demonstrate that their own arguments were couched in similar terms. After Locke formal logic all but disappeared. In Scotland it ceased to be taught in the universities except as an appendage to the 'mental science' which Locke had invented, or as the 'natural logic' of common sense which demonstrated how reasoning actually takes place without examining the internal relationships between the sentences which are the product of this reasoning. In Cambridge logic was replaced by Newtonian mathematics and it survived only at Oxford as a despised part of Aristotelian study.* Philosophy for Locke was a *scientia scientiarum*, synthesising all knowledge and eliminating human vagary and prejudice because it was based on hard facts. Mill in his wisdom saw that this contempt for logic had led to much of the confusion in the rationalism of his father's generation. He had already in 1828 replied to an article extolling the lost art by Whately, the most vigorous mind of the Oriel Common Room in its great days, but Mill was uninterested in the old Aristotelian logic which Whately was revising. His own plan was far-reaching. It was nothing less than a scheme to establish the logic of the natural and the social sciences together.

Mill had no use for the syllogism. Reasoning of the kind: All men are mortal, Socrates is a man, therefore Socrates is mortal, did not increase knowledge, because if you accepted the premise, *ipso facto* you accepted the conclusion. Knowledge could be increased only by reasoning inductively from particular instances to a generalisation. Generalisations of this kind could be called true because they were shorthand descriptions of perceived facts. Mill frankly admitted the difficulty raised by Hume that we could never be certain that an induction was true in that one vital fact, which was an exception to the rule, might have been overlooked; but he replied that if the whole method of induction was invalid, then all science would be false: which was absurd. The uniformity of Nature ensured that scientific laws were true; and the uniformity of Nature was not an *a priori* axiom but an empirical generalisation proved by scientific laws.†

* The universities could quote Locke in their support. In 1637 Descartes had written disparagingly of the syllogism, and following him Locke said: 'This way of reasoning discovers no new proofs, but is the art of marshalling and ranging the old ones we have already. The forty-seventh proposition of Euclid is very true; but the discovery of it, I think, not owing to any rules of common logic. A man knows first, and then he is able to prove syllogistically. So that syllogism comes after knowledge, and then a man has little or no need of it. . . . And if a man should employ his reason all this way, he will not do much otherwise than he, who having got some iron out of the bowels of the earth, should have it beaten up all into swords, and put it into his servants' hands to fence with, and bang one another.'

† The agnostics used Hume to defend themselves against the charge of materialism. They did not declare, like the German materialists, that the universe could be explained solely in terms of force and matter, because the only impression we gain of the outside world is through our senses: space and time are merely mental forms imposed upon chaotic sense impressions. Therefore, God *may* exist and miracles *may* occur. But the agnostics then turned to Mill's argument from the uniformity of Nature and declared that both these contingencies are so unlikely, that we are justified in rejecting them.

The circularity of this argument did not disturb Mill. He proceeded again to by-pass Hume and discover a law of causality: such a law must exist, he argued, because large numbers of events could be shown to have causes.*

But induction is inapplicable to the social sciences: the sands of society are too vast and shifting to admit experiment followed by inference and generalisation. Mill was dissatisfied both with his father's simple interpretation of society as a collection of individuals each bent on their own happiness and with Macaulay's pseudo-empirical criticism of his father's methods. Here, Mill was influenced by the first avowed sociologist, Auguste Comte, whose ponderous Positive Philosophy argued that since every science from mathematics to biology had emerged from the darkness of theological interpretation through the dusk of metaphysics into the pure light of positive or scientific enquiry, so likewise the science of society must emerge. The laws of society, said Mill, can be found by the historical or 'inverse deductive' method. They will not be 'true' in the sense that inductive scientific laws are true. But they can be checked against the other laws, found by the 'direct deductive' method, in such social sciences as Political Economy and what Mill called Ethology or the science of national character. Yet the point to note is that with all this lip-service to sociology, Mill and Comte both agreed that the dynamic which *changed* society was not economic or other kinds of impersonal law, but man's *mind*. Every change in society is preceded by a change in men's beliefs or store of knowledge. This is why *On Liberty* pleads for tolerance lest bigotry suppress a fruitful idea which might be the decisive factor in pushing society forward. This thesis encouraged Stephen and his fellow rationalists to treat falsehood as the enemy of human progress.

Put in popular terms, what were the arguments that Stephen had at his disposal after reading Mill? Firstly,

---

* To put Mill's thesis another way: the only method of enquiry which will yield truth is the scientific method, for it alone is capable of showing that certain conclusions and no others can be drawn from a particular series of experiments unless one assumes that Nature is not uniform; and though Hume is right in denying that we can discover the *necessary* relation between cause and effect, we are nevertheless justified in talking of those causes and effects which we can perceive.

that there are not different modes of thinking but different premises from which you can argue; that the dichotomy between heart and head, faith and reason, is inadmissible. Mill has re-emphasised the unity of truth. Secondly, that this unity is not to be found in some metaphysical reconciliation of empirically deduced fact with theology: Science alone can give us true propositions. A generation brought up on the *System of Logic* was likely to respect Huxley. Indeed, this conception of science as a system of absolute and inflexible rules which scientists discover, is the basis of the nineteenth century rationalist metaphysic. And thirdly, that beyond scientific truth, illuminated brightly, there lies a prairie of knowledge over which the shadows lengthen and merge into perpetual night on the horizon. In the foreground the shadows are receding as social scientists till the soil and gather in their first crops. But on the horizon lies barren soil useless to cultivate. There one may discern the corpses of many thousands of books on ontology and the nature of God. Why should we further waste our energy on such vain tasks of speculation? Let us rather work on land which will provide us with knowledge and in due time harvest the fruits of a complete science of society. 'When this time shall come, no important branch of human affairs will be any longer abandoned to empiricism and unscientific surmise: the circle of human knowledge will be complete, and it can only thereafter receive further enlargement by perpetual expansion from within.'

Mill's message is full of hope and aspiration. Add to this elixir the Evangelical insistence on sincerity and plain-speaking, and there is a potion to startle the senses. Truth exists in a palpable form for Victorian rationalists. In the best of all the agnostic novels, Olive Schreiner's *The Story of an African Farm*, a stranger who is passing across the veldt tells the German farm boy, Waldo, the parable of a hunter who spent his life stalking a beautiful white bird, the white bird of Truth, whose reflection he had seen in the lake when shooting wild-fowl soaring above him. He sets snares for the bird, the snares of credulity and a cage of a new creed, until he learns that nothing but Truth can hold Truth. And so he leaves the valleys of superstition and sets out to climb the mountains of Reality. On he climbs till he reaches a vast precipice of stone towering above him. Year after year he cuts steps up the precipice until, old and wizened, he reaches the summit—and sees rising above him a yet higher range. But as he lies dying he consoles himself:

'Where I lie down worn out other men will stand, young and fresh. By the steps that I have cut they will climb. . . . They will never know the name of the man who made them. At the clumsy work they will laugh; when the stones roll they will curse me. But they will mount and on *my* work; they will climb and by *my* stair! They will find her, and through me! And no man liveth to himself and no man dieth to himself. . . .'

Then slowly from the white sky above, through the still air, there came something falling, falling, falling. Softly it fluttered down, and dropped onto the breast of the dying man. He felt it with his hands. It was a feather. He died holding it.

We can never catch the bird of Truth itself, but we can discover particles of truth so long as we are not decoyed by superstition or sensuality, so long as we are never deterred by the fear that a new truth can endanger society. 'The question must always be, not whether [the disputant's] argument be positive or negative, but whether it is *true*,' pontificated the lapsed Evangelical Francis Newman. 'The longer I live,' wrote Huxley, 'the more obvious it is to me that the most sacred act of a man's life is to say and to feel, "I believe such and such to be true." ' The hunter was rewarded by the sight of the steps he had cut and the feather that fell into his hands; the hunt itself was unimportant. Lessing had declared that it was the search for Truth that gave life meaning and the hunter happiness, rather than the attainment of truth; but Huxley contradicted him. 'I protest that if some great Power would agree to make me always think what is true and do what is right, on condition of being turned into a sort of clock and wound up every morning before I got out of bed, I should instantly close with the offer. The only freedom I care about is the freedom to do right; the freedom to do wrong I am ready to part

with on the cheapest terms to anyone who will take it of
me.' The passage gains from the Evangelical phrases.
'My only desire,' George Eliot wrote as a young girl, 'is to
know the truth, my only fear to cling to error. . . .'

How can one discern true from false? The answer is
given in that revealing document by W. K. Clifford, *The
Ethics of Belief*. Examine the state of your mind strictly, says
Clifford, and renounce the sin of believing what is pleasant.
Belief is not a matter of taste. Suppose you accuse a man
wrongly you cannot excuse your statement by protesting
that it was made in good faith when in fact you could have
easily obtained evidence of his innocence merely by a little
hard work. You have behaved dishonourably however
sincere your accusation. To plead to a charge of sending
an unseaworthy vessel on a voyage that you thought that
she was well rigged and found is no defence. Why did you
not find out the facts first? Belief is not a private possession,
a 'self-regarding' property, which affects no one else in the
community. Our beliefs influence our fellow men and
create the world in which posterity will live, and false
beliefs poison the air as surely as noxious factory chimneys.
We must not accept the traditional answers blindly. Life
lays on us a duty to ask questions. Clifford may have
recalled the maxim of Jacobi: 'A question rightly asked is
a question half answered,' and he stresses that it is by
asking questions that knowledge has progressed. To stifle
questions because they conflict with an accepted code of
belief is morally wrong and fatal to the development of the
human race. This echoes Mill on *Liberty*. 'No one can be
a great thinker who does not recognise that as a thinker it
is his first duty to follow his intellect to whatever conclusions
it may lead.' But the note has changed by the 'seventies.
Mill argued that truth emerged from the dog-fight in the
market-place of ideas; therefore, since the truest opinion
would win in a fair fight, we must not muzzle opinions, not
even error itself, or we retard human progress. His plea
for tolerance was more sharply defined by his disciples.
True, says Clifford, let us be tolerant, but do not let us forget
our duty to expose error. Whereas Mill seems almost to
forget that belief is related to action, the connection between

the two is uppermost in Clifford's mind.* Leslie Stephen
himself in an essay on *Poisonous Opinions* distinguishes
between toleration and nescience or the sceptical shrug of
the shoulders. John Morley's *On Compromise* is a long
gloss on Mill's defence of dissent—but with a difference.
It is not appealing for toleration of unpopular opinions but
attacking everyone who does not hold them! Open contempt has replaced Mill's fear of the tyranny of majority
opinion. Those who sneer at Roman Catholics for taking
their beliefs on trust, says Morley, are usually the very men
who would never dare dissent from the majority. Huxley
went even further and denounced the tenet that 'toleration
of error is a good thing in itself, and to be reckoned among
the cardinal virtues.' No political, aesthetic or sentimental
defence for sham beliefs could be accepted and Huxley was
proud to reject the consolation of immortality on the death
of his small son when he declared that: 'Had I lived a
couple of centuries earlier I could have fancied a devil
scoffing at me . . .—and asking me what profit it was to
have stripped myself of the hopes and consolations of the
mass of mankind. To which my only reply was and is—
Oh, devil! Truth is better than much profit!'

Hence every event in history, every miracle in Scripture
came to be judged by this hard-headed critical movement.
It emphasised, above all things, the *unity of truth*. As Dean
Buckland, first professor of geology at Oxford, said: 'Truth
can never be opposed to truth.' The strength of the Newtonian tradition, to which Mill belonged, lay precisely in its
explanation that society was governed by the same laws as
obtained in the physical world.† Thus Christian dogma

* The agnostics could find support for their belief in the mid-Victorian
revision of associationist psychology by Alexander Bain. *The Senses and the
Intellect* (1855) introduced the new conception that thinking is silent speech or
motionless action in that all human activity, including thought, is transmitted
by nerve-currents which are related in turn to the nerve system of our five
senses: i.e. man is a mechanism, and thought is just one of the mechanical
processes that connect our actions to our sensations. To feel is to think is to
act. His definition of belief was 'that upon which a man is prepared to act.'

† Locke suggested that ideas in the mental universe corresponded to Newton's particles in the physical universe; and ideas, like planets, are attracted to
each other by a law of gravitation or the principle of association of ideas.
Experience was the basis of all knowledge; the two springs of action (or
Newtonian forces) were observation of the outside world and 'the internal
operations of our minds, perceived and reflected on by ourselves.' On this
basis Locke constructed his mental science.

could not be true and at the same time defy the laws of
geology or common morality; if it could no longer receive
the flood of new ideas pouring down the streams of science
and philosophy, then it must be false. Because the rationalists had found a method to discover truth, the word was often
on their lips. The question they ask is: what is the *evidence*
for believing this to be true? and evidence is defined as
empirical examination of facts. G. M. Young cites Newman's fifth proposition of liberalism as the crux of mid-
Victorian thought: that it is immoral for a man to believe
more than he can spontaneously receive as being congenial
to his mental and moral nature. 'I being what I am, and
the evidence being what it is, am disposed more or less
strongly to think so-and-so.' This is Mill's legacy.

Finally, the discovery of truth alone can ensure moral and
material progress. The dying hunter in Olive Schreiner's
novel consoles himself with the thought that truth is mount-
ing at compound interest and that he himself has added a
digit. George Eliot after a scene with her father on refusing
to attend church had experienced the sensation that she
had joined 'the ranks of that glorious crusade that is seeking
to set Truth's Holy Sepulchre free from a usurped domination.' Throughout her life, the dogmatic Comtist, Richard
Congreve,* remained her friend, and she admired the
intention of Comte's papery Religion of Humanity. The
panoply of the glorious crusade was evoked in the Comtist
calendar by naming each week and every month after a
past benefactor of the human race whose researches had
helped to guide mankind on the journey out of the dark
halls of theology and metaphysics. Humanity was marching
on the road to Truth and one must join the vanguard who

---

* Congreve was the founder of Positivism in England. Brought up an
Evangelical, he became Fellow and Tutor of Wadham College and later leader
of a set of Wadham men who were undergraduates in the later 'forties:
Frederic Harrison; Edward Beesly afterwards Professor of History at University
College, London, chairman of the First International and editor of the Trade
Union newspaper, the *Beehive*; and J. H. Bridges, editor of Roger Bacon's
Opus Majus. George Eliot and Meredith were active sympathisers, Morley
admitted that at one time he was not far off a formal union with the Positivist
Church and Leslie Stephen declared, in a moment of aberration, that had he
been at Oxford he might have been a Positivist. But sympathisers were more
numerous than adherents and it is unlikely that the subscribers to the central
funds ever numbered more than three hundred.

hurled the boulders of doubt and delusion aside. We are all going to Heaven and Van Dyck is of the company. Nor was this progress merely material. The rationalists claimed that they, not the speculative theologians, did most to improve human behaviour. 'Our business here,' Locke had said, 'is not to know all things, but those which concern our conduct. If we can find out those measures whereby a rational creature put in that state, which man is in in this world, may, and ought to govern his opinions depending thereon, we need not be troubled that some other things escape our knowledge.' From associationist psychology arose the notion that human nature could be changed for the better. Since every human thought springs from individual experience, education alone is needed to make him good and sensible. Reward and praise a child when he does good; punish and blame him when he is naughty; and by the association of ideas he will grow up instinctively to realise that his own happiness depends on the degree to which he promotes the happiness of others. As human nature changes society's evils will be remedied; and each generation will inherit a less corrupting environment. By playing a double ruff through dummy and his own hand, man will eventually win game and rubber.

Such, briefly, was the rationalist tradition to which Leslie Stephen adhered. Carlyle, the declared destroyer of shams, taught him in addition, to work not to whine, to accept not to reject life.* He did not accept the tradition uncritically: his nature impelled him to distrust all simplifications. 'A love of truth,' he wrote of Huxley, 'must be considered, if I may say so, as rather a regulative than a substantive virtue. Abstract truth is a rather shadowy divinity, though a most essential guide in pursuing any great enquiry.' Truth for Stephen, especially in later years, was a protean creature changing its shape in each age. The value of his contribution to rationalism lies precisely in these nuances.

---

* Stephen, of course, gravely misunderstood Carlyle. He thought him manly and simple—not perhaps the happiest choice of epithets. Though he deplored his illiberalism and the 'rather pestilent nonsense' which he talked, he admired him enormously and wrote to Oliver Wendell Holmes that he was 'a really noble old cove and by far the best specimen of the literary gent we can at present produce.'

3

So far from being an intellectual match for the rationalists, Stephen's opponents were ill-equipped to meet the challenge. The feebleness of their reply can be explained by the fact that they spoke the same philosophic language as the rationalists: this enabled the opposing forces to make overtures to each other and parley at any time, and, so far from being opposed in dialectic, both the rationalists and the metaphysicians claimed descent from the tradition of Newton and Locke.*

Locke had given birth to two schools of psychology; the associationist school to which the rationalists belonged and the intuitionist school. The intuitionists asserted that judgments and perceptions, not ideas, are primarily important and that certain principles of necessary truth exist if we are to think at all. These were metaphysical axioms such as, 'Whatever begins to exist, must have a cause which produced it'; or logical axioms, or grammatical axioms or even axioms of taste. There were also principles of contingent truth such as, 'Everything of which I am conscious exists' or 'Those things which I distinctly remember really did happen.' From these principles were deduced the 'fundamental laws of human belief.' Man is endowed with special faculties that distinguish him from the beasts of the field by enabling him intuitively to perceive the difference between right and wrong and the truth of these principles. The 'rational' system of metaphysics or 'common-sense' philosophy, which was constructed on these principles, stood almost in the relation of first cousin to rationalism and therefore was susceptible of destruction by Mill. The intuitionists were divided from the rationalists on only one fundamental piece of analysis, namely psychology.

The presence of this common-sense or intuitionist school hindered the propagation of the one philosophical system which could have armed Protestants against the rationalists.

* The two centuries' long hatred of Roman Catholicism had impaired the intellectual armament of the Church. Newman was accused of not putting the truth first because he employed (paraded, indeed, with delight), a different kind of logic which was incomprehensible and repulsive to Englishmen of his time. Kingsley was a muddle-head, but his attack on Newman was justifiable provided that his own philosophical assumptions were accepted.

Kant purported to have destroyed rationalism; but in the process he had also exploded the 'rational' metaphysics of the orthodox defenders of English Christianity. The intuitionists pretended to find something useful in Kant, but Henry Crabb Robinson was right when he predicted in 1803 that the alliance of these philosophers with the Kantians 'will be more out of love to the result than out of a genuine and adequate perception of the abstract truth of the system, and it is possible that this school will be among the last to accede to the new doctrines.' In fact the intuitionists, whose philosophy was a canonization of the moral platitudes of the club and coffee-house, soon realised that Kant undermined them. It was not until 1829 that Sir William Hamilton welcomed Kant's destruction of 'rational' metaphysics and even he tried to reconcile certain of Kant's conceptions with the common-sense philosophy. Coleridge similarly never properly understood Kant. 'Coleridge is still on the side of the systems of ontology' writes Wellek, the historian of Kant's influence in England. 'His spirit has outgrown [ontology] . . . but he could not succeed; he simply did not seem to have the ability to conceive in thinking what he felt he should confess and preach as a person. He made a philosophy out of this incapacity, a philosophy of the dualism of the head and the heart. With a serene indifference to the inconsistency involved, he kept much of the architectonic of the mind as it was laid out by Kant, preserving only the negative part of Kant. . . . Like Hamilton he preaches "learned ignorance." Like Carlyle he preaches divine faith . . .'

This absence of a comprehensive philosophical alternative hamstrung the defenders of the Church. Tied to the same tradition as the rationalists, they were without an adequate reply when Mill carried the development of this tradition a stage further. No doubt Coleridge had a seminal mind; no doubt he influenced many poets and reasoners, F. D. Maurice among them;* but he transmitted a poetic vision rather than a philosophic doctrine in that he translated Kant's Practical Reason as Imagination. His influence, which

* Mill admitted that it was Coleridge's writings which persuaded him in 1840 that the Lockian theory of mental science must be overhauled.

appears so great in literary history, is far less important when
the foundations of Victorian thought are analysed. It may
appear pedantic to suggest that English thought was vitally
affected by ignorance of a single philosopher, and to interpret
the climate of opinion through the morphology of philosophies is gravely misleading. Yet it must be emphasised that
the rationalist attack was all the more convincing because it
appealed to a common standard of reference. Until F. H.
Bradley elaborated his Idealist ethics, until Oxford expounded Hegelianism in the 'eighties and Anglo-Catholics
drew on the armoury of Rome, the rationalists held the
philosophic initiative; their opponents produced no work
which could give as satisfying an answer as the *Logic* to the
relations of scientific truth, economic laws and moral
obligations.*

How near to the rationalists the philosophic defenders of
Christianity could come can be seen by studying H. L.
Mansel's Bampton Lectures; *The Limits of Religious Thought*
published in 1858. Mansel, an Oxford don and later Dean
of St. Paul's, seems to have been born an Idealist; as a child
he used to say, '*My* foot, *my* hand, but what is *me*?' He
became a disciple of Hamilton and brought to the defence
of Christianity the negative side of Kant's criticism of
reason. Mansel argued that every object is known only as
it relates to other objects: thus there can be no knowledge
of the Infinite because the Infinite has no limits, whereas
every finite object is limited by its relation to other objects.
God is the Infinite, therefore we cannot know God. What
can we know of God by the use of our ordinary reason?
Nothing. Accordingly we should not be surprised if some
Christian dogmas appear to us unreasonable or even
immoral. How, then, do we know that God exists? Here
Mansel fell back on the Hamiltonian mixture of Kant and

* How dependent the defenders of religion were on this common tradition
can be seen in the Bampton Lectures of that orthodox theologian J. B. Mozley.
On the question of miracles he follows Hume like a dog snapping at his heels
and at the end biting the hand that feeds him, but intellectually his servant.
Even W. R. Ward, the Catholic convert, remains astonishingly faithful to the
kind of argument in which intuitionists and empiricists engaged.

The great Whewell had produced in 1837 a history and in 1840 a philosophy
of the inductive sciences but it never became a text-book for the intuitionists
because, as an academic work, it lacked the scope and clarity of the *Logic*.

the intuitionists and based his case on axioms and 'special faculties.' We know He exists because we are dependent on Him—which is why we pray—and because our sense of moral obligation, given to us by God, presupposes a Moral Lawgiver. We know He exists because our reason tells us there is an Unknowable and our intuition and common sense create moral imperatives which proclaim His existence. 'It is our duty,' he said, 'to think of God as personal; and it is our duty to believe that He is Infinite. It is true that we cannot reconcile these two representations with each other'; but if our frail reason creates contradictions for ourselves, none exist, we may be sure, for God.

Mansel's lectures were a triumph. He was hailed as a major metaphysician and even the College servants, it is said, thronged St. Mary's to hear him.* But the triumph was ephemeral; like undisciplined cavalry his lectures opened the way to defeat by their victorious charge and were, in fact, the last Anglican attempt to found Christianity on a purely philosophical basis. Mansel was not a first-rate metaphysician: 'C'est un disciple qui ressemble à un maître,' is Nédoncelle's judgment. F. D. Maurice was aghast at the suggestion that God was unknowable, and J. B. Mozley hit the mark when he wrote in a letter of October 1858 that the lectures 'seem to me a blunder though a clever blunder.' Pringle-Pattison commented that, if the inventors of those instruments did not themselves do evil, the first man to use them would surely cut his fingers. The retribution came in 1865 when Mill published his *Examination of Sir William Hamilton's Philosophy*. If I am asked to believe, he argued, that the principles of God's government are so beyond our comprehension that they are not sanctioned (in Mansel's phrase) by 'the highest human morality which we are capable of conceiving,' then I will refuse to worship such a God. 'I will call no being good, who is not what I mean when I apply that epithet to my fellow-creatures; and if such a being can sentence me to hell for not so calling him, to hell I will go.' Mansel's rejoinder in defence did him no good. The future economist,

---

* On the other hand the verger of St. Mary's was said to give thanks that after hearing University sermons for thirty years he still remained a Christian.

Alfred Marshall, who had just taken his degree at Cambridge, said that it 'showed me how much there was to be defended.'* When Stephen dismissed the philosophy of intuitionism, he was thinking in terms of Mill's criticism of Hamiltonian Kantianism. He never criticised Kant's text itself; and no wonder since his opponents in the 'seventies had hardly begun to read it themselves.

4

The study of Mansel might lead one to suppose that the rationalist host, bearing the *Logic* before them, would sweep across the field with banners flying. Such, however, was not the case. We have only to glance at the writings of an extreme rationalist, contemporary to Mansel, to see how eager the rationalists before Stephen's day were to conciliate their opponents.

Herbert Spencer was *not* an other-worldly man. Poetry, mystery, imagination, played no part whatsoever in his life. An evolutionist before Darwin, an analytical psychologist resolving human consciousness into its elementary forms after the fashion of James Mill and Bain and thus denying those 'special faculties' so dear to theologians, Spencer epitomised the limit of pseudo-scientific systemising and *laissez-faire* utilitarianism. To him evolution, so long as it increased personal freedom, was progress; and the state tolerable only so long as it protected private rights, particularly those of Property, the basis of free enterprise. He was the apogee of the mechanist philosopher: everything could be explained in terms of force, and by the Law of Conservation of Energy all change could be shown to be merely a continual redistribution of matter according to a definite law of change, whereby less complicated systems gave way to more complicated systems; nebulae were replaced by solar systems, amoebae by human beings, tribes by nation-states, primitive agricultural economies by the nexus of industrial commerce. Brick by brick he constructed his

* Huxley said that Mansel reminded him of nothing so much as 'the drunken fellow in Hogarth's contested election who is sawing through the signpost at the other party's public-house, forgetting he is sitting at the other end of it.'

Synthetic Philosophy to demonstrate how animate and inanimate matter, the individual and society were related to each other and governed by the same laws. Spencer's cosmogony did not require a God of Design since he was at pains to show that his axioms needed no other proof than the fact that we cannot expel this sense of order (produced by the conservation of energy) from our consciousness; and at this point he might have professed himself an agnostic, in the sense that Leslie Stephen did, by confessing that the ultimate origin of force and matter, and their relation to mind, lay outside human experience. But no; Spencer would have his God. He too called it the Unknowable. Beyond the finite lay the Infinite of which man had no knowledge though he was conscious of its existence. Beyond all matter lay Energy which could not be increased, diminished or affected by man's actions, and hence lay beyond their control. Spencer wedded these two notions and produced a First Cause creating and operating the Universe which was 'a manifestation of an Unknowable Power'; and this Power was defined by calling it 'an Infinite and Eternal Energy whence all things proceed.' What was Spencer's Unknowable? It was not an Hegelian Absolute: for the Absolute was the sum of all existence including all separate and smaller totalities reconciling them with the unique— it was ideally knowable because it was finite—whereas the Unknowable lay outside totality. Sometimes he treated it as a Transcendent Power, a mode of Being higher than human intelligence and will, just as these human attributes are higher and transcend mechanical motion. Sometimes he treated it as an Immanent Substance into which our consciousness lapsed when we died—for a future life was not, according to Spencer, a credible concept. Spencer's Unknowable might be more remote than Arnold's Eternal Not-ourselves making for Righteousness or Comte's Grand-Être; but remote or not, it was a God.

Encouraged by the spectacle of a clergyman openly admitting that reason could tell us nothing about an Unknowable God, Spencer strode towards Mansel, stretching out a hand of comfort and agreement: *omnes eodem cogimur*. But this conciliatory spirit was not confined to him alone.

The incapacity of churchmen to challenge the rationalist premises was matched by the eagerness of the rationalists to find a *modus vivendi*. G. M. Young has described the 'fifties as 'a time of preparation: of deep-seated folding, straining and faulting: old strata and new shifting against each other into fantastic and precarious poises.'* Buckle did not perceive that the historical method which he applied in the first instalment of his *History of Civilisation* (1857) should have led him to question his assumption that a personal God existed and the soul was immortal. On the contrary he concluded that 'in our country the truths of religion are rarely attacked except by superficial thinkers.' His successor, Lecky, was described by George Eliot as one who, while not denying that in certain circumstances and with certain limitations all the radii of a circle are equal to one another, adds that the spirit of geometry must not be pushed too far; or as one who does not know how far he goes but knows that he does not go too far. W. R. Greg in his *Creed of Christendom* (1854) doubted the historical truth of the Gospels, but he continued to call himself a Christian; Fitzjames Stephen observed that this kind of Christian appeared to be much like a disciple 'who had heard the Sermon on the Mount, whose attention had not been called to the miracles, and who had died before the Resurrection.' †
George Eliot herself had 'too profound a conviction of the efficacy that lies in all sincere faith, and the spiritual blight

---

* The main landmarks (in addition to the works mentioned above) in the progress of rationalist criticism in the early Victorian era are as follows. In the 'forties, Chamber's *Vestiges of Creation* (1844), ridiculed by Disraeli in *Tancred*, the influence of Carlyle and the spectacle of three of his disciples, Sterling, Clough and Froude, losing their faith; Francis Newman's *Phases of Faith* (1842) in which Christian dogma was attacked as a series of immoral propositions; the growing appeal of Unitarianism producing a notable theologian in James Martineau; and George Eliot's translation of Strauss' *Leben Jesu*. In the 'fifties the writings of positivists, George Eliot, G. H. Lewes and Harriet Martineau, whose *Letters on the Laws of Man's Social Nature and Development* (1851) achieved a scandalous success; MacKay's *Progress of the Intellect* (1850) popularising Tübingen Biblical criticism. Jowett's commentary on the Atonement in his edition of St. Paul's Epistles (1855), Baden Powell's *Christianity without Judaism* (1857); and lastly in 1859 *The Origin of Species*.

† Morley asserted that Greg's book shook 'the fabric of early beliefs in some of the most active minds' at Oxford, but Justin McCarthy declared that it never made one convert or suggested a doubt to anyone though it was much discussed; it was still only in its second edition eighteen years after publication.

that comes with no-faith, to have any negative propagandism'; her imagination was to be fired, not by the philosophical problems of belief, but by the virtues enshrined in the Christian story—mercy, charity, compassion—though she held that they were not bestowed by God but resided in man. In 1844 Mill wrote to Comte, 'the time has not yet come when it is possible without prejudice to our cause to make open attacks upon theology.' The Wadham Positivists published nothing until 1859, the *Westminster Review* took care not to outrage clerical opinion, and this policy of reticence continued, broadly speaking, to be accepted until Stephen's time. Small wonder that the American freethinker, Moncure Conway, was struck by the way in which English rationalists thought it their duty to conceal their views, and noted how James Martineau was censured by Tennyson and Colenso by Matthew Arnold for publishing their opinions.

How are we to account for this pusillanimity? Why was it left to the men of Stephen's generation openly to oppose religion? The answer is to be found in the political, rather than the philosophical, structure of the two parties. Philosophically the party of religion might be weak, but politically they were far stronger than the rationalists.

In Turgenev's *Fathers and Sons* young Arkady Kirsanov, home from the university with his Nihilist friend Bazarov, decides to re-educate his father: his first step is to remove the volume of Pushkin which his father is reading and to lay in his hands Büchner's *Force and Matter*, the famous Bible of materialism which, published in 1855, ran into fifteen editions by 1884. (Arkady, like many young students, thinks he can change the elder generation by giving them the right books to read.) On the Continent, where the Revolution coloured all intellectual configurations, freethought was an integral part of liberal and socialist theory: a deployment of troops to pin down the clerical wing of the opposing army. The European rationalists fighting autocracy found an appropriate cosmology in the scientific monism forged by the German scientists Haeckel and Büchner, which was less a criticism of Christianity than a brand-new explanation of the universe. Science had become a weapon in the struggle against reaction, gunpowder to blow up the hypocrisies of the existing social order.* The conflict between religion and rationalism was submerged beneath the dissonances of a profounder social discord.

In England, on the other hand, free-thought never became specifically associated with a political movement or party. The Tories depended on the Methodist vote until the middle of the century and looked askance at the Tractarians who, had they been encouraged, might have turned religious belief into a serious political issue. The Liberals accepted the support of free-thinking Radicals, were tied to Nonconformity, and their most famous leader was a High Churchman. Political alignments cut clean across religious differences. Nor were the politically conscious working class necessarily militant freethinkers. One of the themes of Halévy's history of nineteenth-century England is how those groups among the lower classes who hated Anglicanism as a weapon of upper class coercion, found their natural home in the Nonconformist communions, which provided an alternative to the upper-class religion. The freethinkers themselves were untainted by revolutionary ideas: the patient, ethical humanitarianism of the Secularists, who looked to the day when science and knowledge would dissipate want and injustice, belonged to the reformist tradition of the English working class movement.† Freethinkers were never united in a nation-wide body. Indeed, the middle class rationalists dissociated themselves ostentatiously from the vulgar outpourings of the Secularists. Huxley was a devoted lecturer to working men's associations but he refused to intervene when Foote, the editor of the *Freethinker*, was imprisoned in 1883 under the Blasphemy Laws: though he admitted that he had not read Foote's writings, he took it upon himself to pronounce that rightful freedom was not attacked when a man is prevented from coarsely insulting his neighbours' honest beliefs. Stephen had little contact with the Secularists until late in life he became an honorary associate of the

* In 1877 Virchow attacked Haeckel and the Darwinists at a scientific congress at Munich on the grounds that since Social-Democrats supported Darwin, all anti-revolutionaries must renounce him and his works.

† The Secularist Society was formed after the collapse of Chartism by George Jacob Holyoake, the leader of the Co-operative movement. Bradlaugh, the greatest preacher of Secularism, ended his life significantly as a Liberal Member of Parliament orating against socialism.

Rationalist Press Association. George Eliot declared that she had very little sympathy for freethinkers as a class, and Herbert Spencer and Mrs. Lynn Linton* echoed her sentiments. The middle class rationalists observed the streak, faint though it was, of social discontent in Secularism which, they sensed, was different from their own protest, namely that intellectuals must be considered seriously by the political rulers of the country. They were divided from the Secularists by those class differences in temperament and education that can be bridged only by intimate friendship or by a common political affinity. The middle class rationalists apprehended that the political reforms they desired could be achieved within the framework of Liberalism rather than by an alliance with Secularism; they could be achieved so long as public opinion was assured that rationalists were not agitators or subversive, but healthy corpuscles in the life-blood of respectable Liberalism. Thus, though the rationalists might appear to be better equipped for the intellectual contest, the churches held the political initiative. As Stephen said, they assumed axiomatically that if I hit you, it's zeal, but if you hit me, it's blasphemy.

The middle class rationalists were not only political quietists: they deplored all symptoms of an ethical revolution and in morals were as orthodox as their opponents. Whereas in Europe Romanticism bred radical theories of morality and challenging Christian ethics—in the exotic and profound interpretations of life by Baudelaire, Nietzsche, Tolstoy, Treitschke and Marx—in England the religious revival tamed the second generation of Romantics with a

* Mrs. Lynn Linton (1822-98) was a considerable mid-Victorian blue-stocking. In her youth a Radical and agnostic, she oscillated between spiritualism, mesmerism, communism and conservatism, and married her husband (an inoffensive friend of Mazzini's), so she said, on God's express instructions. A. W. Benn commented: 'The gifted lady professed agnosticism with complete sincerity . . . but it was a creed that contrasted rather oddly with her credulous nature.' The best of her many novels is *Under Which Lord?* in which a Ritualist priest shatters the happy home of an agnostic gentleman by setting his wife against him and kidnapping his daughter whom the priest compels to enter a convent when he himself goes over to Rome. Victorian Society would have described the book as 'v'y parful.' She was a vigorous anti-feminist, wrote a famous article for the *Saturday Review* entitled 'The Girl of the Period,' and dedicated a novel in which she attacked Girton College (where one B.A. marries a policeman by proposing to him) 'to the sweet girls still left amongst us who have no part in the new revolt but are content to be dutiful, innocent, and sheltered.'

few exceptions such as Swinburne. Insulated from political
revolution to a greater degree than Continental intellectuals,
Victorian thinkers continued broadly to accept the Protestant ethic, anglicised foreign immigrants such as Goethe
and Kant, and appeared to be unaware of the spiritual
maquis burrowing underground in Europe. This was why the
debate on Christianity was conducted in purely intellectual
terms and why it is right to study the philosophic background
in such detail.

Not until 1869 did the tone of rationalist criticism
change decisively. In that year when Gladstone formed his
first administration which was to disestablish the Irish
Church, to open the universities and to nullify payment of
the church rate, John Morley, who, at the age of twenty-
eight, had succeeded G. H. Lewes four years previously as
editor of the *Fortnightly Review*, published T. H. Huxley's
striking article 'On the Physical Basis of Life'; and Huxley,
searching in the newly-formed Metaphysical Society for a
word which would define his state of mind perceived that
the men who surrounded him were certain that 'they had
attained a certain "gnosis"—had, more or less successfully,
solved the problem of existence; while I was quite sure I had
not, and had a pretty strong conviction that the problem was
insoluble'; so he invented the word Agnostic. The flood-
gates opened and a torrent of books and articles openly
attacking Christianity appeared.* This spate of activity
was not solely caused by political and social change; the
rationalists found that the many strands of criticism appeared

* Morley had published some of Huxley's *Lay Sermons*, addresses delivered
in London, Edinburgh and Manchester, and spreading the gospel of evolution,
before 1869, but he did not abandon a policy of caution until the 'seventies.
The *Fortnightly's* lead was followed by Froude in *Fraser's Magazine*. In the
'seventies Swinburne's *Songs before Sunrise* (1871) and James Thomson's *The
City of Dreadful Night* (1875), Winwood Reade's *The Martyrdom of Man* (1872),
the Duke of Somerset's *Christian Theology and Modern Scepticism* (1872), Mill's
Essays on Religion (1874), Walter Cassels' *Supernatural Religion* (1874), Romanes'
Candid Examination of Theism (1874) were the most prominent books published;
there also appeared as articles the contents of Morley's *On Compromise*, Stephen's
Essays in Freethinking and Plainspeaking and part of *An Agnostic's Apology*, Tyndall's
Belfast Address (1874), Huxley's *Animal Automatism* (1874) and Clifford's
essays. Even Greg's *Creed of Christendom* began to sell and between 1873–83
went through six editions. In 1877 James Knowles, founder of the Metaphysical Society, established a new review *The Nineteenth Century* especially to
discuss religion and philosophical questions and in the second half of that
year every number of the *Fortnightly* contained an attack on theology.

suddenly to be woven together and that on the loom was stretched a tapestry of argument, coherent in design and striking in colour. The two men who emerged as the leaders of the movement and expounded Agnosticism were Huxley and Leslie Stephen.

CHAPTER V

LESLIE STEPHEN LOSES HIS FAITH

WHAT made Leslie Stephen lose his faith? Though he wrote of the change between 1859, when he took priest's orders and 1862 when he resigned his tutorship, he left no clear account of his intellectual development. We know, however, what he had read before 1859—Mill's *Logic*, studied in the 'fifties, did not shake him though his father perceived how dangerous it was—and the clue probably lies in the books published during the crucial period; the content of his agnostic articles also enables us to be reasonably sure of the cause.

It was almost certainly the publication in November, 1859, of Darwin's *Origin of Species*. Apologists express surprise to-day that Darwin's work brought the truth of Christianity into question and are apt to attribute its influence to the fact that so many of the clergy and laity still read the Bible in a Fundamentalist sense. But this is to misunderstand Darwin's significance in relation not only to rationalism but to the whole European tradition of metaphysics stretching from Plato to the eighteenth century.

The metaphysical significance of Evolution has been analysed by Arthur O. Lovejoy in his classic work in the history of ideas, *The Great Chain of Being*. Lovejoy traces the fortunes of a complex of three ideas which for two thousand years gave pattern and coherence to European metaphysics, but desiderated not one but two Gods. The one was a transcendental, other-worldly Idea or Ground, self-sufficient, apart from time or space, uniting all eternal Ideas, a self-contained perfection, needing nothing to complete or to realise Itself. But since the contemplation of such a remote disinterested Being satisfied few and could not explain the peculiar scheme of things in this world, or why the world exists, still less how it changes, another God was required. This was a God whose essence required a

world teeming with living creatures, immanent in the processes of nature and related to our sense of space and time.
These two conceptions of God, though logically opposed,
were united by Plato in the *Timaeus* by the device of
emanationism: the Transcendental God, the goal of all
desires, is perfect Good and therefore envious of nothing;
hence He will wish everything to be as He, and He
accordingly overflows into the imperfect and projects
Himself into the universe. He realises Himself by creating
successively all possible kinds of being for all time, and all
these beings are connected to each other ranged in hier-
archical order as an infinite number of links in a chain. A
rational world is now established; and the presence of evil
is explicable by the fact that the different species of being
are all imperfect, each with its distinct qualities and defects:
even though Nature, red in tooth and claw, permits one
species to hunt and kill another, the hunted had far better
have lived and partaken of the Divine Perfection than never
to have existed at all. On this metaphysical foundation
are raised all cosmological and ontological structures in
European religion.

At the end of the seventeenth and during the eighteenth
century, a factor hitherto relatively unimportant—Time—
impinged upon human consciousness and the idea of the
Chain of Being had to be reinterpreted, to include the
notion of Progress. It was accordingly modified by arguing
that all creatures tend toward God and draw ever nearer to
Him during time; that being finite, they must be able to
perfect themselves since to be static is to deserve extinction;
and that perfection is to be attained through eternal altera-
tion. The Chain of Being, as Lovejoy puts it, was temporalised. Though for a time the unity of the fundamentally
dualistic God was held together, the contradiction became
more and more apparent between a Creator, who being
always the same and acting in accordance with changeless
perfect reason, could generate only one Creation to express
His perfection, and with a temporalised God whose created
world was essentially different at one time from what it was
at another. The order of things in time now began to conflict
with man's conception of the eternal aspect of things. With

the spread of Natural Theology, exemplified by Paley, the God of this world was emphasised at the expense of the Transcendental Idea and Absolute God, and soon there began to creep in the heterodox conception that God Himself was part of the time-process and, no less than the species He had created, was not yet fully self-realised—was not Himself fully perfected.

Yet the belief in an orderly and rational universe might have continued for some time longer had not a new principle been introduced into metaphysics by the Romantic Revival. This was the principle of diversity. Most eighteenth century metaphysicians accepted the principle that all conceivable species had been created and were fulfilling themselves because God could not have created a world lacking one or more of His inventions. They believed that the universe was ordered rationally in accordance with a few simple laws accessible to man's reason; and even if man's reason was too limited to apprehend the full truth, they did not doubt that every species was sanctioned by a Divine reason, however many species there were or were yet to be dis-covered—the greater the number the greater God's glory. The links of the chain of Nature must hold together because the world was internally determined by necessary truths and bound in a fixed relationship to the Absolute God. This belief in the rationality of the world was shaken by the Romantic discovery of diversity. The Romantics denied that all beings must strive towards one ideal of perfection: perfection resided in their essential difference and the world was enriched by these differences. Diversity replaced uni-versality as the principle governing the universe—a diversity which would not fit into a rational scheme of things, for every rational scheme impaired the ideal of perfection. For the Romantics even untruth was a valuable addition to diversity; though some poet's dream might be an illusion, the world was that much the richer, the Creator more fully realised; *le moi* and the unique work of art or imagination were more valuable than any rational whole.*

* Not that the Romantics showed any lack of fertility in conceiving Gods. But the gods of Schlegel, Schleiermacher, Schelling, were heretical creations in the sense that Kant's God was not. Kant too had temporalised Being, and progressive diversification and development was for him the supreme law of

Thus, when the question is put, as it sometimes is, why the work of eighteenth century scepticism had 'to be done all over again' in the nineteenth century—why Hume and Voltaire appeared to have argued in vain—the answer is that this question is framed on too low a level of enquiry. Voltaire may have rejected the notion of gradation between species but he retained the conception of a rational universe. The Deists degraded Christ but they accepted traditional metaphysics. In the nineteenth century, however, not only Christian theology but the metaphysical structure which had existed from Plato was called in question.

Since a century and a half of evolutionary hypotheses culminated in Darwin, why did the *Origin of Species* have such an effect? Partly because Darwin became in a lesser degree what Newton was for his age: the man who had discovered the laws governing a wide but circumscribed field of enquiry on which lesser or less lucky minds had been working for many years. Partly because the hypothesis of Natural Selection, derived from Lyell's geology and Malthus' demography, appeared to have been achieved by employing Newton's methods faithfully; and to readers of the *Logic* a fruitful new hypothesis was now available to be applied deductively to social problems. Just as Newton's prestige was enhanced by the respect accorded to mathematics, so Darwin rose on the breezes of the prestige won for the natural sciences by the staggering discoveries of the astronomers, physicists, chemists, geologists and mathematical statisticians.* But the real significance of the *Origin of Species* lay in its apparent contradiction of orthodox metaphysics. Darwin introduced the idea that *chance* begets order. Fortuitous events, not planned or rational but fortuitous, result in a physical law: the process of natural

---

nature. But he believed that a species could not develop beyond a certain point and, when self-realised, was eliminated in order that the links in the Chain of Being may still conform to each other: cosmic egregiousness was unthinkable because Kant assumed the universe to be rational. *Per contra* the German Romantic philosophers dispensed with the rational cosmos, or rather they dispensed with one part of it. The Hegelian Absolute resided *inside* the universe —it was not an Idea of Ideas existing quite apart from force and matter.

* The unwillingness of scientists such as Lyell, or Darwin himself, to accept the principle of organic evolution added to their reputation for scrupulosity. Huxley admitted that, before Darwin published, he opposed the hypothesis for lack of evidence and looked askance at its advocates.

selection, achieved by minute accidental variations in the
species, breaks the principle of internal determinism so that
the links in the Chain of Being fall apart. Chauncey
Wright, the American naturalist and philosopher, pointed
out that the very title of Darwin's book implied a reversal of
orthodox metaphysics. ' "Origin" now means how things
go from one determinate appearance to another . . . the
word "species" now means not an absolute, but a comparative fixity of character, [so that in Darwin] the two terms
appear with modern non-scholastic meanings. . . .' Thus the
Origin of Species made the world seem less, not more, rational,
and the universe a creation of blind chance, not a 'block-
world' (in William James' phrase) created by an other-
worldly Master Mind. Attempts naturally were made to
escape from the disagreeable situation of existing in a
mechanistic world without a mechanic;* intelligent theologians absorbed evolution by the doctrine of Immanence;
and Henry Adams noted the growth of a new evolutionary
metaphysic of 'Form, Law, Order or Sequence.' Though
evolution is almost the least of the problems facing theologians to-day, Stephen read Darwin as *evidence* that confuted
orthodox metaphysics; by using this evidence empirically
was it not possible to show scientifically that all metaphysical
explanations of the cosmos were worthless?

2

The *Origin of Species* raised a moral, as well as an intellectual, issue in Stephen's mind. Between 1860 and 1862
three events took place which may well have influenced
Stephen decisively. The first was Bishop Wilberforce's error
in 1860 during the famous debate on Darwinism in the Oxford Museum. Accustomed to manipulate ecclesiastical
machinery, the Great Diocesan, a genial and often attractive
prelate, fell into the trap which awaits men of good humour
who become politicians—he made a joke at the wrong
moment. When he asked Huxley which of his grandparents

* Not always very happily: A. R. Wallace, the joint discoverer of Natural
Selection, declared that the mechanism of natural selection, which left no room
for the creation of the soul, was broken with the emergence of Mind: Mind
required a separate act of creation—an argument not very far removed from
Max Müller's rebuttal of the principle of natural selection, namely, that
language separates men from apes.

claimed descent from an ape, the earnestness of Clapham
passed in an instant into the hands of his adversaries; his
levity made Belief an issue of moral rectitude. In the same
year *Essays and Reviews* was published; Rowland Williams
was prosecuted for heresy, Jowett was disgraced and the
future archbishop, Frederick Temple, was admonished by
Tait. Temple replied, 'Many years ago you urged us
from the University pulpit to undertake the critical study of
the Bible. You said that it was a dangerous study but
indispensable. . . . To tell a man to study, and yet bid him,
under heavy penalties, come to the same conclusions with
those who have not studied, is to mock him. If the conclusions are prescribed, the study is precluded.' Finally in
1862 Wilberforce seized on Colenso's exegesis on the Penta-
teuch as an issue on which Evangelicals and High Churchmen might sink their differences and unite against infidelity.*
These two last events probably raised a further question in
Stephen's mind: does not the *evidence* of history tell against
Christianity?

When Carlyle besought his countrymen to close their
Bibles and open their history books, he acknowledged the
new sense of power communicated to him by German
historians. Scholarly historians had lived in England before
the nineteenth century but they had written either narrative
history as sweeping in scope as Gibbon, or works of staggering
erudition in which opponents were suffocated by docu-
mentation. The Germans revealed not only the mysteries
of the past but the shape of the future. The Gothic Revival
taught men to love the past for its own sake, but German
scholars encouraged the belief that history was a new social
science and that behind the appearance of events lay a
deeper reality. They set a new standard of scholarship in
that they were aware of the philosophical problems latent
in writing history, and this imposed a new professional
discipline. What is an historical event? How do we establish its authenticity? Strauss commanded attention by
rejecting the eighteenth century rationalist interpretations

* Three other relevant books were published between 1859 and 1862: in 1859
Mill *On Liberty; Omar Khayyám* (of which Stephen was an early admirer);
and Spencer's *First Principles* (1862).

12

of Scripture, whereby miracles were treated as superstitious accounts for which natural explanations could be
found. After showing how the ancients had faced the same
problems of interpreting religious events in the same fashion
as modern scholars, he concluded that argument about the
facts of Christ's life was irrelevant and that the miraculous in
Scripture was not fiction or exaggeration but myth. He gained
his reputation not simply by his vast learning but by his
grasp of the epistemological implications latent in his subject.

Though Thirlwall and the disciples of Julius Hare
appreciated these interpretative subtleties, the rationalists
naturally stressed the scientific examination of source
material. Sources revealed facts, and from these facts a
chain of evidence could be constructed leading to inescapable
conclusions. Niebuhr had said, 'In laying down the pen
we must be able to say in the sight of God, "I have not
knowingly nor without earnest investigation written anything which is not true." ' The rationalists assumed that
historical truth could be revealed largely through the
techniques of the historian and sought to divorce historical
fact as far as possible from interpretation;* positivist history
continued to gather speed from Buckle's day until 1903
when J. B. Bury pronounced in his inaugural lecture that
history was a science no more, no less.† From these premises
agnostics criticised scripture: Huxley and Gladstone
debated the authenticity of the Gadarene swine story
solely on the plane of historical evidence. History, moreover,
made other studies intelligible in a new way. It related not
only the Bible but also Science to the scheme of things, and
Science reciprocally extended the dimensions of History

---

* Cf. Norman Baynes on the cross seen in the sky by Constantine the Great.
Whether the cross appeared or not, whether it was sent by God if it did appear,
are questions which the historian will answer according to his ontological
interpretation of life; as a *technical* historian, he cannot determine whether it
existed but can only record the statements by his sources for its appearance.

† The conviction that the historian can truthfully state what happened
in the past is instanced by a mistranslation of one of Ranke's most famous
passages. Protesting against partisan historiography inspired by the mistaken
duty of historians to pass moral judgments, Ranke wrote in his first work
of importance in 1824: 'People have thought that it was the duty of the historian to judge the past and instruct the present for the benefit of the future.
The present essay is more modest. *Er will blosz zeigen wie es eigentlich gewesen*'.
These words meaning, 'It merely wants to show what it was really like,'
admitting implicitly interpretation, were translated, 'what actually occurred'
or 'events as they actually happened.'

both back into the past and forward into the future. The story of how these extrapolations of scientific laws made men question what they had formerly regarded as the *facts* on which Christianity was founded, has often been told; geology and biology told the history of the earth before man existed; physics foretold the end of the earth when, devoid of kinetic heat, it would spin frozen round an extinct sun. Finally anthropologists showed how religions arose. The work of the classical anthropologists, Tylor, McLennan and Frazer, belongs to the second half of the century, but in the 'fifties and 'sixties books were appearing in which the comparative method suggested that religions were all animated by much the same myths and rites.*

Here again, Stephen, with Mill's correlation of the natural and social sciences in mind, treated Christianity as an explanation of the origins and development of society, and condemned it as bad sociology.

3

Thus Stephen was ready in the 'seventies to accept the title of Agnostic.† Divided by temperament and in their

* Mrs. Lynn Linton grasped this idea in her girlhood. At the age of seventeen in 1839 she noticed, reading in the garden, that the story of Nisus and Scylla in Ovid's *Metamorphoses* was strikingly similar to that of Samson and Delilah. 'There shot through my brain these words which seemed to run along the page in a line of light: "What difference is there between any of these stories and those like to them in the Bible?—between the loves of the sons of God for the daughters of men, and those of the Gods of Greece for the girls of Athens and Sparta?" ' This reflection so disturbed her that she collapsed on the grass in a dead faint. Similarly, Darwin in the *Beagle* suddenly realised that the sacred Hindu books, the *Vedas*, were strikingly similar to the Old Testament. These experiences caused both of them eventually to lose their faith. When in the *Grammar of Assent* Newman dubiously argued that the Atonement must be a valid doctrine because we find the belief current among savages, Stephen pointed out that it would be more rational to deduce that Christianity was just another religious phenomenon holding doctrines common to other creeds. cf. 'The secret of theology is anthropology.' L. Feuerbach, *The Essence of Christianity.*

† The other leading agnostics were Tyndall, Clifford and Morley. Tyndall echoed Huxley; Clifford was more of an atheist: he looked to the day when we should have as good evidence for the non-existence of God as we have now for the non-existence of a large planet between the earth and Venus; he also prognosticated that physiology would prove the existence of 'mind-stuff' and so end the dichotomy between mind and matter. Morley was more concerned with political measures and sought to remove all obstacles to rational discussion; he led the anti-clerical forces and defined the clergy as intellectual eunuchs who had been rendered 'mentally sterile' by the laying-on-of-hands, a ceremony not unlike the Turkish method of providing 'incomparable guardians of the seraglio.'

methods, Stephen and Huxley never became intimate friends. Huxley was the more famous of the two;* arguing with the authority of Science, he had a flair for controversy, and his articles were more widely read, especially in working class circles. But Huxley was a dogmatic positivist in history and science, and though he gave science a rhetoric of its own by his rapturous description of the scientist devoted to the discovery of useful truth, his very use of a scientific phraseology, soon to be re-defined, dates his work. He repudiated his first definition of agnosticism and took all the meaning out of the word by calling agnosticism the method of following the intellect fearlessly and of not pretending that conclusions were certain which were not demonstrable. The original meaning troubled him in that he was certain of too many things: he had found his own 'gnosis,' the scientific metaphysic of his time. He did not declare, like the German materialists, that only Force and Matter existed; but he did suggest by extending the laws of physics to cosmology that the extinction of the sun, and hence of life on earth, were as demonstrable and verifiable as the chemical properties of water; and he used the argument from the uniformity of nature to state as proven other conclusions far less probable. That truth was not all of the same nature never struck him.†

* And also remarkably, for such a pugnacious man, dispassionate. He voted on the School Board for teaching children the Bible because he believed the Authorised Version to be the heritage of Englishmen.

† The rationalists hardly considered the possibility that 'truths' were of different varieties or that it is convenient to use one set of propositions in one field, but inconvenient to use them in another, e.g. that it is a matter of convenience whether a straight line is defined as the shortest distance between two points or as the line following a ray of light. The churches with Aquinas' condemnation of Averroes before them naturally rejected the possibility; but Clifford might have been expected to explore it. He had pointed out the fallacy in Kant's contention, that space can be proved by the eternal truth of Euclidian geometry to exist independently of our experience, by showing that alternative means of measuring space, such as the non-Euclidian geometries of Lobachevsky and Riemann, exist which are as valid as that of Euclid and can be adopted whenever they prove more convenient. His chapter 'On the Bending of Space' in *The Common Sense of the Exact Sciences* prefigures the general theory of Relativity. He saw that geometry was not absolutely true but depended on multiple postulates: e.g. Euclid's fourth postulate 'All right angles are equal' itself postulates the principle of elementary flatness. Curiously enough, Newman raised this question. Writing with the dispute between Galileo and the Church in mind, Newman said that we cannot decide who was right until we know precisely what motion is. And he added: 'If our sense of motion be but an accidental result of our present senses, neither proposition

Stephen's writings appear by comparison more distinguished, acute and œcumenical. Whereas Huxley engaged in specific controversies and dived into Biblical criticism, Stephen ranged over the whole field of theology and metaphysics and gave meaning and currency to the word which Huxley had invented. In his agnosticism Stephen did not try to prove a particular point in Christian theology or history untrue: theology and metaphysics were not so much untrue as unreal; they simply do not correspond, he thought, to the impression which totality makes upon an educated man's senses. Grasping the wider implications of Darwinism, Stephen constantly returns in *English Thought in the Eighteenth Century* and in his controversial essays to the impossibility of squaring the circle and constructing a system which will include an other-worldly Omnipotent Power and a rational Supreme Being at work in this world deducible by Natural Theology after the fashion of Paley. He passed from dogma and ontology to epistemology, or the dialectic in which Newman and Maurice defended Christianity, thence to the nature of conviction to morality, and presented agnosticism as a composite intellectual structure. The confusion in the churches encouraged him to believe they could not weather the storm of speculation which had broken overhead. It was as if the winds had been loosed from the wallet of Aeolus, and the ship of religion in England was to be blown hither and thither for the next twenty-five years to reappear, when she emerged from the tempest, wearing a different rig and sailing under different colours. Stephen held that she ought to strike them.

---

is true and both are true, neither true philosophically, both true for certain practical purposes in the system in which they are respectively found.' This was the sentence which made Froude renounce Newman—who was, of course, not making a revolution of logic but attempting to extract himself from a moral difficulty. Mark Pattison delivered in 1878 a paper to the Metaphysical Society on 'Double Truth.'

CHAPTER VI

AGNOSTICISM

STEPHEN makes three assertions as an Agnostic. Firstly, dogmatic religious systems are unreal; secondly, evidence does not support belief in God's existence; thirdly, religion demoralises society.

There is a simple answer to theologians. Deny that their subject has any right to exist. The agnostic declares that there are limits to human knowledge and that beyond those limits no man has the right to be dogmatic. Have the theologians, who set out to chart the ocean of infinity, settled anything? Listen to the bedlam within the Churches to-day and you will see that on no single point are they agreed. Theologians define 'the nature of God Almighty with an accuracy from which modest naturalists would shrink in describing the genesis of a black beetle,' yet plenty of sincere Christians and fellow theologians disagree with them. Why should agnostics be ashamed of professing ignorance in matters still involved in hopeless controversy? Even if the theologian calls the metaphysician to his aid, he remains confounded. Spinoza tells us that God is the First Cause and that He is the cause of all effects down to the most remote: this leads us straight to a pantheism in which there is no need of a Revelation and God becomes the cause of evil as well as of good. The doctrine of predestination attempts to overcome this difficulty, but whole armies of pious logicians lie sunk in this Serbonian bog; and if the theologian abandons predestination and argues that the chain of causation is broken by the gift of free will to man, God still remains the source of good and evil, since He alone through bestowing His Grace can make a man good. Either God is not omniscient or else His design is so incomprehensible that men, such as Mansel, can only acknowledge their ignorance so abjectly that they become in spite of themselves agnostics. Nor are the orthodox who desert reason for Revelation less agnostic. They claim that intuitively man can know God;

but whom God will save and whom he will damn, whether the damned will suffer in hell for ever or for a space of time, whether He will grant His uncovenanted mercies to certain gross sinners, they cannot say. Butler admits in his *Analogy* that both Nature and God appear to us unjust. Even as Nature wastes millions of seeds in the fertilisation of plants and animals, so God wastes millions of souls. Why, then, should we be comforted by the Incarnation? Often in this world the helpless and innocent suffer tortures in order, presumably, to fit them for the world to come. If this is true of God, what moral being would worship Him? In fact the whole workings of the universe are shrouded in total mystery. And yet, agnostics who acknowledge this fact are reviled! Until the time when the orthodox can point to a single truth which they have discovered and which will stand scrutiny, agnostics will be content 'to admit openly, what you whisper under your breath or hide in technical jargon, that the ancient secret is a secret still; that man knows nothing of the Infinite and Absolute; and that, knowing nothing, he had better not be dogmatic about his ignorance.'

The agnosticism of the orthodox should not astonish us. For, the whole fabric of Christianity is but a dream, woven out of the pathetic desires of humanity, who suffer beneath the miseries of existence and the perplexities of man's final end. Christianity is distinguished from other religions by the certainty of its message that man shall not die and pass into timeless oblivion but shall live in heaven after a corporeal resurrection. The Christian argues that human existence would be a hideous mockery without this belief. Yet the Jews had no such consolation: God rewarded Job in this life with oxen and asses, and sons and daughters, for his patience. The Christian seeks no such recognition: his portion is in the world to come, where he shall obtain his reward. His reward—but also his punishment; for the ungodly will descend to hell. What is hell? On this point Christians are by no means agreed. Dean Farrar states that, if even a part of mankind were to suffer eternally the torments described by Tertullian, or Dr. Pusey, he would ask God to let him perish as the beasts of the field.

This does credit to the Dean's heart—is not the doctrine of hell, which condemns to punishment the mass of mankind who are not Christians, abominable? But what of the Dean's head? Apparently he is still willing to propagate a religion the majority of whose priests entertain such a belief. Stephen recalled the remark of his eldest brother Herbert to Fitzjames at Eton: 'If you can enjoy yourself [in heaven] when you think of me and my like grilling in hell-fire, upon my soul, I don't envy you.'* If it be admitted that these threats of hell-fire which Catholics have hurled at Protestants and Presbyterians at Socinians, and which have in the past been held to be assured for infidels and unbaptized children —if it be admitted that these threats were the offspring of mistaken zeal, why not admit that the whole fabric of heaven and hell are mistaken zeal as well? Historical Christianity is not a corpus of revealed and unchanging truth, but changes with the times. If hell is to be abolished, or to consist of Judas Iscariot and one or two others, what is to become of heaven? In fact, the whole conception of an anthropomorphic God dispensing justice on the Day of Judgment is outworn, and that of heaven and hell unreal, however poetic. Heaven and hell are preached because Christians, determined to awaken a conviction of sin, consider the most violent assault upon the emotions to be justifiable; and it is precisely because our emotions are so prone to overrule our intellect, that the belief in immortality retains its hold on the imagination. And yet, asks Stephen, what does a thoughtful man feel when he stands by the grave of one he loves? Who does he think speaks the truth from his heart during the service for the Burial of the Dead— the Psalmist who declares that we fade away like the grass and that to live long is but labour and sorrow; or St. Paul with his magnificent rhetoric but tortuous arguments, which seek to convince us against reason that we shall rise incorruptible? As he pursued this argument Stephen paused to

---

* C. E. Norton refers in a letter to a rebuke administered to Stephen by Carlyle for his lack of reverence. Stephen had written to Norton 'the old prophet loves hell and answered me on the authority of Dante that it was made by Infinite Love. To which I could only reply naturally in the words of the good Briton whose parson assured him that whom the Lord loveth he chasteneth, "I wish he weren't so bloody fond of me." '

give his reply. Shortly after the death of his first wife and with a heart laden with sorrow, he wrote, 'Standing by an open grave, and moved by all the most solemn sentiments of our nature, we all, I think—I can only speak for myself with certainty—must feel that the Psalmist takes his sorrow like a man, and as we, with whatever difference of dialect, should wish to take our own sorrows; while the Apostle is desperately trying to shirk the inevitable and at best resembles the weak comforters who try to cover up the terrible reality under a veil of well-meant fiction. I would rather face the inevitable with open eyes.'*

Theology is, then, unreal, the orthodox are unwittingly agnostics, and the Christian morality of rewards and punishments is immoral. It is also anti-social. Christians hold rationalists guilty of the sin of materialism; of neglecting spiritual values and worshipping the carnal. But they are guilty of the vice which Blake condemned. They fear the flesh, identify matter with evil and escape from the world into asceticism. Marriage is regarded as a concession to frailty, a monastery a better society than the world. The ultimate end of man becomes the duty to save his soul and not to do his duty in that station to which he is called. The very men who stand accused of materialism are those who

* The similarity of this passage to a well-known letter of Huxley to Kingsley, written in reply to the latter's condolence on the death of Huxley's small son, is striking. Huxley's letter is dated 23rd May, 1863, and was naturally published only after his death in his biography, which Stephen reviewed. Huxley wrote: 'As I stood behind the coffin of my little son the other day, with my mind bent on anything but disputation, the officiating minister read, as a part of his duty, the words "If the dead rise not again, let us eat and drink, for to-morrow we die." I cannot tell you how inexpressibly they shocked me. Paul had neither wife nor child, or he must have known that his alternative involved a blasphemy against all that was best and noblest in human nature. . . .

'Kicked into the world, a boy, without guide or training, or with worse than none, I confess to my shame that few men have drunk deeper of all kinds of sin than I. Happily my course was arrested in time—before I had earned absolute destruction—and for long years I have been slowly and painfully climbing, with many a fall, towards better things. And when I look back, what do I find to have been agents of my redemption? The hope of immortality or of future reward? I can honestly say that for fourteen years such a consideration has never entered my head. No, I can tell you exactly what has been at work. *Sartor Resartus* led me to know that a deep sense of religion was compatible with the entire absence of theology. Secondly, science and her methods gave me a resting place independent of authority and tradition. Thirdly, love opened up to me a view of the sanctity of human nature and impressed me with a deep sense of responsibility.'

have done most for the improvement of mankind.* A priesthood, Stephen declares, depends on giving the people something they want and its task to-day is to show that it wants to abolish pauperism and not to declare that poverty is a blessing. Moreover, religious belief leads to intolerance. People argue that there is no harm in the Churches supplying what men most desire to hear since consolation is much needed on this earth, yet this argument conveniently neglects the past in whose annals the Churches stand blackened by their lust for persecution. No doubt those days are past. 'The impossibility of organising an effectual persecution now is admitted,' says Stephen, living seventy years before our times. But the authority of the Churches is of a different order from that of the other authorities to whom we every day submit. The authority of science can be checked by analysing its conclusions and premises; the authority of a ruler or assembly is open to the arbitrament, if necessary, of a revolution; but the authority of a Church is illimitable for it purports to come from God himself.† The Church's dogma is the truth, heretics are those who deny the truth and must be exterminated; religion is, therefore, a danger to society. Since the truth of any religion cannot be proved to the satisfaction of a majority of mankind, since it proves to be, on examination, the offspring of a shot-gun marriage between tribal rites and superstitions, let us regard all religions with tolerant scepticism; and let man acknowledge authority in matters of opinion only when authority can be demonstrated.

Religion for Stephen was belief. What did you believe and what did you mean by your belief? Beliefs were concrete propositions having an independent existence; he never saw them as the natural exhalation of a living social organism— as the hopes and fears of society which cannot live without a mythology of some kind.‡ Nor was this strange for Stephen

---

* Stephen did ill to add that it was atheists and materialists who had led the movement for prevention of cruelty to animals. It is difficult to believe that he did not know that this honour belonged to the Evangelicals.

† Stephen may have had in mind Newman's *Essay on Development*. 'Religious error is in itself of an immoral nature.'

‡ Feuerbach had shown how religious belief is adapted as society changes, and had suggested that the question of the empirical truth of Christianity was irrelevant, so long as Europeans required a supernatural belief and Christianity could fulfil that need.

had been taught as a child to treat dogma in this fashion. At the day-school at Brighton he had heard the headmaster question the boys at prayers. 'Gurney, what's the difference between justification and sanctification? Stephen, prove the omnipotence of God.' No wonder he detested Ritualism, 'surely the most vapid form of sacerdotalism ever imposed upon effeminate natures'; he feared that man's love of beauty would quench his thirst for truth. 'Admit that the Pope is not, in the plain sense of words, a judge of controversies but a master of ceremonies, and the difficulty [of accepting Christianity] disappears'; Stephen wanted to return to 'the uncomfortable Protestant habit of demanding statements of fact.' Now, ritual is more than a fine art; it suffuses all communal emotion and helps a man to adjust himself psychologically to his fellow-men. Stephen missed his chance of raising a deeper problem. How can truth of any kind be conveyed to the mass of ignorant mankind and also to the few wise men? Is there to be one religion or several according to caste? Are we to force the wise to acknowledge falsehoods as truth, or in the interests of truth make religion incomprehensible to the mass of mankind? This is the problem raised by Dostoievsky in the Inquisitor's speech. 'Thou didst promise them the bread of Heaven, but, I repeat again, can it compare to earthly bread in the eyes of the weak, ever sinful and ignoble race of man? . . . Or dost Thou care only for the tens of thousands of the great and strong, while the millions, numerous as the sands of the sea, who are weak but love Thee, must exist only for the sake of the great and strong?' The answer a man gives to this question depends on his temperament; as a lapsed Evangelical, Stephen deplored the adulteration of the heavenly bread.

The High Church, until the development of Anglo-Catholicism at the end of the century, gave no answer to Stephen's questions. What of the Broad Church with their contention that Scripture must be reinterpreted? Stephen admitted that there had always been clergymen such as Tillotson or Burnet or Paley ('of whom it is now the fashion to speak with contempt partly caused by his utter inability to be obscure'), who had declared that the Bible and Prayer

Book need not be literally interpreted; and he praised them and their modern followers for their liberalism and sincerity. But how, he asked, can a clergyman to-day get round the 39 Articles? There they stand—the document of dogmas to which he must subscribe. The second Article says quite clearly that the Atonement was a bargain struck between the Father and the Son. To their credit Broad Churchmen find this repulsive, but how do they reconcile subscription to this article with their conscience? No doubt they can plead some legal quibble but surely in *this* matter one is not morally entitled to take advantage of loopholes in the law. 'The practical tendency of Broad Church teaching is not, as formerly, to convince young men that it is possible to be at once rational and Christian, but to convince them that it is possible to be at once rational and clergymen, which is a very different thing.'*

The spectacle of clergymen such as Voysey and J. R. Green quitting the Church after a conscientious struggle to square dogma with history encouraged Stephen in his strictures; and he exposed the weakness in the reasoning of Jowett, Dean Stanley and Kingsley, none of whom was a match for his intellect. With Arnold he was somewhat less successful. Arnold, though he was regarded by his contemporaries as beyond the pale even of the Broad Church, was only one of a number of men who were trying to find a *via media* and preserve certain moral habits even when their historical and dogmatic sanction had gone. 'It seems commonly to be assumed that there is something peculiarly perverse or wrong-headed about this,' comments Graham Hough in a wise passage. 'The objections vary from Chesterton's crude gibe at "those who do not have the Faith, and will not have the fun," to T. S. Eliot's more refined eyebrow-raising at Arnold's attempts to make a purely secular culture do the work of religion. It is surely the objections which are wrong-headed. It is not self-contradictory to say, "This

---

* Sidgwick treated this matter more scrupulously than Stephen. In an essay entitled, *Clerical Veracity* he agreed with such clerics as Rashdall that the clergy were entitled to read metaphor into Scripture where their forefathers had taken the texts literally; but he declared that the dogmas of the Incarnation and Virgin Birth, about which there is no obscurity in Scripture, must be accepted—at any rate by clergymen.

type of conduct is right, though the traditional sanctions for it are wrong." And if one holds this view it is perfectly reasonable to practise the conduct without any sanctions at all, or to attempt to find new and valid ones.' Religion for Arnold was a matter of right *feeling* as well as right conduct; and what he tried to do was to fill the emotional gap created by rationalism. Stephen appreciated Arnold's aim, but thought that religion was nothing unless it answers with certainty the perennial questions that trouble men. Arnold was indifferent to these questions; he had said of F. D. Maurice that he beat the bush without ever starting a hare and Stephen added of Arnold, 'if he started the hare, he did not quite catch it.' But Arnold never imagined that these questions could be answered with certainty by minds temperamentally *ondoyant et divers*. Arnold's approach to religious, as well as poetic, diction was subtle and delicate. 'To handle these matters properly there is needed a poise so perfect that the least overweight in any direction tends to destroy the balance. Temper destroys it, a crotchet destroys it, even erudition may destroy it. To press to the sense of the thing itself with which one is dealing, not to go off on some collateral issue about the thing, is the hardest matter in the world.' When Stephen wrote in his valediction that Arnold was urging us 'to get rid of prejudices in general, not of any special prejudice,' Arnold's departed spirit must have bowed ironically from the fields of asphodel and moly. *That* was exactly what he was doing.

Arnold was no philosopher* and he did not explain how, by what new logic or dialectic, men were to be convinced of the truth of Christian dogma. One theologian, however, had faced this problem in his reinterpretation of Christianity and that was Stephen's old mentor, F. D. Maurice.

F. D. Maurice was the greatest Anglican theologian of the

---

* Stephen rightly made hay of Arnold the metaphysician. Arnold purported to have discovered a super-law of science deducible from other scientific laws: namely that in science we will find a God or Principle by which all things fulfil the law of their being. This debased Aristotelianism was given no quarter; and Stephen replied that science can tell us only the order in which our sensations occur and cannot perform the miracle required by Arnold and authorise an intuitively perceived morality to declare itself an absolute morality. By misunderstanding the nature of scientific law, Arnold was adding modern *Aberglauben* with the left hand as fast as he removed ancient *Aberglauben* with the right.

century and, so far from being a Broad Churchman, always declared that he belonged to no party in the Church. The Church of England, he thought, was not a sect propagating certain beliefs but a good *position*. It did not balance opinions but united opposites: truth was not a series of compromises between extremes, but the union of these extremes. Since the world was full of problems insoluble by formulae, all dovetailed logical systems of dogma were fallacious. From this basis Maurice proceeded to break with the old Evangelical teaching. Man is fundamentally good and sin is an aberration. Before ever the Fall, God created the world in Christ, and Christ is the ground on which humanity rests. Since Christ, not sin, is the basis of human nature, sin is an aberration not a norm; sin is man's determination to live independently of God instead of acknowledging his relation to Him in Christ. In place of the Evangelical insistence on personal salvation Maurice emphasised the salvation of the human race; the Elect are not a set of God's favourites but the whole of humanity restored to its foreordained state of goodness by incorporation into the body of which Christ is the Head. The Bible is not to be interpreted in a fundamentalist sense, but neither is it a set of myths; analytical criticism is at fault when the Bible is treated as a collection of texts and not as the revelation of a Divine Kingdom in which man has a place shown to him by God in Scripture; Scripture explains not only that evil exists but how it is compatible with other facts such as goodness. The Creed means belief in a Name, not in a set of doctrines; all doctrines are reconciled in that Name. The 39 Articles protect us from the tyranny of systems and parties by their very ambivalence. Since Christ and not Satan is the Prince of this world, miracles are manifestations of His order not (*pace* Mansel) violations of order to impress us; they demonstrate that spiritual power is superior to mechanical and the world subject to God and not to Darwinian chance.

Widespread as Maurice's influence was, his attempt to make Christianity at once philosophically and morally acceptable was imperfectly understood by his own contemporaries in the Church. To Stephen he was anathema, and of all theologians whom Stephen handled none got rougher treatment. He portrayed him as intricate, futile, bewildering, a 'melancholy instance of the way in which a fine intellect may run to waste in the fruitless endeavour to force new truth into the old mould.' Sir James Stephen had regarded Maurice's teaching as an attempt to wed 'the gospel to some form of philosophy if so to conceal its baldness. But Paul of Tarsus many years ago forbade the banns'; and his son added that to see Maurice graft Coleridgean metaphysics on to Christianity was like watching the struggles of a drowning creed. Stephen even went so far as to break his own rule of obtaining biographers sympathetic to their subject in the D.N.B. and himself wrote Maurice's life—which C. E. Raven rightly condemns. Why was he so incensed?

It was the epistemological tangle, the perversion by Maurice of the meaning of meaning, which appalled Stephen. Faced with the difficulty that a loving Father condemned His children to eternal torment, Maurice juggled with words and claimed that 'eternal' had nothing to do with time, a solution which, Stephen said, 'was more satisfactory than intelligible.' Maurice held that eternity has no meaning in this world; it can be used only in relation to God and therefore is not a term of temporal duration. It is a word of quality rather than quantity and was used in this sense by St. John, who talks of eternal life and death being known here and now in this world, thus showing that eternal death really means being severed from the love of God. Very well, says Stephen; we now arrive at the proposition: 'God's punishments are not excessive, for eternity, as we know, has nothing to do with time, and therefore eternal damnation means merely separation from the Eternal.' A theologian will wince at the word 'merely,' but Stephen relentlessly asks how this theory differs from the old dogma of hell. Maurice would reply that propositions and dogmas have nothing to do with the matter. We cannot be certain what the word αἰώνιος means, but taking the Gospel message and the course of history as a whole, we may trust in the Larger Hope. To believe firmly that some men go to hell is to acknowledge that Satan and not

Christ is Prince of this world.* This, says Stephen, means that one 'has to learn not a new set of facts or opinions, but a new mode of thinking.' How can we argue about God except in words and by laying down dogmas? When Maurice says that Christ has revealed Himself and not a dogma, we may ask what a revelation of God can be but the revelation of a dogma about God. An anthropomorphic explanation of God is inevitable, as Maurice admitted when he attacked Mansel's Unknowable God; and when Maurice says that we must not confound that which *seems* with that which *is*, we can only answer that what *seems* and *is* are indistinguishable to our relative minds. The confusion between a cognition and an emotion runs through Maurice's work.

Here Stephen stands in the best tradition of rationalist thought; just such a refusal to allow words to carry meanings other than they are given in normal conversation was at the root of G. E. Moore's philosophy at the beginning of this century.† Stephen feared that the logic of language as a means of communication would be destroyed. 'Treat believing as a branch of gymnastics and there is nothing, however revolting, which you may not train yourself to swallow.' The crux of his criticism is his refusal to accept Maurice's tenet of the polarity of truth. This enables Maurice to say that every formula is worthless but also of infinite value when rightly interpreted. Maurice believes that the facts of history support Christianity but watch, says Stephen, how he interprets them. He rejects what he dislikes in other creeds and takes the remainder as a vital principle because it coincides with his beliefs. 'Rightly interpreted' Buddhism becomes a prayer for the Light of the World. 'Rightly interpreted' the fate of the Gadarene

* H. G. Wood admits that Maurice went too far in declaring that 'eternal,' as used in Scripture, has nothing to do with time and that he also forgets that Satan derives his authority from God even if he is not Prince of this world.

† From Stephen's point of view Maurice had solved nothing. Maurice rejected the old Evangelical theology, but he did not agree with Mill that one could not worship a Being who punished His children. In fact, he had broken with the Unitarian faith, in which he was brought up as a child, because it denied the need for atonement. To say that God is too kind and good to punish men is to have 'a feeble notion of the Divine perfections [and to represent] *good nature* as the highest of them.' For Stephen the problem of the morality of a belief in hell (or separation from God's Love) remains.

swine is an illustration of the redemption of men from
brutish passions. Stephen claimed that Maurice had invented
a new tense 'the conjectural preterite.' Buddhists, Moham-
medans, Christians 'will have thought so-and-so' i.e. they
did think so 'if Mr. Maurice's theories be sound.' For
Maurice the desire for a Saviour expressed in other religions
proved the truth of Christianity: for Stephen the incompatibility of other religions with Christianity and the lack
of evidence that the world was being converted showed that
Christianity was merely another product of the human
mind and not the supreme truth. The deepest principles,
according to Maurice, are those which the schoolman and
peasant can both grasp; is not this, asks Stephen, to hold
that 'the ultimate criterion of truth . . . comes to be simply
that it is the doctrine which satisfies at once a bed-ridden old
woman and a high-minded clergyman?'

Maurice had been taught by Coleridge to revere history,
but his inadequate understanding of historiography impaired
his theology.* Nevertheless, his modern apologists often
defend his treatment of history by arguments derived from
Collingwood. According to this analysis, history is not a
chain of evidence based on events and facts, hard, concrete
and tangible, as Newtonian particles; it is a series of situations impossible to interpret unless we get inside the thought
of the past. When this is grasped we shall realise that fact is
not *followed* by interpretation: every fact is automatically
itself interpretation as soon as it is used in narrative or analysis.
Objective history is as obsolete as Newtonian physics
which presupposed a direct relationship between mathematical fact and reality. Maurice was, therefore, right to
reject German Biblical source-criticism which, after 150
years of research, still to-day has not discovered 'the historical
Jesus'—for the simple reason that the Gospels are not
biographies written by detached observers but an expression
of the early Church's faith.† Thus, when Stephen says that

* Frederic Harrison complained that when he tried to teach English history
at the Working Men's College in terms of movements and periods, Maurice
insisted on taking the reign of each king and queen separately.
† Some critics declare that form-criticism, which discloses the tradition of
the early Church, rather than source-criticism, is the most fruitful method of
interpreting the evidence. This kind of Biblical criticism rejects the interpretation of the story of the youth fleeing naked from the arrest of Christ

a scientific doctrine, such as the circulation of the blood, is based on a true relation between facts, whereas Maurice's theology justifies an arbitrary relation between figments, such critics declare that Stephen is basing his arguments on the rationalist fictions of his time; and that Maurice correctly appreciates that the divine revelation of the truth is not deducible from 'facts,' events or in dogmatic propositions. Here the question must be left. Maurice will appear an inspired—though, possibly, a muffled—voice crying in the wilderness to those who accept an Hegelian theory of history and believe that to interpret a part one must comprehend the whole. Stephen will appear nearer the truth to those who believe that we can never form a true picture of the workings of the whole world, and to those who demand that religion be based on historical fact.

The Broad Churchmen's second contention was that Christianity develops; admitting that the theology of past ages often reflected barbaric morality, they declared that Christianity can evolve into a creed acceptable to the civilised world.* Stephen, following Comte, simply declared that Christianity was a perishing species and could not revive. He met the Broad Churchmen with a declaration of faith when he wrote, 'There is no infallible guide and no complete and definitive system of universal truth; but by such means we can attain enough truth to secure the welfare and progress of the race . . . and throw some light upon the great problem, What is the conception of the universe to which the previous history of inquiry

---

(Mark xiv, 51–2) as evidence that the youth must have been Mark as no one else would have recorded the story; because this is an interpretation purporting to answer the unanswerable question, what happened? Instead we should realise that the story is a tradition of the early Church, interpreting a Messianic pattern of events to illustrate the need for courage in the Day of the Lord. Not, *pace* Strauss, a myth; but a tradition governing the minds of those alive at the time and therefore, since we can interpret history only through the thought of the past, the only certain attainable truth.

* Newman's *Essay on Development* argued from a different premise: Christian dogma does not change but, containing perfect truth, expands to include newly-discovered lesser truth. Milman exposed Newman's book as grossly unhistorical; Stephen pointed out that Newman conveniently abandoned the argument from development directly he observed that the temper of his own age was hostile to Christianity. Instead of concluding that Christianity was ossifying, he declared that the age was sunk in wickedness. G. G. Coulton's most fiery pamphlets were directed against the Catholic assertion that dogma never changes.

shows that men's minds are gradually conforming themselves
as they become more rational?' This implies a doctrine of
progress, and arguments from progress are, alas, deplorably
unsatisfactory; when challenged Stephen had to admit that
if truth accumulated, it was odd that so many truths were
extinguished for several centuries and then reappeared,
possibly to be buried again. Not until old age did he
perceive that religion, whether true or false, has its roots
in society and is not superimposed. In 1900 he wrote,
'Modern evolutionism . . . coincides with the Catholic view
so far as it recognises the social importance of the Churches
. . . and parts company with the old "negative" criticism
which regarded creeds as simply false and churches as
organised impostures.' He came reluctantly to agree that
religion corresponded not simply to men's knowledge but
to the whole impression made on them by the world.

2

Religion is belief: but what is belief?—how and why do
we believe that statements are true or untrue?

These questions were the chief subject of discussion by the
Metaphysical Society to which Stephen was elected in 1877.
He had no high regard for this Society, and thought that
four out of five members had failed to pass the *pons asinorum* of metaphysics. In philosophy, as in religion,
Stephen was something of an agnostic. He was delighted
when Charles Francis Adams, son of the American statesman, quoted with approval his aphorism, 'the grave humor-
ists who call themselves historians of philosophy seem to
be at times under the impression that the development
of the world has been affected by the last new feat of some
great man in the art of logical hair-splitting.' Doctor and
saint might argue 'about it and about,' but metaphysicians
could never disguise the most notorious conjuring trick in
theology whereby God, or the Supreme Power, was identified
with the anthropomorphic God of the Gospels. But Stephen
was forced to debate the question of belief when he turned
to examine the ripest example of the *mens theologica* who
threatened reason more direly even then F. D. Maurice.
Faced with the problem of evil in the world which 'inflicts

upon the mind the sense of a profound mystery, which is absolutely beyond human solution,' John Henry Newman declared that uninstructed reason could never solve the difficulty. Logic by itself will never convince men of the truth of any statement and the reasons for conviction are too subtle and complex to be expressed in syllogisms. Religious truth cannot be expressed in logic. 'Life is not long enough for a religion of inferences, we shall never have done beginning if we determine to begin with proof. Life is for action. If we insist on a proof for everything, we shall never come to action; to act you must assume, and that assumption is faith.' Stephen agreed that Newman shows that we believe countless things on insufficient evidence, but Newman asks us to make not simply an *intellectual* act of belief on the evidence before us, but a *volitional* act; we are guilty of lack of faith if we believe by balancing probabilities. We must believe first—'the logic has been felt before it is proved.' Stephen answers that if you 'allow conviction to be influenced by the will, you must admit that a belief morally right may be intellectually wrong.' Newman has simply produced out of the hat a logical device for calling an unanswerable objection a 'difficulty.' Moreover, though he is always pouring scorn on the Protestant conscience, he is compelled to appeal to it in the end when he claims that in man's conscience resides the Illative Sense or 'sensible intuition.' Between Newman's mind and Stephen's yawned a gulf too wide to bridge. Stephen shows where an empiricist cannot accept Catholic dialectic; and he could hardly be expected to agree that propositions for a Catholic are true only when the Church recognises them as such, or take pleasure in Newman's deliberate scepticism which was designed to show that the dynamic of belief is the act of faith. Truth, argued Stephen, is not absolute but conditioned by each age; and though the methods of rational enquiry supersede each other, each generation ought to accept the best obtainable opinion. No doubt evidence strikes men in different ways and divergence of belief is inevitable. No doubt what passed for scientific exactitudes in the past are now exploded. But this should lead us to deduce, not that conviction is absurd, but that dogma is

absurd and toleration necessary; and we should accept as
sound reasoning only that which is capable of being dis-
proved by the very methods which make up its proof.
Whatever we may think of the truth of religion, there can
be only one arbiter in all disputes: if we abandon reason
we are left at the mercy of prejudice—you may call
prejudice, faith or intuition, as you will.

This is the core of the rationalist case. But is conviction
independent of the will as Stephen suggests? Are we
capable, as Huxley and Clifford aver, of coolly weighing
evidence in an emotional vacuum? William James did not
think so. James gave a turn of the screw to the controversy
about belief which was all the more difficult for Stephen to
endure because James himself was an empiricist. The elder
generation of metaphysicians, such as W. G. Ward, had
played with the concepts of Mind and Will and, though
reinforced by a first-class Idealist, F. H. Bradley—ironically
an agnostic—were still circling round the periphery. If
Tyndall states that Matter contains the promise and
potency of all terrestial life, how, asked Ward, does the will
exist? If Huxley argues that man can change Nature by
exercising his will, how does a non-material concept play
a part in the chain of causation? If Science says that life
cannot be spontaneously generated, how is the will spontaneously generated? Relying on Hume to guard them
against the charge of materialism, admitting that we could
never have a perfect induction, the rationalists replied that
Experience alone gave data from which to draw *firm* conclusions, and that the uniformity of Nature gave us good
reasons for not accepting revelations and miracles. The debate resembled a long-range bombardment in which the
rationalists, well dug-in, were secure and their enemy
supplied with the wrong kind of ammunition. But James's
right-wing empiricism turned the flank of the rationalist
position. James wanted to restore the richness and plenitude
of human experience, and his purpose was to justify our
right to believe. 'Your bogey is superstition,' he wrote to
an English rationalist, 'my bogey is desiccation. . . . In my
essay the evil shape was a vision of "Science" in the form of
abstraction, priggishness and sawdust, lording it over all.

Take the sterilist scientific prig and cad you know, compare
him with the richest religious intellect you know, and you
would not, any more than I would, give the former the
exclusive right of way.' When agnostics thunder that it is
immoral to believe unverifiable statements merely because
they give pleasure, they really want to impose laws based
'on nothing but their natural wish to exclude all elements
for which they, in their professional quality of logicians,
can find no use.' Every man, says James, believes according
to his 'willing nature,' and if it is in your nature to believe
in God, then believe, and realise that your belief is justified.
This does not mean that by believing a thing we make it
true. James tried to formulate rules for belief and one of
them was that in certain cases where belief and doubt are
possible, there is often a greater chance of getting at the
truth by believing. Nor should we be dismayed if truths
conflict. For the agnostic unity of truth, James substituted
relativism and pluralism. The world 'is a sort of republican
banquet . . . where all the qualities of being respect one
another's personal sacredness, yet sit at the common table
of space and time.' God is finite, external to the world's
evil, not an Absolute and part of a monist determined
scheme of things. Just as Pascal, living in a society given to
gaming, so James, living in an age of financial gambling,
employs against the agnostics the image of the wager.*
'It [the rationalist theory of belief] is like those gambling
and insurance rules based on probability, in which we
secure ourselves against losses in detail by hedging on the
total run. But this hedging philosophy requires that the long
run should be there; and this makes it inapplicable to the
question of religious faith as the latter comes home to the
individual man. He plays the game of life not to escape
losses, for he brings nothing with him to lose; he plays it for
gains; and it is now or never with him, for the long run
which exists indeed for humanity, is not there for him. Let
him doubt, believe or deny, he runs his risk and has the
natural right to choose which one it shall be.' To refuse to

* Veblen pointed out that religion and gambling are often associated; he
claimed that officers of the Salvation Army comprised a higher proportion of
men with a sporting record than the proportion of such men to the aggregate
of the community.

bet is in fact to bet—you are betting against the field; and
that is a negative and mean approach to life.

Stephen reviewed *The Will to Believe* in the *Agnostic
Annual* of 1898 and in a letter said of James. 'He is the one
really lively philosopher; but I am afraid that he is trying
the old dodge of twisting "faith" out of moonshine.' He was
then too old to meet the challenge of pragmatism—which
indeed was at that date only partially constructed. Pragmatism is the rebellious child of agnosticism. It accepts the
agnostic premise that we must not be dogmatic about the
unknowable, it too rejects immutable monist religion; but it
turns the premise back on its father by arguing that in many
cases we ought to believe rather than disbelieve in a God.
Why not believe in God?—as a concept it is a deal more
satisfactory than other substitutes. And if the unknowable
paradoxically grows vaster as scientific knowledge increases,
we shall soon be left without any verifiable beliefs (except
the most trivial) if we remain agnostics. Stephen did not
grasp that pragmatism could be met only by re-examining
the nature of such philosophical terms as propositions (which
James calls beliefs) and by asking how the truth of these
propositions related to objective fact—the method by which
Agnosticism's younger son, Logical Positivism, set about
bullying its elder brother. He still hoped, like Comte, that
scientific principles could be discovered and applied to
society.

Stephen's agnosticism incorporated the idea that science
will enlarge the knowable. Yet he realised in his old age
that Mill's expanding corpus of truth built on verifiable
propositions was not materialising. He came to agree with
Sidgwick that the field of empirical enquiry was narrower
than is commonly supposed and that the circle of the knowable was contracting. This systole did not, however,
depress him. Like any good rationalist he replied that there
will always be certain ontological questions which can never
be answered satisfactorily by any mode of thought; but
because they were unanswerable this in no way impugned
the value of reason, even though the rationalist in cap and
gown might not be able to speak so authoritatively. In his
review of James's book Stephen suggested that even if the will

influences our beliefs, it could be courted by good reasons; and those good reasons should convince unless someone could supply better ones. Deprived of his cane by the psycho-analysts and the mathematical physicists, the stern parent to-day puts his trust in persuasion.

3

Many men and women—more than is commonly admitted—are not religious: they require no explanation of order in the universe or the relation of its parts to totality, nor are they perplexed by the mystery behind appearance. Others—Hobbes was one of them—require such an explana-tion but see no necessity to explain the world in terms of the supernatural: they prefer to explain it in terms of itself. Leslie Stephen demonstrated that such people should not be asked any longer to believe in Christianity. He armed unbelief with a short-sword to slash theology and vitalised it as a noble conception of life. He showed that theologians may define faith, but cannot engender or secure it. He may appear to have failed to meet the arguments of the apologists as thoroughly as he should have done, but this is an illusion. True, he assumed that they were all concerned with the problem of belief when their *point d'appui* often lay elsewhere, but he was really refusing to play their game. The Catholic will object that he missed the subtlety and complexity of Newman's argument; but that can be appreciated only if a man is more than half way to believing the argument as a whole. A liberal Protestant will feel that Stephen denied the right of the individual conscience to believe in God; but all that Stephen demanded was for the individual to understand what he was being asked to believe. Non-religious men who required a cosmology were no longer compelled to turn with dissatisfaction to Christianity; other explanations existed, none of them watertight, but at least as valid. Chris-tianity could now be regarded, according to Stephen, as a system of thought which no longer satisfactorily explained how the Spirit was related to the Law, Man to Necessity, and Guilt to Redemption; and Stephen denied that these notions lost their meaning without a theological superstructure. In his vindication of non-belief Stephen stated a truth which believers themselves acknowledge. The profoundest religious minds have recognised how difficult it is for some men to believe in God and His goodness. They themselves have often come to believe only through doubt and despair: Father Zossima has no reproach for Ivan Karamazov because he sees that Ivan, though blessed with a soul capable of suffering, is prevented by the limitations of his mind from knowing himself. Stephen justified before the sight of man the non-religious mind.

It was also his purpose to show that no intelligent being had any right to continue to believe in Christianity; or rather that if a religiously-minded man had doubts, the evidence against the truth of Christianity was so strong that he should abandon it. In this he was less successful. For to persuade such a man, you yourself must understand what religion means to him. This Stephen could not do. Religion may or may not be true but it is a reality: in unemotional language we may say that men experience a variety of pleasurable or painful sensations of great complexity under its influence. And here a confusion in utilitarian psychology put Stephen on the wrong tack. Pleasure and pain are not emotions but qualities which emotions sometimes possess and they are not, as Hume thought, synonymous with approval and disapproval. Thus, if you demonstrate that certain religious beliefs will cause a man pain, he may reply that such pain will give him joy, or he may deny that the emotion can properly be described as painful. The utilitarians never touched more than the surface of pleasure and pain. Strange that dedicated to the principle of basing all their conclusions in human experience, they knew so little of its range and variety. Stranger still that Stephen, who declared that all experience comes within reason's province, should not have realised that he who would discuss religion must investigate it. Such a man may hold that God probably does not exist, but he cannot ignore that men have held various ideas of God and that mystics have described their experience of communion with Him. Stephen could never have written William James's *The Varieties of Religious Experience* because he did not understand the religious mind.

Religion is not simply a corpus of truth whose object is to teach men right conduct in *this* world. To define religion as Belief is to define it narrowly. When Stephen called the doctrine of the Atonement repulsive he saw a clear concept, the theory of penal substitution; he did not see the mystical purification through suffering which Dostoievsky beheld. He lacked the imagination—and indeed for a rationalist it requires imagination—to enter into the state of mind that believes that history is meaningless without the Incarnation and that even a life of sin is meaningless without a celestial Judge and Lover. God, not just as a Father and Friend, but as a Lover, was alien to Stephen. His vision of life, as he often admitted, was terrestrial. He did not see it through the artist's eyes as a vale of mystery, at once splendid, tragic and suffocatingly tedious, nor did he regard it with the curious interest of the humanist who relates knowledge to his own experience to reveal various truths, many of them conflicting and contradictory. This does not impugn his thesis that Christianity is simply untrue; but his criticism would have illuminated depths which remain dark when he shines his light uniformly on the subject, eliminating texture, surface and colour so that we see the object and its outline but not the attributes that give it significance and beauty.

Moreover, Stephen's canon of morality was that of popular Protestantism. He neglected the rich variety of Catholicism and significantly choose to examine, among Catholics, Newman and Pascal, the one an Evangelical convert and the other a Jansenist. Stephen took it for granted that the Christian ideal was that of the virtuous man, obeying God's rules (all of which are totally revealed to man), soberly working in the circle of his family, and directed by his conscience to improve the state of the world. The greatest Catholic moralists, however, continually emphasise that man's corrupt reason cannot understand God's judgment. Reprobates, publicans and harlots may stand less in awe of the Last Trump than their earthly betters who have fallen into the more deadly sins of pride and Pharisaism. To enable men to lead better lives is only one of the objects of Christianity. It demands that men should love God and it acknowledges that there are many gateways into His temple through which men can pass to offer adoration. The offerings of the juggler of Notre-Dame or the Bedford tinker are both acceptable in the sight of God. For Stephen the Catholic Church, though no longer the Scarlet Woman, was nothing but the Father of Lies: not an illuminating judgment. Nor did he consider the Orthodox Church. He would have found its morality more shocking than Catholicism since the prophets of the Eastern Church often deny that right conduct is essential to the love of God: indeed that preoccupation with conduct and 'the Law' may be a positive hindrance. Both Puritan and Orthodox see conviction of sin as essential to salvation; but the former intends that it shall waken man to mend his ways, the latter to a deeper experience of God's love. In the unwritten sequel to *The Brothers Karamazov*, Dostoievsky intended Alyosha to 'sin his way to Jesus.' The Russian mystics demand a change of heart not of habits, and suggest that reiterated sin, in any case inevitable, can be valuable if revulsion from sin awakens the sinful heart to a profounder experience of God's grace. When Stephen followed Harnack and dismissed the experiences of the Eastern mystics as 'spiritual narcotics,' he ignored those saints and poets who proclaim that intensity of experience, rather than harmony of interests, gives meaning to life. This is not to suggest that Stephen should have abandoned his ideal. But to convince other men to abandon theirs one must first understand them. Ignoring the splendours and glories of religion and the infinite variety of ways in which it corresponds to men's needs, his critique was in this respect poverty-stricken.

Yet if we ask what sundered Leslie Stephen most effectually from Christianity, while binding Fitzjames to it, the answer is his rejection of the central Christian doctrine of Original Sin. Fitzjames retained his belief in Original Sin, Leslie became a Pelagian. He regarded man as prone, not bound, to evil, but capable of training himself to lead a better life— material conditions permitting. He did not believe in the Perfectibility of Man, or think that evil was caused by priests and kings, or, like Hardy, by a hostile universe. Nor did he in any way countenance the worship of man and his works like either the Comtists or the Aesthetes. But for him the promise and the potency of life lay in man. Desmond MacCarthy is right to say that Stephen, unlike Clough, never associated religion with emotion, for Stephen never saw any need to touch morality with emotion. The emotion resided in, not outside, morality. When a man sinned he blasphemed not against his Maker but against his fellow-men and himself. To accept the doctrine of Original Sin was to turn one's back on the scientific spirit, which in Mrs. Humphry Ward's view, which was endorsed by Pater, 'is for ever making the visible world fairer and more desirable in mortal eyes,' and ultimately to despair of make a better world; it was to despise reason, art and endeavour as vanities and delusion. Stephen held that until this was recognised, our morality would remain warped.

This belief that Original Sin is a doctrine which tends to lead the best minds to despise man is finely expressed in the most interesting of all his religious essays, his study of Pascal. He felt an affinity with the Puritanism of Port Royal, with a Catholic who drubbed those Jesuits who made reservations about the first great commandment that man must love God with all his heart and with all his might. 'Love Virtue, she alone is free' was a message which a Clapham heart could receive, and he applauded the man who attacked casuistry as a system of morality which divorced human actions from their agents. Above all, alone among the great apologists Pascal meets the agnostic on his own ground. To be convinced by St. Thomas Aquinas, Hooker, Bossuet or Butler, a man must accept their fundamental premises. Pascal goes all the way with the sceptic, and Stephen appreciates in glowing terms his honesty and integrity which led him to frame his great question in the form of a bet. Since man knows nothing and can never know anything not even of God, since his reason is frail and his vaunted successes over nature vanities, he must bet, with the spectre of death before his eyes, on the probability that God exists. If he is wrong he loses nothing, if he is right he wins all. Pascal did not stop there, for he admitted that a man even with this logic before him might remain unable to believe and might doubt whether God would praise him for manufacturing pseudo-belief. He had his

answer: submit yourself to the Church, hear Mass and lose
you soul in Her mysteries. 'Naturellement cela vous fera
croire et vous abêtira.'

Stephen then delivered a fine sermon on man's duties.
'I see that Pascal's morality becomes distorted; that in the
division between grace and nature some innocent and some
admirable qualities have got to the wrong side; that
Pascal becomes a morbid ascetic, torturing himself to death,
hating innocent diversion because it has the great merit of
distracting the mind from melancholy brooding, looking
upon natural passions as simply bad . . . distrusting even
the highest of blessings, love of sisters and friends, because
they take us away from the service of the Being who, after
all, does not require our services; consecrating poverty
instead of trying to suppress it; and finally, renouncing the
intellectual pursuits for which he had the most astonishing
fitness, because geometry had no bearing upon dogmatic
theology. The devotion of a man to an ideal which, however imperfect, is neither base, sensual, nor anti-social,
which implies a passionate devotion to some of the higher
impulses of our nature, has so great a claim upon our
reverence that we can forgive, and even love, Pascal. We
cannot follow him without treason to our highest interests.'
The appeal to the heart and abasement of reason forbids
man to fulfil his duty by finding a means whereby intellectual persuasion may become conviction. Instead of
reconciling the heart and the head Pascal separates them
and calls one error. He leaves 'not a final solution but a
problem: How to form a system which shall throughout be
reasonable and founded upon fact, and yet find due place
and judicious guidance for the higher elements. . . ?'

The Agnostic, then, is not just a negative critic. He has a
positive duty laid upon him. The old synthesis is failing,
the new synthesis must be created. What was the new
conception of life that Leslie Stephen offered?

CHAPTER VII

THE MORAL SOCIETY

LESLIE STEPHEN did not intend to replace one religion by another. The spectacle of Comte's Religion of Humanity warned all but the foolhardy against such reckless ingenuity. Convinced that the mob required a mythology in which philosophical truth was immanent, that "morality-intoxicated man" had invented a theocracy and a theology; opposed to liberalism and democracy, denying the right of individual judgment, Comte (since he was convinced that he had laid the foundations of eternal positive truth) wished a priestly caste to ordain the opinions of mankind. Europe was to be split into small republics, each ruled by a triumvirate of bankers; wealth was to be concentrated into the hands of the few, and the workers guaranteed a minimum wage and a seven-roomed house; priests were to act as industrial relations officers and the recalcitrant quelled by public denunciation. The destinies of the Continent were to be guided by the High Priest of Humanity who, strangely enough, was to be M. Comte. Widowhood was to be perpetual, divorce with one exception impossible, and chastity to be preserved during the first three months of marriage. The calendar was to be recast, each day and month consecrated to a great human benefactor. The Comtist mythology was elaborate and symbolic. The Earth should be regarded as an animated object called *Le Grand Fétiche;* Space, *Le Grand Milieu,* represented Fatality. Womanhood was the source of love; Positivist saints might be worshipped *provided* they were women; and in order to develop compassionate propensities to the full, priests were to be compelled to marry and imbibe (like Bishop Proudie) rich draughts of female affection. Prayer, which was to occupy two hours of every day, did not consist in asking for favours but in effusing or pouring out emotion ('Effuse as much as you like,' commented the Secularist, J. M. Robertson, 'but why call it prayer?'). Sacraments and festivals there were in abundance,

culminating in the last, seven years after death, when the
priest delivered public judgment on the departed who, if
found worthy, might be removed from the public cemetery
to *le bois sacré*; indeed, Comte emphasised that the *Grand-
Être* of Humanity was not the sum of human beings past and
present, but 'only those who are really capable of assimila-
tion, in virtue of a real co-operation on their part in fur-
thering the common good'; faithful animals would join
the Elect before 'human manure.' Aves and Paternosters
would be supplanted by their Positivist equivalents; the
Virgin Mother replaced as an object of adoration by
Mme. Clothilde de Vaux, who was to personify Humanity,
but was neither a virgin nor a mother; the Sign of the Cross
by placing the hand in succession upon the three chief
organs, those of Love, Order and Progress. (Comte was
speaking phrenologically.) 'This *may* be a very appropriate
way of expressing one's devotion to the Great Being,' commented the exasperated Mill, 'but anyone who had appreciated its effect on the profane reader would have thought it
judicious to keep it back till a considerably more advanced
stage in the propagation of the Positive Religion.' But Comte
believed that this stage was at hand. In 1862 he would invite
the vicar-general of the Jesuits to a conference which would
force all those who still believed in God to become Catholics
and the remainder Positivists. The High Priest of Humanity
would touch 60,000 francs a year. . . . Far-reaching in its
philosophic influence, Comtism as a religion appeared
grotesque; and it was not surprising that when Richard
Congreve determined to preach theological Comtism in
1879, more than half of his tiny band of disciples seceded
under Frederic Harrison's leadership.

Nevertheless, most rationalists agreed that religious
emotion was valuable. Tyndall admitted in his Belfast
address that religion and art cannot be banished by science:
'It will be wise to recognise them as the forms of a force,
mischievous if permitted to intrude on the region of objective
knowledge, over which it holds no command, but capable of
adding, in the region of *poetry* and *emotion*, inward complete-
ness and dignity to man.'* (198)

They recognised that such emotion not only enables us

to do unpleasant actions because they are right, but also inspires our delight in art.

Stephen agreed that it was the rationalist's duty to found a religion compatible with all known truth and capable of discharging the emotional function hitherto assigned to churches; by this he meant a religion based on empirical fact. This appears to be the proposal of a mind which does not understand that religion provides an answer to those questions to which no scientifically tested answer can be given; but Stephen really meant that religious emotion can be generated by the complexity of the knowable, i.e. by morality, and need not depend upon the mystery of the unknowable. The tenets of his new faith were simple. Religion is valuable in so far as it teaches good conduct: clear away the dross of superstition, the gold will remain. Good replaces God, Christianity dissolves into Morality, he who loses his faith will find it.

'I now believe in nothing, to put it shortly,' wrote Stephen in 1865, 'but I do not the less believe in morality, etc., etc., I mean to live and die like a gentleman if possible.' Again and again the agnostics protest that a man who abandons Christianity can live a life of the severest rectitude.† Lord Amberley, the father of Bertrand Russell, wrote to Kate Stanley a fortnight before they were married:

For if I fail in love and kindliness, you will not: therefore it shall be mine to elaborate theories in written arguments, but it shall be yours to prove by daily, constant example, that Christian virtues in their purest, their most perfect, form may exist apart from the remotest tincture of Christian dogma. Thus shall we strive to increase the charity of men to each other, and mitigate their bitterness. And we will not demand Toleration only at the hands of our friends

* Compare Tyndall's Belfast Address with Wordsworth's preface to *Lyrical Ballads*. 'The remotest discoveries of the Chemist, the Botanist, or the Mineralogist, will be as proper objects of the Poet's art as any upon which it can be employed, if the time should ever come, when these things shall be familiar to us, and the relations under which they are contemplated by the followers of these respective sciences shall be manifestly and palpably material to us as enjoying and suffering beings.'

† The agnostics were provoked to protest. The Rev. Noah Porter's *Agnosticism: a Doctrine of Despair* is a fair specimen of the kind of dreary abuse they endured: 'Sooner or later this agnostic without hope will become morose and surly, or sensual and self-indulgent,' etc., etc.

but, much more, Justice. They shall do us Justice. Let
them be shocked and pained at first if it must be so . . .
but when the first violence of their surprise or their resentment is over, we will ask them if after all, we are worse
than other men; we will ask them to confess, if not at
once by the force of reason, then later by the force of facts,
that the fruits of the spirit may be granted to those who have
flung off the ancient creeds as chaff, and stand upright,
pure and noble without their aid!
    We will ask them: yes! and they shall confess it!

    Confession would be wrung from a society amazed by the
punctiliousness of the agnostic code. Had not a Cambridge
don said of Sidgwick's resignation from Trinity, 'though we
kept our own fellowships without believing more than he did,
we should have felt that Henry Sidgwick had fallen short if he
had not renounced his'? The fallen children of the Evangelicals kept up the old standards. 'Hell is the only right
name for such places,' said George Eliot visiting the casino
at Homburg and she rejoiced to hear that a young woman
who had staked her fortune on the tables would no longer
be able to indulge her pleasure as next year the place was to
be closed. The agnostic, however, did not lead the good
life for his own self-satisfaction but to benefit society as a
whole. We cannot avoid influencing our fellow-men.
'For good or for evil,' wrote Frederic Harrison, 'the inevitable chain is set in motion. By every word we have
spoken, every act we have done, we have helped to accomplish some decision, to clear a problem, to form a character,
to strengthen or weaken some brother or sister.'* They
lived with the fate of future generations hanging over their
heads. 'How pleasant it would be each day to think,
To-day I have done something to render future generations
more happy,' mused the naturalist Richard Jefferies.
Mallock hit the note in his *New Republic* when he made an
earnest guest say to his host that it was more moral to do good

---

* Mrs. Lynn Linton expressed the same conviction as ever dramatically.
She relates how George Cruikshank told her that she personally was responsible for the drunken men and women in the London streets whom they saw
as they walked home after supper. She protested: 'but he insisted on it,
and hung those ruined souls like infernal bells about my neck, tinkling out my
own damnation, because at supper I had drunk a glass of champagne from
which he had vainly tried to dissuade me!'

for Good's own sake than for God's: selfishness would then
perish and be replaced by altruism. Altruism—the word
which Comte invented—was the final virtue. W. K. Clifford
distinguished altruism sharply from piety. 'It is not doing
good to others as others, but the service of the community by
a member of it, who loses in that service the consciousness
that he is anything different from the community.' 'Your
happiness,' he added, 'is of no use to the community, except in
so far as it tends to make you a more efficient citizen.' They
would conquer in the sign of self-enlightened humanitarianism.

The Agnostics, like the lady, seemed to protest too much
because the simplicity of the Faith was deceptive. The
difficulties inherent in the pursuit of altruism appeared like
ominous tokens when the agnostic faith was related to the
Victorian social ideal. The mid-Victorian prescription for a
sound society differs almost as much from ours as did theirs
from the Elizabethan. The Elizabethans thought that the
commonweal depended on the system of church government; in Stephen's time it depended not on the form in
which God was obeyed and worshipped, but on the moral
health of each individual in society. The individual was an
atom bombinating among other atoms and exerting a force
for good or evil over his fellow-men. Possessing a soul, he
could choose freely between right and wrong, and hence
society could improve only in so far as each member was
regenerated; law, literature, commerce, voluntary societies,
such as churches or trade unions, were judged by the influence they exerted over the individual. Does such and such a
reform promote the virtues of self-help, thrift, family
sanctity; does not the ballot weaken moral courage or a
factory act by compulsion destroy that free moral choice
essential to a healthy society by forcing owners to be good?
Whereas in our time harmony in society is thought to
depend on the nation's economic structure, and reforms to
improve society are measured by the amount they are
supposed to increase the material welfare of the people, in
Stephen's time the cure for social disorder resided in
self-improvement.

What institutions or forms of social control exist to

regenerate man? The Law guards the righteous and
punishes evil-doers; but the Law, alas, hinders self-improvement in that compulsion vitiates moral choice; prohibit
the sale of alcohol and there is no merit in not getting
drunk—did not Archbishop Magee, when asked to sign the
temperance pledge, say that he would rather see England
free than England sober? Not the Law, but the Church,
was held in the first half of the century to be primarily
responsible for the moral education of the community.
Dr. Arnold reasoned that though power resided in the State,
wisdom and enlightenment rested in the Church. The
churches, Anglican and nonconformist alike, were justified
by performing a useful function; and the educated classes
dismissed Benthamite anti-clericalism when daily before
their eyes the churches were working miracles of utility by
instilling the ideals of sobriety, respectability, thrift, and care
for the aged, distressed and oppressed. Kingsley might
protest that religion was being used as opium for the people;
rationalists and Tractarians might denounce as immoral
Paley's definition of virtue, 'the doing good to mankind, in
obedience to the will of God, and for the sake of everlasting
happiness'; but the Church was still regarded, particularly
in the countryside, as the arm of the secular law, and
Christianity (as Bentham recognised) the sanction which
made men righteous. Thus when agnostics welcomed the
collapse of dogmatic religion, they were at once asked what
they intended to put in its place. They had to provide a
buoyant yet carefully articulated moral code in order to
convince the clerisy that national morality would not
immediately disintegrate on abandoning belief in God.
This is why in the second half of the century theists and
agnostics such as Mill, Green, Martineau, Spencer, Bradley,
Huxley and Stephen, turn to the study of ethics in order to
find a sanction to replace heaven and hell.

2

Leslie Stephen thought that the first duty an agnostic
owed to society was to find this sanction and his *Science
of Ethics* grows out of a twenty year old quest to find reasons
why men will wish to be good even when they do not fear an

after-life.* The answer grew clearer in his mind as he
watched other men's attempts.

Leslie's own brother, Fitzjames, attempted to answer the
conundrum. He thought precious little of the agnostic
belief that altruism would replace selfishness and man
would lose himself in working for the community; nor did
he welcome the golden age that was to dawn† and he
satirised this undogmatic religion of sentiment in a now
neglected book, *Liberty, Equality, Fraternity*. No doubt
individual agnostics live pure high-minded lives. But society
cannot exist without a moral law; the essence of a law is
the sanction; and the gushing humanitarianism of the
Comtists has no sanction—not even the last of the Benthamite sanctions, the disapprobation of neighbours.
Remove the Christian sanction, which compels the wicked
to conform, and you are left with nothing but man's naked
selfishness. Since Fitzjames believed in Original Sin, he
declared that to base morality on appeals to man's better
nature was to be sentimentally blind. What was the
principle that in fact governed society? Not freedom as
Mill thought, but coercion; and if we examine society we
shall see that coercion in subtle economic and social forms
does in practice enforce standards of conduct. Mill was

* The mood is reflected in the swollen rhetoric of a minor agnostic, G. R.
Bithell, who reminded his fellow freethinkers of their duty 'to busy themselves
in the observation, colligation and classification of phenomena with the
ultimate aim of discovering the invariable law and order which operates
through the universe of mind, intellect and emotion. If he succeeds all is
well: if he fails wholly or partly he must pay the penalty; and the bitterest
portion of that penalty will sometimes be the reflection that children yet
unborn will be made to suffer for his delinquencies.'

† Fitzjames, even more than Leslie, delighted in the struggle itself which
gave meaning to life. He wrote: 'The *Great Eastern*, or some of her successors,
will perhaps defy the roll of the Atlantic, and cross the seas without allowing
their passengers to feel that they have left the firm land. The voyage from the
cradle to the grave may come to be performed with similar facility. Progress
and science may, perhaps, enable untold millions to live and die without a care,
without a pang, without an anxiety. They will have a pleasant passage, and
plenty of brilliant conversation. They will wonder that men ever believed at
all in clanging fights, and blazing towns, and sinking ships, and praying hands;
and, when they come to the end of their course, they will go their way, and the
place thereof will know them no more. But it seems unlikely that they will have
such a knowledge of the great ocean on which they sail with its storms and
wrecks, its currents and icebergs, its huge waves and mighty winds, as those
who battled with it for years together in the little craft which, if they had few
other merits, brought them who navigated them full into the presence of time
and eternity, their Maker and themselves, and forced them to have some
definite views of their relations to them and to each other.'

wrong in trying to divide actions into 'other-regarding' acts
which affect other people and 'self-regarding' acts which
for practical purposes affect only ourselves, and with which
the State has no right to interfere. Mill had to admit that
since no one lives isolated, practically every action will harm
or benefit someone else: Frederic Harrison was far more
right to emphasise that every action harms or helps a brother
or sister. This is why the State cannot avoid actively
enforcing the moral code. Nevertheless, the State cannot
instil Virtue into men and it would be intolerable if, like
the seventeenth-century Calvinist State, it tried to do so.
Some other exterior mystical force is needed; if Christianity
is dying what can it be?

Fitzjames' scheme to give morality claws and teeth was to
invest the Law with new majesty. The Law of the Prophets
must be replaced by the Law of England; punishment
meted out by the courts must supplant the torments of hell
and be transcendentalised into Social Revenge. The degree
of moral indignation with which society views a particular
crime must determine the punishment, and judgment would
appear as a terrifying visitation of Human Wrath in place
of the Divine Anger by which men were no longer awed.
This doctrine of retributive punishment was taken a step
further in F. H. Bradley's idealist philosophy and became
a mystical conception of the criminal willing his own punishment. Now, this idea is relevant in the world of the individual soul which is the province of the novel; Mihail, who
confesses to Father Zossima that he has murdered the
woman he loved, wills his own punishment; Dinah Morris
tries to induce the same state of mind in Hetty Sorrel;
and Billy Budd's captain is faced with the perfect Hegelian
dilemma. Koestler has argued that one of the objects
of Communist state trials is to convince the prisoner of
his guilt: the old Marxist, Rubashov, finally accepts his
own execution as just. But is this conception relevant to
English law? Perhaps; public indignation has prevented
the abolition of the death penalty for murder, and Fitzjames
understood better than Leslie the social tensions which
generate political emotion and sweep aside the papery plans
of reformers. His argument descends from a distinguished

204 LESLIE STEPHEN CH. VII

lineage, being derived partly from Machiavelli but owing
most to St. Augustine and Hobbes. Man, so the argument runs, is unalterably selfish and his wants conflict
with the desires of other selfish men. He cannot perform
even an unselfish act without retaining a tough little nut of
selfishness within him; for if he were wholly unselfish, he
would be trampled underfoot by the ruthlessness of the rest
of mankind. Thus individual selfish egoisms all war against
each other, and society resembles a carnage of struggle and
competition. Hence the object of government is not to
make men good but to prevent them from doing too much
evil. Fitzjames held that man was a compound of Good-
and-Evil in a Heraclitian world of antinomies; and, therefore, to suppose that appeals to liberty and humanitarianism
would change human nature, was ridiculous. Fitzjames was
enraged by the positivists' ignorance of human nature.
Allegedly scientific, they reeked of superstition. Huxley called
the goddess of Humanity, 'as big a fetish as ever nigger
first made and then worshipped.' Mill, too, had satirised
Comte's religion, but was not Liberty, Fitzjames asked, as
great a fetish as the object of his satire? 'Discussions about
liberty,' wrote Fitzjames, 'are either misleading or idle
unless we know who wants to do what, by what restraint he
is prevented from doing it, and for what reasons it is proposed
to remove that restraint.'* Man must be coerced to show
his better nature and the Agnostics and Comtists—who
were no better than a Ritualistic Social Science organisation
—were wrong to think that freedom would make them
righteous.† To argue that altruism must replace selfishness
was to be absurd as a physicist who argued that the object
of mechanics was to alter the law of gravitation. The

* Fitzjames regarded himself as the true disciple of Bentham and Mill as
an apostate. He was right for the principle of utility is not inconsistent with
Hobbism: the interpretation of what is useful will change with each interpretation of human psychology. Fitzjames takes a gloomy, Mill a bright view
of man the political animal.

† Fitzjames was unjust to the Comtists. Frederic Harrison's *Order and Progress*
(1875) is the one political treatise of the period (other than the works of the
English pre-Marxists) which challenges *laissez-faire* economics and argues
that the duty of the State is to promote a moral society even if this leads to
State interference. 'It was Harrison' wrote Beatrice Webb, 'who first explained to me the economic validity of Trade Unionism and factory legislation;
and taught me to resist the current depreciation of the medieval social
legislation.'

Christian sanctions must, therefore, be preserved as long as possible. Nor was Fitzjames alone in this belief. When the German materialist, Ludwig Büchner, rallied Darwin on his silence about the religious issue, he was shocked to hear his host doubt whether the masses were ripe for atheism.

'My brother is preaching to the world at a great rate,' wrote Leslie Stephen to Holmes in 1873, 'and I regret to say that I don't much approve of some of his sentiments. Oddly enough, he has been, in my opinion, a good deal corrupted by old Carlyle.' Leslie replied with two arguments. To shrug off as immaterial the question of Christianity's truth would not do;* to pay lip-service to an exploded superstition would bring morality into disrepute. This was to argue on the same, and not particularly high, level as his opponents and on the familiar presupposition of the unity of truth. The strength of a society's morality does not depend primarily on the truth of the idiom in which it is expressed. Morality is conditioned by idiom, by traditions such as the Common Law, by stability of class and international relations, by tacit assumptions such as the Victorian harmony of economic interests, and by hosts of other factors. The idiom of 'myth' is more complex than it at first sight appears. Instead of examining these factors, Stephen was apt to go off into agnostic bombast and demand how we could prejudge the future when 'we are only laying the foundations of the temple and know not what will be the glories of the completed edifice.'† His second objection to Fitzjames' solution, however, was more securely grounded on Bentham. To apply Fitzjames' theory of punishment to society, argued Leslie, would be fatal; a retributive criminal code must lend itself to grotesque injustices and pander to the horrible pleasure of enjoying the criminal's sufferings; and though the law might sometimes take account of the criminal's state of mind, it

---

* Writing in the *Saturday Review* eighteen months before the publication of the *Origin of Species*, Fitzjames asked: 'What difference can it make whether millions of years ago our ancestors were semi-rational baboons?' The same facts are always with us: how they came to be with us is another question of minor importance.

† He ought to have quoted Mill's *Speech on Perfectibility* where Mill says that those who speak of perfectibility as a dream are usually those who feel that it would afford them no pleasure if it were realised.

should not attempt to express the judgment of God (or society acting as God) upon the criminal.

Leslie, however, had not countered his brother's main argument that morality would decay if the supernatural Christian sanctions dissolved. Moreover, some who had abandoned Christianity, had not abandoned its sanctions. Henry Sidgwick had resigned from Trinity on the ground that he could no longer call himself an Anglican, but did not become an agnostic. Of all the freethinkers Sidgwick had the most open and distinguished mind. His life was spent, whether in the Society for Psychical Research or in the Metaphysical Society, searching for new evidence that God did or did not exist, and at the end of his life he inclined ever so gently to the view that He did. He irritated the agnostics by constantly seeing both sides of the question. 'Sidgwick,' said Stephen after a meeting of the Metaphysical Society, 'displayed that reflective candour which in him becomes at times a little irritating. A man has no right to be so fair to his opponents. . . .'* Sidgwick read a

* The younger generation of rationalists at the end of the century admired Stephen more than Sidgwick, who seemed to them either to be arguing in circles, or splitting the hairs of the obvious; resenting, perhaps, that the battle had been won before their time, they found Sidgwick's behaviour deplorably genteel. In 1898, Walter Raleigh described Sidgwick's role as that of a referee in the duel fought between Faith and Doubt. 'This combat was prolonged and was neither bloody nor decisive. Indeed, so inconclusive was it, that at times it was impossible to distinguish whether the combatants, inextricably entangled with each other, were exchanging blows, or costumes, or compliments. One reason for the mild character of the fray (which perhaps diminished its interest merely as a spectacle) was no doubt to be found in the extremely weak state of health of both the protagonists. The Faith that fought on the one side reminds one of the faith of a Unitarian acquaintance of mine. "We Unitarians," he said, "believe, as you know, in only one God, and often we have the greatest difficulty in believing even in Him." The Doubt that fought on the other was an equal antagonist. Moreover, so extreme was their respect for each other, that they could hardly be induced to stop shaking hands that the battle might begin. Sidgwick's decision as referee . . . was to this effect: that the duel was to be lamented only if it should prove decisive, that so long as it proved indecisive it must necessarily continue and must necessarily be of the greatest utility, and that in the nature of things it must always be indecisive. Some dissatisfaction arose on this judgment but it was met by Sidgwick with an offer to award the victory to Faith on condition that he should be allowed to define Faith. . . . His actual definition, so far as it can be compounded from his remarks, introduced a new and useful subtlety of qualification. "Faith," he said, "is the quality whereby we should be enabled to believe that which we might know to be untrue, could we know anything to be untrue, which, by the operation of Doubt, we cannot." The most decisive result of the whole affair was the unanimous admiration that was expressed for the skill and impartiality of the referee.'

paper to this society showing that physics and metaphysics were not as distinct as the rationalists imagined; and in an address to the S.P.R. he claimed that 'the whirligig of time brings round (*sic*) his revenges and . . . the new professor is "but old priest writ large" in a brand-new scientific jargon.' Hutton and James Ward, Huxley and Leslie Stephen all grew in their several ways a horny intellectual integument never to be cast; Sidgwick not only believed in following reason, he followed it long after his contemporaries were content to rest on their oars. With Sidgwick a continuous process of reasoning led him to believe that unless God existed, the structure of ethics, as he understood it, was contradictory. He did not conclude, *donc Dieu existe*, but merely stated the dilemma. Briefly Sidgwick thought that there were two conflicting ethical principles: the duty to do good impartially to others and the duty to seek one's own good. Both altruistic and egoistic duties lie unconditionally upon each of us, yet they must conflict because in many cases they will simultaneously dictate different courses of action. How can these two principles be reconciled? We all know, Sidgwick argued, that it is really *better* to work for the good of others. The only inducement to be altruistic is the assurance that happiness sacrificed in this life will be made up to us in the next life; so that in the long run we will not have minimised our egoistic happiness by our altruistic behaviour. The Universe includes, not only this world, but the next, and Sidgwick saw them both as a single ethical system. Thus if God does exist, there appears to be rule in unity itself. If, on the other hand, God does not exist and the soul is not immortal, yet another ontological mystery must be admitted; and we need not be ashamed of this incoherence in ethical thought since scientists themselves have to admit inconsistencies between various scientific principles.

Sidgwick had not solved anything by his first postulate. For even if God exists, it does not alter the fact that the two principles are logically incompatible. To throw in a postulate is to disguise the fact that you have abandoned the search for a coherent ethical system. This, however, was not the marrow of Leslie Stephen's criticism. He

objected not to the logic of Sidgwick's argument but to his
whole approach of ethics. It was the approach of the
academic philosopher.* Stephen thought that abstract ethics
bogged the inquirer in metaphysical difficulties such as free
will; one had only to watch Sidgwick trying and failing
to establish that reasonable and right conduct are identical,
or appealing to his consciousness as the infallible arbiter
that there is a strictly incalculable element in volition, to
realise that we must abandon orthodox philosophy for
another approach. Stephen believed that philosophers for
ever fail to distinguish between the cause for an opinion
which is held by society and the reasons which men give
for holding that opinion. In an ideally perfect intellect
they would be identical; but men, by and large, accept the
moral code of the day and invent reasons for acceptance
afterwards. The moral philosopher must drop what Stephen
loosely called metaphysics—Sidgwick strictly speaking is not
a metaphysician; he must turn sociologist.

Thus Stephen believed that by observing society scientifically and discovering what men do and how they act, the
moral philosopher would appreciate 'the indisputable truth
that mankind is engaged in a perpetual struggle for existence
with the consequent crushing out—as we must try to hope—
of the weakest and the worst.' Purely theoretical reasoning
could not find the sanctions which Fitzjames demanded. We
must make Ethics a science; and we could do this only if we
applied the principle of Evolution to moral problems—since
this would reveal how morality had developed and why its
laws were acknowledged. Academic philosophers should
show that the differences between intuitionists and utilitarians were purely verbal; and then demonstrate that a
Kantian categorical imperative was binding upon every
society and that this law could satisfy the utilitarian principle of the greatest happiness of the greatest number.

Stephen turned to evolutionary ethics because he thought
that there was no need to find a *new* sanction to replace
heaven and hell; the sanction had always been inherent in
the cosmic process.

* Sidgwick continued to lecture at Trinity after resigning his Fellowship
and was eventually elected Professor of Moral Philosophy in 1883, nine years
after the publication of his *Methods of Ethics*.

3

The nineteenth century poets proclaimed that Nature
had thrown off her disguise as the rationally ordered
Newtonian cosmos; to each she stood revealed in a different
light. Wordsworth admitted, and Stephen commended his
admission, that while Nature healed and helped men, evil
as well as good resided within her. Baudelaire went further
and declared that this dualism in Nature was so marked
that different men saw not the same, but different, Natures.

> L'un t'éclaire avec son ardeur,
> L'autre en toi met son deuil, Nature!
> Ce qui dit à l'un: Sépulture!
> Dit à l'autre: Vie et splendeur!

This led others to infer from the portrait of Nature red in
tooth and claw, drawn by the naturalists, and from the
revival of Spinoza, that her processes directly contradicted
the Christian ethic. Newton's physical universe, which had
worked for the benefit of man to the glory of the Deity, now
seemed to be inhabited by an impersonal goddess to whom
human values were meaningless. Nature is dispassionate
and neither sad nor joyful, proclaimed Leconte de Lisle.
If you will visit Nature, forget tears and laughter, empty
your heart of such human emotions as forgiveness and
rancour; only then will you be able to understand her
and *goûter une suprême et morne volupté.*

> Viens! Le soleil te parle en paroles sublimes;
> Dans sa flamme implacable absorbe-toi sans fin;
> Et retourne à pas lents vers les cités infîmes
> Le coeur trempé sept fois dans le néant divin.

Goethe declared that ethical and Natural considerations
are for ever divorced.

> Denn unfuehlend
> Ist die Natur:
> Es leuchtet die Sonne
> Ueber Boes' und Gute,
> Und dem Verbrecher
> Glaenzen, wie dem Besten,
> Der Mond und die Sterne.*

* 'For Nature does not feel: the sun shines upon the good and wicked alike,
and the moon and stars upon the criminal as upon the best of men.'

A few, however, asserted that Nature, so far from being ethically neutral, delighted in her wickedness. Sade's doctrine that evil was the Natural Law was reiterated by Swinburne:

Nature averse to crime? I tell you, nature lives and breathes by it; hungers at all her pores for bloodshed, aches in all her nerves for the help of sin, yearns with all her heart for the furtherance of cruelty. . . . Unnatural is it? Good friend, it is by criminal things and deeds un-natural that nature works and moves and has her being . . . if we would be at one with nature, let us continually do evil with our might.

Philosophers seldom listen to poets. The confusion and alarm among the poets should have stimulated philosophers to consider whether analogies between Nature and ethics, or between Natural Selection and social forces, were in any way apposite; when popular confusion on some issue arises, critical philosophers might be expected to analyse the relevance of the questions that are being asked and shift the controversy into another key. But such was not the case. Yet another instance of the indebtedness of Victorian thinkers to the eighteenth century philosophic tradition is their adherence to their forebears' treatment of evolution. Just as, broadly speaking, Voltaire and Paley took an optimistic, and Dr. Johnson and Butler a pessimistic, view of Nature's processes, so on the one hand Spencer, and on the other Huxley, explained man's relation to Nature in the time-honoured manner. Determined to preserve the unity of truth, they continued to treat all experience in the same terms.

Herbert Spencer is the best known of those evolutionary ethicists who deny that there is a necessary antinomy between natural and social laws. He had defined Evolution as the development of all Being from the homogeneous or less complex to the heterogeneous or more complex. Thus the more highly developed a society became, the more highly civilised would be its moral code and behaviour. Why? Because men, by the same process by which variations in the species are transmitted, unconsciously inherit certain fundamental moral intuitions; provided that man preserves a free society at peace with other societies as his environment.

These intuitions become more highly developed as each generation bequeaths to the next the accumulated experience of what is most useful in producing good. Spencer's ethics depend, therefore, on a theory which orthodox biologists have scouted for many years, namely the inheritance of acquired characteristics. As a corollary to transforming Natural Selection into the Survival of the Fittest, Spencer went on to proclaim that the rule of life was that the weakest went to the wall and that the weakest were the worst—a doctrine which, like Predestination, should be, as the Thirty-Nine Articles say, of 'sweet, pleasant and unspeakable comfort' to those who understand the inevitable and beneficent laws of the Universe. Huxley opposed this theory and attacked Spencer in his Romanes lecture *Evolution and Ethics* (1893) which, he said, was 'really an effort to put the Christian doctrine that Satan is the Prince of this world upon a scientific foundation.' He denied that the Fittest was necessarily the Best. In any case 'social progress means a checking of the cosmic process at every step and the substitution for it of another, which may be called the ethical process: the end of which is not the survival of those who may happen to be the fittest in respect of the whole of the conditions which obtain, but of those who are ethically the best.' We must not imitate but combat the cosmic process. Huxley made an important admission which should have disposed of the matter in the published *Prolegomena* to his essay, namely that there was no real resemblance between human society and the process which adapts living beings to current conditions in the state of nature; but he really remained well satisfied with his exposition. Yet Huxley had not answered the question: is there a moral law in human society which will make men do good even when the sanctions of religion vanish? Of course he announced with his accustomed vigour that there was such a law. He admitted that men of every age and country have lamented that the wicked flourish as the green bay-tree while the righteous beg for bread, but this was an illusion. Science knows that morality is 'a real and living belief in that fixed order of nature which sends social disorganisation upon the track of immorality, as surely as it sends physical diseases

after physical trespasses. And of that firm and lively faith it is
her high mission to be priestess.' 'The gravitation of sin to
sorrow,' he wrote on another occasion, 'is as certain as that
of the Earth to the Sun and more so . . . nay it is before us all
in our own lives, if we had but the eyes to see it.' Huxley's
faith lay in the Immortality of Force and Matter and 'in a
very unmistakable *present* state of rewards and punishments
for all our deeds.' George Eliot echoed him when she
declared, 'I have not observed that beastliness, treachery
and parricide are the direct way to happiness and comfort on
earth.' Such statements betrayed the agnostics' anxiety that
people would not believe that ethics were a substitute for
theology. They betrayed it because these statements were
not part of a reasoned argument but were reasons trotted out
to support an attitude.

Huxley's evolutionary ethics are mentioned by way of
contrast with Stephen's treatise which had been published
twelve years previously. Stephen resembles Spencer, rather
than Huxley, in his attitude, though he has no use for the
Spencerian cosmology. He himself paid homage to Darwin
who, he said, had inspired it. It is, in fact, a by-product
of Comte.

4

The *Science of Ethics* opens by arguing that ethical treatises
such as Sidgwick wrote lead the reader into verbal quag-
mires. We must look beyond verbal philosophy. We must
also look, beyond the individual deified by the utilitarians, to
the community in which we may discover the ethical process
at work. This process works through the race (by race
Stephen meant Caucasian, Negroid, etc., distinguishing
morality, a property of the race, from habit or custom,
properties of the nation), and the race forms a 'social tissue'
through which moral qualities are transmitted. This tissue
is composed of individuals, just as anatomical tissue which
physiologists study is composed of cells. The reproductive
organ in society is the family, and ultimately the family is
the seat of morality because it indoctrinates children with
those qualities that give life to the race. Since the law of
Natural Selection compels mankind to become efficient in

all walks of life, including that of conduct, moral qualities evolve to preserve the individual, the community and the race; the social tissue is constantly being modified by evolution so that its various components may be better adapted to promote the health of the Social Organism. This in fact is the process which inspired those changes in Parliament and the legal system which preserved the vigour of the English Constitution.

Morality, then, is generated by social pressure and keeps the social tissue alive: if it grows faint, the tissue perishes and the race is threatened with extinction. In other words a moral rule states a condition of social welfare. For instance, intemperance can be proved scientifically to produce a state of disease in both the individual and society; thus we can prove that courage, benevolence and, with minor reservations, truthfulness and justice are logical necessities. All are essential conditions of social existence. At this point Stephen marries Darwinism to John Stuart Mill. Utilitarianism possesses 'a core of inexpugnable truth,' for what is social welfare but another name for utility? Certain types of behaviour are dubbed virtuous when they are recognised by society to be useful because they preserve the race. Right and wrong are terms expressing reverence for certain rules that existed long before man developed a true moral sense. Utilitarianism, however, has been till now an ethic of pure expediency in that it denies that evil can 'be objectionable as evil or good desirable as good [because it argues that] we must consider morality as a means to some ulterior end.' In Stephen's ethics conduct, considered as a necessary part of social welfare, becomes more than a matter of expediency: it is a vital principle in the survival of the race. Nevertheless, Stephen adds, reverting to the true faith, though the utilitarians are wrong in explaining goodness solely in terms of happiness, social ethics show that the general happiness of the people is the ultimate standard. Health and happiness coincide—not absolutely of course and therefore all efforts in the manner of Sidgwick to prove virtue and happiness identical resemble attempts to square the circle—but, by and large, the current morality produces happiness.

This is the sanction we seek. There can be no sanction such as Fitzjames or Sidgwick demanded. The moralist can point out what things are beneficial and can explain what virtue and vice are, but he can never give a bad man a reason for being good; he can give only good people reasons for being good. Virtue resides within man; and if a man's nature is corrupt, intrinsic reasons for good conduct do not exist. Belief in God and the fear of hell are not real sanctions, but theological superstructures built upon the hard facts of social ethics. Why do the Churches put it about that drunkards may be damned? Because originally drunkenness was seen to be socially evil. 'The limiting and determining cause of the moral objection to vice is in all cases measured by the perception of the social evils which it causes.' In fact these supernatural sanctions, like hell, have always been avoidable because such imaginary penalties can be warded off by equally imaginary remedies such as prayer, absolution or conversion. Thus there is no ultimate motive for good conduct but that of social welfare. Science itself is not the basis of morality but a method of demonstrating that the only basis is the old basis and that the rules governing human conduct have been and will be always the same.

Stephen was proud of his book which he believed to be his one substantial contribution to thought. It seemed to him to resolve the conflict between intuitional and utilitarian ethics and clear away the logical obstructions impeding ethical studies. Yet the *Science of Ethics* (1882) was a complete failure. Why? The answer is that evolutionary ethics are fraudulent, they solve the main problems by evading them. Ethics tell us what we ought to do, they deal with problems of obligation; evolutionary theories tell us nothing about obligation.* When Stephen argues that altruism is really egoism in disguise—that the transformation of men seeking their own pleasure into men seeking each other's pleasure is not a conscious act but an unconscious process effected by Evolution—he expressly denies that men are ever under an

---

* Stephen, Spencer, Sorley and T. H. Huxley have bred successors in A. G. Keller, C. J. Waddington and Julian Huxley; but the same criticism applies.

obligation to act in a particular way. Why should a man
feel under a moral obligation when Nature is doing the job
for him? Conscience in Stephen's ethics has become, 'the
utterance of the public spirit of the race, ordering us to
obey the primary conditions of its welfare.' The law Do
This has become Be This. Directly one substitutes the
phrase, You Must Do This for You Ought to Do This,
ethics ceases to be ethics. Morality has been gelded and all
its potency removed. Follow Stephen's argument and you
can see that he doubles back on his tracks on the question
of conscience. Right conduct, he says, is dictated by the
conscience and the greatest moral reformers are those whose
consciences will not let them rest. Of course, they are
dissatisfied with the moral code of society because the
majority of mankind prefer peace even at the price of
condoning evil. ' "Be good if you would be happy" seems
to be the verdict even of worldly prudence; but it adds in
an emphatic aside "Be not too good." ' That is why men
who break with the world for the world's good must expect
to suffer pain. But how does Stephen square these platitudes
with his definition of conscience as 'the utterance of the
public spirit of the race'? This, of course, is the very
point where ethics come in; and at this very point Stephen
breaks off.

This is the failing of an amateur who has blundered into a
profession which demands rigorous training. Critical, as
opposed to speculative, philosophy was becoming increas-
ingly a task for the professional, and Stephen was not
sharpening his wits every week on those of other philosophers
as Sidgwick was doing in London and Cambridge. Sidgwick's *Methods of Ethics* was prolix, over-subtle, badly-
organised and lacked the literary charm of Bradley's *Ethical
Studies*; yet it is the finest treatise on moral philosophy of
the age, because Sidgwick by his analysis of logical terms,
and of epistemological and psychological questions shows
the reader what he means and how he infers. Stephen failed
to recognise its importance because he fell into the error
of the amateur in thinking that pre-occupation with problems of logical inference is an exercise in academic logo-
machy and that these problems could be swept away by a

bold approach from another flank.* Stephen believed that
his conclusions derived from scientific premises, but when
we examine how he relates facts to values, the scientific
part of the argument obviously does not affect the conclusions at all. Social Health and Happiness coincide—
but how? Virtue and Happiness though not identical are
complementary—in what way? The 'scientific' parts of the
argument cancel each other out before we get to the point
where ethics begin. When Stephen applies the principle
of Natural Selection to human conduct, he is unaware that
he is faced with a choice: are we to concentrate on the
brutal competition of the process or on the advantages
which society gains from this process of change? When
Stephen says that right and wrong are names given to rules
that existed before man had a moral sense, is he saying that
it is right for a tribe faced with starvation to migrate and
pillage the territory of another tribe? When he says that
moral rules are statements of a condition of social welfare
what does he mean by 'welfare'? Hopeless to enquire—
all the terms are used in just as 'oily and saponaceous' a way
as theological terms are used: one cannot grasp them—
'like an eel they slip through your fingers and straight are
nothing.'† They evade the question why one way of acting
should be considered better than another and how goodness
relates to right conduct. When Stephen says that the moral
code on which social welfare depends changes as society
evolves, he does not tell us why nor how high-minded men are
entitled to break the code in order to make it 'higher.' It
is not evolution which sanctifies our conception of right and
wrong; it is the very reverse—morality gives meaning to

* Stephen believed, for instance, that in his ethical treatise he had shown
that the conflict between intuitionists and utilitarians was unreal; and that
they were reconciled by his acceptance of both the standard of utility and the
principle that virtue resides within a man. Had he considered what questions
the two schools were seeking to answer he would have seen that they were
sharply opposed, since utilitarians (Mill, Sidgwick and later Moore) all believe
that the goodness of a state of affairs is the primary ethical concept and that
rightness of actions is a derivative concept, while religious or Kantian ethics
hold that the rightness and wrongness of actions ('What is it my duty to do?')
is primary.
† This is how Lord Chancellor Westbury described Wilberforce's act of
condemnation of the Privy Council's dismissal of the process for heresy against
Rowland Williams in 1861. The words were a malicious play on Wilberforce's
nickname, Soapy Sam.

such words as 'progress' and 'welfare' and hence to the interpretation given by Stephen to the term 'evolution.' The most devastating criticism of this kind of ethics was made by G. E. Moore in *Principia Ethica* when he showed that the structure of evolutionary ethics is built on the assumption that 'to be more evolved' is synonymous with 'better.' Writing of Spencer, Moore said, '*If* he could establish that amount of pleasure is always in direct proportion to amount of evolution, *and also* that it was plain what conduct was more evolved, [his theory] *would* be a very valuable contribution to the science of Sociology; it would even, if pleasure were the sole good, be a valuable contribution to Ethics.' On examination there is no *logical* connection at all between moral standards and the evolutionary process.*

Stephen's book is, therefore, worthless *as ethics*; it is simply an expression of opinion about a scientific process related to ethics by crude biological analogies. You may prefer T. H. Huxley's theory that it is our duty to combat the cosmic process to Stephen's theory that we ought to go along with it; but your preference will depend on your temperament and the society in which you live—in logic there is not a penny to choose between them for they are of the same class of argument. If then the *Science of Ethics* is not ethics, is there something to be said for it as sociology?

In sociology the book takes its place among the works of the social Darwinists. The Darwinists were one of a number of schools, some of which still flourish to-day, who applied to society by analogy scientific 'laws' borrowed from physics, chemistry or biology and claimed that these laws govern the social sciences. Treating society as an organism which like the species evolves, they purported to have found the laws governing its evolution.† Stephen's attempt to find the

---

* The difference between the new analytical reasoning in philosophy and Stephen's adaptation of natural science to ethics can be seen by comparing *The Science of Ethics* to G. E. Moore's *Principia Ethica* (1903) or better still with Bertrand Russell's lecture delivered in Oxford in 1914 on *The Scientific Method in Philosophy*.

† Bluntschli wedded idealism, Spencer and Bagehot physics, to biology. Gumplowicz, the Austrial sociologist, whose *Der Rassenkampf* was published the year after Stephen's treatise, saw the evolutionary process in terms of war between races, nations and groups. Each saw the new social forms produced

scientific laws governing ethics sprang from his desire to
follow in Mill's footsteps and carry out Hume's behest to
*Attempt to Introduce the Experimental Method of Reasoning into
Moral Subjects* (the sub-title to the *Treatise on Human Nature.*)
But Stephen's book is innocent of any empirical reasoning.
Part of it is concerned with anthropological questions, e.g.
how does a sense of morality arise within the tribe? But
he retains the old utilitarian method of arguing from an
abstract concept called 'Man.' The early anthropologists,
however hasty their generalisations and speculative schemes
might have been, were already beginning to collect specimens
of primitive culture and to argue from facts in the way
Stephen advocated but did not follow. Not being a scientist,
Stephen was not interested in the *mechanism* of change in
biology and therefore neglected this problem in his sociology.
As Sidgwick had said in his review of Stephen's book,
the Natural Selection of social tissue could not really account
for any of the changes that have taken place in civilised
Europe during the past two thousand years.

Comte invented sociology. Weber and Durkheim revo-
lutionised it. They surveyed the new territory, mapped the
boundaries and possibilities, invented the methods of
exploitation, and forged the discipline for future pioneers.
In the light of their work Stephen's sociology looks as
antiquated as a penny-farthing. Stephen was wandering
in the field of what is now called social control. How do
law, custom, religion and moral codes govern men's
actions? How are they modified to fit new patterns of
culture? Are we to regard moral obligation as external and
coercive or as an internal discipline created by society?
Perusal of the work of modern sociologists, such as Gurvich,
will indicate the appalling complexity of analysing the
forms, kinds, agencies and means of social control; and will
show that Stephen had wandered not into a field but into a
forest and had lost himself in the undergrowth on its fringes.

---

by the struggle as something 'higher' and each proclaimed that, for instance, the
best institutions had advantages over bad institutions. As Bagehot said,
'Those nations which are strongest tend to prevail over the others; and in
certain marked pecularities the strongest tend to be the best.' Stephen was
playing this game with ethics in order to show that the highest conduct was
sanctioned by evolution.

To follow his rambles in detail would be pointless, but the circles he describes in one particular maze are of interest. By asserting that truthfulness is good in that it promotes social welfare, he unwittingly raised an army of questions. Is everything 'good' which promotes the welfare of one's own society, as, for instance, economic pressure applied to another society in order to maintain the standard of living in one's own? Who is to decide *at the time* that a particular course of action will promote social welfare, and how are they to decide? Stephen's argument leads straight to the Marxist camp where concepts such as goodness and truthfulness are indeed defined in terms of 'promoting social welfare'; and by this means falsehood can be called truth because 'objectively' it can be said to be promoting social welfare. The whole argument rests on the assumption that men can judge better what tends to the health of the social organism than what tends to a good morality. In fact men's grasp of the principles governing the welfare of their society is far less certain than their grasp of the principles employed to categorise human action as good or bad. Needless to say, Stephen would have been horrified to learn that his argument ran towards these conclusions; but the lesson to be learnt from the *Science of Ethics* is that science and ethics are incompatible ideas.

One last question about the book beckons. What satisfaction did Stephen obtain from evolutionary ethics? But, indeed, we know the answer already. It was in making the social sciences do the work of religion. Evolution replaces God. Evolution is the Creator, Man His child; Evolution is an Immanent God or Process at work within the world. Just as a belief in God comforted Newman and reconciled him to the spectacle of evil in the world, so Stephen is comforted by the belief that morality is created and sanctioned by Evolution. Despite his long explanation that no sanction exists which will compel an evil man to do good, he is at pains to show that the sanction really resides in the development of civilisation, and that evil men and societies perish (go to hell) according to the Law. It is not discreditable to adumbrate a new personal metaphysic to replace Christianity if you consider that the Christian myths and concepts such as Redemption and the Omnipotence of God can no longer retain a hold on the intellect or imagination. Even if it is sensibly objected that the new concepts of Progress and Social Tissue, or the relation of biological to moral development, are not readily intelligible to most men and will hardly serve as 'judicious guidance for the higher elements' in a society recently introduced to compulsory elementary education, still, every man works in practice on some kind of vision of his relation to totality. The great religious questions of man's relation to himself, society and Nature, still remain and cannot be dismissed as semantic problems; and if an individual rejects metaphysics as a hopeless attempt to explain that what is true for one is true for all in all times and places, he is at liberty to propound for himself and for others of similar temperament an impression of his relation to the world. William James propounded such a solution, and other solutions which do not require his finite God can be adduced in the light of the individual's knowledge and experience. Turgenev was honest enough when he said, 'My faith is in civilisation, and I require no further creed.' He acknowledged that this attitude was a faith, and though he did not define it, he knew that it involved him in certain moral and intellectual implications. We should not blame Stephen for seeking, and in his evolutionary ethics finding, comfort. To seek reassurance that the scheme of things is somehow rational and 'makes sense' is common enough among men. Regarded in this way, Predestination can give just such reassurance and we should not be surprised that Jonathan Edwards in the end found it 'infinitely pleasant, bright and sweet.' Some analytic philosophers obtain a similar reassurance when they declare that these unpleasant problems can be spirited away by showing that they arise from confusions in the logic of language. Even historians derive comfort from the study of history by setting the hopes and frustrations of their times in perspective beside those of other civilisations in the past and future.

But Stephen wanted, not only comfort, but also certitude in the realm of the uncertain. And this he had asserted was unobtainable. He breaks faith with himself when he seeks to answer scientifically the very questions which he as an agnostic proclaimed to be unanswerable; unanswerable, that is, in a uniform manner which is to hold good for the whole world. Isaiah Berlin has analysed the fallacies that lie behind a recurrent desire by philosophers to obtain infallible knowledge of incorrigible propositions (e.g. Locke's simple ideas or Mill's sensations or Russell's atomistic use of words)—propositions beyond which it is logically impossible to go and which, they tell us, are the one spring of all knowledge. But Stephen's evolutionary law of morality —though it is born of the same desire for certainty—can hardly be regarded in this light. Stephen desires not just the discovery of a basic proposition on which a science of knowledge can be founded, but a law which will govern the moral relations of the individual to society—and this, Stephen had declared while destroying orthodox metaphysics, could never be found. This desire to find metaphysical sanctions gives Victorian agnosticism the appearance of a new nonconformist sect. The power of religion over the very minds which denied it is nowhere more subtly instanced than in Stephen's evolutionary ethics.

CHAPTER VIII

MORAL AND IMMORAL MAN

MORALITY is like a great river, turbulent, foaming, perilous, invading every aspect of life, unable to be confined within the narrow bounds of ethics; ethics are like a canal, constructed to carry water to the right place. The source of this river, which, as Stephen admitted, is not to be guessed from a study of utilitarian ethics, is the conscience. Since Christians believe that man's sense of right and wrong is awakened only through the grace of God who, unwilling to abandon His children, speaks through their conscience and thus is the author of all good deeds in the world, agnostics must show that morality is made by man who daily but inescapably realises that without morality life would have no meaning. No God need be invented to prove that men have the power to recognise good from evil. Nevertheless, here is a problem: morality is pictured by the ignorant as dry and lifeless, religion as moving and convincing. To dissipate this illusion the agnostic must be a two-faced Janus, capable of peering into the intricacies of motive and character as well as judging and expounding ethics. He must show how every man works in practice on some conception of what is valuable; and he must then show how some conceptions are richer than others and how indeed the joy of living resides in acquiring the richest morality or how in sorrow only the richest morality avails. Leslie Stephen comprehended that this could be not demonstrated by saw and precept; how then could this be done?

Stephen found the answer in biography and fiction. Biography is a way of catching morality as it flies: it deals with real men and dispenses with the fallacious eighteenth-century method of setting up a fictitious 'moral' man, the counterpart of Economic Man. Biography is especially illuminating if the subject be a writer. A man's attitude to life is expressed through his books and a novelist, in particular, peoples a world which he implicitly judges. The

novelist's world may be fictitious but because each individual
is placed in a different moral predicament, the novel
presents far truer situations than those beloved by casuists
in which conduct is depersonalised and reduced to a set
of principles. Whereas casuists forget that merely to discharge duties imposed by a code of behaviour does not make
a man virtuous, the novelist judges a man by his motives
and what may be called his moral aroma; morality does
not consist merely of answering teasers such as whether
it is right to lie in order to save a man's life, but is to be
found in states of mind. It withers if reduced to the re-
iteration of noble principles. Emerson had played this game
for what it was worth and morality had not come to life in
his hands.* Biography and the novel show life in motion,
but they help us to appreciate its significance. Sainte-
Beuve had been content to anatomise the psyche and to
style himself a naturalist of souls, but Stephen did not stop
when his curiosity was satisfied; he proceeded to pass
judgment. Despite temperamental differences Stephen was
a lieutenant in the company of critics of which Matthew
Arnold was the captain: literature was the mirror of men's
attitudes to sorrow, vanity, indolence, poverty and death:
the Bible of morality whose texts must be conned. Men's
attitudes naturally change with the times; but though
Stephen agreed that the impersonal forces of history in
many respects dictate the prevailing moral code and erect
a 'municipal law' for each age, which the critic disregards
at his peril, there exists a 'law of Nature' which embraces
all municipal laws.

   Stephen was thus trying to make our sense of value more
precise and he thought that the interplay of these two laws

   * Stephen had been unimpressed when Lowell took him to see the New
England sage, and years later summing up Emerson's achievements he concluded that it was not enough to find effective utterance for the 'simplest
truths.' 'The difficulty of the task,' Stephen wrote, 'is proverbial. A simple truth
is a very charming thing; but it has an uncomfortable trick of sinking into a
truism. If you try to make it something more it is apt to collide with other
simple truths. . . . Proverbs, says Emerson, are statements of an absolute
truth, and thus the sanctuary of the intuitions. They are, indeed, absolute
statements of truth; and for that reason, as Sancho Panza might have pointed
out, you can always quote a proverb on each side of every alternative. . . .
The region of simple truths would seem to be altogether above the sphere in
which controversy is possible.' Emerson had fallen between two stools: he
had neither excogitated a moral system nor shown morality in action.

and the case-law provided by biography and fiction would provide a standard of reference. The doctrine of the two laws is sensible enough and puts heart into all those who have trudged through the twisting lanes of Marxist ethics by exposing such slogans as 'bourgeois morality.' Relativists, who explain morality solely in terms of municipal laws, fail to show why we use 'good' or 'bad' at all, nor why we often consider actions which break the municipal law to be right. Stephen also used biography and fiction to good advantage setting the writer against his age and his books and allowing all three to illuminate each other. The results of this method of enquiry are interesting: we must first observe the categories into which he divided human beings —and we must be prepared for shocks.

2

The first category which Stephen devised was simple: he divided human beings into men and women. The distinction has a biological justification but is quite fatal to the understanding of character. Men must be manly and women womanly; and the slightest androgynous taint must be condemned or satisfactorily explained. Stephen's ideal man is beset with many temptations, sometimes falling but always painfully drawing himself upward and out of youthful folly, determined that the worst that can befall will not break his spirit. Dr. Johnson and Fielding are men. Trollope was 'as sturdy, wholesome, and kindly a being as could be desired,' and the way he accepted the world, even his appalling schooldays, must be admired, when 'a more sensitive and reflective nature [would have revolted] against morality in general or [met] tyranny by hypocrisy and trickery.' On the other hand, manliness is not a synonym for John Bull, and Stephen twits Hawthorne and Taine for claiming that Englishmen must be hewn into this shape. Hawthorne even fell into the error of suggesting that Nelson was not a typical Englishman. Stephen does not bother to argue the point. No truer Englishman of course ever existed, he 'was of the same breed as Cromwell, though his shoulders were not so broad'; mysteriously Stephen ignores the feminine qualities of this Dostoievskian

admiral. Stephen is quick to note the failure of women
novelists to portray a man. He calls Charlotte Brontë's
Rochester 'a spirited sister of Shirley's,' Paul Emmanuel 'a
true woman, simple, pure, heroic and loving,' George
Eliot's Tito 'thoroughly and to his fingers' ends a woman,'
and Daniel Deronda a creation in whom 'the feminine vein
becomes decidedly the most prominent.' Adam Bede is a
thorough man, yet if he 'had shown less Christian for-
bearance to young Squire Donnithorne, we should have
been more convinced that he was of masculine fibre throughout.' Since Adam knocks the young squire down for
carrying on with Hetty, Stephen's standard of masculinity
was certainly high. Yet though he holds that these blemishes
detract from the novels as works of art they strengthen his
estimate of these women novelists as women. Charlotte
Brontë, though sadly unaware of Rochester's moral failings,
is not to be over-blamed: Rochester is the longing of a
woman for a strong man and her work as a whole shows
that she did not lack 'true purity and moral elevation.'
Though George Eliot possesses a masculine intelligence, she
is a real woman, not that most offensive of all beings a
blue-stocking—a feminine prig: her greatest creative
triumphs are those of suffering women and her favourite
theme is what may be called, 'speaking with proper reserve,'
woman in need of a manly confessor. Women must lean
on men for help, and George Eliot's unmanly cringing from
criticism is pardonable because it proceeds from the desire
to be protected by her husband. The androgynous is nearly
always dangerous: Richardson's garrulousness is feminine
and Cleopatra, so we are told, has 'an abundant share of
the masculine temperament'; Rousseau's longing for
enjoyment is as effeminate as his shrinking from pain;
Mill's morality is vitiated by a feminine tenderness. Is
there not something intrinsically ridiculous in the notion
that Keats was killed by the *Quarterly*? Why should a poet
howl under the lash, and his admirers continue to howl,
merely because the walls of Jericho did not at once fall
down before him? Byron's contempt for Keats's pusillanimity was more to the point than Shelley's 'musical
moan.' If Keats was killed by criticism then the only sane

reaction is pitying contempt. After all, is the universe so
much the worse for it? Can't we 'rub along tolerably
without another volume or two of graceful rhymes'? While
millions are starving in body and soul, we cannot afford
to waste many tears 'because a poet's toes have been
trampled in the crush.' As for those creatures who hover
between the sexes, Stephen averred that (making allowances
for the robuster manners of the eighteenth century) Cobham
had expressed the proper way of treating 'milksops' when
he spat in Hervey's hat.

The opposite of masculine is not feminine but morbid.
Morbidity implies the refusal to be manly or feminine; it
is to permit carnal desire or horror of the world to dominate
and pervert the character. Stephen sometimes seems to
use the word to mean almost any emotion not kept rigidly
in control. 'Pope was amongst the most keenly sensitive of
men. . . . Sensitive, it may be said, is a polite word for
morbid.' One cannot read the *Dunciad* without spasms of
disgust. 'Pope's morbid sensibility perverts his morals till
he accepts the worst of aristocratic prejudices and treats
poverty as in itself criminal.' Swift, a terrible example of
extreme morbidity, committed the treason of cursing his
affections instead of lamenting the injury to them, and was
so tormented by an extreme personal fastidiousness, that he
vented his anger in filthy abuse. Donne, like Swift, wrote
filth from remorse: his love poems exhibit a morbid
tendency. The emotion which inspired *In Memoriam* was,
if not morbid, at least abnormal: the loss of a college friend
should hardly cause such immoderate agony and prolonged
depression. Rousseau has a morbid tendency to introspection and a morbid appetite for happiness. Balzac's
artistry is ruined by his morbid tendencies, by his delight
in horrors on which no healthy imagination would dwell.
What could be more revealing than the behaviour of
Balzac's aristocratic ladies who are first morbidly sentimental about their lovers, and then turn to the saccharine
of religion and retire into convents? If we compare Crabbe
with Balzac, we shall of course agree that the scene of repentance which Crabbe contrives at the end of *The Brothers* is
less true and effective than Balzac's treatment of a similar

scene; but then Crabbe is healthy—there is nothing morbid about *him*. Why in Massinger's plays do we enter an un-natural country where goodness is praised but wholesome commonsense absent? Because Massinger's morality is morbid: it can hardly be said that he helps us to 'recognise more plainly than we are apt to do the surpassing value of manliness, honesty, and pure domestic affection.'

When we find someone of Stephen's brains writing shorthand, we ought to pause and ask what the catch-phrases mean particularly since he himself condemned Arnold's *penchant* for slogans and called those who use such banal words as 'objective,' 'subjective,' 'realist,' 'morbid,' pane-gyrists too lazy to define their terms. We should pause, not only because each age uses certain 'municipal' words (to use Stephen's distinction) which denote approval or dis-approval, but because different ages admire and despise different human attributes. The Victorian biographer examined a man's public life and tended to judge him by the way in which he performed the formal duties owing towards other individuals. A quarter of a century ago a different ideal of behaviour obtained, and a man was required to display the virtues of sensibility, personal affection and even humility; earnestness was condemned because it was thought to prevent a man seeing himself in relation to the world; and what Stephen condemned as androgynous was now a matter for sympathy, and even for admiration. The emphasis fell on the unsocialised response rather than on the more public and formal virtues, and hence words, such as sincerity or integrity, which define traits of character, were reinterpreted; and the re-definition of feminine virtues was even more startling. Modern anthropologists declare that human nature expresses itself not as a constant but a variable: that there are few attributes essentially masculine or feminine; that codes of behaviour differ in a marked manner from one class, religion or nation to another; and that in every cultural pattern an ideal type is implicitly formulated. This should teach us not to make hasty comparative judgments, but to observe what are regarded as norms of behaviour and what values are thought to be most important. Thus, we must first ask what Stephen meant by his terms masculine and morbid.

Stephen's first criterion is sexual purity. Like other Victorian moralists he sees loose-living and lust as the hooks which clutch at man and make him lower than the angels. Man can be saved from himself by woman: feminine innocence will rouse man from sensuality—this is how eternal womanhood, thought Stephen interpreting Goethe literally (and wrongly), will draw man upwards. Because the institutions of marriage and the family will perish, and society with them, unless we eradicate 'brutalising and anti-social instincts,' all social forces must be directed to the inculcation of chastity; and since art is a persuasive force, the artist too must play his part—immoral art can never be justified on aesthetic grounds. 'If a man really has the impudence to say that immorality is right because it is artistic, he is either talking nonsense or proposing as a new law of morals what is too absurd to require confutation,' and the critic is justified in fettling up his whip. Nor can we admit the plea that literature is written for men not children; if a man argues that he cannot write for schoolgirls, we should reply that he is writing for men who have ceased to be manly. Nobody should compose poems for human beasts. 'Prudery is a bad thing; but there is something worse.' Novels should not be tracts, but a ruling thought should run through them which will 'purify and sustain the mind by which it is assimilated, and therefore tend to make society so far healthier and happier.' Sterne's prurience, Fielding's laxness and Restoration drama are censured; Balzac's novels 'breathe an unwholesome atmosphere,' and his cynical assurance that success in marriage depends on the wife coolly practising the arts of keeping a husband is compared to the views of a lad fresh from college. On the contrary, love 'not only affords the discipline by which men obtain the mastery over themselves, but reveals to them the true theory of their relation to the universe.' Stephen's views on sex must be judged, of course, historically as part of the process of debrutalising society which owed so much to the Evangelicals. Because the intellectual has a duty to educate his fellow-men, literature must be regarded partly as a textbook to be censored for use in the schoolroom of society. In these matters Stephen was less puritanical than Morley or Greg and no less severe than Arnold. But Arnold, as Lionel Trilling points out, had faced the problem of how man is to subdue the energetic, self-seeking lusts of the flesh and had realised that for the will to command the flesh to obey 'only irritates opposition in the desires it tries to control.' Self-command is not enough; nor is it sufficient for many men or women to know the reasons for good behaviour; only a *habit* of behaviour, a tradition of conduct, learnt in the family (or through religion) in the last resort will prevent misery. Stephen betrays his ignorance of human beings in failing to recognise that control of sexual passion is a psychological problem.* And why does he not recognise this? Because on the subject of sex he neglects his own critical canon. 'Most critics,' he once wrote, 'prefer simply to shriek, being at any rate safe from the errors of independent judgment.' When Stephen discusses sex he begins to shriek: then he rushes in, fists milling, like a small boy in a temper, and most of his blows go wide.

Stephen's second canon is to divide human beings into those who accept and those who reject life. The distinction can be important, but Stephen is too much the slave of Carlyle's Everlasting Yea and Nay. However, he gave a new twist to Carlyle by dividing moralists into two classes. The first is 'distinguished by its firm grasp of facts' and considers man as a loving, hating, instinctive animal, whose reason provides a mask for his passions, and defines virtue as the course of conduct securing the maximum of pleasure. Fine theories do not govern, but provide masks for, our passions; they are really useful as shock-absorbers when interests conflict. Swift is the prototype of this school, but both Bentham and Byron in their different ways adhere to it. Their strength lies in their grasp of fact, their weakness

---

* Stephen might have checked himself had he remembered his *Phaedrus* in which Plato compares the soul to a team of horses driven by the charioteer of the will, the one white and noble representing man's higher aspirations, and the other horse black and ferocious representing his lower passions; yet he allows that even though the souls of men are taken off their guard by their black horse, they may yet learn from sexual passion the rule of love and honour and grow wings to begin their upward journey to the light. But Stephen had learnt mathematics.

in a tendency to cynicism. The other school 'seeks to deduce
the moral code from eternal truths without seeking for a
groundwork in the facts of experience' and holds that reason
will reveal the laws to which mankind will ultimately
conform. Their apogee is Godwin. 'The great aim of moral
philosophy is . . . to end the divorce between reason and
experience, and to escape from the alternative of dealing
with empty but symmetrical formulae or concrete and
chaotic facts.' Stephen tried to effect this union but he
came down heavily on the side of the first school. Their
protagonists are often cynical and apt to condemn theories
which appeal to man's better nature, but by facing facts
they clear the mind of cant and expose shams. Sham is
born of either sentimental hypocrisy (Sterne) or faking
(Defoe) or deliberate blindness and determination to live
in a private world grotesquely remote from reality (Shelley).
The sincere man will fight for his beliefs. Stephen finds
de Quincey full of 'effeminate prejudices and mere flip-
pancies draped in elaborate rhetoric,' lapped in reactionary
dreams of the sanctity of Church and State, pouring out his
spleen on radicals and the French but quite unwilling to
rouse himself from his opium slumber and write a first-rate
book. 'The foundation of all excellence, artistic or moral,
is a vivid perception of realities and a masculine grasp of
facts.' *Wuthering Heights* is a 'kind of baseless nightmare'
because of Emily Brontë's feeble grasp of external facts,
'which we may read with wonder and with distressing
curiosity, but with even more pain than pleasure or profit.'
Stephen distinguishes between those who teach us to accept
facts and those who sneer at them. La Rochefoucauld merely
concocts smart sayings—'the wisdom which he affects is
very easily learnt'—whereas Johnson or Burke, though
they admit that men are less just than they should be,
because reason has less influence than a young idealist
would wish, declare that men are more generous than the
cynics allow because man's blind instincts are far from
being invariably bad. To belong to the first school of
moralists is not to be a reactionary: the man who accepts
facts can change the world. Are we to bestow the same
praise on men who do good to their fellows as on Shelley

whose poetry 'is not the passionate war-cry of a combatant
in a deadly grapple with the forces of evil, but the wail
of a dreamer who has never troubled himself to translate
the phrases into the language of fact . . . whose wrath is
little more than the futile, though strangely melodious,
crackling of thorns'?

The acceptance of sorrow is the touchstone to character.
Shelley and Byron (whose verse 'resembles too often the
maudlin meditation of a fast young man over his morning's
soda-water') do little more than play with sorrow. 'A true
man ought not to sit down and weep with an exhausted
debauchee. . . . He has to work as long as he has strength;
to work in spite of, even by strength of, sorrow, disappointment, wounded vanity, and blunted sensibilities; and
therefore he must search for some profounder solution for
the dark riddle of life.' This is why Wordsworth is among
the greatest moral teachers for the lesson always on his lips
is how to turn sorrow to account. 'The waste of sorrow,'
wrote Stephen after the death of his first wife, 'is one of the
most lamentable forms of waste. Sorrow too often tends to
produce bitterness or effeminacy of character. . . . [It] is
deteriorating so far as it is selfish. The man who is occupied
with his own selfish interests makes grief an excuse for effeminate indulgence in self-pity. . . . The man who has learnt
habitually to think of himself as part of a greater whole,
whose conduct has been habitually directed to noble ends,
is purified and strengthened by the spiritual convulsion. His
disappointment, or his loss of some beloved object, makes
him more anxious to fix the bases of his happiness widely
and deeply, and to be content with the consciousness of
honest work, instead of looking for what is called success.'
Because he teaches this lesson, Wordsworth is the only
poet who will bear reading in times of distress. Because he
accepts life and seeks to give meaning to as much of it as he
can, he is a sound moralist, and a supreme poet.

3

Such were Leslie Stephen's canons of judgment for
human beings. But he did not apply them like a calculus.
On the contrary, he made percipient qualifications even on

a matter such as family affection: trust in a father, he commented, was an excellent thing in daughters but in Elizabeth Barrett's case it amounted to self-deception. He realised that work or pleasant pastimes were often anodynes for sensitive men. Writing of Johnson he said, 'Conversation was to him not merely a contest, but a means of escape from himself.' He could distinguish between a failing and a vice, and understood that a man's weakness sometimes proceeds from goodness of character. He defined vanity as a craving for sympathy and confidence in the sincerity of one's fellows: it was the inverse side of a man's philosophy of life, the value he set on certain qualities of mind and character which he believes to be his own: most vain men were vain of qualities which they did not possess or possessed in a lower degree than they fancy. He also knew that men deceive themselves unconsciously even in their most obvious frauds. 'When [Coleridge's letters] expound a vast scheme for a *magnum opus*, or one of the various *magna opera* which at any time for thirty years were just ready to issue from the press, as soon as a few pages were transcribed, we perceive, after a moment, that they are not the fictions of the begging-letter writer, but a kind of secretion, spontaneously and unconsciously evolved to pacify the stings of remorse.' This is not only acute but wise. Stephen understood that there are different levels of morality and that he who fails to distinguish between them must always be something of a prig. Sir Charles Grandison reminded him of those 'beefy and corpulent angels whom the contemporary school of painters sometimes portray. No doubt they are angels, for they have wings and are seated in the clouds; but there is nothing ethereal in their whole nature.' Grandison's virtue was trivial because he gave the same weight to every moral decision, whether it was the treatment of his horses or his wife; Stephen's last word on him was: 'It should have been inscribed on his tombstone, "He would not dock his horses' tails." ' Whereas Fielding made us love virtue, Richardson made virtue mean standing out for the higher price. Stephen would not blame a man for pitching his morality in too low a key provided he was convinced that the man knew what he was about. He might

have been expected to approve Johnson's dictum that
Chesterfield taught the morals of a whore and the manners
of a dancing master, but instead he praised Chesterfield
for thinking that morality was a subject for cool enquiry,
for asking what the conditions for success in public life were
and giving a common-sense reply. If, said Stephen, you
demand that everything be always judged in relation to
moral standards, as Carlyle did, you defeat your own end:
the ceaseless pursuit of morality leads to a narrow vision of life
because it omits so much that is essential to full development—and indeed, one might add, to the comprehension
of morality.

Such insight reassures the reader and implies that Stephen
will not take a man at face value. He did not condemn but
pitied Swift because his egoism was neither petty nor vain
and because his philanthropy kept breaking through his
misanthropy. Contemplating Swift he stood in awe before
'the spectacle of a nature of magnificent power struck down,
bruised and crushed under fortune, and yet fronting all
antagonists with increasing pride, and comforting itself
with scorn even when it can no longer injure its adversaries.'
Pope, too, had many faults—he 'did not love good women
as a man of genius ought,' he was the incarnation of the
literary spirit, pock-marked with stinginess and spleen: but
his reason directed his passions to a worthy end, his morality
was one of good sense and his religion inspired by good
motives. Stephen would hardly be likely to find the skinless,
spiteful, quarrelsome, frivolous intriguer, Horace Walpole,
a congenial spirit; yet he took pleasure in exhibiting
Walpole's tolerance, scepticism and shrewdness, appreciated
his hatred of dullards and boors, and placed him above the
mass of commonplace writers by virtue of his literary
power: a man of his sensibilities and acumen had reason to
sneer at the world he lived in. Walpole was more than a
personage, he was an interesting phenomenon:

There is an intermediate class of men who are useful as
sensitive barometers to foretell coming changes of opinion.
Their intellects are mobile if shallow; and perhaps their
want of serious interest in contemporary intellects renders
them more accessible to the earliest symptoms of superficial

shiftings of taste. They are anxious to be at the head of fashions in thought as well as in dress, and pure love of novelty serves to some extent in place of genuine originality. Amongst such men Walpole deserves a high place; and it is not easy to obtain a high place even amongst such men. The people who succeed best at trifles are those who are capable of something better. . . . [Walpole's] peevish anxiety to affect even more frivolity than was really natural to him, has blinded his critics to the real power of a remarkably acute, versatile, and original intellect. We cannot regard him with much respect, and still less with much affection; but the more we examine his work, the more we shall admire his extreme cleverness.

Cleverness! It is not often that we hear this quality praised by Stephen's contemporaries. Stephen practically always overcame any natural repugnance he may have had for certain kinds of mental and moral attributes. C. R. Sanders has pointed out the fascination which Coleridge exercised over Stephen. 'That old sinner S.T.C. . . . forever wasting his time in aimless talk,' muddling his intellect by religion, admiring George Herbert's poetry, 'part of a craze which possessed all his set at that time,' was attacked by Stephen for being a slave to opium, deserting his wife, plagiarism, failing to realise his possibilities, for nebulous thinking, and opposing the eighteenth century spirit of common sense. Yet Sanders underestimates Stephen's effort to make a serious judgment of Coleridge's life and work. Stephen's essay is an excellent example of the art of making reservations without obscuring the centrality of the argument. He ridicules his own utilitarian outlook, deplores attempts to judge Coleridge by rule of thumb, and declines to answer whether the author of the *Ancient Mariner* is entitled to neglect his children and break the Ten Commandments; the only advice Stephen offers about the privilege of genius is, 'Don't be his brother-in-law, or his publisher, or his editor, or anything that is his if you care twopence—it is probably an excessive valuation—for the opinion of posthumous critics.' Stephen praises without reserve Coleridge's recognition that the morality of a poem lies in the total effect of the stimulus to the imagination, and rightly calls him the seminal mind of the age. He asks us to pity the man whose vast promise and power in youth ran all but hopelessly to waste, and to recollect that his nature was kind and generous.

Stephen, then, is magnanimous but he reserves a hell for one type of man. This is the Careless Gallio: the indifferent, easy-going man, who consciously shirks his moral responsibilities. Such a man was Sterne who carefully conveyed the impression that all his faults were due to extreme candour and impulsiveness—a judicious device 'by which a man reconciles himself to some very ugly actions.' Stephen's analysis of Sterne's character examines this device which:

> ... provides by anticipation a complete excuse for thoughtlessness and meanness. If he is accused of being inconstant, he points out the extreme goodness of his impulses; and if the impulses were bad, he argues that at least they did not last very long. He prides himself on his disregard to consequences even when the consequences may be injurious to his friends. His feelings are so genuine for the moment that his conscience is satisfied without his will translating them into action. . . . He can call an adversary a dirty fellow, and is very proud of his generous indiscretion. But he is also capable of gratifying the dirty fellow's vanity by high-flown compliments if he happens to be in the enthusiastic vein; and somehow the providence which watches over the thoughtless is very apt to make his impulses fall in with the dictates of calculated selfishness. He cannot be an accomplished courtier, because he is apt to be found out; but he can crawl and creep for the nonce with anyone. In real life such a man is often as delightful for a short time as he becomes contemptible on a longer acquaintance.

What a searching condemnation of the man who is on the make! On the make, not in a ruthless cold-hearted adamant fashion which by its very precision compels an unwilling tribute to conscious clear-headedness; but on the make in the sense of having it both ways, preening oneself on being an honest carefree fellow, yet always in fact having an eye to the main chance. To Stephen, as to Bloomsbury, being on the make was one of the nastier vices; and according to Stephen, it is often the result of that conscious indifference to morality which is the unforgivable sin. So long as a man has a good heart or a 'firm grasp of facts,' he is redeemable. For instance, a man may be pardoned for breaking a moral law which he refuses to recognise as binding, provided his action proceeded from an open heart; but if he announces that questions of value do not concern him, he is not only a stupid liar—for value is implicit in all our actions and opinions—but a worthless coward in that he has abdicated in the face of the most difficult, but the most meaningful, challenge presented by life.

Yet what of Rousseau who tried to justify his 'hideous avowals of downright depravity' by arguing, 'like all sentimentalists,' that the exaltation of the immediate sensation is to be the rule of life? Stephen was quite incapable of comprehending Rousseau's state of mind, but once again he struggled to be fair and asked in the end a pertinent question: what is the result of abandoning oneself to the satisfaction of the immediate feeling? It meant, in Rousseau's case, the inversion of normal thought. He had to invent a metaphysic which defied common sense by arguing that everything was right in a transcendental sense because everything in an actual sense was wrong. Man is everywhere in chains and the chains make him free. Moreover, abuse of the emotions brings its own reward: we cannot live by feeling alone and if we try to do so, we develop abnormally—the emotions grow malignantly like cancers and emaciate the spirit which nourishes them. Rousseau constantly protests that he is in love; but he is not in love with a beloved object so much as in love with love itself. Here Stephen not only makes a sound judgment on Rousseau but also an act of imaginative insight into the psychology of the promiscuous. He does not begin to appreciate the shades of distinction perceived by the French moralists—for example by Mme. de La Fayette or Constant or Stendhal. But he is aware that the habit of falling in love frequently, with different and everchanging objects, often leads to a preoccupation with the sensation of being in love, which in time becomes more important than the object which provides the sensation: the beloved is a mere excuse for setting in motion a series of complicated feelings—the

enjoyments of these feelings and not of the beloved becomes the end. Though this is not (as Stephen suggested
it was) an invariable concomitant of promiscuity, which can
take various forms not all of them by any means damaging,
Stephen had laid his finger on one of the weakest joints in
the armour of the romantics.

Who then shall be saved? Above all men, thought
Stephen, Dr. Johnson. Johnson who hated cruelty and
injustice as much as anarchy; who despised optimism and
found the world miserable but never whined; who called
ugly things by their right names, attacked the cant of
calling luxury bad or poverty 'want of riches'; who overcame the torments of his youth and the temptations of
Grub Street. Johnson might have rejected life but he
accepted it; no one had a firmer grasp of facts; no one
ever had a more open heart. To dwell on Johnson's manners
or his rudeness is to be trivial—what do they matter beside
his profound goodness of heart? For Johnson was humble—
he did not judge people by their earthly attainments but
loved poor creatures like Levett. Opposed as Stephen was
to Johnson's religion, toryism, method of reasoning, manners
and habits, no man in the past so unreservedly won his
praise and affection.

4

Magnanimous reservations are to be praised; but is there
not latent in these reservations a confusion of thought
ruinous to Stephen's position? His analysis of Swift provides
the clue: Stephen concluded his examination not with a
judgment, but with a picture of his own state of mind: a
state of mind which expressly excluded judgment. The
spectacle of Swift filled him with awe. Swift was set, not
against a moral standard, but in the panorama of mankind.
So also with Gibbon, who appeared to have solved the
problem of living so satisfactorily that his life had an
aesthetic appeal outside the scope of moral judgment—a
thought, Stephen admitted, which undermined the temple
of Morality. So also with Fielding, an especial trial to
Stephen. Fielding not only pitched the average strain of
human motive too low, but came perilously near to saying

that good instincts were everything and that a moral code strangled spontaneity of action: to accept this was to hold that vice was only objectionable when complicated by cruelty or hypocrisy. Should Fielding be condemned? Stephen, who wanted to acquit him, gave it up. 'Really to know the man, we must go to his books.' And to pardon the 'stains' in his books we must go to the man whose life showed his goodness of heart. Stephen was troubled that Fielding's books did not show that vice necessarily leads to moral disintegration: similarly Defoe's crooks 'always speak like steady respectable Englishmen' and never seem to be tortured by remorse. Yet how does Stephen square these criticisms with his dictum, 'Until you admit that human nature is in some sense a contradictory compound, and can take delight in the queer results which grow out of the [antagonisms in a man's nature], you are hardly qualified to be a student of autobiography'? When looking at the *spectacle* of man we 'take delight in queer results.' Exactly. But is this not to award the palm to Sainte-Beuve and to admit that judgment is not necessarily the most important act of the moralist?

Here, then, is a deadly flaw in the scientific demonstration of Moral and Immoral Man. These two ways of observing human beings are to some extent contradictory but Stephen will neither face this contradiction nor attempt to resolve it. He is not merely making a literary judgment on the relation of a novelist to his characters but demanding, like Huxley, in the voice of the preacher rather than the analyst, that vice must be shown to bring its own reward. We become uneasy for fear that, not simply the dichotomy of morbid and masculine, but the whole method of moral analysis is proving unsatisfactory. And this uneasiness deepens into a suspicion that Stephen is not putting the truth first. Tolstoy wrote: 'To tell the truth is a very difficult thing; and young people are rarely capable of it.' One of the reasons why young people find it difficult (as Stephen was never tired of pointing out) is that they belong to Stephen's second class of moralists, so anxious to change the world that they select those arguments which best further their desires. Is not Stephen guilty of the same fault? The champion of the mature man who faces unpalatable facts is too ready to thunder from the pulpit rather than pause to unwind the coiled springs of human action. He suffered from a defect we seldom associate with Victorian scholars, lack of knowledge; and he lacked it because he was afraid to dig for it.* We do not, he argued, study the lives of great men as scientific psychologists but in order to have a vivid presentation of some interesting type of character. In order to have the second one must study in the spirit of the first—or at least become, like Sainte-Beuve, a naturalist of souls. To understand human beings one must mine the depths of personality and see the man first as a unit. And then one must go further and analyse those shifts and changes of the consciousness, which impart different hues to actions which previously had appeared bright, hard and tangible, so that they defy attempts to fit them into an intelligible design. Psycho-analysis, Proust's theme that time makes the stable *ego* unrecognisable, D. H. Lawrence's exploration of the personality, are all instances of the way in which this kind of analysis has become more complex since Stephen wrote. But the point is that he is not prepared to embark on this kind of analysis at all. No wonder; for the deeper one digs, the harder his kind of moral judgment is to make and to regard as an ultimate judgment.

In truth the moralist must cultivate both faculties: the faculty of judging and saying, Here is corruption, here is goodness, and the faculty of analysing and accepting the spectacle which is revealed. He must be a humanist, and a humanist is always being surprised by human beings in the right way—they are always more curious and diverse than he has yet foreseen and his surprise keeps his imagination supple. The moralist who is not a humanist is always being surprised in the wrong way; he finds his moral categories too narrow to contain the variety of experience, he is shocked by what he finds, he makes his moral judgments too early

* This distaste for truth is curiously reflected in an essay in which he considers whether intimate material such as the Browning love-letters should be published; after many pages of argument he comes to no conclusion except to suggest that if a biographer be permitted to see such letters (and it is doubtful whether such permission should necessarily be granted) he should not communicate their contents to the public, but merely use them to formulate his own opinions.

and they petrify. Stephen will not accept the fact of variety. Love for him must be equated with monogamous bliss and when, as in many lives, it appears in the guise of a destroyer he averts his eyes. He will call Angelo in *Measure for Measure* a hypocrite; but Angelo is not a hypocrite but a man suddenly possessed with a desire more powerful than his own will—a wicked desire, no doubt, but which must be understood. Stephen too readily assumes that conduct is the most important moral criterion. He thought the contemplative life incomparably inferior to the life of action, almost an immoral existence;* and yet we know that many of those men and women who are able to infuse others with their sense of values do so, not by their actions or even by persuasion, so much as by a curious faculty of *emanating* goodness and wisdom. Nor does Stephen understand, as a humanist must, the value of temperament. Temperament is the source of *fascination,* and imparts a clarity and force to the personality compelling us to admire the spectacle of the man's character. It can create such a disparity between a man's conduct and what he professes his purpose to be, that his successive actions appear bafflingly contradictory; but it can also give to his actions and utterances qualities, such as spontaneity, which are not susceptible of Stephen's kind of moral analysis. Stephen felt that George Eliot was in error when she allowed the spiritual and idealistic Maggie Tulliver to fall in love with the 'mere hairdresser's block,' Stephen Guest, but whatever may be our criticism of George Eliot's presentation of this situation in the last part of *The Mill on the Floss,* we cannot criticise her on these grounds: girls of Maggie's temperament notoriously fall in love with just such inapposite men. And when one thinks of the Russian novelists one cannot conceive how Stephen would have judged their vision of human beings. What would he have said of a man who sins despite himself or who cannot express himself except through sin—what would he have made of Dmitri Karamazov or of Lermontov's Hero of Our Own Time, Pechorin? Stephen's narrowness was accentuated by his provinciality; of all his

---

* 'To recommend contemplation in preference to action is like preferring sleeping to waking.'

published essays only those on Rousseau and Balzac are about foreigners. This is a failing: the foreign presents new problems of moral interpretation and presents a challenge to the imagination. Not only could he not re-adjust himself to a foreign standard of values, but he could not imagine what it was to lack will-power. Recollect his remark about Angelo; and ask whether Stephen had ever known that order of temptation. His own will was so strong that he could not conceive that some men had better ride out a storm than battle against it. The moralist who is also a humanist must resemble Baudelaire's *hypocrite lecteur— mon semblable—mon frère*.

This lack of imagination is a disease which, as Lionel Trilling has said, is endemic in the liberal mind. The liberal intellectual is always trying to establish principles, lay down rules, make distinctions in which to contain and order the welter of experience. It is a noble endeavour, but because he demands that no set of principles shall ever appear to contradict another set, he soon gets caught and governed by the rules of his own creation. This was what Stephen objected to in his second school of moralists, the Godwins, who force the facts to fit their principles. Yet he himself unwittingly got imprisoned by his categories: his demand to face the facts concealed the important premise that he chose what facts were to be faced. It was this atrophied liberal imagination that D. H. Lawrence, Yeats and E. M. Forster all in their different ways were attacking. It was the hidden assumptions on which the conclusions of such men as Stephen were based which Bernard Shaw exposed when he filed the petition in bankruptcy of the firm of Victorian Rational-Liberalism and asserted that its prospectus, which showed society as a union of individuals evolving towards a higher conception of life and obeying laws framed by middle class moralists, was fraudulent. Shaw urged us to distinguish between men with ideas and impulses and those with habits and principles. What Eric Bentley calls the struggle in his plays between human vitality and artificial system is a demand not to place people in different classes, labelled hero and heroine, thief and coward, and to see reality as a contrast between black and

white, but to see it as all colours of the rainbow and people
as those who have (or have not) so much vitality and variety
that they overflow the beakers into which the social scientists
and categorising moralists would pour them. This inability
to see human beings *in movement,* this failure to appreciate
change, variety, evanescence and contradiction as natural
and healthy is disturbing. Stephen saw people as static
and moulded: his ideal human being, against which he
measured people, was reducible under analysis to a set of
principles. He was too easily perturbed by a man whose
ideas conflicted and whose actions seemed to be inconsistent;
he did not understand that such conflict produces the very
tension in the mind that gives birth to morality. Because his
imagination was deficient, he could not put himself by an
act of intuitive sympathy into the situation of the character
he was judging. Pity commiserates with the common lot
of man and extends sympathy to particular suffering from
a distance: Stephen was often moved to pity. Compassion
enters into the suffering of the afflicted: this Stephen lacked.
He lacked what Hardy called

>   That high compassion which can overbear
>   Reluctance for pure loving kindness sake.

That is why he fails to convince us that the moral life, as he
defines it, is rich and comprehensive enough to satisfy our
demands.

5

The great moralist must be more than a psychologist: he
must also criticise society. Even as he appeals to men
through his knowledge of the human heart to change
themselves, so by observing the workings of the moral code,
the structure of society, and the assumptions which men
commonly make when dealing with social problems, he
must ascertain the disease in society and suggest remedies.
The moralist, it is sometimes said, must be a social engineer.
This is too limited a term in that it suggests that the moralist
must concern himself intimately with the details of political
reform and that reform is the only way to change society.
Henry James and Matthew Arnold suggested no practical

remedies, but both diagnosed the failings of their times; the remedy lay in the removal of the corrupt consciousness in their readers, and in nothing else. Nevertheless, the 'seventies and 'eighties were years in which the prevailing political ethos, the system of duties and privileges on which institutions were built, and the economic structure, were all being criticised by the younger school of liberals, by the Fabians and the imperialists. Alfred Marshall did not abandon the moral sciences for economics by accident; economics became for him the study which bore most obviously on moral problems. T. H. Green realised the necessity to recast political theory in order to justify the new collectivist legislation. Bernard Shaw believed that customary morality was meaningless unless the structure of society was changed; prostitution is an evil, but Mrs. Warren's Profession was only a more dramatic example of the moral situation of the whole working-class who, according to the Fabian doctrine of rent, were paid a bare subsistence allowance and no wage at all.

To these debates Stephen made practically no contribution and his stature as a moralist is by that much the less. His utilitarian and positivist spirit did not permit him to indulge in that kind of social criticism in which Arnold excelled; nor could he be expected at his age to understand Shaw's dazzling antics; but he should have at least noticed T. H. Green's political philosophy. He wrote the three-volume *English Utilitarians* in 1900 as if Green had never lived; yet no other work of political philosophy as important as Green's posthumously published lectures on political obligation had been written by an Englishman during Stephen's maturity, and to ignore it and Marshall's economics was to ignore the main attempts to give liberalism a new ethical foundation. And by a cruel irony the new Liberalism was conceived in the last place where according to Stephen's calculations it should have been born. Green was a pupil of Jowett, and the Balliol men who sat at the feet of Green or Caird or Nettleship, or later Bosanquet, were taught to ask how far the State should help citizens to lead the good life and how far—if at all—they could live morally without acknowledging that they were part of an organism to which they owed allegiance. Perhaps Oxford was not, as Stephen suggested, merely a Bethel in which prophets thundered; perhaps Jowett by his lectures on the *Republic* and his dabbling in Hegel had done something to reduce the sterile insularity of English political theory; perhaps Asquith, Lansdowne, Milner, Curzon, Morant, and Grey, to name only a few, had learnt under Jowett's Mastership to modify the prevailing political ideology and introduce a new spirit into the Civil Service, while other Balliol men learnt a new doctrine of social service from Arnold Toynbee. Stephen lacked the courage to probe beneath the fatty degeneration of classical economics and philosophic radicalism. The addresses delivered to Ethical Societies, which he republished in *Social Rights and Duties*, are sad stuff, partly glosses on his own ethical treatise, and partly restatements of orthodox utilitarianism under such titles as 'Social Equality,' 'Science and Politics,' 'the Morality of Competition,' which contain some sense but mostly wander round the point. His failure was in a special sense the failure of positivism. Convinced that their carefully constructed empirical systems are not only empirical but logically necessary, positivists often cannot bring themselves to criticise what appears to have been proved once and for all: to do so would be to cast doubt on their whole method of thought. 'A study of the good old orthodox system of Political Economy,' Stephen wrote, 'is useful in this sense, even where it is wrong; because at least it does give a system, and therefore forces its opponents to present an alternative system, instead of simply cutting a hole in the shoe where it pinches, or striking out the driving wheel because it happens to creak unpleasantly. And I think so the more because I cannot but observe that whenever a real economic question presents itself, it has to be argued on pretty much the old principles, unless we take the heroic method of discarding argument altogether. I should be the last to deny that the old Political Economy requires careful revision and modification . . . but . . . it does lay down principles which require study and consideration, for the simple reason that they assert the existence of facts which are relevant and important in all the most vitally interesting problems of to-day.' Here positivism is being used as an argument to preserve, instead of change, the *status quo*; and thus Stephen cut himself off from one of the most important branches of ethical speculation. By and large he declined to meddle with the state of society; he would leave it as he found it.

Nevertheless, we ought to distinguish between Stephen's aim and his achievement. His *point d'appui* is unassailable. He understood far better than many modern moralists that the whole question of ethics hinges on the relation of the individual to the moral code. To justify an action is to relate it to an universal principle: the breaking of a promise can be justified only by an appeal to a further principle which is admitted to override the principle that promises should be kept. For Stephen any view of morality was trivial which failed to take into account whether a man had made the world a better or worse place by living in it; in his view the question always turned on the effect which an individual's actions produced on other people and how they related to the moral code of society.

Such a question is rarely asked to-day; it is either shirked or submerged beneath sociological analysis. During the thirty years following Stephen's death, conduct tended more and more to be seen through the eyes of either Mrs. Webb or Mrs. Woolf. Beatrice Webb depersonalised conduct by treating individuals as cogs in a machine hammering out an ideal. Whereas Stephen, in the spirit of the Charity Organisation Society, held that 'the essential condition of all social improvement is not that we should have this or that system of regulations, but that the individual should be manly, self-respecting, doing his duty as well as getting his pay, and deeply convinced that nothing will do any permanent good which does not imply the elevation of the individual in his standards of honesty, independence and good conduct,' the Fabians prided themselves on ignoring 'the poor' and compiling the statistics of poverty and thereby determining the means of eliminating that curse. Conduct for Beatrice Webb came to mean the social behaviour of groups or the degree of self-sacrifice which an individual should make in the service of the community. ('Asquith is deplorably slack, Grey is a mere dilettante, Haldane plays at political intrigue and has no democratic principle, Perks is an unclean beast. . . .'). The girl of Radical nonconformist stock who described in *My Apprenticeship* the moral dilemma in which she found herself living without vocation or creed, and severed by her father's wealth and comfortable upper middle-class milieu from the purposive groups in society; who set out to discover her function in life and the secrets of human nature among her poor dissenting relations in a mill-town; who, like Stephen, thought that the religious faith which gave so many of the poorer classes their sense of honesty, industry and value, was certain to decline and needed to be replaced by some new gospel of conduct—this girl became the woman whose life, despite the triumph at large of Fabianism, was in detail a series of political defeats at the hands of Lloyd George, MacDonald and the rest owing to her lack of knowledge of human nature and the sources of power, and ended with her conversion to the religion of Marxism in which the moral problems which had inspired her to follow her career appeared to be solved by the dehumanised, complex, political organisation of Soviet Russia. And though English Socialism did not follow in her steps, it produced, after the ephemera of guild-socialism and pluralism, no new analysis of the relation of the individual to society such as exercised Mill and Green.

At the other extreme from Beatrice Webb, Virginia Woolf revealed the complexity of the morality of experience —of the moment of apprehension—of the inner life. For her, life was shapeless, baffling and disheartening though redeemed by visions of beauty which appeared to give it meaning—though the meaning was inexpressible. She showed what virtues she admired, but how these virtues related to society, to something larger than the individual consciousness, was an insoluble mystery. Human beings might be united in protesting against poverty or war, but the tone of their protest—a man's active committee-managing benevolence and a woman's pity and love for the destitute—were so hopelessly different in quality that they defied relation. Surely to pontificate about moral codes and social action was impossible. E. M. Forster, a more didactic moralist than Virginia Woolf, saw the world as a vital mess of delusion and affirmation; for him the world of moral principles was less important than the world of personal relations which transcends morality. Here again the world of politics, the structure of society, the code of behaviour seemed to be so amorphous and barbarous, that the moralist was driven to emphasise the claims of the individual upon, rather than the duties he owed to, the community. In terms of social conduct this led to politics, governments and routine behaviour, being regarded as dreary, aimless and stupid to the point of irrationality; and, as Keynes candidly admitted, a view of life which denied that the rightness of actions in any sense depended on their social consequences, and a conception of rationality which denied that quality to the mass of human beings, in the end proved unsatisfactory.*

The dissatisfaction in being unable to visualise man in a moral relationship to society has long haunted the present century. In their different ways D. H. Lawrence and the gentle Lowes Dickinson recognised that man's relationship to society must be redefined; and perhaps Shaw's redefinition was the most œcumenical attempt, though his perversity hid much of the profundity. The tension created by the divorce between ethics and society gave Marxism impetus in the 'thirties, and in the 'forties Sartrian Existentialism—that singular emanation in France of the English nonconformist conscience—was a bizarre attempt to justify the duties to society which are inescapably binding upon individuals, who, whether they like or not, are forced to commit themselves. Thus, he who criticises Stephen's morality should first be sure that he is not standing to one or other side of the problem and interpreting it in terms of Mrs. Webb or Mrs. Woolf. He must stand, as Stephen did, and face it squarely; and if he cannot produce a moral synthesis between man and society superior to that of Stephen, he should at least respect Stephen's attempt and integrity. Stephen's greatest virtue was to recognise that morality does not consist in rules nor moral education in

* Julian Bell's collected papers express the concern of his generation to relate liberalism to society and his dissatisfaction with a morality which omitted what his grandfather considered to be all-important.

precept; but that it is a way of life learnt unconsciously in the family where all that is most valuable in this kind of education is taught. He also held that the only way to justify good conduct was to give good reasons why such conduct was desirable; and that if these reasons failed to convince, appeals to religious or other extra-ethical considerations were not to the point. This blend of a traditional way of behaviour, the knowledge of how to decide certain questions so as to be able to act rightly, with a readiness to submit this way to rational criticism is the hall-mark of a good moralist; he was a man with a conscience, not with something on his conscience; and his own behaviour testified that his morality was integral to his personality and part of a social tradition, and not constructed out of propositions and principles, each one a contradiction of the man who professed them.

CHAPTER IX

LITERARY CRITICISM

In 1937 Desmond MacCarthy delivered the Leslie Stephen lecture, and chose Stephen as the subject. It was the first assessment of any importance which had been made since Maitland's biography and, though appreciative of Stephen's qualities, MacCarthy characterised Stephen as the least aesthetic of noteworthy critics, in that he discoursed more on human nature and morals than on art, and declared that he was hamstrung by a puritanism which made him demand that an author must show that he 'has been moved himself' before the reader can respond wholeheartedly; no marvel then that he was blind to the peculiar delight in reading Sterne which is evoked by Sterne's 'elegant ambiguity' towards emotion, 'a state of mind (Shandyism) in which we enjoy together the pleasures of extravagant sensibility, and a feeling that nothing much matters.' Moreover, happy as many of Stephen's observations were, he could not record a thrill or communicate any emotion he had derived from literature. Despite his efforts to be dispassionate and his hatred of loose enthusiasm, he was so swayed by his reverence for certain qualities, such as those of domestic affection, that the equilibrium of his criticism was upset. This, in effect, led Stephen 'in whom the exercise of the intellect was a passion' to make judgments which amounted to little more than saying 'Be good, sweet maid, and let who will be clever.'

Two years later a critic of a very different school, Q. D. Leavis, replied. She stigmatised MacCarthy's praise as an insult to Stephen's memory and declared that what Mac-Carthy condemned as critical defects were really virtues. Stephen was to be praised for not recording thrills, for despising aesthetic criticism and for believing that criticism was 'a process of the intelligence.' He was also to be praised for thinking like Henry James that the value of a work of art depends on the quality of the writer's make-up. 'Art is not immoral,' Q. D. Leavis commented, 'and everything is not as valuable as everything else.' Stephen's contempt for eulogy was to be commended and his belief in reason led him to the sound conclusion that poets who preached should have a sound philosophy. She described MacCarthy's lecture as 'an insolent performance' and claimed that if the study of humanities at Cambridge 'has any justification for existing it is in standing in the eyes of the great world— as it does—for a critical position descended from Leslie Stephen and antagonistic to Mr. MacCarthy.'

Some scholars still nurture within their breasts the belief that virulence is the surest way of bringing opponents to their senses. Possibly; but Q. D. Leavis' article has the merit of starkly revealing the main controversy in English criticism. MacCarthy believes that Stephen's analyses of novels and novelists do not tell us the real reasons why a work of fiction is good or bad 'any more than a naturalist's description of a beast necessarily throws light on its value to man'; and Q. D. Leavis replies that, on the contrary, Stephen is able to tell us precisely that, because he appeals to a 'serious' view of life and attends to the writer's idiom and technical devices instead of attempting to find some aesthetic theory to justify his taste. In other words, what is the critic's function and how should he judge a work of art? Such a question rarely concerns French critics who have inherited a critical tradition; and in Germany literature is customarily interpreted by such critics as Gundolf or Strich in terms of a complex philosophic structure built upon Hegel or Nietzsche or Marx. In England, however, where literary criticism has only recently been acknowledged as much more than an agreeable pastime, the fundamental questions of value and function are still matters for debate.

Listening to the voices of the English critics there rises in the mind's eye the spectacle of a Chamber of Deputies, semicircular and heated, with Apollo, by now weary and aged in the president's chair, vainly tinkling a bell to restore order. At first sight no clean alignment of parties is visible since Dr. Johnson or Coleridge are liable to speak from any part of the Chamber depending on the motion at issue. But when the motion of the critic's function is put, something near to a division can be observed. At the end of the benches on one side, the Romantic critics, Hazlitt and Swinburne, rise and gesticulate exuberantly; but no one pays much attention to them now. Near to them, however, is a solid block of critics among whom we can recognise Desmond MacCarthy and the Bloomsbury circle. They speak in a most cultivated and entertaining manner to the following effect: Most of us, says their spokesman, are journalists or lecturers who prefer to express our views through the medium of the essay and regard literary criticism as the by-product of other work. We are men of the world living in London and can claim at least to be urbane, (Matthew Arnold shakes his head), and not to make our judgments solely in the study. We set life against letters. (Here Dr. Johnson, sitting on the other side of the Chamber, nods vigorously and interjects, 'What should books teach but a knowledge of life?') Some of us are artists and criticise from a first-hand experience of the mystery of creation. Though we speak as a bloc we are, of course, creatures of diverse views and, recognising this to be so, we appeal to the great Romantic principle of Diversity. Perhaps the Lamb-Swinburne faction has brought this principle into disrepute but, stated soberly, it amounts to this. No critic can be infallible or impartial: his judgments proceed from a personal vision of artistic and moral excellence. Why, then, spin webs of orthodoxy, why lay down elaborate critical canons? All efforts to establish one's own views as orthodox are a vanity. If this is true of the critic, how much more so is it true of the artist! His works are the unique children of an unique imagination and experience. The fascination of literature, in fact, lies in its astonishing variety. What is the use, asks Strachey, of complaining that Racine is less great than Shakespeare when he worked in a different medium and was descended from a different artistic tradition? Should it not be realised, says Forster, that novelists cannot be fitted into simple categories? Is not every work of art, pleads Virginia Woolf, born of an original imagination and ought not the critic to concern himself with the creative act, the birth-pangs, the struggle of the artist to solve certain technical problems? The critic's

duty is to communicate to the reader the particular vision
of the artist, not to award good and bad conduct marks. 'It
is the critic's business,' says Raymond Mortimer, a pupil
of MacCarthy, 'to discover and expose the merits and
defects of a work; but after this analytic process he must
remember that the work itself is a synthesis, in which the
defects are frequently inseparable from the merits.' The
value of a work depends on the intensity of the artist's
experience and on the quality of the language by which he
communicates his experience. Thus, when asked what the
function of criticism is, the answer is simple. It is to enable
the reader to enjoy literature, to encourage him to read and
realise that to miss reading Homer, or Blake, or Proust, is
to miss an emotional experience and the chance of understanding a peculiarly vital way of regarding life. Criticism
is the homage paid to creators by the uncreative. What can
it be but a branch of *belles-lettres*, an illumination of art by a
civilised mind—civilised having already been defined by
Clive Bell—a mind cultivated by reading the literature of
many countries for many years and thus entitled to invite,
but no more than invite, the reader to accept certain
conclusions?

At this point from the other side of the Chamber Matthew
Arnold spoke. I have always, he began, lamented the
absence of an Academy in England; and to show the state
of mind an Academy could inculcate, permit me to quote
Sainte-Beuve: 'In France the first consideration for us is
not whether we are amused and pleased by a work of art or
mind, nor is it whether we are touched by it. What we seek
above all to learn is, whether *we were right* in being amused
with it, and in applauding it, and in being moved by it.' I,
alas, was too little of an Academician and I am told that the
critical terminology I used was deplorably vague. I looked
to T. S. Eliot, who also turned to a French critic for a
pièce justificative and quoted Remy de Gourmont at the
beginning of *The Sacred Wood*: '*Ériger en lois ses impressions
personnelles, c'est le grand effort d'un homme s'il est sincère*'; and
he has carried the process of making critical judgments a
stage further by demanding that personal perceptions must
be modified by viewing them in the light of the Catholic

tradition of Western Europe. But he speaks not as the
president of an Academy but as a poet whose criticism is
written partly in the service of his poetry. His authority is
derived not from his critical method, but from his distinction
of mind, his rejection of argument by persuasion in favour of
argument by assertion, and from his theological compass
which gives him certainty of direction. As for I. A. Richards,
he indeed tried to sharpen criticism by introducing logic
and psychology as techniques in constructing a theory of
value; and in the universities they now analyse literature
in terms of texture, pattern, symbolism and ambiguity.
But he fell short of my ideal and renounced his quest for a
theory of value in *Practical Criticism.** Where then is my
Academy? Not among the academicians in the universities
the majority of whom I note with regret, but hardly with
surprise, sit on the other side of the Chamber—though, to
be sure, they edge as close as possible to the middle. Why
is no discipline admitted in criticism such as exists in other
fields of learning? Why is no corpus of doctrine accepted
against which newly-propounded judgments are set?

Here the editors of *Scrutiny*, F. R. and Q. D. Leavis, rose
and informed Arnold that in their periodical his ideal of
an Academy of criticism had been realised. For in *Scrutiny*,
literary criticism had been treated as a corpus of doctrine
wherein the rulers of the Academy determined the relative
value of poets and novelists and laid down the correct
approach to literature, while the disciples were encouraged
to elaborate techniques and amplify their masters' conclusions. An attitude of mind was proposed, a critical
language adumbrated, techniques were carefully elaborated,
and all analysis designed to establish once and for all
what works and which authors were significant, important
and valuable; how they related to each other and took

* Richards concluded his analysis of the foundations of aesthetics, communication and value by writing in 1929: '*Critical* certainties, convictions as to the
value, and kinds of value, of kinds of poetry, might safely and with advantage
decay, provided that there remained a firm sense of the importance of the
critical act of choice, its difficulty, and the supreme exercise of all our faculties
that it imposes'; and he added: 'The lesson of all criticism is that we have
nothing to rely upon in making our choices but ourselves. The lesson of good
poetry seems to be that, when we have understood it, in the degree in which
we can order ourselves, we need nothing more.'

their place, not in a system determined by abstract considerations, but in an organisation in which everything was 'placed.' Thus, though a writer's reputation might be revalued or adjustments made in the Hall of Fame, a hierarchy of merit was erected and the paths by which criticism might develop were meticulously mapped. Criticism was held to be useless unless judicial, elegant writing condemned as 'substitute-creation' and the tradition of *belles-lettres* as trivial and foetid; much that passed for criticism was shown, after the fashion of Eliot, not to be criticism; and a distinction was drawn between criticism and other literary studies, such as the examination of the sociological content of literature, which, though approved, were not primarily concerned with establishing judgments of value. The test of value lay partly in the craftsmanship of the writer; but ultimately it depended on the moral content of the work of art and the 'seriousness' of the writer's imagination.* Criticism, then, was not a pastime but a task of supreme difficulty and importance which could not be handled by anyone who had not served an apprenticeship in the Academy. The Deputies were also informed by a clerk that this kind of criticism had taken root in American universities, where the emphasis on method and approach chimed harmoniously with the German academic tradition imported during the nineteenth century, and was displacing the traditional method of treating literature solely as a field for scholarly research into its history and origins. For though this criticism did not purport to be scientific and scorned Aristotelian categories, it was in Mill's sense positivist and looked to the time when this 'important branch of human affairs will be [no] longer abandoned to empiricism . . . [and can only] receive further enlargement by perpetual expansion from within.'

All this time Leslie Stephen sat in perplexity next Arnold but occasionally moved to the other side of the Chamber.

---

* Eliot also used the word 'serious' when he pronounced Villon's *Testament* to be more serious than *In Memoriam* and (singular judgment!) *Amos Barton* than *The Mill on the Floss*. But whereas in *Scrutiny* seriousness appears to mean a profound concern with moral problems, in Eliot it means the possession of a citadel of belief from which to set off perceptions to advantage—the profoundest kind of belief being assumed to be Catholicism.

He heard Q. D. Leavis claim him as a forerunner. A forerunner only. 'We were grateful to Leslie Stephen not so much for what he wrote—though that was considerable —as for what he stood for, implied and pointed to.' This suggested that he was cast for the role of John the Baptist; and since Advent Sunday is not Christmas Day, some critics thought that he might more properly sit near his daughter among the *belles-lettres* critics. Should the critic *ultimately* elucidate works of art and praise each writer who succeeds in his object, however slight that object might be? Or sickened by the vagaries of personal taste, should he set each writer's individual vision of life against an all-comprehensive vision of moral excellence and range artists in merit round a throne in a heaven, built (according to the opponents of this method) to his own design? How important is it to show that certain works are less good than others? And if we are to judge works through moral vision, is it possible to make that vision so commanding and inclusive that 'under that Almighty Fin, the littlest fish may enter in'? The difficulty in answering these questions made Stephen and many other critics hover uneasily between the two camps. Quoting Gide's observation that in French literature we hear a perpetual dialogue between 'the ancient tradition, the submission to recognised authorities, and free thought, the spirit of doubt. . . .' Martin Turnell observes that this dichotomy has forced French writers to choose between two dogmatic positions which distorts their values; and similarly English critics, Stephen among them, often suffer by believing that they must take sides. How, then, does Stephen conduct himself in this debate? What were his criteria?

2

Stephen was Arnold's disciple. Like Arnold he conceived the critic's role to be that of a judge. Like Arnold, he judged a work of art by the moral content and approved his master's dictum that literature was a criticism of life. Like Arnold he declared the highest poetry to be written in the grand style on lofty themes. He, too, deplored the anarchy of contemporary criticism; according to Stephen critics lashed themselves into fits of rhetoric, or swallowed authors whole, or, like Hazlitt, made judgments determined by their own whims or resembled liberal theologians in that they were for ever defending the latest aesthetic doctrine. Stephen appreciated that Arnold had taken judicial criticism a stage further than Johnson who, in Stephen's opinion, considered merely whether an author 'had infringed or conformed to the established rules and passed sentence accordingly'; and though Stephen was irritated by Arnold's use of catchphrases, he apologised for failing to take him as seriously as he deserved and added that Arnold's criticism would have to be taken into account by every man 'who believes in the importance of really civilising the coming world.' Arnold was beyond question the greater critic. His vision is more commanding and sweeping, his ability to focus on a minute point more impressive, his judgments more authoritative. With Stephen the reader's eye is too often taken off the work of art by the shift in emphasis from the work to the author's life and the relation of both to his times. Moreover, a great critic should move with ease between prose and poetry: Stephen rarely criticised poetry and when he did he left off where he should have begun. Nevertheless, Stephen did for English fiction what Arnold had tried to do for poetry: he analysed each author and introduced order into the chaos of opinion about the novel. That was a sufficient task.

At first sight Stephen appears to belong to the classic English tradition of *belles-lettres*. He wrote essays for the *Cornhill* and other periodicals which were later published as books. Yet throughout these books, and more particularly in an article entitled 'Thoughts on Criticism by a Critic,' he was pre-occupied by problems of method. He was not satisfied merely to give another opinion or to play the game according to the old rules. No more than Arnold did he think out a theory of criticism, a consistent statement of principles, and his work suffered by containing notions, reflections, half-conceived plans and unrelated *obiter dicta* which fall short of that architectonic of judgment which a great critic should possess. But he wished to dispel the confusions in contemporary criticism by treating literature in the positivist spirit which he had learnt from Mill. Mill was the second source of Stephen's literary criticism: the Mill who had written so perceptively about Wordsworth and Coleridge, and who was for ever trying in one field of thought or another to divert the course of the river of Imagination so that it might fertilise the desiccated plains of Utilitarianism. Mill taught Stephen that a disciplined analytical intelligence can operate profitably upon literature and that the true positivist is not a crude lout wielding an axe of chop-logic. Mill's attempt to combine the methods of Coleridge and Bentham, to which Stephen paid attention in the third volume of the *English Utilitarians*, taught Stephen how to employ the analytic scientific approach on material in which imagination and intelligence are blended in different proportions from those found in the philosophical works which he dissected so masterfully.

Thus when Stephen wished to define the first quality which a critic should possess, namely the scientific approach, he qualified the word 'scientific.' The critic must first acquire an Arnoldian calm of mind and 'before abandoning himself to the oratorical impulse, should endeavour to classify the phenomena with which he is dealing as calmly as if he were ticketing a fossil in a museum. The most glowing eulogy, the most bitter denunciation, have their proper place; but they belong to the art of persuasion, and form no part of scientific method.' He might be led to an author by sympathy or enthusiasm, but when he sought to justify his emotions he should rid himself of personal bias and become an independent spectator. Ticketing a fossil, however, Stephen bafflingly announced, did not mean giving it a ticket. 'Nothing is easier than to put the proper label on a poet—to call him "romantic" or "classical" and so forth; and then, if he has a predecessor of like principles, to explain him by the likeness, and if he represents a change of principles, to make the change explain itself by calling it a reaction. The method is delightfully simple, and I can use the words as easily as my neighbours. The only thing I find difficult is to look wise when I use them, or to fancy that I give an explanation because I have adopted a classification.' Stephen also condemned aesthetic labels

which consisted in using 'such terms of art as "supreme,"
"gracious," "tender," "bitter," and "subtle."' Criticism
could never be an exact science and Stephen gave another
indication that literary laws are flexible and delicate when
he wrote: 'I do not accept with satisfaction the apparently
implied doctrine that poets can be satisfactorily arranged in
order of merit. We cannot give so many marks for style
and so many for pathos or descriptive power.' Tennyson
and Browning could both be admitted to be excellent
without enquiring which was absolutely the better nor was
it profitable to compare Charlotte Brontë with Jane Austen.
By this he meant that direct comparison between opposed
sensibilities was worthless, not that comparison itself was
harmful. Before valuable comparisons could be made,
analysis of the author and his works was essential. Indeed
comparison, analysis and other critical processes were useful
only in so far as they led to the goal of criticism: judgment.

If ever criticism was to be rescued from the wilderness of
personal taste, judgment must be the critic's right true end.
'To admit that all tastes are equally good is to fall into an
aesthetic scepticism as erroneous as the philosophical
scepticism which should make morality or political principles matters of arbitrary convention. . . .' Despite our
ignorance of the taste of posterity the critic should always
try to give a 'strong presumption as to that definitive verdict
which can only be passed by posterity.' By pronouncing
judgment the critic was helping to construct a body of
doctrine analogous to case-law which would enable future
critics to return a truer verdict upon a writer—though
unfortunately the rarity of good critics and their conflicting judgments made general rules difficult to devise.
Critics might blunder, but if they proceeded in a scientific
spirit, their blunders might form 'landmarks for the future,
and not be simple exhibitions of profitless folly and prejudice.' Johnson's attack on *Lycidas* was outrageous yet much
of it was undeniably true, and honest stupidity was far
better than second-rate insincerity. 'I should welcome a
good assault upon Shakespeare which was not prompted by a
love of singularity.' Stephen followed up this plea again
with a qualification. Tradition, in the Arnoldian sense,

counted for much and must be respected. Nor should a
writer be condemned to the gallows for a misdemeanour:
that would be 'to break a painted window in anxiety to
smash the insect which is crawling over it.' Judgment
did not entail hasty condemnation. Nevertheless, Stephen
emphasised, judgment was integral, and not hostile, to the
liberal spirit. The liberal insisted that opinions must not be
advanced by unworthy methods: not that all opinions were
equally valuable. This tenet of Stephen's faith has been
echoed by Lionel Trilling in his appraisal of E. M. Forster's
literary criticism, in which Trilling laments the absence of
this very determination to conquer by the intellect a province
which for so long has been subject to the vagaries of taste.
According to Trilling, Forster's refusal to make impressive
judgments springs from the wrong kind of liberalism,
'which seems to carry itself to the extreme of anarchy, a
liberalism shot through with a sentimentally-literal Christian
morality. It is *laissez-faire* to the ultimate ... a contradiction
of the Western tradition of intellect which believes that by
making decisions, by choosing precisely, by evaluating
correctly it can solve all difficulties.' To refuse to use the
will to solve problems is to shirk the responsibility that is
borne by every man of intellect and courage. Do we not,
Trilling asks, enjoy a greater intellectual pleasure in Eliot's
dialectic and in the effort to dignify the profession of criticism? Does not this approach bestow a new importance
on works of art, a niche in the history of human endeavour?

Trilling would presumably find this quality in Stephen,
who not only made judgments but continually tried to
make critical terms more precise. He was dissatisfied with
critics who imagined that they had added to knowledge by
praising a novel for being 'so like life,' or a novelist for his
'understanding of the human heart.' Stephen took these
phrases and tried to explain what they meant. Moreover,
when Stephen analysed a work of art, he asked questions
about the subject itself. Both Stephen and Pater wrote
essays on Sir Thomas Browne; but whereas Stephen looked
at the man and his work and wrote about Browne, Pater
wrote about—Pater. The question Stephen invariably
asked was: what judgment ought we to make on this

writer? Thus his criticism of the novel was analytical rather than appreciative: he accepted without argument that the reader enjoyed Defoe, Richardson, Trollope and the rest, but asked why some authors were on reflection less satisfying than others—why after enjoying part of *The Mill on the Floss* the reader was disappointed with the end. Stephen was not concerned with what a novel was 'about' nor did he discover the hidden meaning in order to reconcile the reader to its flaws or apparent inconsistencies as Lord David Cecil does in his essay on *Wuthering Heights* or Lionel Trilling on *Howards End*. He was interested in the relation of the author to his subject-matter; and where, as in George Eliot's handling of Maggie Tulliver or Dorothea Casaubon, the author failed to realise where her characters stood in relation to her own moral standard, the failing was noted in order that the reader should understand why he was dissatisfied. In this kind of criticism Stephen excelled: and a critic can excel in this only if he preserves a sense of the appropriate. To this side of Stephen's criticism MacCarthy does little justice, because he does not recognise Stephen's purpose, and asks him to offer what he has no intention of providing.

3

But now we come to the marrow of the affair: what criteria determine the value of a poem or novel, how are we to judge whether it is good or bad and what precisely is to be analysed?

Stephen knew that a critic must concern himself with style and form; he realised that the greatness of a work of art partly depended on choice of words, on the use of imagery, symbols and the relation between the form and content of a work of art. Unfortunately he was incapable of saying anything important about these matters. This particular kind of analysis was beyond him; and this accounts for those passages in Stephen's criticism of poetry where he maundered and hesitated and despaired. To explain why Johnson's judgment of *Lycidas* was wrong would be, he said, 'to go pretty deeply into the theory of poetic expression.' Stephen stayed on the bank and kept dry. Obviously the language and texture of

poetry could not be irrelevant; further he could not
go and dismissed the matter with the phrase: 'The
value of all good work ultimately depends on touches
so fine as to elude the sight.' All that he could say of
Coleridge's melody was that he left it to 'critics of finer
perception and a greater command of superlatives': he
himself could not explain why the *Ancient Mariner* is a great
poem. Arnold convinced the reader by the facility of his
quotations—'this . . . not that,' he said—but Stephen lacked
the taste and authority to make such comparisons. In a
nine-line quotation from *Hellas* he could discern an obvious
use of the *Tempest's* imagery, but could miss a line echoing
a phrase from *King Lear*; and such cases of textual analysis
were rare. He tried at times to bluff the reader by suggesting that the critic who concerns himself with style will
sink into the bright green marshes of aestheticism, and he
satirised Arnold for claiming to determine ethnological
nuances such as the Celtic, Teutonic and Norman elements
in English literature which was surely 'going a little beyond
his tether.' He therefore claimed that poetic excellence
could be measured by the degree of the poet's sincerity
(by which Stephen apparently meant the depth of his
emotion). But how could this be tested? Stephen in desperation cried aloud for an Ithuriel spear to distinguish true
sentiments from false. Since no spear materialised, he
declared: 'It is best to look at each poet by himself. We
need only distinguish between the sham and the genuine
article; and my own method of distinguishing is a simple
one. I believe in poetry which learns itself by heart.' Or,
as he put it in a less naïve moment, 'the thing had to be said
just as it was said.' Then, shaking his head, he admitted
that all these tests were as personal as any he had condemned
in Arnold.

This is not an impressive spectacle; and like a martinet
inspecting troops, Desmond MacCarthy saw at a glance
that Stephen was deficient in part of his equipment as a
critic: Ithuriel had come on parade without his spear.
What is a critic for if not to tell us why certain lines have
power to move? A theory of value cannot be constructed
without analysis of words and style. 'Poetry, my dear

Degas, is made not with ideas, but with words,' and though no one any longer would use Mallarmé's epigram in defence of a theory of 'pure poetry,' ideas and emotions cannot be separated from the imagery in which they are expressed. The common explanation of Stephen's failure, as given by Mackail, is that Stephen had no touch of poetry within himself—though the logic is odd seeing that Mackail accuses Stephen of being too much a Wordsworthian to appreciate Pope. MacCarthy, too, echoes Mackail when he writes that Stephen would have been the last to see in such a phrase as 'Die of a rose in aromatic pain' the best evidence of Pope's genius; unfortunately Stephen quoted this very line in an essay in the *Cornhill*, which he did not republish, as a characteristically 'poetic' line indicating extreme (and morbid) sensibility. The contrary is in fact the reason for Stephen's failure: he had, not too little, but too much poetry in him and drank it in such draughts that he could not savour the delicacies or tell the vintages. Nevertheless, accusations of 'aestheticism' hurled at Mac-Carthy are wide of the mark; and it is strange that Q. D. Leavis who believes that form and content are inseparable, imagery and rhythm functional, and analysis of language essential, should slur over Stephen's weakness. Nor can Stephen be excused on the plea that his concern was more with the novel than with poetry. However closely he analysed the content of novels, he had little to say about plot, the mode of presentation, the variations of pace, the texture of language and choice of materials to create a mood; nor did he appreciate that the key to a writer's morality lies hidden in his language.* Indeed language— the novelist's power to create a world which, often despite ourselves, we accept—is of prime importance; if it were not, why should so many admirably serious writers, who have meditated profoundly on moral problems, fail as novelists?—why, for instance, does Turgenev succeed while L. H. Myers does not?

Stephen, however, suggested another test of value, namely the sociological. The critic, he said, must analyse inductively

* Stephen's essay on Defoe is an exception in that it contains an interesting analysis of the tricks by which this journalist produced an impression of reality.

and start from the facts of experience by first asking what
pleased men and why it pleased them. Literature being a
by-product of society determined partly by the prevailing
demand, he will be able to establish a 'municipal law' for
each age by relating it to the society in which it grew. For
instance, the didactic quality of eighteenth century poetry
is the natural expression of contemporary rationalism and
the absence of lyric poetry may be explained by the fear of
ridicule which possessed the wits of the town. So far so good.
Really great literature, Stephen continued, is produced
when the individual and society are in thorough harmony.
This was a flabby formula and was as weakly applied.
Why, asked Stephen, did Johnson write so badly when he
felt so deeply and talked so well? Was it not that a century
earlier he would have been at his ease, whereas the literary
convention of his day hampered his power of expression
and the Christianity on which he fed was in a state of
inanition and decay? This dubious solution ignored the
fact that directly some powerful characters take a pen in
their hands the wraith of their invisible audience materialises
to paralyse them; and it also minimised the strength of
Johnson's personal religion. Off on another tack, Stephen
defined a great poet as one who was the most perfect type
of the *Zeitgeist* and by distilling the wisdom of the times
uttered thoughts common to all generations. Instead of
calling Shakespeare a genius was it not better to explain
his originality in terms of his power of interpreting the
thought of his age? All this was sadly superficial and did not
help to make the kind of judgment Stephen wanted to
make. And indeed at other times Stephen wrote as if the
sociological study of literature did not provide a test of
value so much as put the critic in the right relation to
the author:

The great poet unconsciously reveals something more
than the metaphysician. His poetry does not decay with
the philosophy which it took for granted. We do not ask
whether his reasoning be sound or false, but whether the
vision be sublime or repulsive. It may be a little of both,
but at any rate it is undeniably fascinating. That, I take
it, is because the imagery which he creates may still be a

symbol of thoughts and emotions which are as interesting now as they were six hundred years ago. The man of first-rate power . . . had no doubt that the truth [of accepted beliefs] could be proved by syllogising: but they really laid so powerful a grasp upon him because they could be made to express the hopes and fears, the loves and hatreds, the moral and political convictions which were dearest to him. . . .

In other words the critic must first learn the 'municipal laws' of the period he is studying in order to avoid being puzzled by archaic expressions of morality or exploded philosophies. He will then be able to make his final estimate of a writer by judging him in the light of a law of nature, deducible from 'universal principles of reason,' which 'is applicable throughout [all literature], and enforces what may be called the cardinal virtues common to all forms of human expression.' With this Stephen arrived at what he considered to be the supreme test of value: the value of a work of art can be measured by its moral content.

Stephen was clear that a writer cannot be expected to preach. Moral content did not imply the hypertrophy of the conscience into a faculty of oracular utterance, but a vision of life so deeply perceived that all the artist's faculties were co-ordinated to express it. In a less happy phrase he told the reader to ask not whether a work of art was moral, but whether it was 'developed by the invigorating and regenerating processes.' We should not complain of a terrifying portrait of vice so long as the author distinctly showed the concomitants of vice; Fielding's novels were flawed by his failure to show that vicious living causes the character to disintegrate in the way that Crabbe did in *Peter Grimes* or, more subtly, George Eliot with Lydgate and Rosamund Vincy in *Middlemarch*. Delighting in squalor and misery, Balzac asked his reader to accept a world, in which the powerful and wicked always succeed and the good and simple are invariably crushed; but because this view of society was utterly at variance with the facts the reader could not respond, no matter how brilliantly he wrote. Charlotte Brontë seemed to see life as a conflict between duty and passion where only a few kindred spirits

achieved happiness in union and the rest devoted themselves to sensuality or making money: such a view was
morbid and unsatisfactory. She could hardly be put among
'the highest rank amongst those who have fought their way
to a clearer atmosphere, and can help us to clearer conceptions'; and though genius is not synonymous with pure
intellect, her work suffered from the comparatively small
circle of ideas in which her mind habitually revolved. Style
alone, the dazzling presentation of a mood, is never enough;
an adult mind can be satisfied only by an adult philosophy
of life.

'The difficulty of feeling rightly is as great as the difficulty
of finding a worthy utterance of the feeling' wrote Stephen
on Gray's *Elegy*, in which he conceived content and expression to be in perfect harmony, whereas Tennyson in the
Idylls 'seems not so much to be inspired by an over-mastering
idea as to be looking about for appropriate images to express
certain ethical and religious sentiments.' This is the clue
to Stephen's taste in literature. He wanted 'simple and
great truths' to be expressed by wise poets and novelists.
Like Arnold, he resented living in an age in which the
lyric or ode, expressing often a vague emotional mood, was
the prevailing form, and which regarded Tennyson with his
'inadequate and even effeminate' religious philosophy as a
sage poet. The best contemporary poets rose only to short
flights and never journeyed serenely evolving a continuous
life-long scheme. Stephen echoed Johnson's dictum that the
greatest writers examined not the individual but the species,
disregarded contemporary laws by rising to general and
transcendental truths, and wrote as the interpreters of
nature and the legislators of mankind; both Fielding and
George Eliot, for instance, presented the microcosm in
such a way as to embody the thoughts and passions of the
macrocosm. On the other hand Charlotte Brontë's Paul
Emmanuel was all too real, a person who gave real lectures
in Brussels on a particular date; and this naturalism was
just as much an error as the unreality of Rochester who was
all too obviously the self-conscious product of an imagination
which had failed.

Was there, then, a modern writer who could sit beside

Shakespeare or Aeschylus or Dante, a writer whose dreams
were not pretty or picturesque and who fused a profound
morality with power of expression? Stephen found Wordsworth to be such a man. The discovery was hardly original.
Following Coleridge, nearly all the serious mid-Victorian
critics—Arnold, Mill, Hutton, Bagehot, Lowell, Church—
placed Wordsworth just below Shakespeare and Milton.
But Stephen's essay on *Wordsworth's Ethics* was the best of the
lot. Arnold mocked him for saying that the poet was 'a
prophet and a moralist as well as a mere singer' and ostentatiously rescued Wordsworth from the Wordsworthians;
but modern criticism has vindicated Stephen. He did not
admire Wordsworth merely because his ethics were 'capable
of systematic exposition.' In his essay he tried to demonstrate
by analysing Wordsworth's ethics how greatness in poetry
depends upon power of mind as well as strength of feeling.
'In practice,' Stephen wrote, 'the utterance of emotions can
hardly be dissociated from the assertion of principles.'
He continued:

The imagination reasons. The bare faculty of sight
involves thought and feeling. The symbol which the fancy
spontaneously constructs, implies a whole world of truth
or error, of superstitious beliefs or sound philosophy. The
poetry holds a number of intellectual dogmas in solution;
and it is precisely due to these general dogmas, which are
true and important for us as well as for the poet, that his
power over our sympathies is due. If his philosophy has
no power in it, his emotions lose their hold upon our
minds, or interest us only as antiquarians and lovers of the
picturesque. But in the briefest poems of a true thinker
we read the essence of the life-long reflections of a passionate
and intellectual nature. Fears and hopes common to all
thoughtful men have been coined into a single phrase.
Even in cases where no definite conviction is expressed or
even implied, and the poem is simply, like music, an
indefinite utterance of a certain state of the emotions, we
may discover an intellectual element. The rational and
the emotional nature have such intricate relations that
one cannot exist in great richness and force without
justifying an inference as to the other. . . .
Now the highest poetry is that which expresses the

richest, most powerful, and most susceptible emotional nature, and the most versatile, penetrative, and subtle intellect. Such qualities may be stamped upon trifling work. The great artist can express his power within the limits of a coin or a gem. The great poet will reveal his character through a sonnet or a song. . . . An ill-balanced nature reveals itself by a discord, as an illogical mind by a fallacy. A man need not compose an epic on a system of philosophy to write himself down an ass. And, inversely, a great mind and a noble nature may show itself by impalpable but recognisable signs within the 'sonnet's scanty plot of ground.' Once more, the highest poetry must be that which expresses not only the richest but the healthiest nature. Disease means an absence or a want of balance of certain faculties, and therefore leads to false reasoning or emotional discord. The defect of character betrays itself in some erroneous mode of thought or baseness of sentiment. And since morality means obedience to those rules which are most essential to the spiritual health, vicious feeling indicates some morbid tendency, and is so far destructive of the poetical faculty. An immoral sentiment is the sign either of a false judgment of the world and of human nature, or of a defect in the emotional nature which shows itself by a discord or an indecorum, and leads to a cynicism or indecency which offends the reason through the taste. What is called immorality does not indeed always imply such defects. Sound moral intuitions may be opposed to the narrow code prevalent at the time; or a protest against puritanical or ascetic perversions of the standard may hurry the poet into attacks upon true principles. And, again, the keen sensibility which makes a man a poet, undoubtedly exposes him to certain types of disease. He is more likely than his thick-skinned neighbour to be vexed by evil, and to be drawn into distorted views of life by an excess of sympathy or indignation. Injudicious admirers prize the disease instead of the strength from which it springs; and value the cynicism or the despair instead of the contempt for heartless commonplace or the desire for better things with which it was unfortunately connected. A strong moral sentiment has a great value, even when forced into an unnatural alliance. Nay, even when it is, so to speak, inverted, it often receives a kind of paradoxical value from its efficacy against some opposite

form of error. It is only a complete absence of the moral
faculty which is irredeemably bad. The poet in whom it
does not exist is condemned to the lower sphere, and can
only deal with the deepest feelings on penalty of shocking
us by indecency or profanity. A man who can revel in
'Epicurus' stye' without even the indirect homage to
purity or remorse and bitterness, can do nothing but
gratify our lowest passions. They, perhaps, have their
place, and the man who is content with such utterances
may not be utterly worthless. But to place him on a level
with his betters is to confound every sound principle
of criticism.

Stephen then considered how Wordsworth's poetry could
satisfy, even though fault could be found with his reasoning
and his conception of childhood and nature. It satisfied
because Wordsworth faced the specific problems of evil in
nature and sorrow by bereavement and also comprehended
the philosophical issues of ethics themselves. Do we not
tire eventually, asked Stephen, of 'musical moans' that
love, spring and joy fade and die, that to-day is not yesterday
and that everything is not as it should be? Wordsworth had
felt these emotions but related them to the facts and suggested
a means of coming to terms with them. He was not content
to state the ideal; like a sound moralist he tried to relate the
ideal to the present state of the world. He distinguished
between the lessons nature teaches us and the interpretation
we impose upon nature. Or again, when he recommended
contemplation as a mental therapy, he made it clear that
contemplation was the prelude to, not a substitute for,
action. Finally Wordsworth alone among his contemporaries
understood the moral necessity to turn grief to advantage
instead of abandoning himself to it.

What, then, was Stephen's canon of criticism? The critic
had first to set the writer's work against his times, then to
set it again the writer's character and through biography to
understand his morality; by this test Richardson's moral
seriousness would be seen to be tainted by the prudential
reckoning of the shopkeeper and Pope to possess many nasty
traits which impaired his poetry. Lastly the man and his
work should be judged against a profound view of morality.

4

Such was Stephen's method; but a critic is as great as his perception, and acuteness of perception, not the technical apparatus which sets off to best advantage the critic's insights, makes judicial critics such as T. S. Eliot or F. R. Leavis worth reading, as anyone who glances at their lesser disciples can see. As with all judicial critics Stephen's bag after a battle over the fields of literature was mixed. The essay on *Shakespeare as a Man* was commonplace though better than that of Bagehot; the psychopathic nature of O. W. Holmes's novels, which explore perversions of character, passed him by; and one is astonished to learn that Balzac's characters are naturalistic, the work of a patient Dutch artist painting every hair on the head and wrinkle on the face with photographic accuracy. We would to-day place *Middlemarch* higher and liberate *Wuthering Heights* from Purgatory. Yet if one wants to 'place' novels, Stephen's essays repay study: his analysis was penetrating and his dissection of Richardson and George Eliot masterly. He could also take a concept such as vanity or humour in his hands like a jewel and toss it to and fro so that it caught the light; and he had the gift of crystallising a piece of analysis into a single phrase, as when he said that to appreciate the rustic humour, which Scott or George Eliot retail, 'we require not a new defect of logic but a new logical structure.' His criticism is full of such comments. On Balzac: 'He did not so much invent characters and situations as watch his imaginary world, and compile the memoirs of its celebrities.' On Swift providing in Gulliver for the man who despises his species 'a number of exceedingly effective symbols for the utterance of his contempt.' On Pope's emotion which 'came in sudden jets and gushes, instead of in a continuous stream.' On the *Epistle to Arbuthnot* in which Pope 'seems to be actually screaming with malignant fury. . . . The most abiding sentiment—when we think of him as a literary phenomenon—is admiration for the exquisite skill which enabled him to discharge a function, not of the highest kind, with a perfection rare in any department of literature.' Such perceptions, which contain within them the act of judgment, substantiate Stephen's claim that the judicial critic is not concerned to measure writers against an inflexible exterior standard. Moreover, his power of self-criticism and humour enabled him to preserve that sense of the appropriate which judicial critics are apt to lose. His humour helps to convince us that he is able to see himself in relation to the world. He pricked pomposity and his own self-delusions with the same lancet. His humour resided partly in the turn of phrase or in a throw-away line: 'At one of my meetings with [Arnold], indeed, I do remember a remark which was made, and which struck me at the moment as singularly happy. Unfortunately, it was a remark made by me and not by him.' Or when he entreated Disraeli to be a little less serious and to spare us Sidonia: '*Coningsby* wants little but a greater absence of purpose to be a first-rate novel.' Or in a vivacity running through a whole essay such as that which treated Landor as a 'glorified and sublime edition of the model sixth-form lad'; or in his mischievous and astonished interest in Emerson's discovery of an Olympian British philosopher called Mr. Wilkinson; or in extravagances which have the true Strachey ring such as the fabulous description of William Godwin and his novels. Or in dilating upon the singular character of John Byrom who would hymn almost any event in verse of a highly moral nature, though his biographer had to explain away his verses on the fight between Figg and Sutton by reminding us that their combat was not 'a brutal prize-fight' but 'an ultra-vigorous assault at arms'; the line, remarked Stephen, seems hard to draw. Dover Wilson has rightly hinted at the debt which Strachey owed to Stephen's irony and sinuous style, and indeed many of the Bloomsbury essayists inherited a felicity of phrase from Stephen: Virginia Woolf's essays show the influence of her father's as well as her mother's style, and Strachey used in biography Stephen's technique of describing a crisis of mind.* Bloomsbury adapted, pruned and chiselled Stephen's prose and gave it a cutting edge.

* Even the tone of voice in which Stephen made an aside was echoed by the Bloomsbury critics and their disciples. Compare Stephen's 'Bishops indeed have fallen upon evil days; they no longer enjoy the charming repose of the comfortable dignitaries of the eighteenth century. But I should dearly like a deanery'; with Raymond Mortimer's 'I am one of the diminishing band who dearly love a bishop. . . .'

Finally, Stephen introduced in England a new kind of literary study: the sociological examination of literature. Literature interested him as a kind of by-product of social activity, the noise made by the wheels as they revolved, and in his old age he wrote, as he lay dying, a course of lectures entitled *English Literature and Society in the Eighteenth Century*.

Stephen was one of the first English critics to show how literary expression is influenced by shifts in the structure of society and by the demands and nature of the reading public. He also showed how a change of taste, usually defined in jargon as a 'reaction,' could be explained in terms of changing social relationships. His book is a prolegomena to a new branch of learning rather than a first treatise—it says too little about too much—and the author regarded the contents as a statement of the obvious ('I hope and believe that I have said nothing original'); and his account of the way literature reflects social change strikes us as too simple. Not that all modern critics, who have followed Stephen, are necessarily more subtle. The crudity of Marxist literary criticism is notorious. Nor are the critics who analyse the so-called dilemma of the modern writer in relation to the reading public much subtler; their sweeping generalisations about eighteenth-century literary patronage or the demands of the Victorian public are certainly not based, as Stephen would have wished, upon empirical examination. Even Edmund Wilson's *Axel's Castle* or Cyril Connolly's *Enemies of Promise* are far too doctrinaire in their social analysis: as the years advance, these books decline to the status of interesting diagnoses of twentieth-century literature by left wing writers of the nineteen-thirties. Still, a generation of research on this subject—in itself a testimony to Stephen—has naturally amplified and refined what he wrote. Moreover, although Stephen saw the relation between society and literature, he did not realise that he must decide from what angle he was to regard it. Literary critics study society primarily to throw new light upon literature: historians of thought prefer to treat literature as one source among many which help them to gauge the climate of opinion. Stephen was by nature an historian of thought and admitted that his own interest in literature had 'always been closely connected with its philosophical and social significance.' This bias would have been unexceptionable had he maintained it consistently; but he did not. He kept changing his angle of vision from the historical to the literary. He wanted to prove that the greatest literature is the best source for understanding the ideas of an age. 'If,' he said, 'we wish to discover the secret of the great ecclesiastical and political struggles of the day, we should turn, not to the men in whose minds beliefs lie inert and instinctive, but to the great poet who shows how they were associated with the strongest passions and the most vehement convictions.' This was to contradict the method he had employed so successfully in *English Thought in the Eighteenth Century*. It is also, unfortunately, a misleading maxim for the historian. The innumerable collections of essays, each of which expounds the ideas of a great Victorian poet or prophet, often purport to analyse the basic assumptions of the age: in fact, they do much to obscure the foundations of Victorian thought. It is precisely the 'ostensible apologists and assailants,' the minor writers and pamphleteers, whom we must study if we are to plot the intellectual configurations of the times. The great writers are, of course, important for the historians of thought; and Lovejoy's disciples go too far when they proclaim that only those writers who are totally obscure to-day can be considered as fully representative of their age—for these scholars 'stone dead hath no fellow.' But it is true that to cull and admire the finest flowers alone does not tell us enough of the soil in which they are planted: the historian cannot botanise, like the geologist he must dig. Unlike the literary critic whose eyes are fixed on the perennial questions of style and morality he must range far wider afield.

Yet despite these defects, Stephen's book was really important. It gave a new twist to literary studies. Firstly, it taught scholars that the history of literature is more than a search for influences and movements; and, secondly, it warned the 'pure' critics that to wrench a poem or novel from its social setting is to neglect the fact that a work of art has a life of its own in Time, and is subject to different kinds of perception in each age, in that the communication between author and reader is constantly changing. By and large, human nature may be a constant, so that we are still able to be moved by Chaucer to-day: but in what way is it a constant and how do our own values, imposed on us partly by our society, affect our appreciation? Our appreciation is different in kind to that of Chaucer's contemporaries or of his readers in any other subsequent century. Stephen stressed that all writing is a response to the world in which the author finds himself and not a response to an abstract world created by the critic himself. He also forces us to consider how intimately literature is bound up with the behaviour, manners, customs, money-sense and the unspoken assumptions of different classes in society, as well as with their current ideologies.*

Lionel Trilling has written: 'The novel, then, is a perpetual quest for reality, the field of its research being always the social world, the material of analysis being always manners as the indication of the direction of man's soul.' Stephen was beginning to deal with this problem, namely how conceptions of reality change as the structure of society itself alters. Inevitably, because his approach was new, he concentrated on describing the changes in society, relating them firstly to the status of the writer and only secondly to his vision of life. Stephen exploded the common orthodox belief that the eighteenth century was a monolithic structure, which owed its stability to the fact, as Carlyle said, that it had settled with the centre of gravity lowest. He showed how literature was inextricably mixed with politics until the fall of Walpole and how it then passed into the hands of men of a lower social class, leaving Horace Walpole, who had conversed in his youth on terms of equality with Addison and Pope, to bewail that literature was no longer written by gentlemen with the single exception of Gray. Stephen's apprehension that the character of literature is to a great extent determined by social tensions, was a landmark in

---

* Stephen has found in his family a successor who relates the arts to society. His grandson, Quentin Bell, has made a sociological examination of the way in which social forces govern fashion in dress and dictate changes in fashion. *Of Human Finery* (1947) attempts by a modification of the concepts Veblen used in *The Theory of the Leisure Class* to subsume the 'municipal' laws which govern fashion in any period under a general system.

criticism. Whatever its failings, his book remains a classic
in literary studies.

Nevertheless, Stephen's virtues have an unfortunate way
of becoming vices. He suffers from a weakness which
afflicts all who believe in 'placing.' Try as he may to be dispassionate the critic inevitably places writers against his own
vision of life. And thus, Stephen while admitting the
faults of, say, Scott or Stevenson cannot resist giving them
an extra pat on the back for aspiring to qualities of which he
approves; and by so doing appears to denigrate, more than
in fact he does, authors with a finer sense of craftsmanship
or of greater imaginative sweep, whom he thinks stand in
a morally feeble relationship to the world.* He applies the
same technique of analysis to Defoe as to George Eliot and
this has the effect of underrating *Roxana* and of minimising
the importance of *Adam Bede*. We all know that the two
books are not on the same level: why then apply the same
technique to each: What we want to be told is the unique
quality of Defoe's book—if it is merely journalism, then
what distinguishes it from bad journalism. The value of
any novelist depends largely on his success in communicating
an imaginative experience and making his reader accept
the world he creates; and so long as these conditions are
fulfilled the critic in the *belles-lettres* tradition is satisfied.
Stephen, however, who asks that this imagined world should
correspond to his own conception of the way the world
works and how it ought to work, is too apt to underestimate
the virtues of intensity of expression, acute sensibility and
creative power. Adherence to method, even when the critic
protests that his method is flexible, inevitably leads to rigidity.
Though Stephen tried to abolish the vocabulary of aestheticism, the use of descriptive terms such as 'subtle,' 'bitter'
and 'tender,' we find in their place the ominous words
'masculine' and 'morbid' appearing with depressing regularity.† The critic cannot avoid using shorthand terms of

* Stephen can suddenly say in a reasonable estimate of Stevenson that he
was a man of genius; and then includes 'an invincible boyishness' as a prominent characteristic of genius.
† Here is Stephen defending in a letter his view of Coventry Patmore. 'I
do think C.P. effeminate. Every man ought to be feminine, i.e. to have quick
and delicate feelings; but no man ought to be effeminate, i.e. to let his feelings

approbation and condemnation; and when Stephen says
'the highest poetry, like the noblest morality, is the product
of a thoroughly healthy mind,' we ought to realise that
such sentences are aphorisms contracting into a span his
critical theory. But we are right to object when the critic
begins to *think* in shorthand and to condemn works of art
which are not susceptible of analysis by his method.
Stephen's concern for sincerity led him to accept without
question Arnold's distinction between 'genuine' poetry
and poetry conceived in the wits: of which Eliot observed
that there is not one kind of poetry but many, and to which
MacCarthy objected when he said that Stephen had missed
the point in Sterne.

The critic, no less than the novelist, has to persuade his
reader to accept his vision of life and literature. Acuteness
of perception—the gift of seeing relations which do not
strike less sensitive minds—is one method of persuasion:
another is his style which is the product of his sensibility.
'The thing had to be said just as it was said.' And here
Stephen again fails. His literary criticism is well, but
not excellently, written. The intelligent, sensible para-
graphs flow on, and end as best they may, the measured
firm pace is never varied, the very vivacities are submerged
beneath this calm and measureless sea. We wait for pages
for one of those phrases which illuminate the argument,
and the argument itself twists and turns, sometimes peters
out, to be revived again at the close. Not that Stephen is
inelegant or ever boring, though he is undeniably prolix.
The disease lies deeper; there is no fire in the belly, no
sense of urgency, of determination to tear down the old
structure and rebuild. He writes well within himself and
we recognise his voice at once; but it does not call us
peremptorily or persuasively enough. His diffidence, his
take-it-or-leave-it, his protestations of inadequacy set up
barriers between him and his reader. And this should
suggest that impressionist critics, whose criticism is also a

get the better of his intellect and produce a cowardly view of life and the
world. I dislike George Herbert because he seems to me always to be skulking
behind the Thirty-Nine Articles instead of looking facts in the face, and C.P.
has found a refuge which I dislike still more heartily. . . . Want of clearness
is a fault in poetry as in everything else, and so is a tendency to conceits. . . .'

triumph of style and whose temperament is inimical to analysis and rigour, add far more to the calling than their opponents will admit. It is not merely, as Trilling suggests, the play of the dialectic, the visible mechanism of the intellect, which dignifies criticism; criticism containing *aperçus* from the sensibility of a Virginia Woolf or a Forster, written in admirable living English, cast into a form which is almost three-dimensional, so clearly can the reader apprehend it—such criticism also makes art more important.

There is another reason why Stephen's criticism disappoints. He despised the whole business. 'Literature is, in all cases, a demoralising occupation, though some people can resist its evil influences. It is demoralising because success implies publicity. A poet has to turn himself inside out by the very conditions of his art, and suffers from the incessant stimulants applied to his self-consciousness.' Research into the lives of the poets had thrown doubt (which we perceive in his criticism) upon the Ruskinian canon: By their fruits ye shall know them. But if, perhaps, the fruits redeemed in part the tortured and twisted lives and fed other men spiritually, the same could not be said for criticism. We must be scientific and give it what dignity we can: but criticism has little value. Stephen would have nothing to do with the modern cant which declares that criticism by pundits, unknown personally to the artist, can put the artist right and help him in the act of creation. 'After all what does a real genius ever learn from a critic? There is, it seems to me, only one good piece of advice which a critic can give to an author, namely, that the author should dare to be himself.' He advised Thomas Hardy never to read critics but to read the writers 'who give ideas and don't prescribe rules.' He even at times doubted the value of his own method. Is inductive criticism really possible? 'All theories upon all subjects can be proved from history'; and he admitted that 'Hazlitt's enthusiasm brings out Congreve's real merits with a force of which a calmer judge would be incapable.' Such scepticism is typical of Stephen's determination to be honest but makes his criticism undeniably less impressive.

And, indeed, it is a far cry from Stephen's disenchantment

with his pastime to the authoritative tone of voice in which
the rulers of the Academy define the correct approach to
literature. Q. D. Leavis is right in seeing the link between
Stephen and modern positivist criticism; Stephen belonged
to the judicial tradition of Johnson–Arnold–Eliot and,
while rejecting the Aesthetic movement, also rejected neo-
classicism or the erection of general principles in Aristotelian
fashion, against which works of art could be measured, in
favour of a way of approaching literature, a doctrine of
procedure, which inevitably is diffuse and contains many
qualifications. Perhaps Stephen qualified and hesitated
partly through the necessity to state what he is *not* saying
as well as what he *is* trying to say.* But if we recollect
Stephen's character, we must admit that these hesitations
proceed from deeper causes. Not only does he bear on his
brow like Cain many of the marks of the *belles-lettres* critic,†
but his failure to understand fully what Arnold meant by
Culture, to penetrate the disguise of languor and preciosity
which that great and refined critical mind at times assumed,
is a defect which betrayed what can only be called a fear
of literature itself. Though far-removed from the puritanism
of John Morley and lesser critics, Stephen is gnawed by
a utilitarian anxiety: what effect will the poet or novelist
produce upon society? And he pictured the effect in terms
of conduct rather than, as Arnold did, in terms of cultivating the mind and awakening the heart. Ultimately he
reasoned about criticism as follows: Criticism is a pastime.
If you engage in it, apply your mind to it, be as precise as
you can, and judge authors and books by their moral
content. But don't give yourself airs or think that you have
done anything important. The whole of criticism is not
worth a groat when weighed against a work of art of an
original philosophical treatise; and they in their turn are
valuable in the degree to which they help mankind to see
truth clearer and to live better.

---

* Compare E. M. Forster's description of T. S. Eliot's prose which 'conveys
something, but is often occupied in tracing the boundaries of the unsaid.'

 † His devotion to the criteria of *belles-lettres* criticism conflicts with his judicial
method. For instance, in praising Raleigh's criticism, he stated the *desiderata*
for a critic of poetry. Firstly, as an essential, a spontaneous love of the poet:
secondly, learning and critical knowledge to reveal new beauties and deepen
the sense of the old. Thirdly, impartiality and power of analysis.

CHAPTER X

CONCLUSION

HE is a man to respect. His virtues were the simple virtues that deserve praise wherever they are found. He was proud of his own country but despised jingos: he hoped to leave some reflections in his books to benefit, not only Englishmen, but all men of good will. He was proud of his family, but nothing of a snob: he wished to leave a memory which his children might honour. This quiet patriotism and domestic piety flowed from a magnanimous spirit. Revenge, envy, and malice were beneath him; he loved his friends and scorned to injure his enemies. With that solid worth and intolerance of impostors, which invests so many of his contemporaries with the grandeur of hoary oaks, *nil admirari* was his precept, the salute to genius his practice. He pitied the weak—he had suffered as a weakling—but he exhorted them to master their frailty, and his own feats of endurance and daring live in the Alpine records as clearly as his moral courage and intellectual honesty are printed in the history of his times. Courage is sometimes tainted with arrogance or brutality, but Stephen was scrupulous in controversy, modest of his attainments, and candid in his agnosticism. His was the purest kind of renunciation, not inspired by hatred of priests or by the desire to destroy the temple and build it in three days. He wanted to change men not destroy them.

Historically he is no more than a representative figure. He was not a seminal mind, but an eminent controversialist and a literary journalist who expounded the liberal-rationalist tradition which he neither modified like Mill nor criticised like Arnold. He was not an original philosopher, but an historian of thought. Nor was he a great figure in the development of the social sciences like Alfred Marshall or James Frazer. If he saw the errors of Comte and Taine in applying the scientific method and gave as many happy examples of what this method cannot achieve as what it can, he did not realise, as Mill did, that the imperative task facing rationalists was to discover how induction and deduction can be applied in the treatment of social phenomena. (Can change in society be measured in other fields than theoretical economics; if not, how far do the social sciences consist of justifications of different arrangements of facts; and how far are these arrangements determined by implicit judgments of value?) A great rationalist introduces a new technique of enquiry; or creates a new department of knowledge; or changes by his discoveries the very nature of the facts on which men previously had worked. Stephen was not in this class; he swam strongly with the stream instead of turning it to irrigate new country. Partly because he lacked supreme originality and partly because he was too anxious to teach the tenets of the faith, he remained an incomparable *vulgarisateur* unable to revise the premises on which he based his teaching. And Stephen knew his own measure. Did he not say that his place would be at most a footnote in history?

Yet, perhaps, there is more to be said for footnotes than Stephen imagined. Stephen was not merely a scholar but a good scholar. In a limited way he said certain things about certain matters or people—on Hoadly, or Richardson, or Paley—which were *right*. He was an intellectual in the sense that other men have followed his judgments. A good scholar is one who not only produces order in some field of human knowledge, but does not obscure the thought of future generations. Great minds, driven by powerful imaginations, construct new systems and change the thought of their generation; but their books have a curious way of being disregarded after a short passage of time. Frazer's *Golden Bough* was an epic; but do modern anthropologists seriously build on that work to-day? Stephen's *English Thought in the Eighteenth Century* is not an epic; but because Stephen says plainly what he is doing, sets himself a limited objective and does not declare, for instance, that some thinker is of a greater *intrinsic* value by reason of his *literary* value, scholars to-day are helped by his book. They continue to take Stephen's works from the shelves because he made his own approach so clear. Though they may be working from another angle, they find Stephen useful because, as a good positivist, he does not disguise his method nor his personal interpretations. He despised obscurity and practised clarity. As a result, those who disagree state the grounds of their disagreement with the respect of men talking to their equal. No serious explorer of eighteenth century thought and literature can ignore Stephen's pioneer work. American scholarship has analysed minutely Defoe's treatment of his sources; but Stephen's essay is still worth reading. He may not perceive that Clarissa is in love with Lovelace, but his dissection of Richardson remains a classic. He had read so widely in eighteenth century prose and entered so completely into the minds of those writers that the points he makes are too numerous and sensible to be disregarded. His judgments outside the eighteenth century also repay study. John Plamenatz in his admirable critical study of the Utilitarians takes Stephen rather than more recent critics as a reference for manœuvre. Even theologians benefit from the clarity of Stephen's arguments: he gives them every opportunity to confound them, there are no weasel-words, no camouflage or deception.

And this is true of Stephen's literary criticism. Not only F. R. Leavis and his disciples praise him warmly. T. S. Eliot in his famous essay on Massinger calls Stephen's work on this playwright 'a piece of formidable destructive analysis,' though he adds that Stephen has not put Massinger 'finally and irrefutably into a place.' Eliot agrees that Massinger's characterisation is weak and that Stephen's objection to Massinger's method of revealing a villain has great cogency, though perhaps the objection is stated in too *a priori* a fashion. No two critical sensibilities could be more obviously opposed than those of Leslie Stephen and Raymond Mortimer. Mortimer owes little to Stephen and his scale of values differs greatly. Yet if their essays on Balzac are compared, the measure of agreement is startling. They both make some two dozen points (Stephen in over eleven, Mortimer in under five thousand words). Both agree that Balzac lived vicariously in an imaginary world and that for him dream and reality were the same; that his view of human nature was nonsensical and that society cannot be

divided in Balzac's fashion into virtuous fools and clever
knaves; that his stories are improbable but thrilling and
that while his ceaseless explanations are intolerable, the
incredibilities do not matter since his vigour and intensity
sweep the reader away. In other words, Stephen did more
than his share to establish that consensus of opinion about
numerous topics which is held by most educated men.
Positivists would say that Stephen increased knowledge,
and anyone who welcomes the increase of knowledge should
pay his tribute. True, the knowledge he increased makes
little stir in the world; but then scholars should expect
tribute from none but scholars and should be well satisfied
if they obtain even that.

Here a distinction must be drawn. Stephen was not a
professional but an amateur scholar, a Victorian gentleman
such as Darwin or Acton, who sat in his own library and
digested its contents without much recourse to the British
Museum. He read his sources, memorised their arguments,
pondered, and then sat down and wrote without the apparatus of card indexes and cross-references. It is a way of
sowing knowledge which invites armed men to spring up
from the soil. Mistaken judgments which could have been
rectified by yet wider reading are but one part of the harvest,
and, naturally, subsequent research has corrected Stephen's
work, particularly in the D.N.B. In his own lifetime Stephen
had to admit that, curiously enough, he had leant too
heavily on what orthodox critics had said of the anti-clerical
revolutionary, Tom Paine; and this error was typical of
Stephen's fondness for subtle and logical thinkers, and his
antipathy to far more influential, but cruder, writers. Yet
how great are the gains of the amateur! With what sweep,
with what concentrated control, what a work of expert
craftsmanship has he written! How his style in *English
Thought in the Eighteenth Century* shames that of our own
generation, how pellucid and natural, how solid without
being heavy, ironical without being flashy, how it coaxes
the reader from point to point on an easy gentle rein!
Stephen teaches a lesson to all scholars in his field. Analytical
history to be read must be readable. The scholar must
subdue that spirit of egoism which tempts him to write for

himself and to forget his reader. He must not only subdue the desire to turn his work into a battle of the books in which the author turns from his task to bite other scholars; he must also assimilate his technique of criticism into the blood-stream or his work will be indigestible. He must put truth first; but over-scrupulous regard for truth can bring a double-edged reward. Determined that every sentence shall say neither more nor less than the truth, the professional literary scholar too often creates a forest of abstract nouns, intersected by critical approaches, in which the reader for sheer weariness lays himself down and dies. Scholars who properly base *own* write solely for other scholars; but historians of thought and literature, and biographers, should settle questions of method, approach and disputed material, in articles in the learned periodicals, leaving themselves free to write for that wider public which it is their duty to consider. Stephen would have rejected the modern priggery which regards wit as a sign of insincerity and style as something which 'gets between' the reader and the truth.

2

Nevertheless, Stephen was more than a good scholar, though when it is asked where he stands in the history of nineteenth-century thought, the answer at first sight is unimpressive. He was an exponent of a tradition of thought which was stricken as he himself lay dying. A rationalist is always a bad life if one wants to insure against the short memory of posterity: his ideas soon become so remote that they are remembered only for their quaintness. Muddlers like the imaginative Coleridge, intricate minds like F. D. Maurice, who meet a crisis by developing a highly personalised dialectic, prophets, seers, even charlatans, have a longer life than the rationalist whose reputation is soon spotted with the death-tokens of a rare article or reference in a work of learning. Nearly everything Stephen wrote which could claim to be a contribution to thought would have to be reinterpreted to-day. But a positivist, such as Stephen, welcomes the extinction of his reputation: to him his future insignificance is a sign that others have built on his work and profited by his blunders. The life, which is unimpressive to posterity, is in his view a life well spent in destroying superstition and selflessly working for the future.

It is an error to consider rationalism as an icy, un-emotional creed, hostile to all that is poetic, imaginative, generous and ardent; the spare and lean athlete is also grace-ful and vigorous. While watching the greatest rationalists at work, the image forms in the mind of a hurdler who glides forward with felicititious ease scarcely seeming to rise or fall. What is condemned as mechanical is in reality an exquisitely co-ordinated mental effort; what is disliked as metallic is the strength of body and mind developed by exacting training; what is despised as unsubtle is that simplicity of the athlete who has mastered his technique and deludes by his concinnity. To succeed means to re-nounce trivial delights and to dedicate the coming years to the pursuit. It is this spirit of self-sacrifice, the challenge to succeed where others have failed, the intense difficulty of excelling and of conquering matter by mind, that inspires youth to follow the calling. The discipline is severe, the mood cool and calm, but the reward is beyond price. The discipline eschews all devices which enable the trick to be performed without hard work and declares war upon rhetoric, phrase-making, hypnotism, and on all those contrivances which spell-binders and mountebanks employ to seduce and impose upon a credulous world. The mood is that of a man, a tiny figure, standing on the beach, the vast uncharted sea of facts stretching before him to the horizon; but who turns to his fellows with noble self-assurance: *cras ingens iterabimus aequor.* The reward is no less than the possession of a part of truth itself. Not the appearance of encompassing the whole of truth which an artist creates and persuades others to accept as an exquisite *aperçu* of life; not the subtle impression of experience which, by its very restraint and horror of drawing conclusions, leaves us nevertheless with an uncanny awareness of how events and people are shaped; but of truths that are independent of personal vagary, solid and substantial, capable of acceptance by all dispassionate men of good will. And if this is an illusion—if in fact such truths can never be proved to exist and if all truth is interpretation, all reality appearance

—then it is an illusion absolutely necessary for the increase of knowledge and the dissipation of envy, hatred and fear, the enemies of man's happiness and greatness. The rationalist temper is one of moderate optimism and even exaltation. The discovery of truths, tangible and in some degree immutable, obtained by relentless analysis, satisfies the self-esteem; and the belief that these truths will light the path to a wiser, happier future inspires the rationalist in his labours, comforts him for the loss of those spiritual analgesics which deaden the senses to unpalatable facts, and fires him with the ardour and eloquence that he is popularly supposed to lack. He too has his vision: the vision of the present forging the shape of the future. And it is a mistake to dismiss his dream as facilely optimistic. The rationalist vision is also tragic. His hopes are blighted by the cancers that breed about the heart: the crassness of human stupidity, the degradation of the evils corrupting society, the dreary aimless courses of peoples and governments, exasperate and frustrate him and whisper that tyranny, misery and calamity are the eternal lot of man. And so, unable to remould the scheme of things nearer to his heart's desire, the rationalist labours on, now in this vineyard and in that, striving to bring order into one small corner of the chaos which surrounds him and to which he inescapably belongs. The belief that order can be created, and the realisation that his own efforts will change little in the world, are the two central facts in his experience that dignify and ennoble him.

Leslie Stephen held to this faith and was proud to acknowledge his debt to the past. He reminded his contemporaries that not they, but their eighteenth-century forebears, had mapped the paths to truth. 'I would never abuse,' he wrote, 'the century which loved common sense and freedom of speech, and hated humbug and mystery; the century in which first sprang to life most of the social and intellectual movements which are still the best hope of our own; in which science and history and invention first took their modern shape; the century of David Hume, and Adam Smith, and Gibbon, and Burke, and Johnson, and Fielding, and many old friends to whom I aver incalculable gratitude. . . .' This historical sense of belonging to a tradition of thought, in which each man had contributed something, but had also erred, and in which philosophical speculation was kept close to earth by common sense and a generous morality, saved Stephen from the vices of ratiocination; he was a rationalist but never a progressive. The progressive shovels all human experience into the machine of the mind and processes it with a scientific method; he has invested in reading and wants a quick return from his money, and hence searches about for a few fashionable theories which will explain all facets of life; indeed without theories he would be unable to progress. Stephen was sceptical of theories but believed in methods which put the individual in the right relation to the facts; he thought that books widened the mind but that quality of mind depended on character and moral education; and progress for him was an incalculable and slow-motioned operation. He not only believed in, but knew how to use, reason.

Some of the steps he took in using reason naturally appear to us in retrospect to be fallacious. Like almost all his contemporaries he drew certain conclusions, which he thought to be logical, and which we should not agree were inferred logically; and he demanded, which we do not, that every true proposition should be shown to be logically necessary. When Stephen said that theology was unreal and had no right to exist, he confused an ethical reflection (that theology is a waste of time) with a logical inference (that theology is logically improper). Theology, however, is a mode of reasoning as valid as other modes of reasoning; as a human activity it is not unreal, nor are its rules dissimilar from those which govern other activities such as jurisprudence; and there is no *logical* reason why men should not use this mode of reasoning, if they please. Yet Stephen was arguing only as his clerical opponents argued when they declared in ethics that the ultimate justification for preferring one course of action to another was that the former accorded with the will of God. To believe that we are acting in accordance with the will of God may comfort and give us strength to act even though the action and its consequences are unpleasant to ourselves; but it is not integral to the logic of *ethics*. Stephen was determined to separate ethics from religion for two reasons. Firstly because to admit enthusiastic exhortation as part of the logic of ethics is to agree with Newman that 'the logic is felt not proved.' Secondly because the acceptance of dogmatic systems of thought cause men to make wrong ethical judgments: the wrong course of action may be chosen because it appears to accord with some dogma or saintly *obiter dictum*, and hence persecution or poverty is justified on grounds which purport to be ethical but are in fact religious. And this was his most valuable contribution to the controversy.

Nevertheless, the positive contributions made by men of Stephen's mould are often less important than the intangible impression which they leave behind them. Material results are only one criterion of good, and if it be asked what influence, what aspirations, what image Stephen bequeathed for future generations to admire and follow, let it be answered by a passage which will serve as an epitaph, written by Lowes Dickinson, who, like Stephen, took pride in what his university sometime produced:

It does not become a Cambridge man to claim too much for his university, nor am I much tempted to do so. But there is, I think, a certain type, rare, like all good things, which seems to be associated in some peculiar way with my alma mater. I am thinking of men like Leslie Stephen . . . like Henry Sidgwick, like Maitland, like one [Frank Ramsey] who died but the other day with all his promise unfulfilled. It is a type unworldly without being saintly, unambitious without being inactive, warm-hearted without being sentimental. Through good report and ill such men work on, following the light of truth as they see it; able to be sceptical without being paralysed; content to know what is knowable and to reserve judgment on what is not. The world could never be driven by such men, for the springs of action lie deep in ignorance and madness. But it is they who are the beacon in the tempest, and they are more, not less, needed now than ever before. May their succession never fail!

NOTES AND REFERENCES

I have included in these notes supplementary information for which there was no space available in the text. For convenience I have abbreviated the editions of certain of Leslie Stephen's works which I have used, as follows—

AA	An Agnostic's Apology and other essays, 1893.
EFP	Essays in Freethinking and Plainspeaking, 1873.
HL	Hours in a Library, 3 vols., 1909.
SB	Studies of a Biographer, 4 vols., 1898.
Eng. Util.	The English Utilitarians, 3 vols., 1900.
Eng. Thought 18th Cent.	History of English Thought in the Eighteenth Century, 2 vols., 1902.
Lit. and Soc. 18th Cent.	English Literature and Society in the Eighteenth Century, 1904.
Sci. Ethics.	The Science of Ethics, 1882.
Sketches	Sketches from Cambridge by a Don, 1865.
SEI	Some Early Impressions, 1924.
SRD	Social Rights and Duties, 2 vols., 1896.
Life of Sir JFS.	Life of Sir James Fitzjames Stephen, 1895.
Life	F. W. Maitland, The Life and Letters of Leslie Stephen, 1906.

Other works of all authors are given in full with dates of editions; unless otherwise stated, editions quoted are printed in the United Kingdom. The number in the left-hand margin refers to the page in the text.

PREFACE
P. v. **'for another'**: H. A. L. Fisher, *F. W. Maitland* (1910), p. 13.

P. v. **'environment'**: *Life*, p. 6.

CHAPTER I
P. 2. **treats them:** The use of the concept 'class' in this connection follows T. H. Marshall's definition in *Sociological Review*, Vol. XXVI, Jan., 1934, p. 60. Cf. Marshall in *Class Conflict and Social Stratification* (1938), pp. 97 *seq.*, where he defines class as a force 'that unites into groups people who differ from one another, by overriding the differences between them . . . and teaches the members of a society to notice some differences and to ignore others when arranging persons in order to social merit.' To use the

word 'class' here is, perhaps, provocative; but if Warner & Lunt *Yankee City Series, Vol. II: The Status System of a Modern Community*, [Yale] (1942), proves anything, it is that analyses of class made in terms of behaviour are too complicated to apply formally to modern highly civilised societies and that for the present 'class' can be used only to convey an impression of a solidity more pronounced than that defined by the term group.

P. 4. **West Indies:** James Stephen married Anne Stent, a woman of taste and literary sensibility. In the West Indies, writes Leslie Stephen (*Life of Sir JFS*, p. 12), he became 'not insensible' to the charms of another lady. ' "I have been told," said James Stephen, "that no man can love two women at once; but I am confident that this is an error." ' Leslie Stephen's account of this affair is tinged with meiosis: in his grandfather's journal on which Stephen drew for the early history of the family, it appears that his grandfather had an illegitimate son by the lady in the West Indies who subsequently became a parson in Buckinghamshire.

P. 5. **'even the Roman Catholic':** J. Stephen, *Essays in Ecclesiastical Biography* (1849), II, p. 313. This is still the best account of the Clapham Sect. J. Telford *A Sect that Moved the World* (1906) is not helpful. See also F. von Hayek's introduction to Henry Thornton, *An Enquiry into the Nature and Effects of the Paper Credit of Great Britain*, 1802 (1939 ed.).

P. 6. **'level of his speech':** ib., p. 293.

P. 7. **'scientific knowledge':** *Life of Sir JFS*, pp. 31–2.

P. 7, fn. **Venns.:** For an account of the Venn family see John Venn, *Annals of a clerical family* (1904).

P. 9. **'devilishly like it':** *Life of Sir JFS*, p. 49.

P. 9. **'sentimentalist and moralist':** ib., p. 33.

P. 9. **'not a simple man':** ib., p. 43.

P. 9. **'not been formed':** *Ideas and Beliefs of the Victorians* (1949) quoted by J. Simmons, p. 411.

P. 14. **'married you':** *Life of Sir JFS*, p. 63.

P. 14. **'smoked again':** ib., p. 61.

P. 15. **'taken out of him':** *Life*, p. 29.

P. 15, fn. **'active and simple':** C. E. Stephen, *The First Sir James Stephen* (1906), p. 76.

P. 15. **home town:** A. D. Coleridge, *Eton in the Forties* (1896), p. 23.

P. 16. **phenomenal:** *Life of Sir JFS*, p. 79.

P. 17. **'perfect devil':** Coleridge, op. cit., p. 42.

P. 17. **philology:** The real instigator of academic and disciplinary reform in the English public schools was Samuel Butler (grandfather of the author), Headmaster of Shrewsbury from 1798–1836; under his teaching the Shrewsbury boys won a far higher number of prizes and honours at Cambridge in proportion to their numbers than the alumni of any other school. Hawtrey continually sought Butler's advice for reforms at Eton many of which the Provost opposed—such as the system of half-yearly examinations whereby boys were deemed fit to move up the school. Kennedy carried on Butler's tradition at Shrewsbury and despite his choleric temperament achieved a fabulous list of classical successes among his pupils; and his notorious Latin grammar was imposed on all public schools by the Public Schools Commission. It was he who argued before the Commissioners that a public school's duty was to prepare boys for the university not to serve as a local school for the townspeople. (See J. B. Oldham, *Headmasters of Shrewsbury School*, 1552–1908 (1937).)

P. 17. **countenances:** C. A. Bristed, *Five Years in an English University* (3rd ed., 1873), p. 337.

P. 17. **standard of scholarship:** For an account of Hawtrey's reforms see H. C. Maxwell-Lyte, *History of Eton College* (1889), pp. 401–9, 473.

P. 18. **'on the subject':** *Edinburgh Review*, Vol. LXXXI, Jan., 1845, p. 228.

P. 18. **'in the world':** *Life of Sir JFS*, p. 81.

P. 18, fn. **'laugh about?':** Coleridge, op. cit., pp. 293–4.

P. 19. **curriculum:** Maxwell-Lyte, op. cit., p. 479.

P. 19. **'law of Nature':** *Life of Sir JFS*, pp. 79–80.

P. 19. **'impressive phenomenon':** *Cornhill Magazine*, Vol. XXVII, Mar., 1873, p. 290. 'Thoughts of an Outsider: The Public Schools.' Cf. *Fraser's Magazine*, NS Vol. IX, Mar., 1873, p. 326, 'University Endowments' (unsigned), by L. Stephen. 'People educated at our old public schools sometimes seem to fancy that boys have been created in order to add to the glories of Eton and Winchester, instead of admitting the opposite point of view.'

P. 19. **'Tunded MacPherson':** For an account of this scandal see Sir Charles Oman, *Memories of Victorian Oxford* (1941), pp. 35–8, in which prefects inflicted thirty cuts quite unjustly on a senior boy. A friend of his father wrote to the *Times*, and within a few days that paper and the *Daily Telegraph* were deluged with letters complaining of the appalling thrashings inflicted on their sons by prefects. The Headmaster of Winchester took action to stop this cruelty, though he rightly refused to expel the prefect because of the public outcry: his description of him, however, as 'a good and gentle boy' aroused some surprise. The headmaster of Shrewsbury from 1866–1908, H. W. Moss, once gave a boy eighty-eight strokes at a flogging which led to a question in the House and a poem in *Punch*; the Governors, after a public enquiry, refused to condemn this action. (Oldham, op. cit., p. 76). The days of Keate were by no means dead.

P. 19. **'their memory':** This is quoted from a second article on the public schools which Stephen did not publish.

P. 20. **'married state':** *Life of Sir JFS*, p. 81.

P. 20. **'Christian simplicity':** ib., p. 81.

P. 21. **'spectators':** 'The Public Schools,' *Cornhill*, op. cit., p. 285. Cf. SB, II, p. 127–8.

P. 22, fn. **poll-examination:** D. A. Winstanley. *Early Victorian Cambridge* (1940), pp. 216–8.

P. 23. **work in all:** W. W. Rouse Ball, *Cambridge Papers* (1918), 'The History of the Mathematical Tripos,' p. 300. Cf. Winstanley, op. cit., p. 160.

P. 24. **different questions:** Rouse Ball, op. cit., pp. 301–2.

P. 25. **'two hours and a half':** Bristed, op. cit., p. 126. C. A. Bristed was an American, who entered Trinity College in 1840, became a scholar and, after missing two years from ill-health which weakened his chances of obtaining a good degree, was placed second in the second class of the Classical Tripos in 1845. His book on Cambridge, written for an American audience, is by far the best near-contemporary account of Stephen's Cambridge, being full of fascinating detail and accurate in its account of the curricula and regulations of the university. Bristed greatly admired the accuracy of Trinity classical scholarship though he thought that

Cambridge, in other ways intellectually superior to Harvard, lagged behind an American university in oratory and in morals. His book is superior to W. Everett's *On the Cam* (1866), a series of lectures, delivered in Boston in more elaborate and rhetorical form, and far less informative.

P. 25. **five thousand pounds in all:** *Sketches*, p. 38.

P. 26. **William Hopkins:** Rouse Ball, op. cit., pp. 308-9.

P. 26, fn. **'this year':** Winstanley, op. cit., p. 411.

P. 27. **'leaving it':** *Sketches*, p. 107. Cf. SEI, pp. 28-30.

P. 27. **honeymoon:** J. E. B. Mayor, *Isaac Todhunter, In Memoriam* (1884), p. 25.

P. 28. **'his part':** *Life*, p. 48.

P. 28, fn. **with Stephen's help:** D. A. Winstanley, *Unreformed Cambridge* (1935), p. 229. Gunning *Reminiscences* (1854), II, p. 28. *Cambridge University Commission and Report* (1852), pp. 180-2. H. E. Malden, *History of Trinity Hall* (1902), p. 241. Stephen held a Bye-Fellowship, a type of Fellowship which originated in the difficulty experienced in estimating, after any considerable accession of wealth, what was the proper sum the College should pay in respect of the newly-founded Fellowship and by how much the stipend of the old Fellowships should be increased. They were used as stepping-stones by young men to the dignity of a full Fellowship. (See *Commission*, op. cit., pp. 187-8.)

P. 28. **Trinity Hall:** G. M. Trevelyan in an introduction to the 1932 edition of *Sketches*, notes that Stephen never mentions the vigorous intellectual life of Trinity and St. John's; but it is not true to suggest, as Winstanley does, that he knew only small College life. Stephen had friends in both these great colleges and the entrée to the best intellectual sets through his brother's and his cousins' friends. His own friends in undergraduate days were the two Diceys, Frank Coleman, (a cousin of Herbert Duckworth), F. V. Hawkins, Howard Elphinstone and W. F. Robinson, none of whom he saw much of later in life.

P. 29. **'incapable body':** Letter to C. E. Norton, 8 Oct., 1898.

P. 29. **'Well struck Parson':** *Life of Sir JFS*, p. 34.

P. 29. **The Sports:** See *Empire Review*, Vol. II, 1902, p. 656, for an account by P. M. Thornton of Stephen's part in starting the University sports.

P. 30. **'from Cambridge':** *Life*, p. 63.

P. 30. **of pleasure:** An interesting article by P. E. Vernon on the psychology of rowing is to be found in *The British Journal of Psychology*, General Section, Vol. XVIII, Pt. 3, Jan., 1928, pp. 317-31.

P. 31. **rowing coaches:** Sir Charles Dilke, who rowed in the 1864 Head of the River crew, greatly admired Stephen as a coach.

P. 32. **'my comrades':** Odyssey, Bk. XI, 77-8.

P. 32. **'the mark':** *Life*, p. 72.

P. 32. **'done so':** ib., p. 60.

P. 33. **munching:** G. F. Browne, *The Recollections of a Bishop* (1915), p. 102.

P. 33. **out of mischief:** *Fraser's Magazine*, NS Vol. II, Dec., 1870, 'Athletic Sports and University Studies,' by L. Stephen, p. 696. Cf. Winstanley, *Early Victorian Cambridge*, op. cit., pp. 416, 421 and *Life*, p. 58. A novel written on this very theme is T. Hughes's *Tom Brown at Oxford*.

P. 34. **'common pump'**: D. A. Winstanley, *Later Victorian Cambridge* (1947), p. 151. Stephen's comment was that six weeks after a poll man had gone down he would be unable to distinguish between a pump and a siphon. Cf. L. Stephen, *The Poll Degree from a Third Point of View* (1863), p. 2.

P. 34. **'muscular Christianity'**: *Life*, p. 77.

P. 34. **trapeze of the intellect**: Cf. L. Stephen, *Life of Henry Fawcett* (1885), pp. 90-3.

P. 35. **'honour triposes'**: *Flysheet*, 28 *May*, 1864, *University Papers*, H.C.1, quoted by Winstanley, op. cit., pp. 153-4. Cf. *The Poll Degree*, op. cit., p. 14.

P. 36. **governing class**: Cf. Stephen's remark that Cambridge should not be turned into an École Normale because it existed to raise the general tone of instruction among the highly-educated classes and to keep the learned professions in touch with the university, and to 'hold out, even to the aristocracy, a hope of improving their minds amongst us.' (*The Poll Degree*, op. cit., pp. 8-9.)

P. 37. **cactus?**: The duty of a university, thought Stephen, was not to make men work but to put them in the way of, and to encourage, study. (ib., p. 4.) The Cambridge system meant a constant disposition to esteem all kinds of knowledge in proportion to their capacity for testing men's abilities. *Fraser's Magazine*, Vol. LXXVII, Feb., 1868, p. 149, 'University Education,' by a Don (L. Stephen). Stephen had no faith in lectures as a method of instruction. He noted sardonically when delivering the first course of Clark lectures that his audience consisted largely of young ladies from Newnham and Girton colleges who in his opinion could have acquired all that he had to say from two or three books in half the time. Cf. Virginia Woolf's inherited contempt for lectures. (*The Death of the Moth* (1942), p. 146.)

P. 37. **'independent course of study'**: *Fraser's*, op. cit. pp. 142-3.

P. 37. **'their minds'**: ib., p. 137.

P. 37. **attached to them**: 'Cambridge men have been accustomed so long to associate improvement in education with increased competition in examinations,' ib., p. 153. Stephen also attacked the system of prizes and sinecure posts: 'the Head of a College would not be missed if he sank into the earth for fifty weeks a year.' (ib., pp. 143-4.)

P. 37. **narrow minded**: D. A. Winstanley took the occasion offered by a reprint of the *Sketches from Cambridge* (1932 ed.) to trounce Stephen for the unfairness of his judgments on his university (see *Cambridge Review*, Vol. 54, 17 Feb., 1933, p. 259). He complains that Stephen makes no mention of the reform movement which had already swept away many abuses; that he jeers at Fellows and Tutors for not searching; that, as G. M. Trevelyan pointed out (see *supra*) he is disdainfully silent about the brilliant literary and classical sets; and that he writes in spite against the place which he had just quitted. To this there are two points to be made. The first is on the facts. Anyone who reads Winstanley's noble researches on nineteenth-century Cambridge will remark how slow and confused was the reform movement and how the Colleges continually hampered it. Winstanley ignores Stephen's articles in *Fraser's* and does no justice to his good sense. A man like Stephen who was ahead of his time should not be attacked for his foresight. It is also true that the standard of Cambridge scholarship *in Stephen's time* was low by comparison with that of the greatest European universities. Stephen did not ignore the Apostles or other sets but wrote about them at length in his biographies of Fitzjames Stephen and Henry Fawcett and in *Some Early Impressions* which gives a more general picture of his undergraduate days and dilates at length upon the literary taste of Cambridge (pp. 33–44). This leads one to the second point, which is more serious, for it raises the question of whether scholars can maintain a sense of proportion. Stephen called his book *Sketches*. It was not intended to be an accurate history of all aspects of university life. It was written after a well-known pattern of which the next best known is *Sketches of Cantabs*, by John Smith of Smith Hall, Gent. (1849) (almost certainly by John Delaware Lewis, see D.N.B. and Dict. of Anon. and Pseudo. Lit. by Halkett & Laing). These books were intended to give amusing portraits of dons and undergraduates, and they succeeded. You may dislike their jocular tone or disapprove of their values, but you cannot sensibly attack their accuracy. Why should they be measured by a standard suitable for Ph.D. theses? Why break a butterfly on the wheel of scholarship?

P. 38. **'in the 'eighties'**: *Life*, p. 76. See also in addition to the two articles cited above, *Fraser's Magazine*, NS Vol. IV., Sept., 1871, p. 269. 'The Future of University Reform,' and NS Vol. IX, Mar., 1874, p. 323, 'University Endowments,' both by Stephen.

P. 38. **an Englishman**: H. E. Roscoe, *Life and Experiences* (1906), pp. 63–4.

P. 39. **'humble exterior'**: *Life*, p. 70–1.

P. 39. **'battle in the world'**: *Sketches*, p. 81.

P. 39. **'all I want'**: T. Hughes, *Tom Brown's Schooldays*, Ch. IV.

P. 39. **'bachelor's degree'**: SEI, p. 34.

P. 40. **with either**: *Life of Henry Fawcett*, ib., pp. 23–5.

P. 40, fn. **'mankind'**: HL, III, p. 321. See *Julian Bell, Essays, Poems and Letters*, ed. by Quentin Bell (1938). Happily all Stephens are always being filled with the urge to write about themselves and their family, with the result that from the Master in Chancery's memoir to the present day we have one hundred and fifty years of published history of this family. This memoir is a fascinating appendix to the history of the intellectual and spiritual development of the descendants of the Clapham Sect.

Stephen was not hostile to originality in the young, which he defined as an irresistible desire for display; he admired the man who was not afraid to make a fool of himself and respected those who were not afraid to be laughed at. *Sketches*, pp. 65–7.

P. 41. **'the species'**: *Life of Henry Fawcett*, p. 95. Cf. *Life*, p. 170.

P. 41. **of the visit**: *Life of Henry Fawcett*, op. cit., p. 85.

P. 41, fn. **'Clearly not responsible'**: T. Thornely, *Cambridge Memories* (1936), pp. 40–1. Cf. F. A. Keynes, *Gathering up the Threads* (1950), p. 53.

P. 44. **'burnt'**: M. Holroyd, *Memorials of the Life of G. E. Corrie, D.D.* (1890), p. 277.

P. 44, fn. **'not he'**: G. F. Browne, *St. Catharine's College* (Univ. of Cambridge College Histories), (1902), p. 223.

P. 45. **'for granted'**: *Life*, pp. 150–1.

P. 45. **'supporting me'**: *The Mausoleum Book*, p. 3, *Life*, p. 132.

P. 45. **'thousand hours'**: *Sketches*, p. 22. SEI, p. 45.

P. 45. **exceptional**: ib., p. 70.

P. 46. **'nobody will'**: *Life*, p. 159. The book is identified by Maitland as C. W. King, *The Gnostics and Their Remains* (1864).

P. 46. **a mockery**: J. H. Newman, *Apologia Pro Vita Sua* (1864), p. 120.

P. 47. **toy:** *Life*, p. 24.

P. 47. **'sacred truth':** *The Mausoleum Book*, p. 8.

P. 47. **garment:** In an article on Lytton Strachey in *Horizon*, Vol. XV,
Feb., 1947, p. 92, John Russell states that the Agnostics
bequeathed to Bloomsbury a 'legacy of honest and tormented doubt.' This is
a false description of the state of mind of Stephen, Huxley, Spencer, Morley
and Meredith or of Sidgwick's theism. The agonised scepticism of Clough and
of the young J. A. Froude can be found again in G. J. Romanes who, before
his death, was again received into the Church—or, of course, in Robert Elsmere.
But the new fashion in unbelief was not one of doubt, or agony.

P. 48. **'religious belief':** Winstanley, *Later Victorian Cambridge*, op. cit.
p. 40.

CHAPTER II

P. 49. **'sensation':** *Life*, pp. 158–9.

P. 49. **bachelor:** Cf. HL, III, pp. 106–8.

P. 51. **the faithful:** *Life of Sir JFS*, p. 129.

P. 51. **Saturday Review:** M. M. Bevington, *The Saturday Review, 1858–68*
[New York] (1941), p. 381, lists Leslie Stephen's
articles written for the paper; four were identified by a marked file copy which
had belonged to Fitzjames; two by Leslie himself; and the remainder by
Bevington.

P. 51, fn. **'Mr. Cunningham':** G. W. E. Russell, *A Short History of the
Evangelical Movement* (1915), p. 117.

P. 51. **Cornhill:** Stephen described the *Cornhill* at this time as 'an unprece-
dented shillingsworth—limited to the inoffensive.'
J. W. Robertson Scott, *The Story of the Pall Mall Gazette* (1950), p. 69.

P. 52. **'root and branch men':** F. W. Hirst, *Early Life and Letters of John
Morley* (1927), I, p. 45, Cf. J. Morley
Recollections, 1917, p. 117.

P. 52. **Froude:** Maitland identifies on p. 171, fn., of the *Life* all Stephen's
articles in *Fraser's* including those not republished, but he
decides not to make conjectures about some articles written between 1866–9
on the grounds that other men were writing in much the same freethinking
style, and because Stephen had decided not to reprint his earlier work. The
article on Voltaire in Vol. LXXVI, Nov., 1867, pp. 541–68, has the true
Stephen ring; a review of Lecky's *History of European Morals*, Vol. LXXX,
Sept., 1869, pp. 273–84, is more doubtful.

P. 52. **'an ass':** *Life*, p. 172.

P. 53. **[The North]:** *The History of the Times* (1939), II, p. 365.

P. 53. **'to England':** ib., p. 376.

P. 54. **'makes four':** *Life*, p. 113.

P. 54. **'his pictures':** ib., p. 120.

P. 54. **indigenous:** Cf. *Essays in Reform* (1867), pp. 86–123.

P. 55. **'public crime':** *Life*, p. 127.

P. 55. **'due authority':** *The Times on the American War*, by L.S. (1865),
pp. 7–8. Stephen's closely reasoned analysis of
the *Times*' policy during the war in just over 100 pages is a brilliant forensic
argument. He accused the paper justly of crass ignorance, vacillation and
oscillation between different policies (p. 33), apologising for slavery and
dissimulating on the issue of emancipation (p. 41), and he had great fun at the

expense of its military correspondent who, even when Sherman reached the
coast, was still prophesying ruin for the North (pp. 81–9).

P. 55. **Wolstenholme:** Virginia Woolf drew the character of Mr. Carmichael in *To the Lighthouse* from Wolstenholme.
In old age he became something of a bore and Stephen irritated his family by
asking the lonely old bachelor to stay in Cornwall with them for the holidays
and then, finding his company tedious, leaving wife and daughters to entertain
him. Wolstenholme was present on the summer holiday in Cornwall (see
To the Lighthouse, Part III), of which Stephen wrote to C. E. Norton, 21 Sept.,
1899, 'I have lost the power of holiday making.'

P. 56. **'vulgar we are':** *Letters of J. R. Lowell* (1894), I, p. 403.

P. 56. **'Mr. Howells':** Van Wyck Brooks, *The Flowering of New England*
(1936), p. 315, fn.

P. 57. **'are making':** *Letters of J. R. Lowell*, op. cit., II, p. 503.

P. 57. **godfather . . . to Virginia:** *New Letters of J. R. Lowell* (1932),
p. 292, cf. also p. 268.

P. 57. **'lovable of men':** *Life*, p. 129.

P. 57. **'needless outrage':** Letter from L. Stephen to C. E. Norton,
dated 15 June, 1903. In a letter of 3 April,
1883, to Norton, he bemoans the 'poor old man' whose 'noble qualities'
are forgotten.

P. 58. **'in the act':** Van Wyck Brooks, op. cit., p. 518, fn.

P. 58. **identical:** Compare *Life*, p. 181, with *New Letters*, op. cit., p. 317.

P. 58. **'altogether':** *Letters of J. R. Lowell*, op. cit., II, p. 186. Cf. ib.,
p. 166, 'I confess to a strong lurch towards Calvinism
. . . that strengthens as I grow older.'

P. 58. **'of it':** ib., I, p. 420.

P. 58. **immigrants:** ib., p. 496.

P. 59. **'of fools':** ib., p. 179.

P. 59. **'whoever was?':** ib., p. 178. See also p. 274.

P. 59. **'somehow':** ib., pp. 258–9. Cf. V. L. Parrington, *The Romantic
Revolution in America, 1800–1860* [New York] (1927),
p. 461.

P. 59. **'of the eyes':** *Letters of J. R. Lowell*, op. cit., II, p. 141.

P. 59. **of Faith:** ib., p. 143. Cf. H. E. Scudder, J. R. Lowell (1901), II,
p. 176. Cf. Lowell's comment on Stephen's essay 'Are
We Christians?' 'I think I should say that you lump *shams* and *conventions*
too solidly together in a common condemnation. All conventions are not shams
by a good deal, and we shall soon be Papuans without them.' *Letters*, II, p. 109.

P. 59. **'a holiday':** Van Wyck Brooks, op. cit., p. 523. This assessment of
Lowell's writing (pp. 311–22, 514–25) is more reason-
able than V. L. Parrington's unnecessarily harsh judgment (op. cit., pp.
460–72). Parrington's partiality for hundred per cent American literature of
the Mark Twain variety leads him to depreciate the value of the aristocratic
New England tradition.

P. 60. **become friends:** *Life*, p. 246.

P. 60. **cowardly:** In a letter to C. E. Norton, Stephen scoffs at Sir G. O.
Trevelyan for carrying on his uncle's tradition of
Whig history whereby all Americans in the eighteenth century are god-
fearing angels and the only good Englishmen were Burke and Fox. See also
SB, I, pp. 174–8, for Stephen's estimate of politics.

P. 60. **'cynicism'**: SB, III, p. 163.

P. 60. **'particular case'**: *Nineteenth Century Review*, Vol. LI, Jan., 1902, 'The Good Old Cause,' by L. Stephen, p. 23. Cf. Virginia Woolf, *Night and Day*, (1938 ed.), Ch. VII, p. 100.

P. 61. **'old don'**: *Life*, p. 179.

P. 61. **'pea in a pod'**: ib., p. 194.

P. 62. **'getting into'**: *The Letters and Private Papers of W. M. Thackeray*, ed. Gordon Ray (1946), IV, p. 230.

P. 62. **'pureminded ... affections'**: *The Mausoleum Book*, p. 12.

P. 62. **'fixed'**: *Life*, p. 181.

P. 62. **'Onslow Gardens'**: *The Mausoleum Book*, p. 8.

P. 63. **'assembled'**: *Life*, p. 196.

P. 63. **'applaud'**: *The Mausoleum Book*, p. 10. For an excellent sketch of Lady Ritchie see Virginia Woolf, *The Moment*, 1947, pp. 156–8.

P. 63. **'any rate'**: ib., p. 10.

P. 63. **'utterly useless ... genius!'**: ib., p. 11.

P. 64. **'chilling criticism'**: ib., p. 17.

P. 64. **'mankind'**: ib., p. 18.

P. 64. **dining room**: E. Gosse, *Books on the Table* (1921), pp. 293–8. *Life*, pp. 268–9. Cf. Virginia Woolf, 'Leslie Stephen,' in the *Times*, 28 Nov., 1932, pp. 15–16, which is amended and reprinted in *The Captain's Death Bed* (1950), pp. 67–73.

P. 65. **'laughter'**: *Life*, pp. 190–1.

P. 65. **'oh!'**: ib., p. 189.

P. 65. **'papists'**: ib., p. 224.

P. 66. **Cornhill**: For the best account of Stephen's connection with the *Cornhill* see Robertson Scott, op. cit., pp. 94–7 *passim*. Since Thackeray's retirement Frederick Greenwood, who was also editor of another of Smith's ventures, the *Pall Mall Gazette*, G. H. Lewes, Dutton Cook, dramatist and novelist, and Smith himself had taken a hand in the editing. Stephen handled contributors better than Thackeray who had been too lenient; W. E. Norris says that 'he made me re-write whole chapters, and he would scrawl all over one's tidy manuscripts.' Stephen himself, says Robertson Scott, wrote so freely that he would sometimes put other initials than his own to his articles. Of his *Cornhill* style, Meredith wrote, 'the only sting in it was an inoffensive humorous irony that now and then stole out for a roll over, like a furry cub, or the occasional ripple on a lake in grey weather.' Under Stephen's editorship, Gosse, Stevenson, Henley, Mrs. Lynn Linton, Mrs. Oliphant, Hardy, Henry James and Meredith first contributed. See also Wilfrid Meynell (*Academy*, Vol. LXVI, 27 Feb., 1904, p. 221) for an account of Stephen as an editor.

P. 66. **'and religion'**: *Life*, p. 258.

P. 66. **unsophisticated**: James Payn, *The Backwater of Life* (1899). Introduction by L. Stephen, p. xxxv. Payn was a Cambridge friend of Stephen and much liked in society: G. W. E. Russell dedicated his *Collections and Recollections* to his memory. He wrote sixty-nine novels and candidly admitted that he wrote that much because 'I should not get so much for one first-rate book as I do for three second-rate ones.' He succeeded Stephen as editor of the *Cornhill*.

P. 66. **Hardy:** *Life*, pp. 275–77. W. E. Norris, *Cornhill*, NS, Vol. XXVIII,
               Jan., 1910, 'Leslie Stephen as editor' complains bitterly of
Stephen's fear of Mrs. Grundy.

P. 67. **'pleasant':** M. Veley, *A Marriage of Shadows* (1888), Introduction
               by L. Stephen, p. x.

P. 68. **'Charles I':** *Life*, p. 202.

P. 68. **'my race!':** ib., p. 297.

P. 69. **'parsons':** ib., p. 235.

P. 69. **blood money upon it:** ib., p. 299.

P. 69. **'has gone':** ib., p. 256.

P. 71. **amendment:** *The Mausoleum Book*, p. 32.

P. 72. **'waste time . . . denunciation':** ib., pp. 34–5.

P. 73. **'companion':** ib., p. 43. Caroline Emelia Stephen had had a sad
               youth. She fell in love with a student at Haileybury
when Sir James Stephen was a professor there, but he never proposed to her,
and he was suddenly sent unexpectedly to India. Her heart was for a time
broken and her health never recovered: she lived at home until her mother
died. She doted on Leslie who admitted that she was like a twin rather than
a younger sister. But Leslie found her circle of Quaker friends 'intolerably
dull,' and she his friends 'worldly.' Leslie admitted that she had 'really great
abilities,' but he underestimated her work. Like all Stephens she wrote a
natural readable style, and her book, *Quaker Strongholds* (1890), is an admirable
exposition of her new-found faith. D. N. Dalgleish has an essay on her in
People Called Quakers (1938). She also wrote about her religion, *Light Arising*
(1908), and the *Vision of Faith* (1911), in which there is a memoir of her by
her cousin, Katharine Stephen, and T. Hodgkin. Her book, *The Service of the
Poor* (1871), grew out of her work with Octavia Hill and her cousin Sarah in the
Metropolitan Association for Befriending Young Servants. The Cambridge
Hegelian, McTaggart, who knew her when she lived in Cambridge at the
beginning of this century, said that had women been eligible for election to
the Apostles, she alone would have been worthy of the honour.

P. 73. **Huxleys:** Stephen was never a close friend of his fellow agnostic,
               T. H. Huxley, but he wrote of him with affection as a
man who had been kind to him when he was in misery.

P. 73. **Pattle sisters:** The sisters married respectively, General Mackenzie,
               Henry Thoby Prinsep, H. V. Barley, J. W. Dal-
rymple, Lord Somers, Charles Henry Cameron and Dr. Jackson. Dr. Jackson
was a nonentity; 'somehow,' wrote Stephen, 'he did not seem to count as
fathers generally count in their families'; he married Maria Pattle in Calcutta
in 1837. The Pattle sisters were granddaughters on their mother's side of the
Chevalier de l'Estang, a page of Marie Antoinette who emigrated to India
after the French Revolution. For an entertaining, but scarcely accurate,
account of their father see Virginia Woolf's introduction to *Victorian Photographs
of Famous Men and Fair Women*, by Julia Margaret Cameron (1926). The
Jacksons had a son who died in infancy and three daughters, Adeline who
married Henry Halford Vaughan, Mary who married Herbert Fisher and
Julia who married first Herbert Duckworth and secondly Leslie Stephen.
Vaughan, who showed no affection for his wife, was Professor of History of
Oxford from which post he retired to write a *magnum opus*; he later gave out
that it had been destroyed by a housemaid's carelessness, but it was suspected
that he had himself torn it up. He published three volumes of commentaries
on Shakespeare described by Stephen as 'most singular instances of misapplied
ingenuity,' and of which one bookseller said that the only man who ever
bought a copy from him was Disraeli. Fisher was tutor to the Prince of Wales
and father of H. A. L. Fisher and Florence, wife of F. W. Maitland.

P. 74. **'smart to me':** *The Mausoleum Book*, p. 22.

P. 74. Holman Hunt . . . Woolner. Hunt and Woolner married two sisters and when Hunt's wife died, he married the third sister in the family. This second marriage led to a quarrel between the two men for both had secretly adored her; and the reason for this adoration (so Stephen relates) was said to be that she resembled Julia Jackson and was indeed often mistaken for her. ib., pp. 22–3.

P. 74, fn. 'rummy effect': Robertson Scott, op. cit., p. 87.

P. 75. proposed: Kind friends had other ideas for their future. Stephen was pressed to consider Julia Marshall later Mrs. O'Brien, and Julia was urged by Mrs. Cameron to marry a widower, Charles Norman, and to cease being dazzled by Stephen's 'vast intellect.'

P. 75. out of the question: Stephen left an account based on their exchange of letters analysing Julia's state of mind. Stephen writes that 'She already loves me tenderly: she dreams of me and thinks of me constantly: and declares that my love is a blessing which lightens the burthen of her life. But this feeling is blended with a fear of the consequences to me. She feels that she is making me more restless; my position is a trying one; she remembers how she has herself thought of women who had men "devoted" to them, who gave nothing and took everything. . . . I suggested that we might continue to live as we were living and yet go through a legal form of marriage, which would give me the right to be with her as much as I desired. She at once pronounced the scheme to be—as of course it was—impracticable.' Julia found it soon impossible to give him up (as her mother urged she should if she could not make up her mind to marry him). 'If I could be quite close to you,' she writes, 'and feel you holding me, I should be content to die. Knowing what I am, it is no temptation to me to marry you from the thought that I should make your life happier or brighter—I don't think I should. So if you want an answer, I can only say that as I am now it would be wrong for me to marry. . . . All this sounds cold and horrid—but you know I do love you with my whole heart—only it seems such a poor dead heart.' Later she asks Stephen to decide for her. He refused: 'the worst thing that could happen would be that she should become my wife and find that she had been mistaken.' He writes to her, 'there is no hurry. You may think of me as I think of Troy (my old collie)—a nice kind loving animal who will take what I give and be thankful. . . .' On the night of the 5th of January, Stephen dined with her and as he rose to go, she suddenly looked up and said, 'I will be your wife and will do my best to be a good wife to you.' Ten days later she wrote, 'My darling one, I feel most commonplace and quiet. The only thing I can't quite believe is that we are not married. . . .'

P. 75. 'adores her': ib., pp. 61–2.

P. 75. 'your mother': Virginia Woolf, *The Times* op. cit.

P. 75. 'ought to be': *The Mausoleum Book*, p. 41. Stephen begins the Mausoleum Book by saying: 'I wish to write mainly about your mother. But I find in order to speak intelligibly it will be best to begin by saying something about myself.' Though the book gives an account of the Jackson family circle, it is largely a justification by the father of himself to his children who, he feared, would fail to understand him. It ends slightly pathetically: 'It comforts me to think that you are all so fond of each other that when I am gone you will be the better able to do without me.'

P. 76. discovering: See A. W. Brown, *The Metaphysical Society* [New York], (1947), pp. 221–2. The first issue in Jan., 1860, sold 110,000 copies. James Payn attributed the drop in sales under Stephen to 'the failure of the literary and especially the classical essay to attract the public,' and to the increased readableness of the daily and weekly press. He guaranteed to make the *Cornhill* popular and Smith reduced its price to sixpence; but the sales still fell. Cf. Robertson Scott, op. cit., pp. 69, 96.

P. 76. **D.N.B.:** Material for the passage on Stephen and the D.N.B. has been drawn from SB, I, pp. 1–36; *Life*, pp. 383, 385, 387, 390, 394; DNB (1912–21), 'Memoir of Sir Sidney Lee.' Robertson Scott, op. cit., Ch. XXI, pp. 243–50. See also *The Times Literary Supplement*, No. 2498 (misprinted 2968), 16 Dec., 1949, p. 819, for further comment on the original conception of the Dictionary and its fulfilment.

P. 79. **crushed him:** It is from this time that Stephen's handwriting deteriorated so badly that misprints, which he failed to notice, appear frequently in his articles in periodicals. W. E. Norris, op. cit., p. 48, tells of one comic instance where Stephen completed a sentence, in which Swift compared something to beef without mustard, with the words 'in a letter to Arbuthnot'; the words were deciphered by the printer as 'or wine without nuts.'

P. 79. **'Ph.D. degree':** A. W. Brown, op. cit., p. 223.

P. 79. **'into slips':** *Life*, pp. 394, 397.

P. 80. **'half work':** ib., p. 402.

P. 80. **succeeding generation:** This was the view of the Harrow schoolmaster and climber, John Stogdon, quoted in Arnold Lunn, *Switzerland and the Alps* (1944), p. 148.

P. 80. **'worship':** L. Stephen, *The Playground of Europe* (1910), p. 39. See Stephen's article, 'Alpine Climbing,' in *St. Paul's Magazine*, Vol. I, Jan., 1868, pp. 470–85, in which Stephen ruminates on the changing attitude to mountains as a study in the history of thought. 'The history of mountaineering is, to a great extent, the history of the process by which men have gradually conquered the phantoms of their imagination.' This is quoted by W. R. Irwin, *Queen's Quarterly*, Vol. 53 (1946), p. 338.

P. 80. **Albert Smith:** Smith gave a popular course of lectures in the Egyptian Hall, Piccadilly, in the early 'fifties which ran for three years and did much to popularise climbing. Cf. Oscar Browning, *Memories of Sixty Years* (1910), p. 93.

P. 80. **four pounds each:** C. Hudson and E. Kennedy, *Where there's a Will there's a Way* (1856), p. 142. Cf. p. xiv. It was at this time that country sports were becoming expensive and more and more the preserve of the upper classes. The cost of mountaineering, which in the 'fifties was about one pound a day, however, rose sharply in the 'seventies, partly due to the development of hotels and other comforts and the cost of guides. Cf. A. Wills, *Wanderings Among the High Alps* (1937 ed.), p. 234.

P. 80. **Alpine Club:** The Alpine Club was composed mostly of professional men of the upper-middle classes. Mr. C. S. Bennett, in an unpublished paper on the Club in this period, which he generously put at my disposal, calculates that in the first twenty years of the Club's existence, there were 432 members of which 149 were lawyers, 103 business men, 70 dons and schoolmasters, 37 clergymen, 31 officers of the army or navy and 30 civil servants.

P. 80. **Alpine Journal:** Stephen also translated Berlepsch, *Die Alpen in Natur und Lebensbildern dargestellt*. He contributed to *Peaks, Passes and Glaciers;* F. Galton, *Vacation Tourists and Notes of Travel in 1860;* and to *British Sports and Pastimes*, ed. A. Trollope.

P. 80. **exploration:** The English Alpinists sometimes saw themselves as Livingstone or Burton or Wills (cf. Frederic Harrison, *My Alpine Jubilee* (1908), p. 120): but though they plugged this theme, no systematic work was carried out as was done by the Deutsche und Oesterreichische Alpenverein in the Eastern Alps.

P. 81. **amateur:** *Playground*, op. cit., p. 76 *seq. Life*, p. 96, however, suggests that he did sometimes climb without guides.

P. 81. **himself**: W. R. Irwin, op. cit., p. 341, takes Stephen's sage warnings against racing too literally. The precept that mountaineers should reduce dangers not exploit them was always trotted out by Stephen; but he enjoyed danger and exposed himself to it as all Alpinists do.

P. 81. **'self-satisfaction'**: J. Ruskin *Sesame and Lilies* (Library Edition, 1905), Vol. XVIII, Lecture I, §35, p. 90.

P. 81. **'silent'**: *Life*, p. 308.

P. 81. **science**: *Playground*, op. cit., pp. 108-9.

P. 81. **Tyndall**: Lunn, op. cit., pp. 138, 156. T. G. Bonney attacked Stephen's attitude in the *Alpine Journal*, Vol. VII, May, 1875, p. 223, as 'sheer Philistinism.' The quarrel and resignation have been followed by similar lamentable incidents in the history of this contentious club.

P. 81, fn. **host**: *Life*, pp. 96-7. *Playground*, op. cit., p. 1.

P. 82. **Olive Schreiner**: Unpublished MS. by Mrs. W. K. Clifford.

P. 82. **'mountains'**: *Life*, p. 92.

P. 83. **morning**: G. F. Browne, *The Recollections of a Bishop* (1915), p. 102.

P. 83. **'en silence'**: *Life*, p. 99.

P. 84. **so speedily**: EFP, pp. 192-3.

P. 84. **for it**: ib., pp. 194-5.

P. 84. **'to retreat'**: *Life*, p. 92. Cf. Frederic Harrison, op. cit., p. 21, 'I never saw a fresh peak but I thirsted to stand on it.'

P. 85. **'meeting'**: *Quarterly Review*, Vol. CI, April, 1857, pp. 285-323. 'Pedestrianism in Switzerland' quoted in W. A. B. Coolidge's edition of J. D. Forbes *Travels* (1900), p. 473. Forbes was the author of the first detailed book in English relating to exploration in the High Alps and is the link between the German scientist de Saussure and the founder of the Alpine Club.

P. 85. **freemasonry**: Cf. C. D. Cunningham and W. de W. Abney. *The Pioneers of the Alps* (1887), p. 25.

P. 85. **'money'**: *Life*, p. 220.

P. 85. **Religion**: T. Carlyle, *Past and Present*, Bk. III, Ch. 12, Centenary ed., 1896, p. 200. C. S. Bennett notes the large number among the first mountaineers who were Old Rugbeians. The school motto, he observes, is *Orando, laborando*.

P. 86. **'accomplish it'**: J. Tyndall, *The Glaciers of the Alps* (1860), pp. 73-74. The spirit of sanctifying play through work inspired both mountaineers and rowing men. Tyndall wrote of a climb up Mont Blanc: 'To some such bodily exertion is irksome, to some painful in the extreme, while to others it imparts the increasing flow of life and energy which is the source of a pleasure fully appreciated by all who, like one or two of our party, could row in a boat on which is depicted the motto "*Labor ipse voluptas*".' Tyndall was referring to E. S. Kennedy who was a don at Caius College.

P. 86. **pursuit**: *Playground*, p. x of 1946 edition.

P. 87. **'take it for'**: *Playground*, op. cit., p. 109. Stephen's jocular jokes, alas, have been inherited by too many literary Alpinists and form part of their stock in trade.

P. 87. **rococo imagery**: Stephen made play with Ruskin's misanthropy which, he averred, influenced his attitude to the Alps. 'The most eloquent writer who, in our day, has transferred to his pages the charm of Alpine beauties shares in many ways Rousseau's antipathy for the social order. Mr. Ruskin would explain better than anyone why the love of the sublimest scenery should be associated with a profound conviction that all things are out of joint, and that society can only be regenerated by rejecting all the achievements on which the ordinary optimist plumes himself. After all, it is not surprising that those who are most sick of man as he is should love the regions where man seems smallest.' HL, II, p. 205.

P. 88. **'shall be!':** *Playground*, op. cit., pp. 273–5.

P. 89. **possibilities:** For other assessments of Stephen as a mountaineer see C. E. Engel, *A History of Mountaineering in the Alps* (1950), and C. W. F. Noyce, *Scholar Mountaineers* (1950).

P. 89. **Sunday Tramps:** *Cornhill*, NS, Vol. XXIV, Jan., 1908, J. Sully, 'Reminiscences of the Sunday Tramps.' Stephen resigned the leadership in 1891 and went out for his last tramp in 1894. Sully comments on the intimate friendship which these walks bred, p. 88.

P. 89, fn. **'climbing?':** Unpublished MS. of Mrs. W. K. Clifford.

P. 90. **'in front':** Letter of Mrs. W. K. Clifford to Miss Vanessa Stephen. 2 Feb., 1906.

P. 91. **'to me':** *The Mausoleum Book*, p. 22.

P. 91. **due east:** A. Birrell, *More Obiter Dicta* (1924), p. 4.

P. 91, fn. **'prisoner':** F. W. Hirst, op. cit., I, pp. 165–6.

P. 92. **gratification:** W. Raleigh, *Samuel Johnson* (1907), p. 3.

P. 93. **die:** Letter to C. E. Norton, 12 Jan., 1902.

P. 93. **'without me':** *The Mausoleum Book*, pp. 91–2.

P. 94. **goal:** W. H. Thompson, *Huxley and Religion* (1905), p. 67.

P. 94. **'exciting topics':** Letter to C. E. Norton, 26 June, 1898. Cf. J. H. Morgan, *Morley* (1924), pp. 180–1.

P. 94. **'in nature':** *Letters of George Meredith* (1912), II, p. 555 (14 Feb., 1904).

P. 94. **Leslie Stephen:** The best short articles on Stephen's character which appeared on his death were those of Frederic Harrison in the *Cornhill*, Vol. LXXXIX, April, 1904, p. 433, reprinted in *Realities and Ideals* (1908) and of Frederick Pollock, *Independent Review*, Vol. III, June, 1904, pp. 48–60. Since then articles have been remarkably scarce. A 1907 reprint of EFP has an essay by James Bryce and Herbert Paul on Stephen's life and work, but it does not amount to much. A. C. Lyall, *Studies in Literature and History* (1915) and J. E. Courtney, *Freethinkers in the Nineteenth Century* (1920), comment briefly on his career as an agnostic and moralist. Sidney Lee republished in *Elizabethan and other Essays* (1928) his Leslie Stephen lecture of 1911, which gives a personal recollection of their collaboration on the D.N.B. S. T. Williams, *London Mercury*, Vol. 8, Oct., 1923, pp. 621–34, considers Stephen as an essayist. E. Gosse, *Silhouettes* (1925), pp. 319–26, claims that Stephen has been unfairly forgotten as a critic. Desmond MacCarthy, *Leslie Stephen* (1937), which he delivered as the Leslie Stephen lecture for that year and Q. D. Leavis's reply to it are dealt with in Ch. IX below.

P. 96. **'to God':** *Ideas and Beliefs of the Victorians* (1949), p. 100.

P. 97. **hospital:** *Life*, p. 126.

P. 97. **slaughter:** ib., p. 436. Stephen spoke strongly against the cant of supposing that the Crimean War had regenerated England. SB, II, p. 237 and HL, III, p. 50.

P. 98. **The Egoist:** In Ch. II of *The Egoist* Meredith describes Vernon Whitford, who was drawn from Stephen, in the well-known phrase, 'Phoebus Apollo turned fasting friar.' Readers of *The Egoist*, however, have been misled by young Crossjay Patterne's encomium of his tutor to the effect that one could depend upon him because he was 'always the same,' e.g. 'If ever a man was all of a piece it was Stephen,' F. W. Knickerbocker, *Free Minds: John Morley and His Friends* (1943), p. 15.

P. 98. **'first rate man':** Virginia Woolf, *To the Lighthouse* (1927 edition), p. 17.

P. 98. **'tyranny in him':** ib., pp. 255–62; p. 306.

P. 98. **'human decency':** ib., p. 54.

P. 98. **'little drama':** ib., pp. 256–7.

P. 99. **'live them down':** *The Mausoleum Book*, p. 44.

P. 100. **'scientific world':** Mrs. Leslie Stephen, *Notes From Sick Rooms* (1883), p. 5.

P. 101. **'impractical':** Letter to Norton, 25 Aug., 1895.

P. 102. **'masculine nature':** *The Mausoleum Book*, p. 44. Cf. HL, III, p. 162.

P. 103. **'agreeable':** Letter to Mrs. W. K. Clifford, 4 Sept., 1884.

P. 104. **'in their heads':** *Sketches*, p. 84. R. E. Sencourt misjudges Stephen's humour when he writes, 'Nothing of a joke appealed to him but the sardonic in it.' Cf. Sencourt, *Life of Meredith* (1920), p. 192.

P. 105. **'to the world':** *The Mausoleum Book*, p. 74.

P. 105. **pause:** Cf. the same honesty in C. Oman, *On the Writing of History* (1939), pp. 218–20.

P. 105. **'old work':** SB, II, p. 158. C. E. Norton gave a different but, I think, less satisfactory explanation of Stephen's lack of inner purpose. In *Letters* (1913), I, p. 436, he writes: 'Struck as usual with Stephen's intellectual sincerity and liberality, and with that temper of indifference to one's own influence, a certain inertness, which, I fancy, is common to men of delicate and fastidious sensibilities and of philosophic disposition, who find themselves in creed and in motive out of harmony with their generation.'

P. 105. **'own legs':** I. Turgenev, *Fathers and Children*, Ch. XXI.

P. 105. **whole story:** Q. D. Leavis in *Scrutiny*, Vol. VII, March, 1939, p. 405, 'Leslie Stephen—Cambridge Critic' takes it as a final judgment and calls it a 'brilliant study in the Lytton Strachey manner of a slightly ludicrous, slight bogus, Victorian philosopher, [which] has somehow served to discredit Leslie Stephen's literary work.' It is difficult to see how the agonising description of the state of mind of a daughter in regard to her father could be conceived as in the Lytton Strachey manner; or, indeed, that Virginia Woolf was preoccupied with debunking her father's character. In an attempt to score a point against Bloomsbury, Q. D. Leavis has omitted to mention the complementary portrait of Stephen as Mr. Hilbery in *Night and Day*, and is apparently unaware of the article in the *Times*.

P. 105, fn. **'still':** Virginia Woolf, op. cit., p. 59.

P. 106. **Walter Pater:** Letter to C. E. Norton, 21 Nov., 1899.

P. 106. **'life-like villain':** *Life*, p. 474.

P. 106. **'discomfited':** *The Times*, op. cit.

P. 106. **'genuine':** ib.

P. 106. **discarded:** C. E. Norton expressed surprise that Stephen should
have defended Gosse when the latter was flayed by
the *Nation* for inaccuracy. Stephen admitted that Gosse was fussy and conceited and not 'in a high rank among friends'; but Gosse had been kind to
him and Gosse should be protected. Letter to Norton, 27 April, 1900.

P. 107. **'antipathy instead':** Florence Hardy, *Early Life of Thomas Hardy*
(1928), p. 238.

P. 107. **'never changed':** *Life*, p. 273.

P. 107. **Newbolt:** See Stephen's appreciative references, SB, I, p. 29 fn.

CHAPTER III

P. 110. **of valves:** The best contemporary assessments of Evangelicalism
as a party are in W. J. Conybeare, *Essays Ecclesiastical
and Social* (1855), pp. 57–164, and an article in *Macmillan's Magazine*, Vol. III,
Dec., 1860, 'The Evangelical Clergy.' An excellent short and suggestive
bibliography on Evangelicalism may be found in C. Smythe, 'The Evangelical
Movement in Perspective' in *Cambridge Historical Journal*, VII, No. 3,
1943, pp. 160–174.

P. 110. **Evangelical origin:** On the contribution of Evangelicalism to the
Oxford Movement see Y. Brilioth, *Evan-
gelicalism and the Oxford Movement* (1934).

P. 110. **His sheep:** An apparent inconsistency obtrudes upon the Evangelical scheme of salvation as preached by Simeon and
Calvinists. If God predestines a man to be among the elect, why should we
evangelise the unredeemed, who are either irretrievably lost or will at some
time during their lives turn to God and show signs of their election? Calvinists,
like disciples of other necessitarian creeds, stand in danger of antinomianism—
the antinomy of a determinate decree of election consequent upon a limiting
of Divine Grace to the elect, and of a universal appeal to human free will,
as if predestination did not exist. It was this doctrine which Wesley rejected,
when he declared that God's grace was not limited, but for all men. The
Wesleyan evangelist must spread God's word in order to melt the hearts of
men frozen with sin which, when melted, could close with God's offer of
salvation. Wesley's Arminianism—though, of course, it finds itself in difficulties in other fields of theology—is a satisfactory logic for the administration
of redemption. How then are we to explain the views of the Calvinist
Evangelicals?

Firstly they held that no man can say who are the elect, even less that he
himself is for certain numbered with them. Thus he must seek out the elect
and awake them to their destiny. He must evangelise to spread God's glory
and show how many, in fact, He was prepared to pardon and receive. He must
evangelise to make sure that he himself did not slip from grace. He must
evangelise for every moment of his time was accountable to God; and in what
more godly way could he spend his hours? Though many will for ever remain
deaf to the Gospel Call, many will be awakened to their real mission in life,
and so the rule of God's saints on earth will be achieved with greater speed.
Secondly the Church of England has always been at pains to moderate its
Calvinist doctrines. Article XVII is explicitly Calvinist, and the English
delegates to the Synod of Dort signed its canons. Yet they were able to interpret
them liberally without straining their conscience, and indeed the Synod itself
inclined to an Infralapsarian rather than to the Supralapsarian interpretation
of Predestination preferred by Calvin. Richard Baxter taught a Calvinism
which held that God provided salvation for all men, some of whom he elects
and others whom he leaves without the necessary grace of repentance and faith
(which none of us have the right to claim), and that thus we have great need of
evangelisers. Simeon appears to have been oblivious to the difficulty. He

was of course aware of the degrading controversy in which Toplady engaged against Wesley on Predestination and rightly saw that the work of evangelising was not furthered or edified by such debates. For a discussion of the matter from the Wesleyan point of view see W. B. Page, *A Compendium of Christian Theology*, (1877), II, pp. 340–57. Cf. *Eng. Thought 18th Cent.*, II, pp. 426–8.

P. 111. **of death:** H. Venn, *Complete Duty of Man* (1779, 3rd edition), Ch. 7–9. *Eng. Thought 18th Cent.*, II, p. 431.

P. 112. **experienced God's grace:** Cf. J. G. McKenzie, *Psychology, Psychotherapy* and *Evangelicalism* (1940), pp. 21 *seq*.

P. 113. **'reply':** Moncure Conway, *Autobiography* (1904), I, p. 396.

P. 115. **'derived':** C. E. Stephen, *The First Sir James Stephen* (1906), pp. 181–3.

P. 115, fn. **odious:** *Life*, pp. 133–4.

P. 117. **'praise':** G. W. E. Russell, *The Household of Faith* (1902), p. 226.

P. 117. **'notice it':** E. M. Forster, *Abinger Harvest* (1936), p. 242.

P. 117, fn. **'mind':** Russell, op. cit., pp. 226–7.

P. 118. **'truth':** SRD, II, p. 244.

P. 118. **'complacency':** Sir J. Stephen, *Essays in Ecclesiastical Biography* (1849), II, p. 305.

P. 119. **'Evangelicals':** G. W. E. Russell, *A Short History of the Evangelical Movement* (1915), p. 124.

P. 119. **'absolver':** ib., p. 83.

P. 119. **'a year':** C. E. Tonna, *Personal Recollections* (1841), p. 24. 'Parents know not what they do, when from vanity, thoughtlessness, or over-indulgence, they foster in a young girl what is called a poetical taste' (p. 25). This fear of literature as a lure which drew man away from God appears frequently in the biographies of the pious. Cf. Benjamin Gregory, *Autobiographical Recollections* (1903), pp. 119–144, in which Gregory tells how he crushed the love of literature which he had gained at his Methodist school, and after his conversion resolutely refused to join his schoolfellows in reading any but devotional books. Cf. the partisan analysis of Evangelicalism by the High Churchman, W. H. B. Proby, *Annals of the Low Church Party* (1888), I, p. 386, who quotes the Evangelical saying: 'Literature is inimical to spirituality if it be not kept under with a firm hand.'

P. 119. **'flesh':** *Macmillan's Magazine*, op. cit., pp. 114, 120.

P. 119. **'spiritual good':** F. Close, *Sermons* (1842), p. 149.

P. 120. **own sake:** V. F. Storr, *Freedom and Tradition* (1940), p. 29.

P. 120. **to God:** R. W. Dale, *The Old Evangelicalism and the New* (1889), pp. 19–26, cf. Dale, *The Evangelical Revival* (1880), pp. 4–8, 24.

P. 120. **ignorance of the world:** A. P. Stanley, *Life and Correspondence of Thomas Arnold* (1880), I, p. 246, fn.

P. 120. **broker:** See W. E. Gladstone, *Gleanings* (1879), VII, p. 222, and J. Tulloch, *Movements in Religious Thought* (1885), p. 51, on Whateley's attack on Hervey, the author of *Meditations among the Tombs*, for trying to explain the incomprehensible mystery of the Atonement in terms of abstract justice. Cf. F. P. Cobbe, *Broken Lights* (1865), pp. 36–7.

P. 120. **undoing:** Cf. F. D. Maurice: 'The Evangelical preaching has been deficient in reverence because it has been deficient in depth,' *Life of F. D. Maurice* (1884), I, p. 335.

P. 121. **Persecution Company Ltd.:** *A Short History of the Evangelical Movement*, p. 114.

P. 121. **strong upon him:** T. Mozley, *Reminiscences Chiefly of Oriel College and the Oxford Movement* (1882), I, p. 99.

P. 121. **Shaftesbury:** E. E. Kellett, *As I Remember* (1936), p. 149 fn.

P. 121. **'vita':** G. M. Trevelyan, *Sir G. O. Trevelyan, A Memoir* (1923), p. 15.

P. 121. **Austin:** C. E. Stephen, op. cit., p. 90. *Life of Sir JFS*, p. 75.

P. 122. **'anchorage':** J. Stephen, op. cit., II, p. 309.

P. 122. **'inquiry':** *Life of Sir JFS*, pp. 127–8. Cf. Rev. John Newton, 'I shall preach, perhaps, very usefully upon two opposite texts, while kept apart; but if I attempt nicely to reconcile them, it is ten to one if I don't begin to bungle.' C. Smythe, op. cit., p. 163.

P. 122. **Record:** The *Record* first appeared in 1828 and after six months of disastrous sales was saved by Haldane, who gave a 'new acrimony to religious controversy' as the *Christian Observer* noted. Sumner, the first Evangelical archbishop of Canterbury, commented, 'The conduct of the *Record* is execrable,' see G. R. Balleine, *A History of the Evangelical Party in the Church of England* (1908), pp. 206 *seq.*

P. 122. **clergyman:** A. V. Dicey, *Memorials* (1925), p. 139. Dicey wrote, in 1895, about the Stephen brothers: 'I am more and more convinced that [Leslie] will live far longer as a writer than his brother. Leslie, whether successful or not, is always trying to ascertain the truth; Fitzjames Stephen is always trying to show somebody else's error; and he often obtains his successes as a controversialist by first misrepresenting, though honestly, the meaning of his opponent, and then confuting an opinion which no one really holds.'

P. 122. **enthusiasm:** *Life of Sir JFS*, p. 221. It is difficult to state what Fitzjames Stephen's state of belief was after, say, 1860. A. W. Brown, *The Metaphysical Society* [New York] (1947), p. 132, states that he would have admitted that he believed in God on the grounds of probability though he had stopped attending Church in 1869. Vanessa Bell, on the other hand, recollects her uncle and aunt coming regularly on their way back from church, to Sunday lunch with the Leslie Stephens during the 'eighties; Fitzjames' wife certainly never discarded her Christianity and her daughters followed her in her beliefs. Fitzjames himself seems to have been deplorably uncertain. In two letters to Lady Grant Duff he states: 'I can sympathise heartily and fully with your perplexity as to the theological cross-examination of your boy—which of them was it? My wife and I determined to take a very definite line with our children, which we have accordingly followed ever since. We take them to church and have family prayers, which my wife reads.' Leeds, 1 April, 1875. *Per contra:* 'I have just been reading my Spectator, which always gives me a mild satisfaction. It is about the nearest approach that I ever make now, except on circuit, to going to church.' Athenaeum Club, 22 Nov., 1879.

P. 124. **'than dull':** DNB (1922–30), p. 261.

P. 124. **'faith':** J. M. Keynes, *Two Memoirs* (1949), pp. 84, 97.

P. 126. **'contemplating':** Desmond MacCarthy, *Portraits* (1949 edition), pp. 164–5.

P. 127. **mania:** *Eng. Thought 18th Cent.*, II, p. 430 ff.

P. 127. **'spirits':** HL, I, p. 291.

P. 127. **'and sweet':** ib., p. 284.

P. 128. **'head':** *Life of Sir JFS*, pp. 309–10.

P. 128. **complicated subject:** See H. Butterfield, *The Whig Interpretation of History* (1931), Ch. III, esp. pp. 54–63. The connection between puritanism and empirical science in the seventeenth century deserves more careful examination before generalisations such as that of Stephen can be made. It is, however, significant that of those foundation members of the Royal Society about whose religious beliefs we have evidence, over sixty per cent had puritan or parliamentary affiliations during the civil war; and all the ten original Enquirers who met in 1645 and subsequently formed the nucleus of the Royal Society, were puritans.

P. 129. **'shackles':** T. H. Huxley, *Collected Essays* (1894), V, p. 13.

CHAPTER IV

P. 130. **rougher texture:** *Sketches*, p. 138.

P. 130. **clear the mind:** See F. Pollock, *For My Grandson* (1931), p. 64, on disinterested Cambridge discussion.

P. 131, fn. **'bees':** J. Pope-Hennessy, *Monckton Milnes* (1949), I, p. 24.

P. 132. **'polish':** *Sketches*, p. 139.

P. 132. **humbug:** SB, II, pp. 126 ff.

P. 133. **'opinions':** SB, II, pp. 156–7.

P. 133. **old Fellow:** E. Abbott and L. Campbell, *Life and Letters of Benjamin Jowett* (1897), II, p. 149.

P. 133. **'play acting':** C. Oman, *Memories of Victorian Oxford* (1941), p. 235.

P. 134. **politics:** He snatched Arnold Toynbee from Pembroke ('Balliol, sir, is a kidnapping College. . . .'), Abbott and Campbell, op. cit., p. 65.

P. 134. **'obstruction':** ib., p. 213.

P. 134. **his day:** Part of Jowett's opposition to research was inspired by his mid-Victorian liberal hatred of sinecures.

P. 134. **'hate learning!':** ib., p. 132.

P. 134. **'merit':** Oman, op. cit., p. 234. Other interesting studies on Jowett, in addition to those cited *supra et infra* are A. C. Swinburne, *Studies in Prose and Poetry* (1894), A. M. Fairbairn in *Contemporary Review*, Vol. LXXI, Mar., 1897, and G. M. Young, *Daylight and Champaign* (1937).

P. 134. **for poetry:** W. H. Mallock, *Memories of Life and Literature* (1920), p. 64.

P. 134. **suicide:** ib., pp. 56–60.

P. 135. **'Church of Christ':** W. H. Mallock, *The New Republic* (1889 edition), Bk. I, Ch. 3, p. 59.

P. 135. **'authentic Christianity':** ib., p. 52.

P. 135. **'former establishment':** ib., Bk. II, Ch. 2, p. 123.

P. 135. **corrupt:** ib., Bk. I, Ch. 4, p. 80.

P. 136. **'masculine':** SB, II, p. 124. Stephen often praised Jowett in his articles e.g. 'Jowett did more than any other to stimulate the intellect of the rising generation.' *Fraser's Magazine*, NS, Vol. II, Dec., 1870, p. 700.

P. 136. **'early years':** ib., p. 157.

P. 137. **but sincere:** See Stephen's admirable analysis of Jowett on the Atonement, ib., pp. 134–5.

P. 137. **'a dodge':** Abbott and Campbell, op. cit., I, p. 131.

P. 138. **truth at all:** Cf. A. H. Sayce, *Reminiscences* (1923), p. 87, who agrees with Stephen's judgment on Jowett. Jowett's remark that study for its own sake is a waste of time enraged Mark Pattison, who replied by describing Oxford as 'a lively municipal borough.'

P. 138. **'them all':** SB, II, p. 143. The root of Stephen's argument is that Jowett in the end abandons metaphysics which should be studied 'to enable the mind to get rid of them.' Hence he bases himself on common-sense rationalism and history; but he abandons his base, as soon as he has settled, by a series of subterfuges and appeals to 'mystery.' He is not a Hegelian or a Coleridgean, and he cannot be excused by reason of his adherence to an intuitionist school of philosophy; therefore he cannot complain when attacked by Christians who thought that he was sinking the ship or leading, in Carlyle's phrase, 'an exodus from Houndsditch.'

P. 138. **the stake:** A. Birrell, *More Obiter Dicta* (1924), pp. 8–9.

P. 138. **'a rope':** *Life*, p. 114.

P. 138. **'quite a genius':** Abbott and Campbell, op. cit., I, p. 342.

P. 139. **'of roguery':** SB, II, p. 153.

P. 139. **that God:** *Ideas and Beliefs of the Victorians* (1949), pp. 403–09.

P. 139. **and fiction:** SB, II, p. 152. James Payn, *The Backwater of Life*, Introduction by L. Stephen, pp. xix–xx.

P. 140. **'especial province':** E. Hodder, *Life and Work of the First Earl of Shaftesbury* (1886), III, p. 166.

P. 140. **'not reason at all':** SB, II, p. 282.

P. 140. **'warm hearts':** Quoted from Marshall's Inaugural Lecture of 1885 by J. M. Keynes, *Essays in Biography* (1933), p. 255.

P. 140. **'impartial enquiry':** SB, III, p. 103.

P. 140. **'other subjects':** *Sketches*, pp. 32–3.

P. 140, fn. **is serious:** Cf. *Fraser's Magazine*, NS, Vol. IX, June, 1874. 'Mr. Ruskin's Recent Writings,' by L. Stephen. Huxley, too, took time off to defend classical economics and establish still more strongly his reputation for respectability. Cf. his article on Henry George *Collected Essays* (1901), IX, pp. 147–87, 'Capital—the Mother of Labour.'

P. 141. **'his system':** *Life of Sir JFS*, p. 123.

P. 141. **'swear by':** M. Carré, *Phases of Thought in England* (1949), p. 312, quoted from D. Masson, *Recent British Philosophy* (1867), p. 8.

P. 142. **syllogism:** I have found particularly helpful on Mill, O. A. Kubitz, *Development of John Stuart Mill's System of Logic* [Illinois] (1932) in the *Illinois Studies in the Social Sciences*, Vol. XVIII, No. 1.

P. 142, fn. **'bang one another':** J. Locke, *Essay Concerning Human Understanding* (1690), IV, 17.6.

P. 144. **'from within':** *Logic*, VI, 10.8. For a comparison of Comte's and Mill's positivism see T. Whittaker, *Reason and Other Essays* (1934), pp. 48–55. Stephen analyses the *System of Logic* with customary clarity in *Eng. Util.*, III, pp. 75–157.

P. 145. **'holding it':** Olive Schreiner, *Story of an African Farm*, Pt. II, Ch. 2

P. 145. **'true'**: *Fortnightly Review*, NS, Vol. XIV, Dec., 1873, pp. 741–2. F. W. Newman was reviewing the 3rd edition of Greg's *Creed of Christendom*.

P. 145. **'to be true'**: L. Huxley, *Life and Letters of T. H. Huxley* (1900), I, p. 217.

P. 146. **'of me'**: T. H. Huxley, *Collected Essays*, (1894) I, p. 192. Cf. W. McNeile Dixon, *The Human Situation* (1942), p. 342.

P. 146. **'to error . . .'**: J. W. Cross, *Life and Letters of George Eliot* (1885), I, p. 103.

P. 146. **Ethics of Belief**: W. K. Clifford, *Lectures and Essays* (1901), II, pp. 163–205.

P. 146. **'may lead'**: J. S. Mill, *On Liberty* (1859), Ch. II, p. 62.

P. 147. **'cardinal virtues'**: Huxley, *Life*, op. cit., I, p. 358.

P. 147. **'much profit!'**: ib., p. 217. Cf. Carlyle, *Frederick the Great* (Complete Works), 1897–1901, VIII, p. 240. 'The vital all-essential point, what we may call the heart's core of all Creeds which are human, human and not simian or diabolic . . . that it is not allowable, that it is dangerous and abominable, to attempt believing what is not true.'

Even Jowett approved of a lady who wrote to him saying, 'We Liberals should not talk about Freedom, but about truth—that is the flag under which to fight.' Abbott and Campbell, op. cit., I, p. 299.

P. 147. **'opposed to truth'**: *The Bridgewater Treatises* (1836), W. Buckland, "Geology and Mineralogy" I, p. 595.

P. 147, fn. **'act'**: A. Bain, *The Senses and the Intellect* (4th edition, 1894), pp. 356–8. See Carré, op. cit., pp. 316–17, who explains this point.

P. 147, fn. **'by ourselves'**: Locke, op. cit., II, 1.2.

P. 148. **'so and so'**: G. M. Young, op. cit., pp. 106–7.

P. 148. **'domination'**: J. W. Cross, op. cit., I, p. 106. George Eliot told Jowett that she was never a Comtist but as they were a poor unfortunate sect she would never renounce them. (Abbott and Campbell, op. cit., II, p. 182.) She continued to subscribe to Positivist funds until her death.

P. 148, fn. **Stephen . . . Positivist**: *Life*, p. 172.

P. 149. **'our knowledge'**: Locke, op. cit., I, 1.6, quoted by Carré, op. cit., p. 288.

P. 149. **'enquiry'**: SB, III, p. 196. Note the revolt of Henry Adams against this devotion to truth by the Darwinists. He wrote of himself in the 'sixties: 'Henry Adams was one of the first of an infinite series to discover and admit to himself that he did not care whether truth was, or was not, true. He did not even care that it should be proved true, unless the process were new and amusing. He was a Darwinian for fun.' *The Education of Henry Adams* (1917), pp. 231–2.

P. 149, fn. **'produce'**: *Life*, pp. 228, 231–2. Carlyle was one of Stephen's gods, though he disagreed with him, misunderstood him and got up against him. Writing to Norton (Letter of 29 Dec., 1873) he says, 'I regret very much my position to the old prophet but I cannot help it. Whenever I see him it is the old story: I like him, indeed I might say, I feel a strong affection for him but he always rants at me. . . . I think that he dislikes me.' (Cf. also *Life*, p. 377–8.) Stephen wrote his life in the D.N.B. and in an article entitled the *Decay of Literature* he paid tribute to the effect of

Carlyle's style. 'You might return from the strange gloom and splendour of the *French Revolution* or *Sartor Resartus* revolted or fascinated; but to read it with appreciation was to go through an intellectual crisis; and to enter into this spirit was to experience something like a religious conversion. You were not the same man afterwards. No one ever exercised such a potent sway over the inmost being of his disciples.' On the relation between Carlyle and the utilitarians see E. E. Neff, *Carlyle and Mill* [New York] (1924). How far utilitarians could misunderstand Carlyle may be appreciated by reading E. R. Bentley, *The Cult of the Superman* (1947), Ch. 1–3.

P. 151. **'new doctrines'**: Quoted by R. Wellek, *Immanuel Kant in England*, 1793–1838 (1931), p. 26.

P. 151. **'divine faith'**: ib., pp. 134–5.

P. 152. **'What is me?'**: M. Nédoncelle, *La Philosophie religieuse en Grande Bretagne de 1850 à nos jours* [Paris] (1934), p. 35.

P. 152, fn. **his servant**: Carré, op. cit., p. 341. For W. G. Ward see A. W. Brown, *The Metaphysical Society* (1947), pp. 56–9.

P. 152, fn. **Whewell**: Whewell held that while numerous instances of cause and effect might prove the generality of an induction they could not prove its universal application: that could be achieved only by employing in Cartesian style the additional use of the necessary truths of arithmetic and geometry. Mill replied that geometry is never more than approximately true and that the truth of arithmetic depended on the convention that every unit is exactly the same size as every other which again in real life was not true. As regards geometry Mill was to receive support from contemporary mathematicians when non-Euclidean geometry penetrated to England; as regards arithmetic, contemporary mathematical opinion was against him, cf. Kronecker's dictum: 'Integral numbers are made by God; everything else is the invention of man.' (Sir W. Dampier, *A History of Science* (4th edition, 1948), p. 465.) Mill appreciated that geometry, if studied as a branch of pure mathematics, must be hypothetical—it can be true only if studied as a branch of physics; but he did not realise that arithmetic is continuous with pure logic and independent of experience. Mill contradicted his own argument on number (contained in *Logic* III, 11, 14), in Ch. VII of the *Examination of Sir W. Hamilton's Philosophy*, curiously enough at the instance of a peculiarly fallacious argument by Fitzjames Stephen in his review of Mansel's metaphysics (republished in *Essays by a Barrister*). See an interesting note by C. E. Whitmore, 'Mill and Mathematics,' *Journal of the History of Ideas*, VI, Jan. 1945, pp. 109–12.

P. 153. **'with each other'**: H. L. Mansel, *The Limits of Religious Thought* (1858), p. 89.

P. 153. **'un maître'**: Nédoncelle, op. cit., p. 36.

P. 153. **fingers**: Nédoncelle, op. cit., p. 75, quoted from S. Pringle-Pattison, *Scottish Philosophy* (1885), p. 177.

P. 153. **'I will go'**: J. S. Mill, *An Examination of Sir William Hamilton's Philosophy* (1878 edition), p. 129.

P. 153, fn. **Christian**: T. H. S. Escott, *Social Transformation of the Victorian Age* (1897), p. 398.

P. 154. **'defended'**: J. M. Keynes, op. cit., p. 163.

P. 154, fn. **'end of it'**: *Life and Letters of T. H. Huxley*, I, p. 202.

P. 155. **was a God**: Agnostics were divided on the question of whether to deify the Unknowable, cf. Huxley's remark to a friend, 'the more I think of it the more I am convinced that there must be something at the bottom of it all.' (George Forester, *The Faith of an Agnostic* (1902), p. 81.) Cf. L. Büchner's condemnation of agnostics. 'Faith in the Unknowable is the distinctive feature of Agnosticism.' (*Last Words on Materialism*, trans.

by J. McCabe (1901), pp. 116, 149, which Forester thinks is unfair.) Büchner declares that absolute existence without manifestation is non-existence, but Forester argues that there may be a manifestation unknown to us or that Büchner's dichotomy of Force and Matter may be two sides of the same thing which we may call God.

P. 156. **'precarious poises':** G. M. Young, op. cit., p. 172.

P. 156. **'superficial thinkers':** H. T. Buckle, *History of Civilization* (1857), I, p. 694. Cf. *Fortnightly Review*, N.S., Vol. XXVII, May, 1874, pp. 672–95, in which Stephen censures Buckle for this remark. Nevertheless even Stephen did not go far enough for J. M. Robertson who criticises this review in his work on Buckle. Stephen noted ruefully on the proof copy of his article, 'I think he may have found a blot or two.'

P. 156. **go too far:** G. Eliot, *Essays and Leaves from a Note-book* (1884), p. 201, quoted by A. W. Benn, *The History of English Rationalism in the Nineteenth Century* (1906), II, p. 247.

P. 156. **'Resurrection':** *Life of Sir JFS*, p. 213.

P. 156, fn. **'minds at Oxford':** A. W. Benn, op. cit., II, p. 66.

P. 156, fn. **McCarthy:** J. McCarthy, *Reminiscences* (1899), II, p. 325.

P. 157. **'propagandism':** Cross, op. cit., II, pp. 343. Joan Bennett, *George Eliot, Her Mind and Her Art* (1948), Ch. IV gives an excellent analysis of George Eliot's agnosticism.

P. 157. **'theology':** *Lettres inédites de John Stuart Mill à Auguste Comte*, ed. L. Lévy-Bruhl (1899), p. 307. Cf. pp. 403, 447. See *On Liberty*, op. cit., Ch. II, pp. 97–8, where Mill writes 'Opinions contrary to those commonly received can only obtain a hearing by studied moderation of language, and the most cautious avoidance of unnecessary offence, from which they hardly ever deviate, even in a slight degree, without losing ground,' i.e. the interests of truth and justice demand restraint. This reticence led to a serious misunderstanding between Mill and Carlyle over the former's religious views: see *Letters of J. S. Mill*, ed. H. S. R. Elliot (1910), I, pp. 87–93.

P. 157. **their opinions:** M. Conway, op. cit., II, pp. 47–8. An account of the works of minor rationalists during the 'fifties is given by T. H. Bastard, *Scepticism and Social Justice* (1877). They show how far the rationalists were on the defensive and what lines of advance they were exploring.

P. 158. **Blasphemy Laws:** J. M. Robertson, *A Short History of Freethought* (1899), pp. 385–9, gives an account of the major prosecutions.

P. 158. **honest beliefs:** *Life and Letters of T. H. Huxley*, II, pp. 406–7.

P. 158, fn. **Virchow:** W. Boelsche, *Haeckel, His Life and Work*, trans. by J. McCabe (1906), pp. 145 and 171. Darwin was regarded in conservative scientific circles in Germany as an anarchist blowing up the work of a generation of careful classifiers, *vide* the speech of Keferstein, Professor of Zoology at Göttingen at the scientific congress of 1863.

P. 159. **George Eliot:** *Life and Letters of T. H. Huxley*, II, p. 343. Max Müller, delivering a Hibbert lecture entitled 'Atheism a Spectre' before Dean Stanley in the Jerusalem Chamber at Westminster Abbey, drew a distinction between religious and vulgar atheism. Vulgar atheists baited priests. M. Conway, *Autobiography* (1904), II, p. 365.

P. 159. **Herbert Spencer:** S. Dark and R. S. Essex, *The War against God* (1937), p. 73.

P. 159. **and Mrs. Lynn Linton:** G. S. Layard, *Mrs. Lynn Linton; her life, letters and opinions* (1901), pp. 243, 334–46.

P. 159. **it's blasphemy:** SB, III, pp. 202–4.

P. 159, fn. **'credulous nature':** Layard, op. cit., p. 202.

P. 160. **'insoluble':** T. H. Huxley, *Collected Essays*, V, pp. 238–40. Huxley came to define agnosticism, however, as no more than a method of thought, i.e. empirical enquiry. It 'is not a creed but a method. . . . Positively the principle may be expressed: In matters of the intellect, follow your reason as far as it will take you, without regard to any other consideration. And negatively: In matters of the intellect do not pretend that conclusions are certain which are not demonstrated or demonstrable. That I take to be the agnostic faith, which if a man keep whole and undefiled, he shall not be ashamed to look the universe in the face, whatever the future may have in store for him.' (Pp. 245–7.)

R. C. Churchill in *English Literature and the Agnostic* (1944), claims (pp. 17–18) Shakespeare, Jonson, Dryden, Swift, Pope, Fielding, Gibbon, Burke, Coleridge, Wordsworth, Burns, Peacock, Lamb, Byron, Hunt, de Quincey, Hazlitt, Keats, Shelley, Arnold, Mark Rutherford and Jefferies as agnostics. Only the last-named qualifies. This is sheer idiocy: to use the term agnostic in this fashion is to make a useful word meaningless and to out-do even A. W. Benn, the admirable but over-enthusiastic historian of nineteenth-century rationalism.

CHAPTER V

P. 162. **Origin of Species:** In *Essays in Biography*, pp. 161–2, op. cit., J. M. Keynes suggests to the unwary reader that Mill's *Examination of Sir W. Hamilton's Philosophy* was the decisive factor in the loss of faith by James Ward, Alfred Marshall, Sidgwick and Leslie Stephen who in 1865 'was still an Anglican clergyman.' Technically Stephen still remained a clergyman until 1875, but Mill's book can have done no more than confirm him in his agnosticism. Maitland suggests that Stephen had not read Mill's *Logic* by 1855 when he was ordained deacon, and notes that Sir James Stephen had foreseen how 'dangerous' it was (*Life*, p. 135); but Stephen had certainly read it by 1859 when he was ordained priest.

Stephen admired Darwin as a god but was too modest and diffident to make his acquaintance. Darwin did not know Stephen well enough to spell his name correctly when Stephen's article on the theological implications of his work appeared in *Fraser's Magazine* in 1871. Writing to Chauncey Wright, the American naturalist and philosopher, Darwin adds a postscript. 'Do you ever see *Fraser's Magazine*? There is a startling article on Divinity and Darwinism by, I suppose, Y. L. Stevens, who married one of the Miss Thackerays.' (*Journal of the History of Ideas*, Vol. VI, 1945, p. 34, 'Chauncey Wright, Darwin and Scientific Neutrality,' by P. P. Wiener.)

Stephen refers to the Wilberforce-Huxley debate in SB, III. He also cited J. R. Green's intense indignation with Wilberforce in the *Letters of John Richard Green* (1901) which he edited. Green who had been influenced by Ritualism as a youth and had taken Holy Orders with some misgivings, was just on his way to his first curacy under Mrs. Humphry Ward's future father-in-law in the East End of London when it occurred. He followed Stanley's Broad Church party for a time but took the opportunity afforded by ill-health (he had contracted tuberculosis) to resign his living in 1869 and, in order to avoid giving pain to his former friends, made no public avowal of his agnosticism (p. 71). He seems still to have been undecided for in 1871 he declared that he did not know until he had seen the Voysey judgment whether he would be able to take further preferment (p. 281). 'He seems to have thought that for a gentleman who openly denied the doctrine of the Trinity to be deprived of his living was an unjust or at least an injudicious restriction on clerical liberty' (Benn, op. cit., II, p. 345); at all events he broke with the Broad Church on this issue. In his *Short History of the English People*, he affirmed his faith in mid-Victorian Radicalism in bringing 'every custom and tradition, religious, intellectual and political, to the test of pure reason' (1889 edition), p. 605.

P. 162. Great Chain of Being: Any summary, so short as that *supra*, of so influential a book must be inadequate. For a *resumé* of articles on pre-Darwinian evolutionary theories, see P. P. Wiener, *Evolution and the Founders of Pragmatism* (1949), p. 245.

P. 164. fully perfected: See Stephen on Pope's metaphysics, HL, I, p. 122.

P. 165, fn. its advocates: *Life and Letters of T. H. Huxley*, I, pp. 168–71.

P. 166. 'non-scholastic meanings': Quoted by Wiener, op. cit., p. 7.

P. 166. Immanence: See C. C. J. Webb, *A Study of Religious Thought in England from* 1850 (1933) for an account of the Immanentist movement. In *Stones of Stumbling* (1893), pp. 207–27, Tollemache speaks of personal immortality not being literally true, but as being a process by which we are gathered back to God and *in* God.

P. 166. 'or Sequence': *The Education of Henry Adams* (1928), p. 231.

P. 166, fn. apes: Benn, op. cit., II, p. 167.

P. 167. 'precluded': Randall Davidson and W. Benham, *Life of A. C. Tait* (1891), I, p. 291.

P. 168. 'is not true': G. P. Gooch, *History and Historians in the Nineteenth Century* (1913), p. 19.

P. 168. interpretation: The extent to which Comte influenced Mill's historiography may be judged by reading Mill's review of Michelet's *History of France* (*Edinburgh Review*, Vol. LXXIX, Jan., 1844, pp. 1–31), in which Mill cites Larcher, Carlyle and Guizot as representing Comte's three stages in historiography; Mill thinks Michelet to be an excellent *scientific* historian in that he combines the gifts of poetry, reliability and ingenious interpretation, and thus illuminates the general laws which explain order and causation in historical phenomena.

P. 168. historical evidence: The controversy presents a remarkable instance of argument from evidence. Gladstone declares that Huxley has insulted the Lord by suggesting (on the best Liberal principles) that anyone who wantonly destroys another's property is guilty of a misdemeanour of evil purpose; but, *per contra*, the destruction of the Gadarene swine was legitimate because Jews were forbidden under Mosaic Law to keep pigs. Huxley examines his authorities carefully and replies that Gadara was in fact a Hellenic and Gentile town, and therefore the inhabitants had a right to keep pigs; since we may assume that Christ would never have wrongfully harmed such men, we may dismiss the story as false—unless one chooses to assume that Christ broke 'the first condition of enduring liberty [which] is obedience to the law of the land.' Further animadversions on pig-keeping habits in Galilee, the administrative boundaries, the social structure of Gadara, and Schürer's interpretation of Josephus, leads Huxley to declare that all the best opinion agrees that the synoptic Gospels are not independent but are founded on a common source and hence the story rests on legend or the observation of a single observer; and, while, *pace* Hume, there is no *a priori* objection against the miracle, such frail evidence for its occurrence is wholly insufficient. And Huxley added the singular prophecy: 'Whether the twentieth century shall see a recrudescence of the superstitions of medieval papistry, or whether it shall witness the severance from the living body of the ethical ideal of prophetic Israel from the carcase, foul with savage superstitions and cankered with false philosophy, to which the theologians have bound it, turns upon their final judgment of the Gadarene tale.' Note how Gladstone fights on Huxley's ground and argues too from historical evidence. Cf. also on this miracle Huxley, *Collected Essays*, V (pp. 303–8).

This is a characteristic Huxley argument. The feeding of the five thousand is possibly true; but why should he believe it to be so on the contradictory evidence available (ib., V, p. 206)? The Agnostic does not doubt Christ:

he doubts the evidence given for Christ having said or done certain things (ib., p. 220). Huxley noted the admission by Christians that some Biblical stories were not literally true, and asked why it was still anathema to tell schoolchildren that Jesus had a human father (ib., p. xi); eventually, he suggested, Christians will boast that since faith is not in touch with fact at all it will be inaccessible to infidel attacks (ib., IV, p. 217).

P. 168, fn. **appearance:** N. H. Baynes, *Constantine the Great and the Christian Church* (1930), p. 9. Cf. *Journal of Theological Studies*, Vol. I, pp. 24–37, 'Some Current Conceptions of Historiography and their Significance for Christian Apologetics,' by N. Sykes for a discussion of this problem.

P. 168, fn. **'gewesen':** L. von Ranke, *Geschichten der romanischen und germanischen Völker von 1494 bis 1514* [Leipzig] (1874), Vorrede vii. The words were translated by G. P. Gooch as 'What actually occurred' in *History and Historians*, op. cit., or as 'events as they actually happened,' Gooch, *Cambridge Modern History*, Vol. XII, Ch. XXVI, p. 824. Ranke meant no such thing. He was not a positivist but a moderate Hegelian who believed that diligent research would reveal the divine order in history, i.e. his vision was that of a process in history in which certain facts were more important than other facts. The famous phrase was coined as a protest against historians, such as Leo, who assigned to history 'the task of judging the past, of instructing the present for the benefit of the future.' See *The Times' Literary Supplement*, Nos. 2519, 2521, 2522 of May–June, 1950, in the last number of which Dr. Gooch supports his translation by arguing that Ranke's pictorial sense was so weak and, like most writers before 1848, his sociological interest so little developed, that it would be inappropriate to suggest that he had any feeling for what 'the past was really like.'

P. 169. **and rites:** Cf. Evans Bell, *Task of To-day* (1852) which compares the Bible and the Koran and *A Was I Hind* or *A Voice from the Ganges* (anon.) (1861), which dilates on mistranslations in Scripture.

P. 169, fn. **Mrs. Lynn Linton:** Layard, op. cit., p. 36.

P. 169, fn. **Darwin:** *Life and Letters of C. Darwin* (1887), I, Ch. 8, esp. pp. 307–8.

P. 169, fn. **other creeds:** EFP, p. 98.

P. 169, fn. **'anthropology':** L. Feuerbach, *The Essence of Christianity*, trans. Marian Evans (1881), p. 270.

P. 169, fn. **'seraglio':** Quoted by W. Staebler, *The Liberal Mind of John Morley* [Princeton] (1943), p. 48. Cf. W. K. Clifford, *Lectures and Essays*, II, p. 237. 'I can find no evidence that seriously mitigates against the rule that the priest is at all times and in all places the enemy of all men.'

P. 170. **not demonstrable:** See Huxley, op. cit., V, pp. 238, 245–8, 313–34. Note Huxley's admission that he does not like saying that anything is unknowable, p. 311.

P. 170, fn. **Clifford and Kant:** W. K. Clifford, op. cit., II, 'The Philosophy of the Pure Sciences,' pp. 301–409.

P. 171. **œcumenical:** Stephen accepted the current rationalist interpretation of science as, not only the sole corpus of verifiable truth (which is right), but also the only method of description which laid down 'the base, to which all other truth in so far as it is discoverable must conform' (which is either a repetition of the first proposition or false). In HL, I, p. 25, he refers to thought-transference as 'a superstition . . . in which Boswell, if not Johnson, fully believed.' Nevertheless, he used this argument infrequently in his analysis of religion. It is interesting to compare his approach to the question of the immortality of the soul with that of Huxley. Huxley argues from Hume that we must reject miracles such as the Feeding of the Five

Thousand since the evidence for its occurrence appears contradictory and flimsy although there is no *a priori* reason for its falsity. The soul cannot be 'deduced by scientific methods of reasoning from the facts of physical or psychical nature,' and that such evidence as exists suggests that immortality is a delusion, for it is a law of nature that living matter is always dying, is being resolved into its lifeless constituents, and cannot live unless it dies.' (The Physical Basis of Life, *Fortnightly Review*, Feb., 1869, reprinted *Lay Sermons*, 1880, p. 132.) Stephen on the other hand concentrates on the unreality of the conception. He points out that it is exceedingly difficult to imagine a soul without a body—a difficulty shared by theologians who in the past have consigned souls to a most corporeal hell. If it is objected by the Mauriceans that this is mere imagery, what remains of the concept when the imagery is banished? Consciousness comes to us only through our senses. 'It is impossible even to understand emotions in an eternal state where nothing happens and no action is rigidly possible.' (AA, p. 152, *passim*.) If we believe in the immortality of the soul, why do we not accept the Hindu belief in its preexistence and therefore in its transmigration? An agnostic is prepared to admit that the soul may be immortal, but he can see no reason why it should take the precise form taught by the Church. Stephen is struck by the futility of dogmatising: Huxley by the fact that the conception of immortality is contrary to the laws of science, and that such evidence as we possess does not support belief in the conception. Huxley lets the reader suppose that the laws of science will almost lead him to a verifiable proof, whereas Stephen in *The Vanity of Philosophising*, although he repeats his very proper belief that science is true, not because one can participate in its discoveries, or even understand them, but because its conclusions are independently verifiable, says, as the title implies, that the debate is fundamentally hopeless; he came to agree with Sidgwick, who argued in the Metaphysical Society that the field of empirical enquiry was narrower than commonly supposed. (SRD, II, pp. 208–23.)

P. 171, fn. **'respectively found'**: J. H. Newman, *Sermons chiefly on the Theory of Religious Belief*, 1844, pp. 350–1. AA, pp. 179–80. J. A. Froude, *Nemesis of Faith*, 1904, p. 172.

P. 171, fn. **Pattison:** See A. W. Brown, op. cit., pp. 85–90, for an analysis of Pattison's paper.

CHAPTER VI

P. 172. **'black beetle'**: AA, p. 5.

P. 173. **unjust:** Cf. Stephen's reply to an article by Gladstone who criticised his writings on Butler, *Nineteenth Century*, Vol. XXXVIII, Nov., 1895, pp. 715–39, and Vol. XXXIX, Jan., 1896, pp. 106–22.

P. 173. **'ignorance'**: AA, p. 41.

P. 173. **astonish us:** Stephen noted A. J. Balfour's admission 'I do not suggest that the doctrine of the Incarnation supplies any philosophical solution of [the problem of evil in the world],' and annotated his copy of the *Foundations of Belief* with sardonic word 'Modest.' Stephen's copy of Balfour's book is to be found in the London Library where he succeeded Tennyson as President in 1892.

P. 173. **final end:** AA, 'Dreams and Realities,' pp. 86–126.

P. 173. **beasts of the field:** ib., p. 98.

P. 174. **such a belief:** Stephen had no love for Farrar, and writing to Norton on the death of Dean Stanley, for whom he expressed real regret, said that he feared Farrar would be the next Dean of Westminster since he 'is just the man to impose upon a rhetorician like Gladstone.' (Letter to Norton, 26 July, 1881.)

P. 174. **'envy you'**: *Life of Sir JFS*, op. cit., p. 84.

P. 174, fn. **'fond of me'**: Letter to Norton, 16 Nov., 1873, cf. *Letters of C. E. Norton* (1913), II, p. 19.

P. 175. **'open eyes'**: AA, pp. 91–2.

P. 175, fn. **'responsibility'**: *Life and Letters of T. H. Huxley*, I, p. 220, reviewed by Stephen in the *Nineteenth Century*, Vol. XLVIII, Dec., 1900, pp. 905–18, reprinted in SB, III, pp. 188–219. Stephen refers to the letter to Kingsley, SB, III, p. 212.

P. 176. **intolerance**: AA, pp. 242–337, 'Poisonous Opinions.'

P. 176. **'admitted'**: AA, p. 274.

P. 176. **demonstrated**: EFP, p. 352.

P. 176, fn. **'immoral nature'**: J. H. Newman, *Essay on Development* (1878), p. 357.

P. 177. **'omnipotence of God'**: *Life of Sir JFS*, p. 73.

P. 177. **'effeminate natures'**: EFP, p. 7.

P. 177. **'disappears'**: ib., p. 51.

P. 177. **'statements of fact'**: ib., p. 48.

P. 177. **'and strong'**: F. Dostoievsky, *The Brothers Karamazov*, Bk. V, Ch. 5.

P. 177. **'obscure'**: EFP, p. 37.

P. 178. **sincerity**: ib., 'The Broad Church,' p. 7, 26. C. E. Raven, *Christian Socialism* (1920), p. 81, complains that Stephen accuses F. D. Maurice and Broad Churchmen of being cheats. This does not do justice to Stephen's constant attempt to acknowledge the sincerity of the Broad Church and at the same time make his point that they were (unconsciously) deceiving themselves intellectually and morally.

P. 178. **'different thing'**: ib., p. 40.

P. 178, fn. **by clergymen**: H. Sidgwick, *Practical Ethics* (1898), pp. 142–77. Morley took Stephen's line on this matter, cf. *On Compromise* (1874), pp. 72–6.

P. 179. **'valid ones'**: G. Hough, *The Last Romantics* (1949), p. 136. Cf. G. M. Young, *Daylight and Champaign* (1937), p. 250.

P. 179. **'catch it'**: SB, II, p. 120. R. H. Hutton took the same line as Stephen upon Arnold's religion from a Christian standpoint in *Contemporary Thought and Thinkers* (1894), I, p. 217, 'Mr. Arnold must choose between two alternatives. He must evaporate the whole . . . or he must take the personal language about God as straightforwardly as he takes the moral language about man. It is not criticism at all, it is playing fast and loose with language in the most ridiculous manner, to regard the long series of passionate appeals to God . . . as mere efforts of poetry while all the words describing the moral conceptions of men are interpreted with scientific strictness,' see *P.M.L.A.*, Vol. LVI, 1941, 'R. H. Hutton,' by Gaylord C. Le Roy, for a useful article on Hutton's criticism.

P. 179. **'in the world'**: M. Arnold, *On Translating Homer, Last Words* (1862), p. 10.

P. 179. **'special prejudice'**: SB, II, pp. 95–6 *seq.*

P. 179, fn. **right**: Arnold had no right to mock Herbert Spencer by saying that no one was likely to say 'the Unknowable is our refuge and strength, our very present help in trouble,' when he defined God as a Stream of Tendency Not-Ourselves Making for Righteousness (cf. *Literature and Dogma*, 1893 edition., p. 31; *God and the Bible* (1884 edition), Preface, p.

xxvii). James Martineau was on to this, as was Stephen (*An Ideal Substitute for God* (1878), pp. 8–12, 24–5; and SB II, p. 112). By far the best analysis of Arnold's religious views is, of course, L. Trilling, *Matthew Arnold* (1949), pp. 317–368, which deals implicitly with most of the points which Stephen raises.

P. 180. **F. D. Maurice:** For this passage, I have drawn on both A. R. Vidler, *Witness to the Light* [New York] (1948) and H. G. Wood, *F. D. Maurice* (1950). For a survey of recent work on F. D. Maurice, see A. R. Vidler, *The Orb and the Cross* (1935), p. 85.

P. 180. **position:** Quoted by Vidler, op. cit., p. 208, from *The Kingdom of Christ* (Ev. ed.), II, p. 329.

P. 180. **the Head:** ib., p. 52.

P. 180. **contemporaries in the Church:** See Vidler, op. cit., pp. 1–5 and Wood, op. cit., pp. 1–12, for diverse contemporary opinion on Maurice's teaching.

P. 181. **'old mould':** EFP, p. 20. Cf. C. R. Sanders, 'Sir Leslie Stephen, Coleridge and Two Coleridgeans,' *P.M.L.A.*, Vol. LV, Sept., 1940, in which Stephen's references to F. D. Maurice are collected. See also *Fortnightly Review*, NS, Vol. XV, May, 1874, pp. 595–617, 'Mr. Maurice's Theology,' by L. Stephen, and *Eng. Util.*, III, pp. 453–62. *Life*, pp. 240–1.

P. 181. **banns:** *Life of Sir JFS*, p. 127.

P. 181. **condemns:** C. E. Raven, op. cit., p. 77, fn.

P. 181. **'intelligible':** SEI, p. 66.

P. 181. **'the Eternal':** *Fortnightly Review*, op. cit., pp. 614–5.

P. 181. **'merely':** Wood, op. cit., p. 100, comments that this word shows the great gap between the two minds.

P. 181. **Larger Hope:** Cf. Hallam Tennyson, *Tennyson, A Memoir*, 1897, I, p. 322, in which Tennyson expresses disappointment that the translation of the Revised Version had not changed 'everlasting' into 'aeonian' or some such word.

P. 182. **'mode of thinking':** *Fortnightly Review*, op. cit., p. 610.

P. 182. **Maurice's work:** ib., pp. 600, 604. Stephen (wrongly) called Maurice a mystic using the word in Goethe's sense to mean one who taught the scholasticism of the heart, the dialectic of feeling.

P. 182. **'to swallow':** EFP, p. 152.

P. 182. **of the World:** *Fortnightly Review*, op. cit., pp. 606–7, p. 609.

P. 182, fn. **of this world:** Wood, op. cit., pp. 102–4. A most scrupulous assessment of the worth of Stephen's criticism will be found at pp. 77–128 which, though it naturally differs from mine, treats Stephen honestly.

P. 182, fn. **'of them':** *Life of F. D. Maurice*, II, p. 15, quoted by Wood, op. cit., p. 29.

P. 182. **'preterite':** *Fortnightly Review*, op. cit., p. 605.

P. 183. **'clergyman':** ib., p. 615.

P. 183. **fact and reality:** See *Cambridge Journal*, Vol. II, Feb., 1949, pp. 288–300, 'Some Reflections on a Contemporary Problem Raised by Science and Religion,' by I. T. Ramsey, which puts the anti-positivist view clearly, though I think it to be misleading in its sketch of nineteenth-century historiography.

P. 184. **revive:** AA, pp. 194–203, 234–9. Algernon Cecil, *Six Oxford Thinkers* (1909), pp. 83–4, makes the point that Stephen always assumed that what was fittest to survive was necessarily the Best.

P. 184, fn. **attainable truth:** On form criticism I have found M. Dibelius, *From Tradition to Gospel*, trans. by B. L. Woolf (1934) most helpful; also B. M. Easton, *The Gospel before the Gospel* [New York], 1928, and A. Schweitzer, *The Quest of the Historical Jesus*, trans. by W. Montgomery (1910).

P. 184, fn. **Coulton:** Two good examples of Coulton's dialectic are *St. Thomas Aquinas on the Elect and the Reprobate* (1927) and *Infant Perdition in the Middle Ages* (1922).

P. 185. **'more rational?'** AA, p. 241.

P. 185. **'impostures':** *The Nineteenth Century: a Review of Progress* (1901), 'Evolution and Religious Conceptions,' by L. Stephen, p. 380.

P. 185. **pons asinorum:** Berkeley of course. The first paper on 12 June, 1877, was on 'Belief and Evidence,' and the second on 11 Mar., 1879, on 'the Uniformity of Nature.' The one argues that although false beliefs may satisfy those who act on them, we must not let our assent outrun evidence, for that would create a dangerous precedent; the other that we cannot conceive nature to be anything but uniform or we would be faced with a negation of thought. See A. W. Brown, *The Metaphysical Society* [New York] (1947), pp. 135–6, 221–3, 333, 335.

P. 185. **'hair splitting':** *Life*, p. 417. The quotation is to be found in AA, p. 309.

P. 186. **'human solution':** J. H. Newman, *Apologia pro Vita Sua* (1864), p. 378.

P. 186. **'is faith':** J. H. Newman, *Grammar of Assent* (1889), pp. 94–5. *Eng. Util.*, III, p. 495. AA, p. 223.

P. 186. **'intellectually wrong':** *Eng. Util.*, III, p. 496 *et seq.* Perhaps the best contemporary answer to Stephen on Newman's theory of Belief is R. H. Hutton, *Cardinal Newman* (1891), Ch. V.

P. 187. **periphery:** Bradley, though an Idealist, was an agnostic. His Absolute is not equated by the notion of God; God, together with other concepts such as Goodness or Nature, is included within the Absolute in which they obtain perfection. For a characteristic statement of Bradley's position in regard to immortality see F. H. Bradley, *Appearance and Reality* (1906), p. 509 fn.

P. 187. **exist?:** J. Tyndall, *Fragments of Science* (1899), p. 191. For Ward's argument see A. W. Brown, op. cit., pp. 56–9.

P. 188. **'right of way':** R. B. Perry, *The Thought and Character of William James* (1936), II, pp. 246–7.

P. 188. **'no use':** William James, *The Will to Believe and Other Essays in Popular Philosophy* (1897), pp. 10–11.

P. 188. **'space and time':** ib., p. 270.

P. 188. **shall be:** W. James, op. cit., fn. p. 94–5.

P. 188, fn. **community:** T. Veblen, *The Theory of the Leisure Class* (1899), pp. 297–8.

P. 189. **Agnostic Annual:** This periodical was edited by Charles Watts from the 'Propaganda' of Rationalism at Johnson's Court in 1884. Most of the articles are of an inconceivable dullness; the best are by F. J. Gould, G. R. Bithell, Edward Clodd and J. McCabe. Stephen in his review reiterates his thesis that our intellect and not our will disposes us to believe one way or another. He defended Clifford against James's charge that he was more eager to avoid error than find truth by claiming that Clifford merely held that certain hypotheses explain facts better than their rivals and of these we should take notice. Of course, Clifford went far further than this. James and Stephen also diverge on the nature of fact. James, echoing Feuerbach, finds that faith creates facts and that a sceptic may deny only the worth of the facts of Christianity to himself. Stephen asserts that so far as religion depends on assertions of fact it is clear that the facts are not dependent on our wishes but on logic. In an unpublished letter to William James, 15 Feb., 1898, he says, 'You, (as I fancy) say that there is no "conclusive" evidence (I say none of any kind) for a certain belief. You infer that a man has a right to hold either the negative or the positive creed. My reply is that he has a right to hold *neither*. By Agnostic I do not mean a negative creed but an absence of all opinion; and that I take to be the only rational frame of mind.'

P. 189. **'moonshine'**: *Life*, p. 445. In the same letter to Norton there is a characteristic comment by Stephen on Santayana, which Maitland excluded. Stephen detected an illogicality in Santayana, who had said that nothing is objectively impressive. 'How the devil should it be? Nothing impresses which does not impress.'

P. 193. **'spiritual narcotics'**: AA, pp. 159, 167.

P. 194. **'mortal eyes'**: W. Pater, *Essays from 'The Guardian'* (1905), p. 69, quoted by G. Hough, op. cit., p. 155.

P. 195. **'abêtira'**: SB, II, p. 277. Arnold in the preface to *God and the Bible*, op. cit., p. xii, exclaims about this phrase, 'Did ever a great reasoner reason so madly?'

P. 195. **'highest interests'**: ib., p. 281.

P. 195. **'higher elements'**: ib., p. 284, cf. AA, pp. 338–80, EFP, pp. 360–2.

CHAPTER VII

P. 196. **'morality-intoxicated man'**: J. S. Mill, *Auguste Comte and Positivism* (1865), pp. 139–40.

P. 196. **Fatality**: 'Our images of all sorts,' writes Mill (ib., p. 194), 'down to our geometrical diagrams, and even our ciphers and algebraic symbols, should always be figured to ourselves as written in space, and not on paper or any other material substance. M. Comte adds that they should be conceived as green on a white ground.'

P. 197. **'common good'**: A. Comte, *Catechism of Positivist Religion*, trans. by R. Congreve (1858), p. 74.

P. 197. **and Progress**: ib., p. 143.

P. 197. **'Positivist Religion'**: Mill, op. cit., pp. 154–5. An excellent short account of Comte's religion may be found in B. Willey, *Nineteenth Century Studies* (1949), pp. 187–203; admitting Comte's eccentricity, Prof. Willey praises the scope and nobility of his system, but I find it hard to regard the religious and prophetic part of the system as more than the outpouring of an egomaniac.

P. 198. **'to man'**: J. Tyndall, *Fragments of Science* (1899), II, p. 196.

P. 198. **'if possible'**: *Life*, pp. 144–5.

P. 198, fn. **'self-indulgent'**: G. R. Bithell, *The Creed of a Modern Agnostic* (1883), p. 147.

P. 199. **'confess it!'**: *The Amberley Papers*, ed. Bertrand and Patricia Russell (1937), I, p. 341.

P. 199. **'renounced his'**: J. W. Cross, *Life and Letters of George Eliot* (1885), III, p. 214.

P. 199. **'such places'**: ib., III, p. 170. Cf. Esther, sister of F. D. Maurice, rejoicing in the fact that some children who had been kept by their parents from going to church for fear of catching measles, had succumbed. 'I am *very glad* they are so ill; it is a well-deserved punishment. . . .' Augustus Hare, *Story of My Life* (1896), I, pp. 202–3.

P. 199. **'or sister'**: F. Harrison, *The Creed of a Layman* (1908), p. 89. Cf. W. K. Clifford, op. cit., II, p. 169, 'An awful privilege, an awful responsibility, that we should help to create a world in which posterity will live.' Arnold and Morley admired Turgot for being 'filled with an astonished, awful, oppressive sense of the *immoral thoughtlessness* of men; of the heedless, hazardous way in which they deal with things of the greatest moment to them; of the immense incalculable misery which is due to this cause,' J. Morley, *Biographical Studies* (1923), p. 90. The responsibility for their utterances hung just as heavily upon those who had abandoned their faith, as on Christians. Cf. Francis Newman, 'It is a sad thing to have printed erroneous fact. I have three or four times contradicted and renounced the passage . . . *but I cannot reach those I have misled.*' (F. N. Sieveking, *Francis Newman* (1909), p. 342.) What is this but an echo of his brother? 'A man publishes an irreligious or immoral book, afterwards he repents and dies. . . . Shall *he* be now dwelling in Abraham's bosom, who hears on the other side of the gulf the voice of those who curse his memory as being the victims of his guilt?' (5th University Sermon, 'On Justice as a Principle of Divine Governance,' quoted by G. W. Faber, *Oxford Apostles* (1936), p. 260.)

P. 199. **'more happy'**: R. Jefferies, *The Story of My Heart* (1883), p. 120.

P. 199, fn. **'dissuade me'**: G. S. Layard, op. cit., p. 87.

P. 200. **for God's**: W. H. Mallock, op. cit., Bk. I, Ch. IV, p. 83.

P. 200. **'citizen'**: W. K. Clifford, op. cit., II, p. 94.

P. 201. **'everlasting happiness'**: W. Paley, *Moral and Political Philosophy*, Bk. I, Ch. VII (*Coll. Works*, 1838, III, p. 20).

P. 202, fn. **'delinquencies'**: *Agnostic Annual* (1896), article by G. R. Bithell.

P. 202, fn. **'each other'**: *Essays by a Barrister* (by J. F. Stephen) (1862), pp. 318–9.

P. 203. **moral code**: J. F. Stephen, *Liberty, Equality, Fraternity* (1873), p. 131 and pp. 158–88. Cf. B. Lippincott, *Victorian Critics of Democracy* (1938), pp. 134–66.

P. 203. **Social Revenge**: Huxley agreed with Fitzjames. 'As to whether we can fulfil the moral law, I should say hardly any of us. As there are men born physically cripples and intellectually idiots, so there are some who are moral cripples and idiots, and can be kept straight not even by punishment. For these people there is nothing but shutting up, or extirpation.' (*Life and Letters of T. H. Huxley*, II, p. 306.)

P. 204. **Machiavelli**: See *Discourses on the First Decade of Titus Livius*, Bk. I, Ch. 12, for a disquisition on the utility of religion.

P. 205. **Hobbes**: Fitzjames Stephen's essay on Hobbes in *Horae Sabbaticae* (1892), II, pp. 1–54, is far more illuminating than Leslie's book on Hobbes in the English Men of Letters Series: Fitzjames had studied philosophic conservatism—see the essays on Maistre in the third volume.

P. 204. **'worshipped'**: *Life and Letters of T. H. Huxley*, I, p. 301.

P. 204. **restraint:** *Liberty, Equality, Fraternity*, p. 182.

P. 204. **righteous:** ib., p. 122.

P. 204, fn. **'legislation':** B. Webb, *My Apprenticeship* (1929), p. 145.

P. 205. **atheism:** L. Büchner, *What is Materialism?* (1897), p. 147.

P. 205. **'old Carlyle':** *Life*, pp. 230–1.

P. 205, fn. **'baboons':** Quoted in *Life of Sir JFS*, p. 375.

P. 205. **'edifice':** EFP, p. 360. A comparison between the views of the two brothers, as expressed in EFP and *Liberty, Equality, Fraternity*, was made by Henry Holbeach in *St. Paul's Magazine*, Vol. XIV, Feb., 1874, pp. 193–220.

P. 205, fn. **realised:** *Speech on Perfectibility* (1828), reprinted in O.U.P. World's Classics edition of *Autobiography* (1924), p. 290. Huxley was at one with Fitzjames: he thought it monstrous to dangle the prospect of perfectibility in the face of mankind when they lived within a solar system in which life would for certain be extinguished according to the second law of thermodynamics. (*Collected Essays*, IX, p. 44.)

P. 206. **the criminal:** SRD, II, pp. 55–93.

P. 206. **'opponents':** *Life*, pp. 333–4.

P. 206, fn. **'referee':** The quotation is from an unpublished paper by Raleigh. G. U. Coulton observed that this spirit of excessive impartiality in Sidgwick cost Maitland his Fellowship at Trinity: Sidgwick, who was an elector, was so impressed by Maitland's work, with whose conclusions he agreed, that he voted against him, fearing that his powers of impartial judgment had been impaired. And note Maitland on Sidgwick's lectures. 'He always gave us of his very best; not what might be good enough for undergraduates . . . but the complex truth just as he saw it, with all those reservations and qualifications, exceptions and distinctions which suggested themselves to a mind that was indeed marvellously subtle, but was showing its wonderful power simply because, even in a lecture room, it could be content with nothing less than the maximum of attainable and communicable truth.' H. A. L. Fisher, *F. W. Maitland* (1910), p. 8. The ethical revolution, however, which divides Bloomsbury from the Victorians, is marked by the change of attitude to Sidgwick. Though Bertrand Russell admired him (*Unpopular Essays*, 1950, p. 214), G. E. Moore, like Raleigh, was unimpressed (*The Philosophy of G. E. Moore* (1942), pp. 16–17). Moore and his disciples found Sidgwick 'inhuman.' Keynes wrote to Lytton Strachey in 1906 on reading *Sidgwick, A Memoir*: 'There is no doubt about his moral goodness. And yet it is all so dreadfully depressing—no intimacy, no clear-cut, crisp boldness . . .' R. F. Harrod, *The Life of John Maynard Keynes* (1951), pp. 116–17.

P. 207. **'jargon':** A. W. Brown, op. cit., p. 246. Cf. *Henry Sidgwick—A Memoir* (1906), Appx. II, pp. 608–15.

P. 207. **their oars:** See A. W. Gore's tribute to Sidgwick. *Henry Sidgwick—A Memoir*, p. 557.

P. 207. **contradictory:** ib., pp. 600–8. Cf. *Mind*, N.S., Vol. X, Jan., 1901, pp. 1–17. 'Henry Sidgwick,' by L. Stephen: *Hibbert Journal*, Vol. XXXVII, Oct., 1938, pp. 25–43, 'Henry Sidgwick,' by C. D. Broad. Broad considers Sidgwick's mistaken appeal to the nature of scientific postulates in *Five Types of Ethical Theory* (1930), pp. 244–56.

P. 208. **'the worst':** *Fraser's Magazine*, N.S., Vol. XI, Mar., 1875. 'Sidgwick's Methods of Ethics,' by L. Stephen, p. 325.

P. 209. **Baudelaire:** *Spleen et Idéal*, 'Alchimie de la Douleur,'

P. 209. **de Lisle:** Midi.

P. 209. **Goethe:** Das Goettliche.

P. 210. **'our might':** A. C. Swinburne, *William Blake, a Critical Essay* (1906),
p. 175 fn, quoted by Mario Praz, *The Romantic Agony*
(1933), pp. 283–4.

P. 211. **'unspeakable comfort':** Book of Common Prayer, Article XVII.

P. 211. **'scientific foundation':** *Life and Letters of T. H. Huxley*, II, p. 359.

P. 211. **'ethically best':** *Collected Essays*, IX, p. 81.

P. 212. **'priestess':** ib., p. 146.

P. 212. **'see it':** *Life and Letters of T. H. Huxley*, II, pp. 219–20.

P. 212. **'our deeds':** ib., I, p. 241.

P. 212. **'on earth':** George Eliot, *Essays and leaves from a note-book* (1884),
p. 62.

P. 213. **social welfare:** *Sci. Ethics*, p. 450.

P. 213. **'inexpugnable truth':** ib., p. 356.

P. 213. **'ulterior end':** ib., p. 358.

P. 214. **'it causes':** ib., p. 460.

P. 214. **egoism in disguise:** Stephen is not an egoistical hedonist. He
maintains that men do whatever is easiest
for them to do, and that it is often easier for a man to sacrifice his happiness to
that of others owing to the pressure of public opinion and his own upbringing.
Stephen had learnt from Darwin that all living organisms are induced to act
in a particular way from a multitude of causes.

P. 215. **'welfare':** ib., pp. 350–1.

P. 215. **'too good':** ib., p. 418.

P. 215. **'of the race':** Stephen wants to show that all attempts to persuade
a bad man to be good are doomed to fail, i.e. that
there is no sanction. But this leads him to say that a virtuous man has no
reason for being more virtuous than the social code. Stephen shows that
truthfulness is good because it promotes social welfare. It is at this point that
Marxism rears its head and we are forced to ask: is everything that promotes
social welfare good? The answer depends on the meaning attached to the
words 'welfare' and 'promotes.' Stephen would, of course, have put certain
spiritual values, e.g. human dignity and self-respect before material needs.
R. H. Hutton made the excellent point that while men often are unable to
discern clearly how to ameliorate material conditions or fathom the principles
which tend to the vitality and health of society, they understand moral laws,
which are far more clearly defined in their minds (*Criticisms on Contemporary
Thought and Thinkers* (1894), I, p. 155).
Moreover (*Sci. Ethics*, p. 163), Stephen tells us that 'ought' exists only for the
virtuous. If a virtuous man acts below his standard yet conforms to the moral
code, he is still a highly (perhaps even a higher) moral being. Indeed he
proves that science and what most men mean by ethics are incompatible.

P. 215. **breaks off:** *Queen's Quarterly*, Vol. 55, 1948, pp. 450–63, contains
a useful article by J. A. Irving on 'Sir Leslie Stephen,
Evolution and Ethics.' There is also an admirably concise exposure of evolutionary ethics in *Cambridge Journal*, Vol. I, May, 1948, pp. 465–73, 'World-
Stuff and Nonsense,' by S. E. Toulmin, to which I am indebted.

P. 216, fn. **primary:** Moore's ethics, though utilitarian in the primary
concept, of course reject hedonism. Mill thought
that the goodness of a state of affairs means pleasantness; Sidgwick that
although goodness does not mean pleasantness it is an *a priori* truth that all

good states are pleasant; Moore that there are many characteristics other than pleasantness of a state of affairs which make it good and that all a moral philosopher can do is to give a partial list of such characteristics.

P. 217. **'to Ethics':** G. E. Moore, *Principia Ethica* (1929 edition), p. 54.

P. 218. **two thousand years:** *Mind*, Vol. VII, 1882, p. 577. Stephen admitted that Sidgwick was right in pointing out that his sociology derived from Comte rather than from Darwin (*Life*, p. 352) and claimed that he appreciated Comte's greatness more fairly than the scientists such as Huxley who fulminated against Comte's religiosity. Comte's influence on Stephen is not surprising; nearly all the hard-thinking minds of the 'sixties felt the pull—among them Sidgwick's (see *Mind*, N.S., Vol. X, Jan., 1901, p. 4 fn.)

P. 218, fn. **'the best':** W. Bagehot, *Physics and Politics* (1873), p. 43.

P. 220. **'further creed':** Quoted by B. Bosanquet, *The Civilization of Christendom and Other Studies* (1893), I, p. 63.

P. 221. **all knowledge:** *Proc. Aristotelian Soc.*, N.S., Vol. L, 1949–50, pp. 157–88, 'Logical Translation,' by I. Berlin.

CHAPTER VIII

P. 223. **municipal laws:** *Lit. and Soc. 18th Cent.*, p. 6.

P. 223, fn. **'is possible':** SB, IV, pp. 136–8.

P. 224. **'be desired':** SB, IV, p. 205.

P. 224. **'and trickery':** ib., p. 176.

P. 224. **'so broad':** HL, I, pp. 164–5.

P. 225. **'of Shirley's':** ib., III, p. 21.

P. 225. **'and loving':** ib., p. 18.

P. 225. **'a woman':** L. Stephen, *George Eliot* (1902), p. 139.

P. 225. **'most prominent':** HL, III, p. 206.

P. 225. **'throughout':** ib., p. 207.

P. 225. **'moral elevation':** ib., p. 23.

P. 225. **manly confessor:** HL, III, p. 207.

P. 225. **by her husband:** *George Eliot*, pp. 145 *seq.*

P. 225. **'masculine temperament':** HL, II, p. 155. Landor exhibits a 'masculine simplicity,' ib., p. 294.

P. 225. **tenderness:** *Life of Sir JFS*, p. 316.

P. 226. **'in the crush':** *Cornhill*, Vol. XXXIV, Nov., 1876, 'Thoughts on Criticism by a Critic' (by L. Stephen), p. 558.

P. 226. **Hervey's hat:** HL, I, p. 328.

P. 226. **'for morbid':** *Eng. Thought 18th Cent.*, Ch. XII, p. 350.

P. 226. **'criminal':** *Lit. and Soc. 18th Cent.*, p. 134.

P. 226. **filthy abuse:** L. Stephen, *Swift* (1909), p. 31.

P. 226. **morbid tendency:** SB, III, p. 47.

P. 226. **prolonged depression:** ib., II, pp. 228–9.

P. 226. **happiness:** HL, III, p. 236. The text reads 'retrospection,' a misprint, I believe, for 'introspection.'

P. 226. **into convents:** ib., I, p. 213.

P. 227. **about *him*:** ib., II, p. 54 ff.

P. 227. **'domestic affection':** ib., p. 159.

P. 228. **man upward:** Stephen took the final lines of *Faust* in the normal Victorian sense, that eternal womanhood ennobles man and makes him better. Goethe's conception, however, was utterly different. He was describing the two principles in life: the masculine which is active and creative but for those very reasons destructive and sinful; and the feminine which is passive, loving, suffering and redeeming. Both are needed in the world. Thus Faust, the sinful man, is saved by Gretchen's love and sacrifice. Faust is admitted to Heaven for Gretchen's sake, because she has atoned for his sins through her love. Goethe's idea was religious, not ethical, and, characteristically, the Victorian rationalists could not distinguish between the two.

P. 228. **'anti-social instincts':** *Cornhill*, Vol. XXXII, July, 1875, 'Art and Morality' (by L. Stephen), p. 94.

P. 228. **'confutation':** ib., p. 92.

P. 228. **'something worse':** ib., p. 94.

P. 228. **'healthier and happier':** ib., p. 101.

P. 228. **'unwholesome atmosphere':** HL, I, pp. 211–13. Cf. L. Stephen, *Pope* (1914 edition), p. 14.

P. 228. **universe:** ib., III, p. 35.

P. 228. **the Evangelicals:** For an excellent study of the change in manners between 1780 and 1830, see M. J. Quinlan, *Victorian Prelude* [New York] (1941).

P. 229. **W. R. Greg:** Cf. his *Literary and Social Judgments*, 1869, esp. pp. 146–84, 'French Fiction: The Lowest Deep,' in which the novels of Victor Hugo, Eugène Sue, A. Dumas and Georges Sand are unsparingly attacked. 'The inspiration of French fiction—the source from which flow half its deformities, its vile morality and its vitiated taste, is the *craving for excitement* that has so long been characteristic of the nation' (p. 150). After declaring that 'of course we can give no quotations' (p. 155), he proceeds to quote liberally from their works, and is particularly irate that God is mentioned as the mainstay of a religion of 'affection and emotion,' never as a Guide, a Governor and the apex of a Creed (p. 182). Greg has also some hard words for Kingsley's preoccupation with sex (pp. 133–5). For Morley see his famous review of Swinburne's poetry in *Saturday Review*, Vol. XXII, 4 Aug., 1866, pp. 145–7.

P. 229. **to control:** Quoted by L. Trilling, *Matthew Arnold* (1949 edition), p. 347, from M. Arnold, *St. Paul and Protestantism* (1870, 2nd edition), p. 49.

P. 229. **'independent judgment':** L. Stephen, *Johnson* (1887), p. 189.

P. 229. **'of facts':** HL, II, p. 256.

P. 229, fn. **light:** *Phaedrus*, pp. 255–256 D.

P. 230. **'experience':** HL, II, p. 257.

P. 230. **'chaotic facts':** ib., p. 258.

P. 230. **'rhetoric':** ib., I, p. 250.

P. 230. **'grasp of facts':** ib., II, p. 160.

P. 230. **'or profit':** ib., III, p. 25.

P. 230. **'easily learnt':** ib., II, p. 174.

P. 231. **'of thorns':** ib., III, pp. 90–1.

P. 231. **'soda-water':** ib., II, p. 261.

P. 231. **'of life'**: ib., p. 262.

P. 231. **'success'**: ib., p. 279.

P. 232. **self-deception**: SB, III, pp. 23–7.

P. 232. **'from himself'**: HL, II, p. 27. Cf. *Pope*, p. 46. 'Popularity is more often significant of the tact which makes a man avoid giving offence, than of the warm impulses of a generous nature.'

P. 232. **vanity**: SB, II, p. 78; HL, III, pp. 239–40; *Johnson*, p. 86.

P. 232. **'remorse'**: HL, III, p. 330.

P. 232. **'whole nature'**: ib., I, p. 74. Cf. *Lit. and Soc. 18th Cent.*, p. 162.

P. 232. **'tails'**: ib., pp. 70–1.

P. 233. **'adversaries'**: *Swift*, p. 185. Cf. *Pope*, pp. 158, 210.

P. 233. **'man of genius ought'**: HL, I, p. 114.

P. 234. **'cleverness'**: ib., p. 350.

P. 234. **common sense**: C. R. Sanders, op. cit., p. 795. *Life*, pp. 315, 388.

P. 234. **'critics'**: HL, III, p. 328.

P. 235. **'longer acquaintance'**: ib., pp. 160–1.

P. 236. **'depravity'**: ib., p. 226.

P. 237. **Morality**: ib., p. 247. SB, I, pp. 148–9. How, asked Stephen, could one censure Colly Cibber who delighted in exposing his own failings, or Rousseau when he declared that he had nothing to be ashamed of? HL, III, pp. 236–7. Cf. HL, III, p. 79, and *George Eliot*, p. 204.

P. 238. **'to his books'**: ib., II, p. 172.

P. 238. **'respectable Englishmen'**: ib., I, p. 15. Had Stephen forgotten honest Iago?

P. 238. **'autobiography'**: ib., III, p. 233. Cf. ib., p. 264.

P. 239. **character**: SB, III, p. 31.

P. 240. **Angelo**: HL, II, p. 156.

P. 240. **'hairdresser's block'**: *George Eliot*, p. 104.

P. 240, fn. **'waking'**: HL, II, p. 271.

P. 241. **foreigners**: Of the essays in *Hours in a Library* and *Studies in Biography* over fifty per cent deal with subjects in the nineteenth century and thirty per cent in the eighteenth century. Only thirteen per cent in any way criticise poets as poets and only one single essay (that on Balzac) is concerned solely with a foreign author. *The Importation of German* is a note in literary history and the treatment of Rousseau perfunctory.

P. 241. **liberal mind**: See L. Trilling, *E. M. Forster* (1941), Ch. I, and *The Liberal Imagination* (1951).

P. 241. **pour them**: See E. R. Bentley, *Bernard Shaw* [New York], 1947, Ch. III.

P. 244. **Toynbee**: Klaus Dockhorn, *Die Staatsphilosophie des englischen Idealismus* [Bochum] (1937), especially II Teil, 'Die Wirkung der Lehre' is interesting and informative on the extent of Green's influence on particular individuals.

P. 244. **'to-day'**: SRD, I, pp. 131–2.

P. 245. **'good conduct'**: ib., p. 219.

P. 246. **'unclean beast'**: B. Webb, *Our Partnership* (1948), p. 232.

P. 246. **mill-town**: F. R. Leavis in his useful introduction to *Mill on Bentham and Coleridge* (1950), rightly shows the line of descent through Mill and George Eliot to Beatrice Webb, but does not carry the argument further than the years of *My Apprenticeship*.

P. 246. **impossible:** See Joan Bennett, *Virginia Woolf* (1945), Ch. IV.

CHAPTER IX

P. 249. **'of noteworthy critics':** D. MacCarthy, *Leslie Stephen* (1937), p. 11.

P. 249. **'moved himself':** ib., p. 16.

P. 249. **'much matters':** ib., p. 15.

P. 249. **'be clever':** ib., p. 44.

P. 250. **'everything else':** *Scrutiny*, Vol. VII, March, 1939, p. 407. 'Leslie Stephen—Cambridge Critic,' by Q. D. Leavis.

P. 250. **'to Mr. MacCarthy':** ib., p. 406.

P. 250. **'value to man':** MacCarthy, op. cit., p. 46.

P. 251. **urbane:** It was, of course, the lack of urbanity that Matthew Arnold deplored in his essay on 'The Literary Influence of Academies' in *Essays in Criticism*, I; but Arnold there used the word in a peculiar sense to denote that lack of agreement on values, the lack of a tribunal of cultivated taste—the anarchy which he opposed to culture.

P. 252. **'the merits':** R. Mortimer, *Channel Packet* (1942), p. 57.

P. 252. **'by it':** Arnold, *Essays in Criticism* (1895 edition), I, p. 48.

P. 253. **Scrutiny:** A useful critical estimate of the aims of this periodical will be found in *The Importance of Scrutiny*, ed. E. R. Bentley [New York], 1948.

P. 253, fn. **'nothing more':** I. A. Richards, *Practical Criticism* (1929), pp. 299–305, 351.

P. 254. **'from within':** See Ch. IV *supra*, p. 306.

P. 254, fn. **Mill on the Floss:** T. S. Eliot, *The Sacred Wood* (1923), p. 43.

P. 255. **'pointed to':** Q. D. Leavis, op. cit., p. 404.

P. 255. **'spirit of doubt':** Quoted by M. Turnell, *The Novel in France* (1950), p. 414.

P. 256. **aesthetic doctrine:** HL, II, p. 84. SB, IV, pp. 208, 249.

P. 256. **'accordingly':** *Lit. and Soc.* 18th Cent., pp. 3–4. G. U. Ellis in *Twilight on Parnassus* (1939), pp. 63–89, chooses to attack Stephen on the grounds that it is valueless to consider the sociological aspect of literature, since poets are influenced not by their 'age' but by other poets. He accuses Stephen of thinking that the poet owed more to the Reform Bill than to Apollo, and of suggesting that the middle class, so far from often ruining authors by imposing their prejudices and taste upon them, raised the standard of literature by extending the reading circle. The argument is not worth while considering since Stephen made no such claims and to rend one book from the corpus of his criticism and to cite it as the essence of the whole, is ludicrous, though not perhaps surprising from a critic who discerns the quality which makes the nineteenth century unique is that it is 'an acquisitive age.'

(Cf. Stephen's irony about the very method of which Ellis complains. HL, II, p. 83.)

P. 256. **'coming world'**: SB, II, pp. 104, 109. Stephen did not pass over the famous phrase about literature being a criticism of life without a sigh at such lack of precision: if poetry is to replace much of 'what now passes with us for religion and philosophy,' it could hardly be at the same time criticism. But Stephen added that much of the ridicule which Arnold suffered for the phrase was inspired by men 'apparently unable to distinguish between an epigram and a philosophical dogma.' Cf. pp. 89–91.

P. 257. **'scientific method'**: HL, III, p. 1.

P. 257. **'classification'**: ib., p. 338. Cf. ib., II, p. 46, where Stephen says that the scientific method depends on observation not on *a priori* theories. 'The true business of the critic is to discover from observation what are the conditions under which a book appeals to our sympathies, and, if he finds an apparent exception to his rules, to admit that he has made an oversight, and not to condemn the facts which persist in contradicting his theories.'

P. 258. **'subtle'**: ib., II, pp. 83 and 167.

P. 258. **'descriptive power'**: SB, II, p. 81, and HL, III, p. 6.

P. 258. **'convention'**: *Cornhill Magazine*, Vol. XXXIV, Nov., 1876, 'Thoughts on Criticism by a Critic' (by L. Stephen), p. 568.

P. 258. **'posterity'**: ib., p. 563.

P. 258. **'prejudice'**: ib., p. 566.

P. 258. **'singularity'**: HL, II, p. 25.

P. 259. **'crawling over it'**: 'Thoughts on Criticism by a Critic,' p. 566.

P. 259. **'all difficulties'**: L. Trilling, *E. M. Forster* (1944), pp. 147–8 and pp. 140–1.

P. 259. **'human heart'**: HL, I, p. 204. Cf. II, p. 167.

P. 260. **'poetic expression'**: *Johnson*, p. 189.

P. 260. **'the sight'**: *Pope*, p. 198.

P. 261 **'superlatives'**: HL, III, p. 334.

P. 261 **King Lear:** ib., p. 82. The line 'By which they have been, are, or cease to be' recalls *King Lear*, I, 1, 115.

P. 261. **'his tether'**: SB, II, p. 93 ff.

P. 261. **Ithuriel spear:** HL, I, p. 101.

P. 261. **'by heart'**: SB, II, pp. 81–2.

P. 262. **to appreciate Pope:** J. W. Mackail, *Pope* (1919), pp. 7–14. Cf. Francis Thompson, *Sir Leslie Stephen as a Biographer* (privately printed by Wilfrid Meynell in 1915, written probably before 1902), in which Thompson calls Stephen natively prosaic and unimaginative. 'Throughout his writing one cannot but be conscious of a certain hardness, a lack of moist light,' which is only partly counterbalanced by a strenuous fairness of mind permitting him to reach the aesthetic in poetry in a 'reflex way.' Thompson called Stephen's essay on Arnold the best ever written by a critic on an author with whom he was not in native sympathy. Thompson's essay pronounces upon Stephen the judgment of the 'nineties.

P. 262. **sensibility:** 'Thoughts on Criticism by a Critic,' p. 558. MacCarthy, op. cit., p. 20.

P. 263. **pleased them:** *Lit. and Soc. 18th Cent.*, p. 5.

P. 263. **and decay?:** HL, II, pp. 9, 11, 29–30. Cf. MacCarthy, op. cit., pp. 16–19.

P. 263. **his age?:** *Lit. and Soc. 18th Cent.*, p. 17.

P. 264. **'dearest to him':** ib., pp. 11–12.

P. 264. **'human expression':** ib., p. 6.

P. 264. **'regenerating processes':** *Cornhill*, Vol. XXXII, July, 1875, 'Art and Morality' (by L. Stephen), p. 101.

P. 265. **'clearer conceptions':** HL, III, pp. 27–8.

P. 265. **'the feeling':** ib., p. 109.

P. 265. **'sentiments':** SB, II, pp. 202–3. Tennyson, Stephen complained, is no sage poet such as Aeschylus, Shakespeare, Goethe or Dante: he cannot write poetry transfused with philosophy (pp. 234–5). The essay is written in defiance of the popular respect for Tennyson's gnomic qualities and concludes that the early Tennyson is superior to the later. Stephen may 'place' Tennyson satisfactorily; but he conveys little of the extraordinary qualities of the earlier poems.

P. 266. **'mere singer':** HL, II, p. 256. *Essays in Criticism*, II, op. cit., pp. 148–54.

P. 266. **'principles':** ib., p. 252.

P. 268. **'principle of criticism':** ib., pp. 252–5.

P. 269. **Bagehot:** SB, IV, pp. 1–44; W. Bagehot, *Literary Studies*, I, pp. 37–86.

P. 269. **photographic accuracy:** HL., I, pp. 190–1.

P. 269. **'logical structure':** ib., III, p. 202. Note the way Stephen exposes the deficiencies of de Quincey's humour (HL, I). He demanded that 'the imaginative humorist must in all cases be keenly alive to the "absurdity of man"; he must have a sense of the irony of fate, of the strange interlacing of good and evil in the world, and of the baser and nobler elements of human nature' (HL, III, p. 159).

P. 269. **'celebrities':** ib., I, p. 188. The text reads 'memories'—a misprint, I think, for 'memoirs,' which, like numerous other misprints, Stephen never corrected.

P. 269. **'contempt':** *Swift*, p. 178.

P. 269. **'stream':** *Pope*, p. 189.

P. 269. **'literature':** ib., pp. 106, 210. Lytton Strachey quoted this phrase with approval in his Leslie Stephen lecture of 1925 on Pope (*Characters and Commentaries* (Phoenix edition, 1936), p. 295).

P. 270. **'not by him':** SB, II, p. 77.

P. 270. **'first-rate novel':** HL, II, p. 107.

P. 270. **'sixth-form lad':** ib., p. 313, 'only,' Stephen added, 'with an unusually strong infusion of schoolboy perversion.'

P. 270. **'assault at arms':** SB, I, p. 91. The most extravagant passages occur in SB, SEI and *Sketches*.

P. 270. **from Stephen:** J. Dover Wilson, *Two Critics of Wordsworth* (1939), pp. 20–1. For a characteristic approach to a biographical subject in the Strachey manner see SB, III, pp. 225–8.

P. 270, fn. **'bishop':** SEI, p. 98, and R. Mortimer, op. cit., p. 18.

P. 271. **'nothing original'**: *Lit. and Soc. 18th Cent.*, p. 26.

P. 272. **'significance'**: ib., p. 2.

P. 272. **'convictions'**: ib., pp. 12–13.

P. 273. **'man's soul'**: L. Trilling, *The Liberal Imagination* (1951), p. 212.

P. 274, fn. **'boyishness'**: SB, IV, p. 210 *seq.*

P. 275. **'healthy mind'**: HL, I, p. 219. Cf. HL, II, p. 254.

P. 275. **of the wits**: Cf. T. S. Eliot, *The Use of Poetry and the Use of Criticism* (1933), p. 98.

P. 275, fn. **'conceits'**: *Life*, pp. 314–5.

P. 276. **'self-consciousness'**: SB, III, pp. 31–2 *seq.*

P. 276. **'be himself'**: *George Eliot*, p. 147.

P. 276. **'rules'**: *Life*, p. 290. Stephen thought that 'Sainte-Beuve and Mat. Arnold (in a smaller way) are the only modern critics who seem to me worth reading—perhaps, too, Lowell.'

P. 276. **'from history'**: HL, II, p. 104.

P. 276. **'incapable'**: ib., p. 88. Cf. 'Your impartial critic or historian is generally a man who leaves out of account nothing but the essential,' ib., p. 132.

P. 277, fn. **'unsaid'**: Quoted by L. Trilling, *E. M. Forster*, p. 146.

P. 277, fn. **analysis**: SB, IV, p. 90.

CHAPTER X

CONCLUSION

P. 280. **manœuvre**: J. Plamenatz, *The English Utilitarians* (1949).

P. 280. **'a place'**: T. S. Eliot, *The Sacred Wood* (1923), p. 123.

P. 280. **startling**: The comparison between Mortimer and Stephen is reasonable as Mortimer is also a literary journalist who takes pride in his profession. See *Channel Packet*, p. 7 and pp. 46–57.

P. 281. **Tom Paine**: Mr. M. M. Bevington, who most generously shared with me the fruits of his learning on the Stephen family, remarked that Stephen was too strongly reared in the tradition of Burke to appreciate how completely Paine's common-sense reasoning destroyed Burke's theory of contract. See Stephen's admission that Moncure Conway had proved that he, Stephen, had accepted a worthless source in his assessment of Paine. (*Fortnightly Review*, NS, Vol. LIV, Aug., 1893, pp. 267–81.)

P. 282. **blunders**: Cf. 'Thoughts on Criticism by a Critic,' p. 566.

P. 284. **'gratitude'**: HL, III, p. 338.

P. 286. **in fact religious**: S. E. Toulmin, *The Place of Reason in Ethics* (1950), discourses on this question in Ch. 11–14.

P. 286. **'never fail!'**: Quoted by J. M. Keynes, *Essays in Biography* (1933), pp. 302–3.

INDEX

The following abbreviations have been used: Sir Leslie Stephen: LS; Sir James Fitzjames Stephen: JFS; Footnote: fn.